John McDermott is a writer/video ........ ........ Hendrix memorabilia collector and h......

Eddie Kramer was Hendrix's original producer/engineer and was responsible for three "classic" and four posthumous Hendrix albums.

*Praise for HENDRIX:*

'The facts about the greatest guitarist of all time – a classic Hendrix book'

— Paul McCartney

'The book really had an emotional impact on me. It takes you to Hendrix himself'

— Peter Frampton

# HENDRIX
## SETTING THE RECORD STRAIGHT

John McDermott with Eddie Kramer

WARNER BOOKS

A *Warner* Book

First published in the USA in 1992 by Warner Books, Inc.
and in Great Britain in 1993
by Little, Brown and Company
by arrangement with Warner Books, Inc. New York
This edition published in 1994 by Warner Books
Reprinted 1996, 1999, 2001

Copyright © 1992 by John McDermott

A CIP catalogue record for this book
is available from the British Library.

ISBN 0 7515 1129 3

Typeset in Palladia by Leaper & Gard Ltd, Bristol
Printed in England by Clays Ltd, St Ives plc

UK companies, institutions and other organisations wishing
to make bulk purchases of this or any other book
published by Little, Brown should contact their local
bookshop or the special sales department at the address below.
Tel 020 7911 8000. Fax 020 7911 8100.

Warner Books
A Division of
Little, Brown and Company (UK)
Brettenham House
Lancaster Place
London WC2E 7EN

www.littlebrown.co.uk

For Laura, whose love and support never wavered

—J. McD., Dedham 1992

I would like to thank my parents Sonny & Minna Kramer for providing me with a musical education and environment which enabled me to appreciate all types of music without prejudice.

I would also like to dedicate this to my children, Alex and Lara, who, maybe, when they read this book, will appreciate what their father has Experienced.

—E.H.K., Rhinebeck 1992

# Contents

# Acknowledgments

In writing a book over so long a period of time, Eddie and I have had the distinct pleasure of meeting and interviewing a seemingly endless number of fascinating individuals. We are grateful for their input and support for the project. No less enjoyable was the manner in which many of our interviews were conducted. These circumstances, among others, included Eddie pinning a lavaliere microphone on Joe Boyd as we careened through London traffic; a twelve-hour, herculean combination Chinese food and prime rib feast with Buddy Miles; Crosby, Stills and Nash each alternating – between vocal overdubs no less – to volunteer anecdotes about Jimi; Paul and Linda McCartney, at the height of their 1990 U.S. tour – in a gracious show of hospitality – receiving us at home and abroad; Stevie Nicks speaking with us as she and her staff frantically packed for a Fleetwood Mac tour of Australia; and capping off a magnificent afternoon of reminiscences with Chas Chandler with some Old 80 at the bar of the Bay Hotel in Cullercoates, Newcastle.

The following are just some of the people who took time out to speak with Eddie and me: Leslie Aday, Tunde and Taharqa Aleem (Albert and Arthur Allen), Carmine Appice, Dan Armstrong, Bob Babbit, Frank Barselona, Jeff Baxter, Danny Blumenauer, Tony Bongiovi, Joe Boyd, Stefan Bright, Al Brown, Terry Brown, Baird Bryant, Randy California, Jim Capaldi, Paul Caruso, Jack Casady, Ed Chalpin, Chas Chandler, Neville Chesters, George Chkiantz, Larry Coryell, David Crosby, Monika Dannemann, Spencer Davis, Leon Dicker, Alan Douglas, Tom Edmonston, Kathy Etchingham, Mike Finnigan, Robert Fitzpatrick, Tom Flye, John Gardiner, Jerry Goldstein, Michael Goldstein, Keith Grant, Gerry Guida, John Head, Michael Hecht, John Hillman, Elliot

Hoffman, Tom Hulett, Abe Jacob, John Jansen, Andy Johns, Glyn Johns, Les Kahn, Henry Kalow, Steve Katz, Linda Keith, Marta Kellgren, Kim King, Al Kooper, Howard Krantz, Bob Krasnow, Bob Kulick, Kevin Laffey, Joe LaNostra, Arthur Lee, Bob and Kathy Levine, Mark Linett, Jim Marron, John Marshall, Paul Marshall, Dave Mason, Roger Mayer, Paul and Linda McCartney, Eugene McFadden, Terry McVay, Buddy Miles, Jeff Mironov, Mitch Mitchell, Tom Moffat, Nigel Morgan, Graham Nash, Mike Neal, Stevie Nicks, Dave Palmer, Peter Pilafian, Faye Pridgeon, Noel Redding, Barry Reiss, Jim Robinson, Shimon Ron, Tony Ruffino, Ron Saint Germain, Don Schmitzerle, Abby Schroeder, Alan Schwartzberg, Daniel Secunda, Mickey Shapiro, Linda Sloman, Joe Smith, Chris Stamp, Mark Stein, Gerry Stickells, Stephen Stills, Bill Stoddard, Chris Stone, John Storyk, Ron Terry, Ed Thrasher, Willie Vacarr, Larry Vaughan, John Veneble, Johanan Vigoda, Chuck Wein, Steve Weiss, Judy Wong and Herbie Worthington.

Enough can't be said to describe the time and effort each one of our contributors gave to this project. To help "set the record straight" (and, as many told me, only half jokingly, to spare them from having to do any more interviews in the future) we spent days poring over details with Hendrix's closest associates, and many – like Bob and Kathy Levine, Chas Chandler, Jim Marron and Gerry Stickells – went well over and above the call of duty, sharing memories and their lively – and often contradictory – opinions, as well as providing us with updated information or long-lost contact numbers. In London, Linda McCartney threw open her magnificent photo archives to us. In Los Angeles, Herbie Worthington tirelessly helped track down an amazing number of key contributors. Jim Robinson and Judy Wong did the same, as did Tony Bongiovi in New York.

Eddie and I also extend our gratitude to the following individuals who have helped us at various intervals throughout: Peter Frampton for the phone tip and John Regan for the laughs. Jimmy and Joanne Waldo for putting up with Eddie in L.A. Lynn Kramer, Nick and Will Fenton and Paul Stone for putting up with Eddie in London. Billy Cox for his support. Alan Selby and Richard Flanzer for their tour of Electric Lady. Eric Barrett – for his "official Eric Barrett stamp of approval." Don Adler, Jan Owen and Fred Talmadge from Warner Films. In memory, Carol Appleby, who orchestrated a reunion between Eddie and Noel that was long overdue. John Hammel, Geoff Baker, Mary McCartney, Sylvie Tata, Shelagh Jones and all the gang at MPL. Kevin Stein – for his early and continued support. Danny Goldberg, Arthur Spivak, Ian Kimmet and Ilene Cherna Bellovin for "connections." DeWitt Nelson, Jim Fahey and Dan Neer from Neer Perfect Productions. Virginia Lohle/Star File Agency Inc. for her unstinting enthusiasm. Ron Weisner and Richard Ogden – for taking time out of their hectic schedules to speak with us and to see that our needs were met. D.A. and Fraser Pennebaker for screening footage from their library. Byron Parham from the Nixon Presidential Library. Steve Lang from the Warner Bros. Tape Library. David Cugnasca from A.W. Chesterton. Promoters Phil Basile and Shelly Finkle. Craig Inciardi from Sotheby's.

A deep measure of gratitude is due Mark Lewisohn for his considerable contribution, without which our manuscript would have truly suffered. Mark's combination of enthusiasm, patience and diligence, as well as his noted penchant for accuracy and detail, were a much welcomed assist.

Kudos are in order for Warner Books' own Ellen Herrick, Karen McDermott and Anne Milburn, whose support and encouragement brought us to Warner. Special thanks are also due Charlie Conrad, our editor, who nurtured this project with patience and enthusiasm, and whose helpful editorial advice throughout broadened our perspectives and improved our manuscript considerably.

Special thanks to Ben Dewey for reviewing the manuscript, improving our introduction and providing helpful editorial advice and suggestions throughout. Both Eddie and

I are grateful for his sustenance and encouragement.

Eddie and I would also like to acknowledge Peter Shukat, as well as Jeffery Hafer, Marsy Kupfersmith and all those at Shukat & Hafer. Their conference room often doubled as our New York interview facility.

With regard to research, August Angerame, Kevin Bond, Harvey Daniels, Bob Elliott, Barry Gruber and Bruce Pates are Hendrix archivists who volunteered their time and effort over the years to swap articles, clippings, photos and tapes to help the project. A number of others also took time out to assist; they include: Nona Hatay, Shane Gates, Jay Dolan, Leland Stein, Maury LaPrade, Mike Chase and Dietmar Schmischke.

Innumerable hours of interviews were ably transcribed by Robin Bianchi, Diane Bullwinkle and Paula Lyons. Special thanks to George Cuchural and Bill Rothfuchs for their computer assistance.

Thanks to Leo Branton, Alan Douglas and Al Hendrix.

Thanks to all, and to those not named, including the McDermott family, who never ceased to encourage and support me. Enjoy!

# Preface

I started work on this project more than seven years ago, unsure of its ultimate shape and form. On the heels of the shoddy 1980 album release *Nine to the Universe*, I wanted to explore what I considered to be the strange dichotomy that existed within the Hendrix ranks. Despite the steady stream of such increasingly inferior Hendrix releases, why did those involved in Hendrix's finest recordings – Chas Chandler, Mitch Mitchell, Noel Redding, Billy Cox, Buddy Miles and Eddie Kramer – refuse to be associated with the recordings? So I contacted Eddie Kramer, Hendrix's respected engineer; we began a friendship and I began an amazing and enjoyable seven-year voyage.

At first, during that initial meeting, Kramer was tentative, sticking to general observations and memories that I had already gathered from previous research. But I was struck by something he said: "I want to set the record straight about Jimi Hendrix." This goal, Kramer instructed me, could only be achieved by contacting all of the key people who had helped orchestrate one of the most brilliant and exciting careers rock music has known. *Setting the Record Straight* promptly became not just this book's title but our focus.

While Eddie Kramer played a crucial role in the creation of Jimi Hendrix's personally authorized recorded legacy – from the breathtaking *Are You Experienced?* to *The Cry of Love* and the construction of Electric Lady Studios – this book could not have been crafted from his personal experiences alone. To explain the multifaceted Hendrix phenomenon with the recollections of a single source is impossible. Therefore, to best provide the complete picture of Jimi Hendrix, we have searched out each of his associates and evaluated their roles within his life or career.

With that in mind, this book is best described as a

retrospective account of the myth, music and legacy of Jimi Hendrix. Frustrated with the previous accounts of his life and career, Eddie Kramer and I looked to create a narrative consisting primarily of firsthand testimony, rather than a third-person profile. Each interview, save for an occasional phone conversation, was conducted *with* Kramer present, an undeniable assist. Together, we contacted every member of Hendrix's management team still living, gathering such a volume of remarkable new information that even Eddie came away with a new insight into the life and career of the man with whom he worked so intimately:

Originally, I found myself on the "inside," yet twenty years later, having now had the opportunity to look at things objectively, my knowledge, understanding and appreciation of this incredible man has increased immeasurably.

Working in the recording studio with Jimi, my function may best be described as "co-conspirator," which specifically meant creating new sounds, lending support and encouragement and capturing his creativity on tape. Equally challenging and engaging was blending the considerable talents of Mitch Mitchell and Noel Redding, as well as Billy Cox and Buddy Miles, into his groundbreaking music – whose final results couldn't have been imagined when we began.

While I was definitely aware of outside influences affecting Jimi's moods, there were aspects of his life and loves that I had no idea about. One of the distinct pleasures of participating as heavily as I did in the research phase of this project was discovering the depth of Jimi's preparation for recording sessions. The detailed notes he made about the inner complexities of his songs and how they should work and sound were a revelation to me. Though I am often described as having been Jimi's "translator" in the studio (a description that only partly defines my role, as Chas Chandler was quite successful at this during the early stages of Hendrix's career), I can honestly admit to learning a great deal from Jimi. I remember sitting alone with him in the darkened control room of Electric Lady Studios, listening intently as he made a heartfelt attempt to describe what "Electric Church" music truly was, what it meant to him and what its components were. Though I didn't let on to him, a great deal sailed over my head as I struggled to grasp how I could help him reach this deeply felt personal goal. It was during these times that I let his magnificent talent and spirit guide *me*.

In the end, he was a wonderful man, someone I revered, respected and sometimes even feared. I sincerely hope that the world's perception of Jimi Hendrix, specifically the image of the stoned-out, undisciplined musician (a notion I have never believed) has been – as far as I'm concerned – permanently altered. This man was very much aware of what was going on around him emotionally, politically and even business-wise, which, unbeknownst to me at the time, all came out in his music.

If John and I have done anything with this book, I hope we have captured the essence of what it was like to have been part of that creative process.

Since a massive portion of Hendrix's legacy is rooted in the arcane business practices of the music industry, Eddie and I interviewed all of the key participants still alive today, our sole rejection coming from current Warner Bros. Records Chairman Mo Ostin, who has chosen not to speak about any Warner-Reprise artist – from Hendrix to Frank Sinatra – while he remains associated with the company.

While Hendrix's lasting achievements are rooted firmly in his music, *how* his fame was achieved is a fascinating, complex tale. In developing the Experience, Michael Jeffery and Chas Chandler, employing disproportionate measures of foresight and audacity, eschewed many of the traditional steps along the path to fame and fortune. Hendrix's management, aided by Track Records – a small, tenacious, London-based independent record label – incorporated many of the same sales and promotional techniques (i.e.: hype) that had successfully launched stars as diverse as Fabian and the Beatles. This time, though, they stretched and exceeded, as members of the press would unfailingly recall, the limits of both morality and decency while fully cognizant of their audience's maturity and sophistication. Apart from Hendrix's overtly suggestive stage gyrations, no less potent was the underlying issue of race, the Experience's interracial, intercontinental pedigree drawing considerable interest from fans and critics alike.

Unlike Motown, the self-titled "Sound of Young America" or, to a lesser degree, Stax, and artists such as Aretha Franklin and Wilson Pickett, Hendrix burst on the London pop music scene without the slightest of warnings, armed with his irrefutable talent and a sound and look entirely his own – a culmination, not unlike his own musical influences, also synthesized from white rock n' roll, soul, jazz and blues.

This blurring of musical and cultural styles was an essential element of the Hendrix appeal. Not only was he free of slavish devotion to any previous or existing musical or social movement, *he* himself seemed synthesized, a true personification of Americana – from the Boy Scouts and football to his stint as a paratrooper in the U.S. Army's 101st Airborne Division. Neither the brooding bluesman of lore nor the fresh-faced heartthrob carefully nurtured and protected by professional handlers, Hendrix's résumé depicted a steady, unspectacular, modestly capable musician desperate for his shot at the brass ring.

Considering his sudden transformation to J-i-m-i and the success that ensued just months later, it seems unthinkable that Hendrix could have languished so miserably as a low-level member of the Greenwich Village folk and pop scene until fate beckoned – materializing here in the form of Animals bassist Chas Chandler. The sheer immensity of Hendrix's metamorphosis seemed impossible to believe, and his story seemingly a myth fabricated by his media-savvy management team. It made for great PR, the fading pop star (in this instance, Chandler) uncovering an even greater artist buried within the club circuit his own career had long surpassed.

Before Chas Chandler discovered him in 1966, Hendrix – despite his considerable ability and intense desire to succeed – was hamstrung by a paucity of organizational skills. Fronting Jimmy James & the Blue Flames, Hendrix seemed mired in mediocrity, destined for obscurity. Though his makeshift combo sometimes included the likes of Randy California (later of Spirit), Jeff Baxter (later of the Doobie Brothers) and John Hammond, Jr., the Blue Flames' progress – and that of their leader – was restricted by the combined weight of poor wages, limited cash flow and low morale.

Unlike Buddy Guy, Howlin' Wolf, Otis Rush or Muddy Waters, Hendrix had yet to develop a distinct identity or a core audience of any significance. While his idols had cultivated their following from Chicago's gritty South and West sides, Hendrix's relocation to the predominantly white folk clubs of Greenwich Village seemed anomalous. Though many top blues artists included stops at the Village's Cafe Au Go Go on their tour itinerary, their stronghold was drawn from neighborhood bars, taverns and function halls. In addition, in choosing Greenwich Village as his musical base, Hendrix eschewed New York's top dance spots, including such venues as the Cheetah, where, as a member of Curtis Knight & the Squires, he had once created a minor stir with his stage show, an outrageous combination of virtuosity and bravado.

Hendrix's fortunes changed that afternoon when Chandler walked into the Cafe Wha? No longer the freak guitar player pushed to the stage's backline until his novelty act was needed, Hendrix was molded by Chandler as a star of the first magnitude. Without a single recording on which to base his claim, Chandler cast Hendrix as the leader of an exciting, albeit undefined, new musical movement, and then completed the transformation by creating the act, the Jimi Hendrix Experience.

Previous articles and books about the Hendrix phenomenon have often cast him sympathetically as an unwitting dupe, dominated by his all-white charges whose sole interest was based firmly on Hendrix's ever-increasing ability to generate income. While this condescending interpretation reflects the extreme viewpoint, subtle shadings of this belief have now permeated the Hendrix myth, diluting his many achievements and leaving his considerable fan base intrigued and confounded.

Who then was Jimi Hendrix? As was the case with many artists of the 1950s and 60s, public knowledge and understanding of Jimi Hendrix was shaped primarily by way of promotional and publicity releases. During his all too brief four-year career as a major artist – especially the first two under the shared stewardship of Michael Jeffery and Chandler, aided and abetted by bandmates Mitch Mitchell and Noel Redding – Hendrix flaunted his manufactured image skillfully, enraging the establishment as the antihero of the embryonic counterculture while fast developing a large, devoted following. Jeffery and Chandler were relentless – and often shameless – in their efforts to establish the Experience as a full-fledged member of rock's elite. Jeffery's notorious business acumen, especially when blended with Chandler's sensibility and unshakable faith in Hendrix's artistic capabilities, complemented Jimi and his Experience perfectly, masking Hendrix's natural personality behind the charismatic appeal of "Jimi" and the promise of an "Experience."

While Hendrix's management may have skillfully manipulated the media during his lifetime, in the years following Jimi's death, with Chas Chandler cast adrift, and no strong voice emanating in his defense, Hendrix's reputation fell victim to sensationalism and opportunists bent on their own individual agendas. Hendrix's much vaunted organization fell apart almost immediately, as the balance of power began to tilt against Jeffery. Each tabloid headline seemed directly aimed at destroying his fragile legacy, spanning from rumors about his pathetic demise – a childish Eric Burdon openly discussed suicide as a possibility on British television just days after Hendrix's death – to the hodge-podge of posthumous albums and films issued without any semblance of order or historical perspective. The cumulative effect would prove devastating, as so much of the Hendrix legacy – even at the time of his death – was already rife with confusion. The last two years of his life were marked by astonishing artistic achievements and devastating personal and professional failures, not the least being the breakup of the Experience and his 1969 arrest for heroin possession.

Shortly after Michael Jeffery's death, when Alan Douglas assumed control of the Hendrix tape closet in 1974, a new publicity campaign was unleashed, this time trumpeting the discovery of the so-called lost tapes, a cache of some 300 reels of multitrack recording tape. It was these tapes, Douglas and publicist Ken Schaffer told *Time, Newsweek, Rolling Stone* and anyone else who would listen, that would finally shed some light on Hendrix's true intentions, specifically his desire to replace his rhythm section and embrace more free-form musical styles such as improvisational jazz and blues. While Douglas may have wanted to clarify Hendrix's true intentions, the posthumous albums he has issued – particularly *Crash Landing* and *Midnight Lightning* – did more to confuse the legacy than anyone could have imagined.

Cursed by a ceaseless parade of increasingly inferior releases, the Hendrix legacy remains in dire need of direction and definition. Sadly, Jimi's untimely death occurred just as crucial projects – principally the completion of Electric Lady Studios and his long overdue fourth studio album – were within sight. Save for the continuation of projects already set in motion by Jimi himself, neither Michael Jeffery nor Alan Douglas had any concrete idea as to Hendrix's future projects and ambitions. With only interviews and publicity literature available for scrutiny (each laden with Hendrix's typically cryptic public speech), fans and critics alike have only the speculation of "what might have been" to stoke the fires of interest. While an understanding that Hendrix *was* a complex, compassionate, intelligent artist firmly committed to his craft has survived, his many achievements have been all but crushed by the trappings of psychedelia and the lurid details of the 1960s drug culture.

In the 1990s, Hendrix remains an enigma, an innovator forever frozen in time at the age of twenty-seven. As rock n' roll continues to feed on his best ideas, devouring successful techniques of the past to fit the video age, Hendrix's popularity continues almost undiminished. He remains, via his music and dress, a figure of rebellion, an outlaw mainstream America still struggles to absorb.

Sadly, the promotion of Hendrix's music today seems purely one-dimensional, narrowcasted to his most rabid admirers – white guitarists – whose unabated devotion keeps the estate of Jimi Hendrix financially secure by gobbling up each new posthumous release trumpeted by such well-intentioned journals as *Guitar World* and *Guitar Player*. This connotation of Hendrix as the deacon of heavy metal and the grand gadgeteer of the electric guitar has caused many to overlook his considerable abilities as a songwriter, including the poetry weaved into such beautiful ballads as "Little Wing," "Drifting" and "Castles Made of Sand." And although Hendrix's musical fingerprint extends to such obvious admirers as Robin Trower and the late Stevie Ray Vaughan, his considerable influence on black music is irrefutable, as the works of Prince, Parliament/ Funkadelic, Jon Butcher, Digital Underground, Living Colour, Ernie Isley, Cameo, and the Time continue to prove.

While voodoo and other exotic aspects of the African-American heritage may be evident and perhaps even essential ingredients of the Hendrix sound and appeal, his music *arrives* to fans and those still uninitiated via Classic Hits radio, the bane of American radio programming. Ironically, Hendrix, one of the first artists to embrace FM radio, had he lived, would have seen his legacy trapped by the rigid format that shapes current American rock n' roll radio. As an icon of the late 1960s, Hendrix receives steady AOR (Album-Oriented Radio) and Classic Hits airplay, yet the only songs seemingly selected for broadcast can all be found on a single disc, *Smash Hits*. (Understandably, this remains his best-selling album, just outscoring *Are You Experienced?*)

Therefore, to best understand one of the most talented artists of our time, to counter the many misperceptions of Hendrix's legacy and, ultimately, to "set the record straight," one must examine not only Jimi's entire body of work but also how his fame was created and exploited. Rock n' roll, jazz, blues and R&B, despite a continuing series of technical advancements over the last twenty years, are still struggling to define and clarify Hendrix's majestic abilities.

# Introduction

Some years back, *Rolling Stone* featured on its cover a picture of Jim Morrison and the text, "He's Hot, He's Sexy, He's Dead." The subsequent marketing success of the Doors and record sales of their catalogue many years after Morrison's death underline the continuing fascination with legendary figures from the 1960s. In retrospect, it may seem that Creedence Clearwater Revival was the most aptly named group of the era, subject as we all are now to the permanent wave of revival. There are some figures from this era who cannot be repackaged, but must be revealed. They are outsized figures, whose achievements defy attempts at trivialization. Because their influence was so profound, myths and legends cloud the actual facts of their lives and circumstances. But most important, their messages are either confused or mislabeled, or worse, relegated to the status of mere innovators of style. Jimi Hendrix is such a figure. Sad to report, his legacy has either been misconstrued, tampered with or disfigured by half-truths and fabrications.

Born John Allen Hendrix, the first child of Al and Lucille Hendrix, on November 27, 1942, in Seattle, Washington, Jimi, or Johnny as he was then called, never met his father until the fall of 1945, when, as a serviceman in the U.S. Army, Al was finally discharged. Johnny's early years were difficult, as Lucille, still only in her late teens, struggled with the demands and responsibility of motherhood. Though they had married before Al had shipped out, the couple had never lived together and, as a result, Lucille and young Johnny were transients, shuffling between family and friends and trying to survive.

When Al Hendrix did return, young Johnny had been placed in the care of a family in Berkeley, California. Al's marriage to Lucille was fast disintegrating, as passions and needs influenced by the fear of impending war had long

1

since dissipated during Al's nearly four-year absence. Determined to claim the son he had never seen, Al traveled to Berkeley, retrieved Johnny and brought him home to Seattle. A short while later, Al Hendrix began matters anew, and on September 11, 1946, renamed his son James Marshall Hendrix.

Though shy and somewhat introverted, Jimmy participated, like most boys, in sports and other community activities, but nothing captured his interest more than music. His first string instrument was a battered ukulele, followed by an equally timeworn acoustic guitar, but as he later recalled, his initial experiments with music came from the mouth. "My first instrument was a harmonica, when I was about four. Next, though, it was a violin. I always loved string instruments and pianos, then I started digging guitars – it was the instrument that always seemed to be around. Every house you went into seemed to have one lying around."

Entirely self-taught, and unable to read music, Hendrix practiced incessantly. While in high school, he joined the Rocking Kings, playing rock n' roll, blues and the top R&B hits of the day at local legion halls and community centers. "My first gig was at a National Guard Armory," Hendrix later recalled. "We earned thirty-five cents apiece and played stuff by people like the Coasters."

Hendrix's earliest influences encompassed a wide variety of musical styles. "I liked Buddy Holly, Eddie Cochran, Muddy Waters, Elmore James, B.B. King," Jimmy explained. "The first guitarist I was aware of was Muddy Waters. I heard one of his old records when I was a little boy and it scared me to death because I heard all these sounds. It was great. The *Grand Ole Opry* used to come on, and I would watch that. They used to have some pretty heavy guitar players. But I didn't try to copy anybody. Those were just the people who gave me the feeling to get my own thing together."

At seventeen, Jimmy failed to complete his senior year at

Garfield High School, choosing instead to enlist in the armed services. "I figured I'd have to go sooner or later," Hendrix explained in 1968, "so I volunteered to get it over with. When I joined, I figured I might as well go all the way, so I signed with the Airborne."

Following training in California, Hendrix joined the 101st Airborne Paratroopers in Fort Campbell, Kentucky, where – as a member of the elite "Screaming Eagles" squad – he made twenty-five successful jumps and attained the rank of private first class during his thirteen-month stint. On his twenty-sixth, however, he suffered a broken ankle and was honorably discharged soon after.

Despite the thrill of jumping from an airplane (the pleasure, he would later admit, "came when you found you had landed safely"), Hendrix had soured quickly on army life, his personality not being suited for the rigid discipline, modest pay and limited social opportunities that came with the lifestyle. "I hated the army immediately," he would later state. "It was very boring. I was lucky to get out when I did. Vietnam was just coming up. When I got out, I didn't have anything to show for it all, so I wasn't going home."

Hendrix did make one key contact during his relatively brief stay in the forces, becoming friends with Billy Cox, a fellow serviceman and musician, forming with him the King Kasuals, an R&B combo that performed at Fort Campbell's service clubs and also at other small, non-military-affiliated venues like the Pink Poodle Club in nearby Clarksville, Tennessee.

Invalided out of the army, Hendrix's discharge started him on his journey, first with Billy Cox and the continuing King Kasuals and later as a sideman, backing a host of top R&B stars. "I started playing all around the South," Hendrix later recalled. "We had a band in Nashville, Tennessee, and I got tired of that because they didn't want to move anywhere. So I started traveling around."

Hendrix landed in New York, and promptly won the $25 first prize in an Apollo Theater amateur contest. During another visit to the famed theater, Hendrix met Fayne "Faye" Pridgeon, a fixture on the Harlem music scene, and each was immediately attracted to the other. "Jimi thanked me for getting him backstage to see Sam Cooke," remembered Pridgeon in 1982. "He referred to Sam as 'what's-his-face'! We started to walk home, talking all the way to my mother's place on Central Park West. I went on in with Jimi and he got all excited about her blues records. She had the low-down stuff ... Ruth Brown and beyond, Muddy Waters, Lightnin' Hopkins, Earl King, Junior Parker and folks like that, and Jimi loved those people. He got out his guitar and played along with some of the records, and then we got him to have some food. It didn't take too much coaxing, because at that time he wasn't used to having meals too regularly, and he ate and ate. After my mother eased us out, we went to the Hotel Seifer where I was staying with a girlfriend. The Hotel Seifer was where all the up-and-coming entertainers lived, it was the next stop before downtown. We spent the night together, and after that he never left, he just moved in with me. It wasn't hard because he was carrying all his possessions around in his guitar case. He didn't have underwear. He wasn't into jeans. He had these shiny black pants, a very thin, little jacket, and high-top boots."

With Faye being popular on the Harlem music scene, Hendrix made the rounds on her arm and, as a result, his ability as a guitarist was quickly noticed. Some three weeks after their meeting, the Isley Brothers were in Harlem for an engagement at the Palm Cafe. During their stopover, Ronnie Isley mentioned to Tony Rice, an associate of soul legend Joe Tex, that the group needed a guitarist. Rice knew of just the person, a young phenomenon from Seattle who had just come to town, and arranged for a meeting.

Despite backing from the Palm Cafe's jealous and largely unsympathetic house band, Hendrix sailed through his audition. Suitably impressed, the Isley Brothers offered the shy, struggling guitarist a position in their band. "The Isley Brothers asked if I'd like to play with them," Hendrix would later remember of his itinerant musician days. "I did that for a while, but I got very bored playing behind other people all the time. I quit them in Nashville and went on a tour with B.B. King, Jackie Wilson and Sam Cooke. Then I got stranded in Kansas City because I missed the bus. I was in Kansas City without any money when a group came up and brought me back to Atlanta, Georgia, where I met Little Richard and started playing with him for about six months. I got tired of that and played some shows with Ike & Tina Turner before I went back to New York and played with King Curtis and Joey Dee. I just got tired. Man, I couldn't stand it anymore."

Hendrix's many stints as a sideman to the stars, while it barely kept him fed, padded his résumé (which, in retrospect, seems more impressive today) and provided him with an inexhaustible supply of material for his repertoire. Hendrix's synthesis of rock, soul and blues was honed night after night, and although he continued to refine his craft, each group that recruited his services demanded that he not pursue ideas above his station. As a result, Jimmy landed back in New York, frustrated, broke and hungry, thoroughly disillusioned by the endless grind of the rhythm & blues personal appearance circuit.

While his short stint with the Isley Brothers proved to be his most successful as a sideman to date, Hendrix redirected his career away from that of hired hand to developing his own style and sound. "I was trying to play my own thing," he would later explain. "But I was working with people like Little Richard, the Isley Brothers and Wilson Pickett and they didn't like too much of that feedback. I was kept in the background, but I was thinking all the time about what I wanted to do. [That's why] I'd join a group and quit them so fast. I dug listening to Top 40 R&B but that didn't necessarily mean I liked to play it every night."

In joining Curtis Knight & the Squires, Hendrix, though not an equal creative partner with Knight, was finally allowed to exert some control over his sound and, ultimately, his role within the band's music.

While Knight, in the years following Hendrix's death, may have shamelessly promoted himself as both his best friend and guiding musical inspiration, their collaboration *did* elevate Hendrix's career, and – at least initially – proved beneficial for him, as the Squires' tours kept him clothed and fed and provided him with intermittent access to the recording studio. Many of the Squires' earliest recordings – however crude – were serious attempts at cracking *Billboard*'s elusive top 40 chart. Tracks such as "How Would You Feel?" (trumpeted by Knight as the first black-rock protest song), "Gotta Have a New Dress" and "No Business" now provide a fascinating insight into the development of the distinctive Hendrix sound. Membership in the Squires brought an additional benefit too, Hendrix enjoying his first record label credit, another clear sign that despite Knight's name on the marquee, he was now an essential ingredient in the modest R&B combo. (Indeed, neither Knight nor any of the other Squires would ever replicate the small level of success they enjoyed during Hendrix's brief tenure.)

Despite any modest progress made with Knight, economics soon forced Jimmy Hendrix back on the road, first in November 1965 for a quick ten-day tour backing Joey Dee as a member of his Starliters, then as a member of the famed saxophonist King Curtis's Kingpins. In May 1966, though, Hendrix returned to New York and briefly reprised his duties with Curtis Knight, joining the Squires for an extended engagement at the city's hottest dance spot, the Cheetah. Privately, Hendrix knew that this reunion was a temporary measure, a much needed financial stopgap that would tide him over until he could launch his own group. Within the gaudy decor of the Cheetah, however, sat someone who would finally recognize the spark within him.

In recent years, Linda Keith had become a top London fashion model, her soft features and endearing eyes symbolizing the upheaval in a fashion world now immersed in all things British. Where the Beatles had smashed a great many cultural barriers, the staid capital of the old empire had fallen into a love affair with its new, mod self. In the heady atmosphere of swinging London, Linda Keith had ensnared one of rock's young royalty, Keith Richards. When the Rolling Stones set off to tour America once more in 1966, Linda accompanied Richards to New York, but here her journey concluded, Richards invoking the unwritten rule that girlfriends not travel with the band.

Using his paid-for hotel suite as a base, and with her passion for American blues whetted by Greenwich Village's bustling scene, Linda conscripted two native New Yorkers, Roberta Goldstein and Mark Kauffman, to escort and direct her to the city's trendiest night spots. One sure stop on any such journey would always be the Cheetah. While certainly not a blues band by any definition, Curtis Knight & the Squires – the evening's attraction – were known to sprinkle more than a few blues numbers into a set top-heavy with covers and soundalike Top 40 hits. Jimmy Hendrix, the Squires' lead guitarist, was about to be liberated from his heretofore directionless pursuit of success.

Explains Linda Keith: "I was sitting near the back of the Cheetah when I noticed in the back line of Curtis Knight's band a guitarist whose playing mesmerized me. After the set, I had Mark check him out and see if he wanted to come have a drink with us. Fortunately, he did."

As the four exchanged small talk at the table, Linda grew increasingly intrigued with Hendrix, whose polite and painfully shy demeanor immediately separated him from the typical rough and tumble blues-man. His stint with Curtis Knight, Hendrix informed Linda matter-of-factly, was an afterthought, a job that wasn't that important to him. His plan, he announced somewhat halfheartedly to his new friends, was to strike out on his own and establish his own band. As he would soon return to the bandstand, Linda and Jimmy made plans to get together again, to establish whether someone from her impressive network of friends might be of some help.

Hendrix was taken with Linda. Her assertiveness, not unlike Faye's, impressed him, and their friendship accelerated rapidly. They spent hours talking and listening to music at Goldstein and Kauffman's apartment on 57th Street. "He was living uptown in Harlem, but he would stay at the 'Red House' [Goldstein and Kauffman's apartment was decorated almost entirely in red, complete with red velvet walls and leopard skin decor], as we called it, for days on end," Keith recalls. "I would play loads of music, trying to motivate him, something he desperately needed. It seemed silly, me a middle-class white girl playing *him* the blues."

With Linda Keith's encouragement, Hendrix combed Greenwich Village's folk-pop scene for willing conspirators eager to join his planned group, Jimmy James & the Blue Flames, he being "Jimmy James." Along with Keith, Goldstein and Kauffman, Hendrix's tiny band of supporters also included Paul Caruso, a harmonica player, and Terry Noel, a local artist and DJ whose extensive record collection would prove invaluable.

As Hendrix strived to establish himself as bandleader Jimmy James, he became a fixture, if not an odd sight, walking the streets of the Village, guitar slung across his back. "You knew there was something about that guy," remembers Tom Flye, whose own band, Lothar & the Hand People, was fast developing a cult following. "He would walk down Bleecker Street with his guitar over his shoulder like a lumberjack."

In the finest Maxwell Street tradition of Muddy Waters, Hendrix − occasionally with Paul Caruso contributing on harmonica − would often grace passersby with an impromptu performance for tips and encouragement. "He loved to play on the streets in the Village," recalls Linda Keith. "I always wanted him to sing, but he wouldn't. So I would. I think it was the excruciating sounds that came from me that finally made him say, 'Oh all right, I'll do it!' He really believed that he couldn't sing." Keith's encouragement didn't stop there, however, for she would also play him song after song by Bob Dylan, subtly showing him that it was not the actual quality of the voice but the tone and sentiment of the delivery that counted.

At first Hendrix struggled with Keith's assertive direction, not wanting to lower his guard and risk being hurt or embarrassed or both. Afraid to lose his new friendship, Hendrix maintained a secret double life, setting in motion a defense mechanism to ensure that his two very different worlds would never collide. His relationship with Linda Keith, the first person who had recognized his potential as an artist, exemplified this conflict. "We were not a couple," emphasizes Keith. "I was not his girlfriend, I was still dating Keith Richards. I was interested in Jimi's music and desperate for it to be fulfilled. He needed motivation and direction because, emotionally, he was almost completely lacking in confidence and terribly indecisive. He would muster this sort of false bravado to protect himself, but beneath that hard, external shell lay the real Jimi. He was confused about his ethnic identity and there was a great conflict between his musical roots and desire to play the blues and then wanting to be this sort of middle-class pop star. I was always pushing him to play the blues and he was rejecting that, in part because his great influences were Buddy Guy and Otis Rush, and he felt that he could not match up to them, certainly not in terms of his vocals.

"His personal life was just as splintered," continues Keith. "He seemed petrified to make an honest commitment to anyone. He would be in Manhattan with me and then uptown with Faye Pridgeon. At first, Jimi would only refer to her as 'Auntie Faye,' not in a deceitful way, but nonetheless I was never quite sure if she was his aunt or his girlfriend. There would always be a twinkle in his eye when he would say he'd have to go uptown and see Auntie Faye. As it was, his life in Harlem was strictly off-limits to me, but I think that Faye and I must have provided Jimi with separate halves of a whole emotional need."

With his now formed Blue Flames, a loosely bound aggregation of white players from the Village's pop-folk scene, finally in place, Hendrix was able to secure an occasional gig at the Cafe Wha? He was also a frequent participant at the Night Owl's afternoon jam sessions, where musicians who took part were given a free lunch, a policy perfectly suited to Hendrix's lack of organizational skills, as, under one roof, he could snatch temporary shelter, food and the opportunity to interact and exchange ideas with other musicians. "Needless to say, a lot of starving musicians – and Jimi was a regular – were jamming there," explains Kim King, lead guitarist in Lothar & the Hand People (and later, as an assistant engineer to Eddie Kramer, a Hendrix employee at Electric Lady Studios). "We had jammed a bunch of times before, but one time he came in with these killer series of chords – no song, no title, no nothing – just a great series of chord progressions. We played this every day for hours, until Jimi suddenly disappeared. I later found out when, sometime thereafter, I heard him described as 'England's newest sensation,' that those chords had been to 'Hey Joe.' "

"Hey Joe" had been one of the handful of covers that dominated the Blue Flames set lists. According to Linda Keith, Hendrix had been working hard on composing a couple of blues numbers – including "Red House" – but wasn't yet confident enough to mix them into his regular show. With his band tenuously in place and gigs scattered about the Village, Linda was determined to showcase Hendrix, so that he might be rescued from his haphazard surroundings as soon as possible. But cautious of his fragile emotions, and wanting to spare him a much dreaded face-to-face rejection, her first plan was to merely document one of the Blue Flames performances in the hope of creating a résumé of his many talents. Explains Keith: "We were trying to record a demonstration tape live from the Cafe Wha?, but it was a very amateur effort. We couldn't afford to bring Jimi into a studio." Despite the good intentions, the demonstration tape idea – as well as the tape itself – was scrapped.

Desperate for someone to recognize Hendrix's talent before he gave up and rejoined another R&B package tour, Keith played her trump card, deciding to have Jimi audition for someone she felt would immediately grasp Hendrix's potential: Andrew Loog Oldham.

As manager and producer of the Rolling Stones, Oldham had quickly garnered a reputation as one of Britain's fastest-rising music entrepreneurs. Having already launched Immediate Records, his own record label and outlet for some of the many bands in his stable, Oldham, Keith was hoping, might sign Hendrix to a development contract, whereby he could continue to hone his craft while being assured some modest means of financial assistance. Oldham placed great faith in Keith's judgments, as, apart from the considerable clout she carried as Keith Richards's girlfriend (Oldham had, in fact, introduced the couple to each other), their own friendship dated back to school days in north London, long before the Rolling Stones had been established.

With Oldham's interest piqued, Keith delayed matters until Hendrix could secure a gig at the Village's Cafe Au Go Go, which, at least to the casual observer, would be far more impressive than the cave-like Cafe Wha? Keith then approached the next hurdle, outfitting Hendrix with a decent instrument to use for his audition. She explains: "Jimi desperately wanted to play a Fender Stratocaster, as had his idols Buddy Guy and Otis Rush [who also played his upside down]. From the hotel suite we were sharing, I borrowed a new, white Stratocaster from Keith Richards, though I must admit the circumstances were actually less savory than that. I never actually told Keith that I had taken the guitar because he was away on tour. Jimi used that guitar for his first audition and thereon in. I doubt Keith ever knew it was missing."

Now armed with Richards's Stratocaster, while still noticeably reticent to sing, Hendrix performed with great gusto for the Stones' mentor, incorporating all of his time-tested, flamboyant stage moves into his frenzied, eclectic mixture of blues, R&B and rock. Out in the audience, Oldham sat decidedly unimpressed with Keith's discovery. "Andrew was absolutely turned off and didn't want any part of him," admits Keith. "He thought Hendrix was a wild man who just didn't have it." After the Blue Flames' performance, herself disheartened by Oldham's outright rejection, Keith did her best to console Hendrix, whose confidence was obviously bruised.

Hendrix's next Cafe Au Go Go showcase came soon after, with Seymour Stein [now president of Sire Records], another friend of Linda's, volunteering to check out her discovery. "He wasn't as negative as Oldham had been, but he didn't want any part of him either," recalls Keith with amazement.

Twice rebuffed, Hendrix grew resigned to failure as well as a little miffed that Keith would expose him to such rejection. Keith, on the other hand, vowed to press on. She says, "I couldn't believe these people weren't seeing what I was seeing. To me, Jimi's talents seemed so clear."

Having tried unsuccessfully to interest Oldham and Stein – her best resources – and soon due to return to London, Linda's options were limited. One evening, however, while relaxing with Goldstein and Kauffman at the popular night spot Ondine's, Keith was introduced to Animals bassist Chas Chandler. Marbled within their conversation was Chandler's declaration that he intended to try his hand at record production. Hearing this, Linda immediately suggested Jimmy Hendrix and, judging his interest sincere, Keith implored Chandler to see Hendrix for himself. He agreed.

As the tall, husky bassist for the Animals, Bryan "Chas" Chandler had enjoyed a degree of success most people would envy. Although his group posed no threat to the Beatles, or even the Rolling Stones for that matter, they were popular and enjoyed a considerable worldwide following. The roots of the Animals were entrenched in the blues masterworks of black Americans, a musical style in which many of Newcastle's working poor took solace. Their idols were outlaws, artists such as Howlin' Wolf and John Lee Hooker, whose music, while excluded from the mainstream, thrived in neighborhood taverns and function halls. The Animals fostered this rebellious image when, as one of the leading bands of the British Invasion of 1964, their version of "The House of the Rising Sun" raced up the charts, capturing the number one slot in the face of Beatlemania. In person, the Animals were the antithesis of the Beatles: dark, rough and earthy.

By the summer of 1966, riding high upon their eighth *Billboard* top 40 hit, "Don't Bring Me Down," the thrill of success had paled for Chandler. Although the Animals had never again managed to crack the exclusive top 5, the course had been steady. None of the Animals were rich; far from it. And since none of them had shown any particular skill for songwriting, their income was minuscule, a 2 percent record royalty rate in Britain and 1 percent abroad – split among the five members. Touring was no better, as each Animals tour would invariably end in debt. Aside from weekly wages and a fund of memories, Chas Chandler had little to show for his work.

Weary of the package tours and their interminable flights and bus rides, Chandler knew it was time to shift gears. Though his knowledge of the music industry was limited, he wanted to be a record producer. Never an instrumentalist of any particular merit, his decision was based principally on his desire to reestablish home in England and maintain a career in music. What struck Chandler about becoming a producer was that the producer was the leader, the man in whom both the band and its management placed their faith. A quintessential "man's man," Chandler was a sturdy, level-headed, hard-drinking Geordie with a tireless work ethic and strong family roots. His personal timetable was put into gear during this summer; then, by September 1966, the original Animals disbanded.

In July of that year, the Animals had grouped in New York, preparing for their final tour of North America. "I had gone there about a week ahead of time to see some friends," recalls Chandler. "The night before we were to play in Central Park, someone played me Tim Rose's version of 'Hey Joe,' which had been out for about nine months in America. I was so taken by it that I vowed, 'As soon as I get back to England, I'm going to find an artist to record this song.' Later that evening, we went out to a club called Ondine's. As we walked in, Linda Keith came walking out and we stopped to talk. She told me she was going out with this guy in the Village that I had to see. It hadn't been public, but all of my close friends knew that I was getting into record production after the Animals' impending split and Linda suggested that her friend might be just the guy to start with. So I made arrangements to meet her the next afternoon. I went down to the Village again and saw Jimmy James & the Blue Flames perform at the Cafe Wha? It just so happened the first song Hendrix played that afternoon was 'Hey Joe.' After his show, we just sat and talked for about an hour. I told him that I was going off on a tour with the Animals, but I would be back in a week or so. I then left saying, 'I'll come back to New York and if you still feel like it, I'll take you to England and we'll start.' He said, 'Fair enough.' "

"The Animals," recalls their road manager Terry McVay, "finished their tour with Herman's Hermits on August 6, 1966, in Atlantic City. We were all going to New York to visit friends and catch our breath before leaving for London. On the 7th, Chas asked Dave Rowberry [Animals keyboardist] and me to come to the Village and see this musician. I said, 'Sure! A free beer? Why not!' He took us to the Cafe Wha? Dave Rowberry had come from a jazz background in England and wasn't really a rock n' roller. He didn't know what he was looking at and neither did I. This guy was playing the guitar backwards, upside down and making all these strange noises. Chandler looked at us wide-eyed and said, 'What do you think? I'm thinking of taking him back to England, managing him and making an act.' All I could manage was, 'Interesting.' He then asked me again, 'What do you think?' I blurted, 'I haven't a clue what he's doing but I think it's great!' "

After the show, the trio accompanied Hendrix across MacDougal Street to a pub. There, Chandler told him about his background and what he planned to do for him in Britain. Hendrix was shy, and while grateful for the beer and kind words, he quizzed Chandler about British musicians, asking specifically whether Chandler knew Eric Clapton. Sensing that he had now found common ground, Chandler promised not only to introduce Hendrix to Clapton but told him that Clapton would be just as impressed – if not more – by his abilities. Chandler could sense that he had breached Hendrix's defenses and was now communicating musician to musician. Hendrix had recently known disappointment, yet there was an intangible component within Chandler's presentation that captured his imagination and bolstered his desperate desire to succeed. Yes, he told Chandler, he would be willing to go and give it his best shot.

Walking back with Hendrix to the Cafe Wha?, where he had to perform another set, both Chandler and McVay were taken by Jimi's guarded optimism, each noting his modest, slightly suspicious acceptance of Chandler's offer. Instead of gushing with joy, Hendrix had kept his emotions in check, voicing concern about inadequate equipment and what the possible reaction of British musicians to this untested Hendrix-Chandler-"Hey Joe" combination might be. Hendrix also cautioned Chandler about his voice, telling him that he simply "couldn't sing." Chandler refused to be dissuaded, however, confident that the image he had in mind bore little comparison to anything Hendrix's Jimmy James & the Blue Flames were currently doing or had ever conceived.

Having now found the artist he wished to produce,

Chandler was eager to set his plans in motion. "He called me and set up a meeting," recalls Leon Dicker, attorney and U.S. representative for Yameta, the Animals' parent company that, among other duties, administered the group's Bahamian tax shelter account. "There in my outer office, sitting alongside Chandler, was a gentleman dressed in an Indian-styled outfit. I invited them in and we discussed Chandler's plan. Chas wanted me to advance him money from his account so that he could take Hendrix to England and, ultimately, produce and manage him." Despite the Animals' legendary reputation for excess, Dicker sensed Chandler's enthusiasm to be legitimate, and not the result of a misguided whim. Moreover, Dicker was intrigued by Chandler's protégé. "I was immediately impressed with Hendrix," he recalls. "He was shy, but well spoken with a wonderful personality. I gave Chas the money and offered to do everything I could to help them."

Having gained both Dicker's support and an advance from Yameta, Chandler's progress was interrupted when initial efforts to locate Hendrix's birth certificate failed. "To obtain a passport for Hendrix," continues Dicker, "we had to find his birth certificate, but the authorities told me no such man was ever born. 'He's standing right here in my office!' I yelled into the phone. A couple of weeks passed until one of my old classmates from college, who lived in Seattle, intervened. There *was* a certificate, but it had been filed under John Allen Hendrix, the name his mother had given him when his father was away in the service."

In the interim, unwilling to waste time or opportunity, and while formulating his strategy for London, Chandler pressed on, accompanying Hendrix to the Blue Flames' last few remaining gigs scattered around Greenwich Village. "Chas Chandler brought Hendrix to our office in early September 1966," remembers music publisher Abby Schroeder. "Hendrix didn't have a passport, didn't have a birth certificate and didn't even have real shoes. They came to us because we had offices in both New York and London and Chas felt comfortable with that. We signed him up right away even though he didn't have a thing on tape with him. I just knew something was going to happen with that guy."

While awaiting Hendrix's passport, Chandler observed his performances with a keen eye, continually searching for ideas. Away from the stage, Chandler and Hendrix became closer, growing to know and understand each other, a bond that was sure to be tested during their critical first weeks abroad, where Chandler would have to back up his promises with action. Though the task ahead was, at the very least, daunting, Hendrix placed his complete trust in Chandler, respecting his take-charge authority and accepting his sincerity as wholly legitimate – which, indeed, it was.

Having endured repeated viewings of Blue Flames performances, Chandler's initial reaction was proven correct: Hendrix needed a clean break and a new supporting cast if his considerable talents were to be exploited properly. Though the Blue Flames were satisfied in their choice of music and were capable musicians – especially Randy California, then only fifteen years old – they were ragged and unfocused. As he listened, usually alone in the back of a club, Chandler couldn't help but wonder where the catch was. While Hendrix had vaguely described previous commitments to various band leaders and "managers," it was clear that any previous attempt to launch his career or improve his surroundings had been ineffectual. Though Chandler prided himself in his ability to discern hit music, he had no such reputation for discovering talent. Hendrix's talents seemed so striking, why hadn't anyone else taken notice of him before?

For Hendrix, his deliverance from the Blue Flames couldn't come soon enough. The group had represented little more than an attempt to disengage himself from the rut of backing other artists. But though one might have expected his new mood to swing between elation and nervousness, he approached Chandler's offer with indifference. "I might as well go [to England] because nothing much is happening here,"

Hendrix would later recall as being his frame of mind at this time.

Financially, he was badly off, barely surviving on miserable pay and the kindness of his tiny band of supporters, namely friends like Faye Pridgeon and Linda Keith. "We were making something like three dollars a night," Hendrix would later complain, "and you know ... we were starving." Recalls Faye Pridgeon: "Jimi and I had gone through some hard times. We were down to our last dollar and debating whether we should buy the cat some food or share a hot dog. The ASPCA made the decision for us: they charged us our last dollar to take the cat away because we couldn't feed it."

Hendrix's faith in his own ability remained unshakable, however, and grateful that Chandler had offered him an opportunity, Jimi went out of his way to please him. "He was so worried about making a good impression," says Faye Pridgeon. "One night I met Chas Chandler, John Hammond, Jr., and Mr. and Mrs. John Hammond, Sr. [Hammond Sr., long-respected talent scout and producer for CBS Records, was renowned for signing such luminaries as Billie Holiday, Robert Johnson, Charlie Christian, Aretha Franklin, Bob Dylan and, later, Bruce Springsteen to the label.] We were in this little bar in the Village, nibbling on black bread and drinking beer. Jimi was so nervous. I still have the scars on my thigh where Hendrix dug in his fingernails under the table every time I would just try to join in on the conversation. He wanted me to meet John Hammond, Sr., because he thought they were wild about him. That really impressed him."

With his passport finally secured and outstanding bills settled by Chandler, Hendrix was ready for England. Without a work permit and nothing more to go on than Chandler's reputation and pledge of unwavering support, he left New York on September 24, 1966, destined, he hoped, for better things. "Hendrix, Chandler and I sat in economy, three abreast and flew to London," remembers Terry McVay. "Part of my checked baggage was a white Stratocaster, because Jimi didn't have a work permit. Being a British resident, I could walk in without a problem."

Despite McVay's deception, British immigration officials initially refused to grant Hendrix the required work permit. Chandler argued vehemently on his behalf, describing him as an American recording artist of considerable stature. Immigration officials took a more suspicious view, no doubt noticing that Hendrix had stuffed what seemed to be the entirety of his possessions into a carry-on flight bag. After much debate, though, the authorities conceded, at least partially, granting Hendrix a seven-day non-work permit, sparing Chandler the indignity of sending Hendrix home without his stepping foot out of the airport. Later, in London, Chandler was able to secure all of Hendrix's necessary visas and work permits.

During the flight, Hendrix had again reiterated his concern that British musicians might not be as receptive to his music as Chandler had been. Wanting to quell his apprehensions, Chandler's first move was to pay an unannounced visit to Zoot Money, a musician and longtime friend whose flat was en route from the airport into central London. Though they arrived there just shortly before 11 A.M., most of Money and his Big Roll Band's gear was strewn about his apartment, ready to be transported to their gig that evening. Money's welcome was warm, though, just as Chandler had anticipated. Whereas John Mayall served as a respected blues mentor for aspiring British musicians, Money performed a similar, albeit less publicized, role. Yet instead of replicating the gritty blues of John Lee Hooker, J.B. Lenoir and Howlin' Wolf, his music was deeply influenced by the swinging rhythm and blues stylings of Joe Turner and Ray Charles. At Money's insistence, right there in the flat, Hendrix jammed with members of his Big Roll Band (whose ranks included a young Andy Summers, later of the Police) reworking blues classics and recent soul hits for nearly three hours, leaving all involved astounded.

Afterward, as the two made their way toward London,

Chandler could sense Hendrix's relief. Having been accepted so readily by Money and his band, it was as if a huge burden had been lifted from Jimi's shoulders. Now it was time to channel all of his energy toward achieving his dream.

# 1 CRAFTING THE EXPERIENCE

> *"It's me, Dad. I'm in England. I've met*
> *some people and they're going to make me a*
> *big star. We changed my name to J-I-M-I."*
>
> – Jimi Hendrix

**H**aving arrived in London with Hendrix in tow, Chandler immediately set out to establish him as "an item." As he recalls, Hendrix had not been in the country a week before he was afforded his first big break. "Late in September, before we had even had a rehearsal, I had bumped into Jack Bruce and Eric Clapton down at the Cromwellian Club. They had recently formed Cream, and asked what I was doing, because news was out by then that the Animals had broken up, so I told them about Hendrix. They said, 'Why don't you bring him to Regent Polytech on Saturday [October, 1, 1966] for a jam?' I told them that this wouldn't be fair. 'You're mates of mine,' I said, 'you can't let me do this to you. This guy is really extraordinary.' They said if he was that good, I *had* to bring him.

"When we got there Ginger Baker was a bit uptight, but he was an old pal of mine, we had known each other at that stage for ten or eleven years, and backstage he said that Hendrix could jam with them if Clapton stayed on stage. He wanted this because if Eric stayed on stage and then it all went wrong, he could pull it out." Baker's conditions were respected. Regent Polytech was an important gig for the "cream" of Britain's white R&B enthusiasts. Partway through the set, Jimi went on, opening with "Killing Floor," his frenzied arrangement of Howlin' Wolf's recent Chess single. "Clapton stood there and his hands dropped off of the guitar," recalls Chandler. "He lurched off the stage. I thought, 'Oh God, it's happening now.' I went backstage and he was trying to get a match to a cigarette. I said, 'Are you all right?' and he replied, 'Is he that fucking good?' He had heard ten bars at the most. Within a week, he had his hair frizzed and would come by our flat anytime that he had a spare moment, to be with Hendrix."

Considering the circumstances – he had no band and no original material – Hendrix couldn't have wished for a better introduction to the small, close-knit London music scene. In addition, his debut had come unexpected and without hype. This fortified the air of mystique and anticipation that Cream's glowing praise would create.

Working from the apartment Jimi would share with Chas and his wife Lotta, Chandler and Hendrix plotted their next move. With Chas burning for Jimi to record Tim Rose's "Hey Joe," plans were made to audition a support group. Hendrix would also need a recording contract. Enter Michael Jeffery, Chandler's own manager during his tenure with the Animals and now his partner. "When I came back to England Jeffery said to me, 'Strictly speaking, you are still signed to me and anything you do I've got commission on it. I'll tell you what – I'll put Eric Burdon and the new Animals with the Alan Price Set into a pot and you put Jimi Hendrix and his group into the same pot and we'll share it 50-50.'

"I knew what I wanted to do, and that was to produce Hendrix. I knew very little about the business, only what I thought should be done with an artist, but when it came to negotiating contracts, I thought, 'Well Jeffery can do that and I'll do this.'"

Using his Animals connections, Chandler was, at the same

time, helping to assemble the lineup for Eric Burdon and the new Animals. "I was looking for drummers and bass players, even though I didn't know what the band was going to be or what kind of lineup it would have. We were just looking for musicians." Hendrix's criteria were just as simple. "I was thinking of the smallest pieces possible with the hardest impact," Jimi would later explain. Animals road manager Terry McVay remembers the auditions too. "I had access to the Animals' blue van in which there were two SE 100 top-brand amplifiers and one Foundation, single eighteen-inch bass amplifier. That's what we were using for the auditions." At the same time, Hendrix was struggling to find adequate sound equipment for himself. "I took him to Shaftesbury Avenue, 'Music Alley' as we called it, where all the music stores were," remembers McVay. "He blew up Burns amplifiers, Selma, Sound City, everything in sight; everybody in the stores would stop and look. It became a daily routine, go to the store to look for a new amp and then go to the auditions. He would plug into the borrowed SE 30s and say, 'I hate this shit.' I'd laugh and say that it was all we had!"

Word had spread through the London club scene about the auditions for the new Animals, while hopeful candidates from outside the city learned of the opportunity via advertisements in *Melody Maker*. One of those aspirants was a twenty-year-old rhythm guitarist from Kent, Noel Redding.

"It all came to a point in the summer of 1966," says Redding. "I wasn't getting enough work and thought I'd change from guitar to drums. I used to play drums a bit in those days when there weren't any drummers, so I thought I'd sell my guitar and amp and get some drums. But I was on the way up to London on the train from Kent when I got a *Melody Maker* and saw an ad announcing auditions for Eric Burdon and the new Animals. I had met Eric six months before in a club, when he had jammed with the band I was in. So I went around to this office – I think it was the Harold

Davison Organisation – and they said, 'Oh yes, the audition is at the Birdland Club. Turn up tomorrow.' So I went back to Kent on the train and back again the next day to this place. Burdon vaguely remembered me. I played guitar for him; he liked it and asked me to stick around for a while. So there I was waiting, when Chas Chandler came up to me."

Chandler's account is somewhat different: "One day this kid with the same haircut as Hendrix turned up at the office asking to audition as the new guitarist for the Animals. I said that I was sorry, I had just fixed the last guitarist yesterday, Vic Briggs had joined and there was no room, but how did he fancy playing bass? He said, 'I'll do anything. I'm absolutely skint!' So we went straight down to Birdland. I happened to have a bass, a Gibson EB4, and told him that I was looking for a bass player for this guy I had brought over from the States. I knew Jimi was down at the club screening musicians and I told Noel that he might want to permanently pack in the guitar and go to bass after seeing him. Noel had never played bass before but he played for about two hours. Hendrix said, 'Fine, I like this guy. He's the first one.'"

"I sat in with this colored gentleman, a drummer and a keyboard player," continues Redding. "We played two-chord sequences, that's all, just a couple of chord sequences, and afterward the colored gentleman said to me, 'Oh I really like you. Do you want to play with me?' I said, 'Well, I can't really play bass, you know,' and he replied, 'Look, can you come back tomorrow?' I said, 'If you give me ten shillings, yes.' So I got the ten shillings and went back the next day, was taken to the office, saw Chas Chandler and Mike Jeffery, and they offered me a job. They also said that they were looking for a drummer. For that first audition the drummer was Aynsley Dunbar and the piano player was Mike O'Neill, from the Gladiators. So we came back to London and tried out a couple others, including a guy from up north who was very good."

"It came down to two drummers," recalls Terry McVay.

"One was Mitch Mitchell, the other Aynsley Dunbar. I knew Aynsley from the Mojos and Mitch from the Riot Squad. The Mojos were a part of the Liverpool scene. That was in 1964 when I was working with Goldie and the Gingerbreads [another Michael Jeffery-managed act]. We had done a tour and a lot of those gigs were with the Riot Squad so I had gotten to know Mitch."

"Chas introduced us to this guy – Mitch – who had just left Georgie Fame & the Blue Flames," remembers Redding. "We rehearsed for three or four days, learning things like 'Have Mercy,' 'Johnny B. Goode' – old things – 'If You Need Somebody to Love' and 'Hey Joe.'"

"One night Hendrix and I went to a club called Blaises, and Jimi got up to jam with Brian Auger," Chandler recounts. "While he was on stage I started speaking to Johnny Hallyday, the French singer, and his father Lee. Lee said, 'Johnny's going out for his first French tour in five years in France. Have you got a band together for this guy? He could be a support act.' I said yes even though I hadn't – I only had the bass player fixed. Lee said that they started their tour in ten days' time and if we joined them in Nice, we could do the whole tour. So we sat and did a deal that night. Jimi and I went back to our apartment and tossed a coin to see who was going to be the drummer [Dunbar or Mitchell] – we couldn't make up our minds. We had to start rehearsals, the tour started in only ten days. We were lucky, Mitch won the flip. We rang him the next morning and immediately started rehearsals to get an act together for the Johnny Hallyday tour.

"Mitchell had played it safe during the auditions," says Chandler, "he didn't show all he could do. But as soon as he was told the job was his he started opening up. We decided there and then that we weren't going to bring any other musicians in. It just sounded so clean, so exciting and new. We said, 'The hell with it, we don't need anyone else right now!' We had discussed every option but it was just the way it fell down. There was no master plan."

With Mitchell and Redding now in place, Chandler and Hendrix began brainstorming names for the newly formed trio. Chas had been unimpressed with Hendrix's former moniker, Jimmy James & the Blue Flames, and wanted to make a clean break from the past. Chandler did not want the group's name to ensnare them to one particular style of music. He viewed the Blue Flames tag as too down-home blues-like, and besides, Mitch had just left Georgie Fame's Blue Flames, and British fans were bound to be confused – at least initially – by the two distinctly different groups. After some gentle prodding, Hendrix agreed to drop Jimmy James and utilize his given name, although changing the spelling of his first name to J-i-m-i. "We racked our brains trying to think of a name for the group," recalls Chandler. It was he who coined "Experience." Hendrix at first was reluctant, but Chandler was sure it suited his artist perfectly.

With their touring place secured, Chandler immediately took the group into the studio to record "Hey Joe": "Jimi and I literally used the recording session as a test, to take Mitch and Noel into the studio and see how they worked. Although we completed the backing, the track was still not finished before we went to France because we couldn't get the girls' vocals right. I ended up going from one studio to another, trying to get different girls to put the vocals on. I nearly screwed it all up because my master tape was one-inch four-track [most London studios used half-inch four-track tape] and it took sessions at three different studios, Pye, CBS and De Lane Lea to complete." "Hey Joe" would finally be completed after the group's return from France, on October 23, 1966, with the Breakaways on background vocals.

With the backing track for "Hey Joe" recorded to Chandler's satisfaction, the group departed for France. Accompanying them, at Redding's suggestion, as road manager was his close friend, ex-car mechanic Gerry Stickells. The Jimi Hendrix Experience was set to debut – even though they still had no original material ready. "Johnny Hallyday was a master manipulator of an audience," says Chas Chandler. "Hendrix and I used to sit at the back of a hall and say, 'Look what he's doing, look at that.' He used to do a long set, party at a club he would rent after a gig and then sing for another two hours. Hallyday had that sense of outrage, but he could make it funny and amusing at the same time. And though Hendrix knew all of the routines, somehow watching a Frenchman put a little extra grace into the tricks and licks helped him refine his stage act. We benefited so much from it. Really, the Hendrix Experience's entire act – the entire basis of the act – was established on that Johnny Hallyday tour, no question about it."

Despite the group's short sets – only four or five songs – the French audiences took to them. Gerry Stickells recalls the initial crowd reaction as "good, but it was kind of like, 'What the hell is this?'" Despite their brief appearances, they had, according to Noel, "gone down a storm" in Evreux on the 13th and Nancy on the 14th. The enthusiasm and momentum was growing stronger each night. The real test would come when the tour reached the Olympia in Paris. The pressure was on, as Hendrix acknowledged in a later 1967 interview. "Paris Olympia is worse than playing the Apollo. Four days after we got together we were playing the Olympia, the biggest thing in Europe. The reception was great and we played four songs. We got it together with [just] 'Midnight Hour,' 'Land of 1000 Dances,' 'Everyone Needs Someone to Love' and 'Respect.' We never played those songs except one other time, in Germany."

With a sold-out Olympia awaiting, Chandler desperately wanted not only to establish the Experience but also Hendrix himself as a major new star. "We worked out a great entry for him," explains Chandler. "Mitch and Noel were on the stage and we announced Jimi, who was standing in the wings. We did an old blues trick, Georgio Gomelsky did a stepped introduction, something like, 'Ladies and gentlemen ...' and Jimi, still in the wings, let loose a quick burst of notes, 'From Seattle, Washington ...' and Jimi's guitar roared again, 'We have a ...' and Jimi would play again. This went on for ages before Jimi walked out with one hand in the air, still playing, and when the audience suddenly realized that all of this great guitar sound was being played one-handed, they went bananas."

Fueled by their triumphant success in France, the group returned to England to prepare for their London club debut at the Scotch of St. James. The showcase gig may as well have been closed to the public, with musicians and industry personnel packing the club to get a firsthand look at what would soon be London's newest sensation. The French gigs had jelled the trio much faster than anticipated. At the very least, Chandler knew that the three-man concept was working. With a strong performance at the Scotch on October 19 the Experience could work around the London clubs as a legitimate attraction rather than merely a curiosity. "The Scotch was a small place," remembers Gerry Stickells, "but we were trying to impress big agents such as Dick Katz and Harold Davison. The club owner kept trying to get me to turn down Hendrix's amp. I kept saying I would do so at the end of the next song, but as each one ended I ran to the bathroom to hide!"

Having extended their live repertoire to include Don Covay's "Have Mercy" in addition to Howlin' Wolf's "Killing Floor" and "Hey Joe," the Experience were a smash success once again. London's rock cognoscenti, so fervent in their adulation of authentic American blues and R&B performers, accepted Jimi immediately. As raw and frenzied as his Scotch performance was, Hendrix was clearly unique, miles apart from the likes of blues guitar greats like Hubert Sumlin and Earl Hooker. Hendrix exuded the very passion and conviction that British audiences loved in America's best blues and R&B artists, and combined this with a stage show of which only Howlin' Wolf and T-Bone Walker had shown flashes, and a new electric sound that Buddy Guy had only hinted at.

Their name quickly established in London, Chandler immediately took the Experience back into the studio to finish "Hey Joe." Hendrix later described the song's evolution. "Chas was sure it would be a hit. It was the first time I had ever sung on a record actually." Recording a strong lead vocal track from Hendrix took patience and repeated efforts. Capturing Jimi's modest, appealing voice was crucial to the single's success, and a listen to the song's session tapes relays some of the nervous energy Hendrix channeled into his performance. Having completed "Hey Joe" as the debut single, Chandler needed a B side. "'Stone Free' was the first thing we cut after France," he remembers. "Jimi wanted to put 'Land of 1000 Dances' on the B side but I said absolutely no way – you will sit down tonight and write a new song. So he sat down that night and composed 'Stone Free,' the first Experience song he ever wrote."

Recording "Stone Free" was decidedly less complicated than "Hey Joe." With little money available to pay for experimentation, Chandler essentially recorded a strong basic track with a live feel, fueled by Hendrix's incessant rhythm playing and Redding's driving bass. Overdubs were simple, specifically Mitchell's inventive percussion, harmony vocals from Hendrix, as well as additional guitar. "They seemed like ten-minute recording sessions," remembers Gerry Stickells. Indeed, "Stone Free" today is decidedly low-fi when compared to Hendrix's later sonic masterworks, but what Chandler did capture, with little financial or technical support, was the energy and enthusiasm behind the Experience. Chas was convinced of the prospects for "Hey Joe"; "Stone Free," on the other hand, was the first glimpse at Hendrix's potential as a composer.

With two songs completed, Chandler and Michael Jeffery secured the services of noted British press agent Les Perrin. It would be Perrin's job, Jeffery decreed, to "set the publicity machinery in motion and inform the press that an unusually capable artist had been found and brought to England." Seeking the record deal, Jeffery first approached Decca, meeting with its A&R representative Dick Rowe – best known, if a trifle unfairly, for turning down the Beatles. The meeting proved to be equally as futile, as Rowe dismissed "Hey Joe" and "Stone Free" outright. Perhaps if Jeffery had remembered Rowe's quip to Brian Epstein, published in the Beatles manager's autobiography *A Cellarful of Noise* – "groups of guitarists are on the way out" – he might have saved the trip.

Chandler had better success, securing a contract with Track Records. "I did the deal with Kit Lambert at the Scotch of St. James nightclub. The VIPs were playing there that night, and being friends of mine I brought Hendrix down to jam with them. Kit was there and nearly knocked over the tables trying to get across to me. He was such an outrageous guy: we wrote out the deal on a beer mat at the Scotch."

The pairing of London's hottest new act with Track Records, an aggressive new independent label, seemed on its face a perfect match. As Chris Stamp, co-owner of Track, recalls, Hendrix's talent and originality were just too good to let slip by. "When we saw Hendrix we said that we wanted to be involved with this guy as managers, producers or whatever. We couldn't get in as producers because Chas was producing. We couldn't get in as managers because Michael Jeffery was managing. So we said, 'Fuck it, we have a record company,' and we talked to Jeffery, Chandler and Hendrix about a record deal. We hadn't actually started the company yet. We had been talking to Polydor about the desperate need for an independent label: the big companies would not go along with any of the thinking happening at that time. Polydor had just come to Britain from Germany so they were the obvious ones to go to because they were just starting and they had money. We had taken The Who to Polydor, that was our in. We broke our Who deals with Decca and London Records and signed them to a recording contract and production deal. One of the things we offered to Jeffery and Chandler straight off – which we didn't have the right to do – was to guarantee Hendrix two performances on *Ready Steady Go!* Michael Jeffery also forced us to give them one thousand pounds sterling, which at the time was a lot of money for us, but he wouldn't do the deal without some kind of an advance, just to show good faith.

"As it turned out," continues Stamp, "Jimi's first record was released on the Polydor label because the Track label wasn't actually ready – though the deal was. We wanted to release it before Christmas to catch that market and coincide with one of the dates we had set for *Ready Steady Go!*" Having promised Hendrix two appearances on the program, Lambert and Stamp were forced to live up to their brag. After some gentle arm-twisting, they did indeed set up an engagement for December 13, 1966.

With a recording contract secured, the Experience rehearsed daily at a second floor studio on Savile Row, run by a friend of Eric Burdon's. Hendrix was now sharing Chas's apartment at 43 Berkeley Street, and it was here that the two strengthened their already close friendship.

At first quiet and painfully shy, Hendrix's quick wit and sense of humor gradually surfaced. Says Chas: "The legend of him now is as this sort of tragic figure. My memories of Jimi are always with a smile on his face. We laughed all the time. The only tragic thing about Jimi was his death. He had an enormous capacity for life and was great fun to be with. We did nothing but sit at home and talk about his songs and his career."

With Chandler imploring Hendrix to write new material, the Experience left for gigs in West Germany. Although the pay was nominal, the Experience had been booked to play two shows a night at the Big Apple Club in Munich. The idea, according to Gerry Stickells, was to "tighten up the band and work in some new material." In addition to honing stage versions of "Hey Joe" and "Stone Free," the Experience added a rearranged version of B.B. King's "Rock Me Baby" and a stunning interpretation of Dylan's "Like a Rolling Stone." The German audiences loved them, particularly Hendrix's wild stage presence. As Chandler explains: "The thing that made it work was Jimi's sense of humor, the laugh that went with it. It was outrageous, but in a humorous way. You had to take it seriously but you couldn't."

What Hendrix did take seriously, according to Chris Stamp, was the cultivation of his look. "No one realized how hip Jimi was. He was *super* hip. Hendrix wanted to immediately acclimatize himself with hip London, *he* wanted to do that. Chandler wasn't really your man for the gig there – this isn't a knock on Chas, but for that area Jimi went to places like Granny's and got all of his look together. He just knew all of those things instinctively and his whole look changed overnight."

# 2 TAKING LONDON BY STORM

*"After the gig at Croydon [February 6, 1967], Hendrix never looked back. At Croydon, the audience was shocked. It wasn't just excitement, I think they were numb!"*

– Chas Chandler

**W**ith only two gigs booked for the remainder of November, the Ricky Tick Club in Hounslow on the 16th as well as an important press reception and show at the Bag O'Nails in London on the 25th, Chas and Jimi had decided to record each new song Hendrix had completed. Working with his Stratocaster and a small Vox amplifier at Chas's apartment, Jimi began to develop the riffs and rhythm patterns for songs such as "Can You See Me" and "Remember." Living with Chandler also began to have a pronounced influence on Hendrix's lyrics and poetry, as Jimi was soon exposed to Chandler's penchant for science fiction. "I had dozens of science fiction books at home," says Chandler. "The first one Jimi read was *Earth Abides*. It wasn't a Flash Gordon-type, it's an end of the world, new beginning, disaster-type story. He started reading through them all. That's where 'Third Stone From the Sun' and 'Up From the Skies' came from. He used to do the lyrics and I would try to make them a bit more ambiguous."

As determined as Chandler and Hendrix were to succeed, it wasn't exactly all work and no play, as Chas recalls. "We used to play Risk for days on end, having a game going all the time. All four of us played: me, Jimi, his new girlfriend Kathy Etchingham, and my wife Lotta. There was always a table with the game set – if we went out we used to leave it until we came back and sometimes it would last three, four or five days. Of course, after a while you got to know how each person played and it became even more fun because you knew what the other people were up to."

Graham Nash, a member of the Hollies at that time and a longtime friend of Chandler's, befriended Hendrix soon after he settled in London and took part in many a game. "Jimi," relates Nash, "was a great Risk player – and no slouch at Monopoly either!"

The gig and press reception at the Bag O'Nails proved to be a coming-out party for London's rock n' roll elite, and the Experience, fortified from their daily rehearsals, once again lived up to the challenge. Their stint at the Big Apple Club had tightened the band, especially the interplay between Hendrix and Mitchell, whose playing had continued to evolve. Stemming from his love for American jazz, his style was essentially self-taught. Working at Marshall's Music Shop (owned by amplifier creator Jim Marshall) as a young teenager, Mitch sat in with Screaming Lord Sutch's backing group and Johnny Kidd and the Pirates, who would pass through the West London store. Later, while playing in a band that featured Jim Marshall's son on saxophone, Mitch caught a glimpse of British jazz pianist Georgie Fame. "We used to play upstairs at the Whisky A Go Go above the old Flamingo Club on Wardour Street," recalls Mitch. "One night I heard something going on so I went downstairs and saw Georgie Fame, playing piano. That was before [his] Hammond organ period, and I thought 'Oh yeah!' and that was my first exposure to Mose Allison and things like that. I wasn't particularly aware of anything else, but when I heard Georgie Fame's band I was really interested. I thought, 'Yeah, I really want to play with that band.' Well, years passed and I eventually did."

After working in various London studios as a session drummer, Mitch joined Georgie Fame & the Blue Flames in the spring of 1965. It was during his eighteen months with the Blue Flames that Mitch developed his reputation as a drummer fluent in both jazz and rock. In addition to the obvious imprint jazz powerhouse Elvin Jones had on his style, Mitch also had Ginger Baker's dexterity. Not a hard drummer in the Keith Moon or later John Bonham tradition, Mitchell gripped his sticks in the style of jazz idols such as Ronnie Verral, and used a small drum kit – especially in the studio. In October of 1966, Fame disbanded the present lineup of the Blue Flames. The next day, Mitch received the call from Chas Chandler about auditions for his new artist. Shortly thereafter, he was in the Experience.

But was London's hottest new group a true band? Both Mitchell and Redding were suitably impressed by Hendrix's considerable talents, but what exactly were their roles? Chandler was obviously dedicated, he had worked hard for the band right from the start. But unlike Jimi, whose friendship with Mitch developed out of mutual respect, Chandler thought of Mitchell and Redding – much to Mitch's chagrin – as employees first. Chandler made no bones about Hendrix's role in the group. He was and forever would be the star. Along these lines, Michael Jeffery also saw the prospects of marketing the act. Jeffery had replaced members of the Animals at their peak without any loss of popularity. In his mind, it was and would be the Peter Noones, Eric Burdons and Jimi Hendrixes that generated all of the excitement and money. "Jeffery was very specific as to who Yameta signed to exclusive contracts," says John Hillman, Yameta's director as well as Jeffery's personal attorney. "Hendrix was the only one to receive a share, and that's just how Jeffery – and Hendrix – wanted it." As for Hendrix, he had made considerable progress in his three months abroad. For once, he was being treated with respect and given an opportunity to succeed. For the first time he was the star, not the sideman; he was encouraged, not ignored. Irrespective of their status with Yameta, Jeffery or Chandler, on personal and musical levels Hendrix would treat Mitchell and Redding as equals – just as he had always wanted to be treated himself.

The Experience's show at their Bag O'Nails press reception had stunned the celebrity-studded audience, whose presence was not lost on the group. As Redding explains: "In those days, you only played thirty-five or forty minutes. I remember being in the dressing room afterward and when John Lennon walked in, I nearly fainted. Then McCartney walked in, and Donovan walked in. I was on the floor by then!"

Aside from the gaggle of musicians wishing to meet and speak with Hendrix following the performance was a young electronics enthusiast, Roger Mayer. "Hendrix was playing and I was floored," he says. "It was like everything I had ever imagined. I just went up to him and started talking, telling him what I did. I had been in electronics since 1963 and was totally into avant-garde sounds. Jimi asked me to come down to a gig he was playing at Chiselhurst Caves on December 16, 1966, near London. So I went there and brought some of my devices such as the Octavia [which boosted a guitar's octaves to various levels]. He tried them out backstage and was thrilled. When I had met Michael Jeffery, he was the type of person that I made out very quickly that I didn't want to deal with. I just wanted to make sure that I received expenses for research and development – I never got salary, I just got paid for making the things. I did things for Hendrix, but not for Jeffery."

As Lambert and Stamp had promised, the Jimi Hendrix Experience soon made their television debut, appearing with Keith Relf and the Merseys on the penultimate episode of *Ready Steady Go!* Complying with the British Musicians Union ban on lip-synching, Hendrix, with Mitchell and Redding miming accompaniment, sang "Hey Joe" live. As tame as the performance seems today, the Experience clearly exposed the era's transition from British pop to a new, more sophisticated and harder-edged sound. The Beatles had started the process earlier that summer with the release of "Paperback Writer" and "Rain," but, at least at this stage, the Experience lacked the refinement and facility that the Fab Four's recordings routinely featured. It wasn't "Hey Joe" alone that caught the viewers' imagination, it was the group, obviously different from anything else they had ever seen. Intentional or not, the coupling of a genuine black American artist with two aggressive young Englishmen had created a dynamic combination. At once, Hendrix appealed to England's maturing legions of rock, blues and R&B followers.

Chandler would be proven correct: "Hey Joe" became a hit single. But it also masked the true potential of the group. "Hey Joe" was a well-intentioned, calculated attempt to compete with the status quo of the British pop scene. Despite the group's and Chandler's limited technical experience in the recording studio, their arrangement of "Hey Joe," and especially of Hendrix's own composition "Stone Free," far and away exceeded the likes of Cream's recent debut single "Wrapping Paper." Within both "Hey Joe" and "Stone Free" Chandler had successfully incorporated Hendrix's striking guitar and, by mixing it to the fore, made Jimi's ability on the instrument the record's most obvious characteristic. The rigid adherence of "Wrapping Paper" to standard pop structure negated Baker's, Bruce's and especially Clapton's much vaunted virtuosity.

For Chris Stamp and Kit Lambert, Track Records had been their reply to the burgeoning London rock scene. But as Stamp explains, despite the fact that the audience was now growing older, they still responded to the same marketing techniques (i.e. hype) that had reeled them in just a few years before. "Chandler was sure that 'Hey Joe' would be a winner," remembers Stamp, "but all of the imagery [behind the Experience] was basically done at Track. We brought in six of the top London photographers, people like Roger Law, David King and David Montgomery. We had these great black-and-white posters, featuring provocative shots of Hendrix posing bare-chested. Track was doing a semi-management job but that was because Kit and I were managers who operated a record label. That was our thinking. Our strategy was to get you an appearance on *Ready Steady Go!* rather than an advance [against artist royalties]."

What *Ready Steady Go!* achieved for the Experience was to make people outside of London aware of this visually striking and exciting group. Hendrix's dynamic stage charisma had been attracting small but growing praise in the capital but it was through television that the Experience and Jimi Hendrix startled not only England's rock n' roll fan base but the working press. As an almost direct result of the group's television debut, "Hey Joe" entered the chart published by *Record Mirror* at 38. Just two days after "Hey Joe" was released, Blaises club was packed with London's rock n' roll elite. With members of the Beatles and the Rolling Stones in attendance, Hendrix roared through "Killing Floor," "Rock Me Baby" and "Stone Free" using all of his stage moves – playing guitar one-handed, behind his back, through his legs, behind his head and with his teeth. Interspersed among the frenzied uptempo material were the slower numbers, "Like a Rolling Stone" and "Hey Joe." Hendrix sang with conviction and confidence. Although only one song, "Stone Free," was an original Hendrix composition, "Like a Rolling Stone" teemed with emotion, as if he had lived and endured each line, each verse. Even "Killing Floor," the group's opening number, overwhelmed the packed club. Howlin' Wolf had never sounded like this. "Killing Floor" was not only an opening forum for Hendrix's outlandish stage show but a far more exciting, high-velocity, reworked interpretation.

After the show, Hendrix, Mitchell and Redding were swamped by the likes of Paul McCartney, John Lennon and Brian Jones. These people, thought Redding, "were *our* idols and they wanted to meet us!" In fact, they were enamored with Hendrix. So much so that Gerry Stickells accidentally clobbered Lennon, clogging the club's narrow walkway, over the head with Mitch's bass drum while trying to remove the band's gear. Hendrix so impressed the Beatles and the Stones that they went out of their way to mention Jimi and the Experience in public. "We got a tremendous amount of help from people like Mick Jagger, Paul McCartney and John Lennon," recalls Chandler. "They would rave about Hendrix and turn the entire course of an interview around just to talk about him."

With this continued endorsement, "Hey Joe" began to creep slowly up the British charts, though, as Chas recalls, it seemed to be moving a bit too slowly. "Kit Lambert was a great operator. The week 'Hey Joe' started selling, the Bee Gees had a massive record out. It was going up the charts at such a rate it had to be number one. Track was a little independent label whose records were pressed and distributed by Polydor. 'Hey Joe' broke and we were told that all of the machines were tied up pressing the Bee Gees record. Kit went down to the pressing plant and stood at the machines putting pound notes on top of them until the operators switched over to 'Hey Joe.' He had a roll of pound notes and just kept doing it until all of the operators switched."

No stranger to unorthodox measures himself, Michael Jeffery was determined to see that "Hey Joe" receive ample exposure on British radio. To guarantee continued play on some of Britain's influential pirate stations, Jeffery, unable to barter with "Hey Joe" – a cover song – as a bribe, dealt away a portion of Hendrix's publishing royalties for "Stone Free." Abby Schroeder, with whom Jeffery had already signed to administer Hendrix's publishing, was livid. "Jeffery was so desperate for airplay," recalls Schroeder, "that he allowed himself to be blackmailed. He explained to me that this process had worked successfully once before and, to ensure heavy pirate airplay, one had to give up a piece of the action. I told him that splitting publishing copyrights wasn't like cutting up a pie. There were other ways to get airplay without sacrificing your artist's work."

As "Hey Joe" gradually scaled up the British singles chart, Hendrix had yet to finish writing – let alone record – the Experience's follow-up. "'Purple Haze,'" Chandler recalls, "was written December 26, 1966, at the Upper Cut Club. The Upper Cut was owned by Phil Walker, his first venture after retiring as a boxer, hence the club name. It was actually written in the dressing room of the club that afternoon. The gig was at 4 P.M., a press function for the club. He started playing the riff and I said, 'Write the rest of that!,' so he did." Chandler refutes suggestions that Hendrix was under the influence of LSD at the time, deflating a much perpetuated myth that "Haze" came as the result of some "Purple" psychedelic potion. While Hendrix was no stranger to drugs, especially speed and marijuana, the Experience's first formal introduction to drugs, Chas recalls with a laugh, came later that week. "After the group's New Year's Eve show at Stan's in Folkestone, Kent, Redding's hometown, they all planned to stay with Noel that night." It was this same party that reportedly inspired Hendrix to write "Fire" as he huddled near the Redding fireplace frigid from the bitter English cold.

With its signature riff completed, Hendrix began to edit down his "Purple Haze" lyrics in preparation for recording. Chandler had provided Hendrix with shelter, opportunity and encouragement. In return, Hendrix loosened seemingly self-imposed restraints on his abilities. Not quite confident enough to address his spirituality, so prevalent in his later work, Hendrix pared down such phrases as "Purple Haze, Jesus Saves" rejecting them as too personal. As Chandler has described, Hendrix's early efforts at songwriting were intensely private. Songs were created from Hendrix's poetry, an interest he kept a virtual secret. Some years later, during the long construction of Electric Lady Studios, Hendrix spoke with studio president Jim Marron about his admiration for the poet e.e. cummings. While Hendrix was never a voracious reader, cummings's lyrical style, exotic imagery and liberal use of colors struck a chord within him.

The difference between "Hey Joe," with its recording serving as an audition for Mitchell and Redding, and "Purple Haze" was a marked one, says Chandler. "'Purple Haze' probably took longer to record than any of the earlier records. With 'Hey Joe,' I didn't know how to run the place. I was just a dumb bass player trying to become a producer. With 'Purple Haze,' Hendrix and I were striving for a sound and just kept going back in, two hours at a time, trying to achieve it. A lot of the background sound on 'Purple Haze' is actually a recording being fed back into the studio through the earphones held around the microphone, moving them in and out to create a weird echo. It wasn't like we were in there for days on end. We recorded it and then Hendrix and I would be sitting at home saying, 'Let's try that.' Then we would go in for an hour or two. That's how it was in those days. However long it took to record that one specific idea, that's how long we would book. We kept going in and out."

These spur-of-the-moment ideas included the oohs and aahs, provided by Redding, who laughingly recalls Chandler sending him to the vocal booth to contribute them. As absurd as they may have been, they made the final version what it was. "Purple Haze" wasn't the only song under construction at the time. Hendrix had been composing a long poem about relationships between men and women – Hendrix was a vocal opponent of traditional marriage – which became a song started and completed the same day. As Chandler recalls. "'51st Anniversary' was recorded on January 11, 1967. That was the B side. A great recording, I always loved that song. It features five guitar overdubs all linking in together, to sound like one guitar. Hendrix was brilliant. We would record on four-track, premix down to two-track, fill those up, and overdub again."

"51st Anniversary" also prominently featured Hendrix's

lead vocal, a difficult victory for Chandler. "I had arguments with him about where his voice should go," Chandler says. "He would always want to bury his voice, but I loved its rhythm and thought it was great."

With just two original compositions under his belt, Hendrix's "51st Anniversary" lyrics were similar in feel to those of "Stone Free." Note the same pulsating bass technique utilized by Redding for "Purple Haze." Not to be overlooked either were the stinging closing guitar notes, which would later reappear in "Highway Chile." Not only were the ideas coming fast and furious, "51st Anniversary" featured Hendrix's first real injection of attitude into his recordings, most notably his fake joint smoking (which appears not once but twice) and his bold aside "That was the good side baby, here comes the bad side." While tame in comparison to "Fire" and its "Move over rover, let Jimi take over," it did signal Hendrix's first combination of his stage persona with the Experience's outrageous (by 1966 standards) image.

"Hey Joe" was a clever reworking of Tim Rose's composition. "Purple Haze," on the other hand, was Hendrix's own first A side, his first real test as a composer. Having alerted Britain's rock audience to his talents via "Hey Joe," "Purple Haze" had to be even more impressive lest he and the Experience risk halting their fast-growing momentum.

While the group continued to score minor triumphs such as placing "Hey Joe" on the charts and appearing on *Ready Steady Go!*, their lack of cash flow dogged Chandler and Jeffery. They had only enough money to pay for recording sessions at lesser-known studios, and even when they could record, they had to compromise, taking late nights or an hour or two at a reduced rate. While they were playing almost every night through January in London, the pay was nominal. "We were doing clubs like the 71/2 for seven pounds," recalls Redding. Their transportation was even less glamorous: "They drove themselves in Mitch's car and I drove the van," says Gerry Stickells. As "Hey Joe" continued to inch up the charts, the Experience performed the song, with the Breakaways on background vocals, on BBC-TV's influential *Top of the Pops*, and gave their first, albeit brief, television interview. Looming large on the group's horizon, however, was a concert set for January 29, 1967, at Brian Epstein's Saville Theatre, in London. Scheduled to appear on the same bill were fellow Track recording artists The Who, along with two other bands, the Koobas and Thoughts. "Kit and I had a lot to do with who went into the Saville on Sunday nights because things were much smaller then," says Chris Stamp. "It wasn't like Kit and I had this great power. We knew Vicky Wickham from *Ready Steady Go!* and she was working for Brian Epstein, booking the Saville. We booked The Who and brought the Experience in as support for them. This was Hendrix's most prestigious London gig to date."

A beautiful old-fashioned theater, the Saville was full to capacity, its audience aware of Hendrix and the Experience from their important television appearances and press interviews. As was becoming the custom, the Beatles dropped by the group's dressing room before and after the gig, offering their support and admiration. Judging by the reception accorded them, the Experience had truly arrived and were already on the verge of becoming, apart from the Beatles and the Rolling Stones, the biggest thing in England. Their compact forty-minute set included "Killing Floor," "Have Mercy," "Can You See Me," "Like a Rolling Stone," "Rock Me Baby," "Stone Free," "Hey Joe" as well as a new addition, a charged rendition of the Troggs' recent hit "Wild Thing" – complete with Hendrix thrusting the neck of his Fender Stratocaster against and through his legs and across the face of his battered Marshall 4 × 12 speaker cabinets.

This new and dynamic stage show was perfectly suited for larger venues such as the Saville. Hendrix was physically imposing as he played guitar. (His stage show had been perfected over years, first alone, shaped during countless hours of private practice, and then as part of support bands behind R&B pioneers Little Richard, the Isley Brothers and

Ike & Tina Turner, among others.) His act, even the way the group looked, was a clever combination of superior ability and an element of surprise capable of astonishing even the most seasoned rock n' roll admirer. With most of his following too young to have seen Chuck Berry in his prime, the Experience stunned audiences who had previously considered Keith Moon kicking over his drum kit the consummate act of civil disobedience.

Within the Experience, there seemed an element far more threatening than England had ever before seen. For the Beatles, performing stock-still incited rioting; for the Stones, Mick Jagger's gyrations whipped young girls into an uncontrolled frenzy – regardless of what either group was playing. With the Experience, Hendrix had never played with this much passion and enthusiasm in his life, as each performance drained years of stagnation and frustration from him. His ability, stifled and suppressed behind such lesser talents as Curtis Knight & the Squires, expanded in an incredibly short time. He had won the total support and admiration of London's best musicians on the strength of rearranged blues and R&B standards. His only original composition to date, "Stone Free," as brilliant as it was, was still only a B side! Chandler's support of and commitment to Hendrix challenged him into making the most of his first real opportunity for public acceptance and success.

# 3 CLEARING A PATH

*"Jimi and I used to sit up at night and think of who we could offend tomorrow to get into the headlines."*

—Chas Chandler

Leaving Hendrix in Chandler's hands, Michael Jeffery left for America. While in New York, he began to investigate possibilities for an American recording contract for Hendrix, as well as severing any outstanding contracts and agreements. Before they had left for London in September of 1966, Chandler and Jeffery had settled a handful of such obligations – booking agreements and the like – out of their own pocket. The total sum, as Chandler recalls, came to less than $500. At the same time, Hendrix told his charges that in addition to contracts he had signed as a "session man," he had also signed a recording contract with Henry "Juggy" Murray, Jr.'s, Sue Records, and a management contract with Copa Management, a company that Murray was involved in.

Unable to settle these before they had left for Europe, Jeffery wrote to Marshall & Vigoda, a New York law firm that had occasionally represented both him and the Animals. Paul Marshall was a prominent, respected music industry attorney, and Jeffery looked to his firm to find Juggy Murray and buy out any agreement that bound

45

Hendrix to him. The process was all the more frustrating because Hendrix hadn't retained any copies of the agreements that he had signed. Acting as an agent for Yameta, the Bahamian tax shelter corporation developed for the Animals by British attorney John Hillman, Jeffery had signed Hendrix to a recording, management and publishing contract. Hillman deducted 10 percent of all revenues generated by Yameta's artists to maintain the shelter. Jeffery deducted a staggering 40 percent of Hendrix's earnings (he also received additional compensation to act as Yameta's "exclusive talent representative"). Chandler's name was not on Hendrix's original management contract signed December 1, 1966; Jeffery had the contract amended June 5, 1967, finally awarding Chandler his half of Jeffery's 40 percent share. Mitchell and Redding, unbeknownst to them, were actually on salary. Though their pay for each performance was calculated as if on a 50-25-25 basis, they had no signed agreement with Yameta entitling them to such a rate. Theirs was a verbal agreement with Hendrix, Jeffery and Chandler, *despite* the fact that they were signed to Yameta as "employees."

Chandler, and to a lesser degree Jeffery, had been funding the Experience with money each had earned from the Animals. Establishing Hendrix in England had proven to be a costly undertaking. It was imperative that Jeffery secure an American record deal that would include, at the very least, some sort of cash advance. Since August 1966, Jeffery and Chandler, under the auspices of Yameta, had paid off most of Hendrix's outstanding obligations in New York, put him up there and paid his living expenses until his passport and birth certificate were located, installed him in London at the White House, the Hyde Park Towers, and Chas's home in Ringo Starr's Montagu Square duplex, paid all of his London living expenses, developed a supporting group, hired a road manager and publicist, purchased stage equipment and paid for recording studio costs – all without any obligation from Hendrix to repay them should he not succeed. However, what Hendrix and Yameta did have in writing was a "tacit understanding" with regard to recouping sums advanced by Yameta to Hendrix. This tacit understanding meant that, should the Jimi Hendrix Experience become successful and financially self-sustaining, Yameta would deduct all of its costs incurred in establishing the artist. Jeffery and Chandler were strapped for cash, and even this clause, despite the group's early triumphs, brought no financial relief. The group wasn't to be financially self-sufficient until March 1967.

As Marshall and Vigoda began tracking down Juggy Murray, Hendrix further exasperated Yameta. "I remember the situation very clearly," recalled Michael Jeffery in 1968. "We took him to a club in London where they were playing records, and one evening Hendrix proudly said, 'Hey, listen to this one. I'm on there somewhere.' I got a bit agitated, obtained a copy of the record, and said, 'What do you mean you are on it?' He said, 'Oh, it was made when I was playing with this group, the Squires.' I started questioning him in depth about this group and what his relationship was with them. I said, 'Are you sure you have no other pieces of paper around?' He said, 'No, I did sign something as a session man or something like that ... forget it, it doesn't mean anything.'" Regardless, Jeffery instructed Marshall & Vigoda to obtain quitclaims for any recordings Hendrix may have participated in with the Squires on RSVP Records, the label on the single he had purchased. He then instructed Leon Dicker, Yameta's American attorney and representative, to forward Marshall & Vigoda the sum of $2,500 to secure all necessary quitclaims.

Johanan Vigoda, Paul Marshall's partner at the time, was asked by Jeffery to help secure a recording contract for a new act he was representing. "One day Jeffery came to our office to talk about getting a record deal for this black guitarist he had found. He showed me some reviews from things like *New Musical Express* as well as these pictures that had Hendrix in a cape and under his arms, like a wrestler, two white guys' faces. Jeffery was convinced that Hendrix was a great star and would become a phenomenon."

Vigoda, who had represented Juggy Murray in the past, found him in Chicago and instructed him to find his contract with "Jimmy James" or "Jimmy Hendrix." Murray had fallen on hard times despite the fact that Sue Records had released a number of superlative singles by such R&B artists as Baby Washington, Derek Martin and Ike & Tina Turner. In fact, Sue was on the verge of financial collapse, having filed a bankruptcy petition under Chapter 11 on December 29, 1966. From a deposition completed by Beldock, Levine, & Hoffman on December 5, 1967, Murray described the following: that Vigoda and the firm of Marshall & Vigoda had represented him since the spring of 1965; and that he was summoned to Vigoda's office on January 20, 1967, at which time Vigoda had him endorse a check for $1,500 (Murray did not remember the name of the payee). At Vigoda's request, Murray then turned the check over to Vigoda, and Vigoda gave Murray $750 in cash, obtaining a receipt from Murray. Simultaneous to this Murray signed two assignments on behalf of Sue Records Inc. and Copa Management Inc. stating that up to that time neither Vigoda or Jeffery had seen a copy of the contract between Hendrix and Sue Records because Murray had been unable to locate same. (It would not be until August 1967 before Murray actually found a copy of his original blank contract forms and not until that October that he was able to personally deliver to Jeffery the original agreements.)

For the purpose of completing the assignments, though, Murray attempted to reconstruct from memory the terms of the contract. For Jeffery, the whole affair had been a messy, albeit necessary, exercise. For Juggy Murray, it had meant a net gain – he needed the $750 to pay a personal mortgage. Sue Records was a one-man operation, forced to survive on a record-to-record basis with little or no consistent cash flow. Despite having signed Hendrix on July 27, 1965, he had never recorded any material with him and had shown no plans to do so in the future.

With Juggy Murray out of the way, Jeffery and Vigoda

looked to settle any claim RSVP Records might have had over Hendrix. RSVP was a small New York-based independent label run by Jerry Simon. Simon's involvement with the Squires had officially begun February 19, 1966, when RSVP signed Curtis Knight, leader of the Squires, to an exclusive recording contract. Knight had recorded a number of finished songs, featuring the Squires, for Ed Chalpin's PPX Industries during 1965 and early 1966. PPX president Chalpin was best known in the music industry as the producer of "soundalike" records – cover versions of the top hits of the day, prepared for countries all over the world. He recorded these records as well as his other artists such as Curtis Knight, at his own facility, Studio 76.

On March 15, 1966, RSVP Records entered into an agreement with PPX Industries, obtaining a license to manufacture and sell in the United States and Canada two recordings, "How Would You Feel?" and "Welcome Home." Since Curtis Knight with the Squires was recording for Jerry Simon, he deemed it necessary to put the group under written contract, doing so on June 10, 1966. The Squires' lineup included Napoleon Anderson, Nathaniel Edmonds, Marian Booker and Jimmy Hendrix. Pursuant to the June 10, 1966, agreement, they recorded seven songs: "The U.F.O.," "I'm a Fool for You Baby," "Ballad of Jimmy," "Gotta Have a New Dress," "Hornet's Nest," "Knock Yourself Out" and "Your Love." RSVP issued one 45 rpm record of two titles, "Hornet's Nest" and "Knock Yourself Out" – the single Jeffery and Hendrix had heard at the London club – which had indifferent results. The record label mentions Hendrix only as a co-composer, not as a recording artist.

The lack of success dulled Simon's interest in the Squires, so when contacted by Johanan Vigoda, Simon negotiated Hendrix's release from RSVP. He discussed with Jeffery the seven songs, inaccurately referred to in the agreement as "six master sides," agreeing that none "have heretofore or will hereafter be released commercially in any matter or form using the name Jimi Hendrix in connection therewith."

This provision was the essence of the agreement. As far as Simon was concerned, he had no further interest in Curtis Knight & the Squires. "As a matter of fact," Simon would later say, "if Jeffery had so requested, I would have sold the master tapes themselves to him at the time, but neither one of us considered that to be essential."

So with a check dated January 23, 1967, Jeffery acquired the rights to the seven sides for $500. All things considered, the week was considered a success. Jeffery had, he thought, secured all of the assignments necessary to free Hendrix from his prior commitments. In addition, he had fully briefed Vigoda to pursue an American recording contract, outlining the structure of Yameta and its relationship with regard to himself, Hendrix, the Experience and Chandler. Yameta's American representative, Leon Dicker, was to be kept abreast of Vigoda's progress, as Jeffery had to rejoin the new Animals tour.

Back in England, the Experience immediately resumed touring, a process easier said than done, says Gerry Stickells. "The New Cellar Club in South Shields [February 1, 1967] had a revolving stage. That was the first time we used a Marshall 200 watt amplifier and it blew up on stage. We had only one 100 watt Marshall for the PA system and both Jimi and Noel had to play through it. They were singing and playing all through the same amp. The next morning I had to drive all the way down to Marshall's to pick up parts, then drive all the way back to the Imperial Club in Darlington for the next night's gig – and there wasn't much motorway in those days!"

The next day, Chandler brought the band to De Lane Lea Studios to record a new song Hendrix had written about his girlfriend, "The Wind Cries Mary." Chandler recalls: "That was written about Kathy [Etchingham] – her middle name was Mary. For sheer fun, 'The Wind Cries Mary' is my favorite track. Neither Mitchell, Redding nor I had ever heard the song before but we finished recording it in twenty minutes!"

With Hendrix and Chandler sharing an apartment, the creative relationship between artist and producer continued to grow outside of the studio. As Chas recalls, "In the initial stages, I changed a lot of the lyrics. He would come up with a lyric and I would make suggestions; in general, editing them down. His songs tended to be six or seven minutes long and we would get them down to three or four minutes. We all felt that that improved them. The basic thing was editing, I was acting as if I was the editor of a newspaper, getting everything concise."

The session for "The Wind Cries Mary" also saw the recording of one of the group's stage staples, "Can You See Me." An uptempo rocker, drawn from simple R&B chord sequences, "Can You See Me" was given serious consideration as a B side for "The Wind Cries Mary." While the latter may have been completed in only twenty minutes, the Experience's limited finances dictated how much time they could allot per song. As Mitch Mitchell would later describe, Chandler shared duties as producer and comptroller, a difficult task requiring great sensitivity. "It caused a lot of problems at the time because Hendrix had very specific ideas about what was required and the sound that he wanted. A lot of the early things were basically done in two or three takes. Chas never let us forget that the Animals' 'House of the Rising Sun' was made for forty pounds and sold a million copies." While engineer Dave Siddle tried his best to accommodate the band's evolving ideas about their sound (a listen to the panning of the bass near to the end of "Can You See Me" will provide one example), Chandler was hamstrung by a lack of money: overlooked in the song's mixing was a sloppy insert edit of one of Hendrix's reverb-drenched notes.

Lack of finances wasn't Chandler's only concern (he was already selling his own bass guitars and calling in favors to pay for recording time): De Lane Lea Studios was having problems with its neighbors over Hendrix's love of volume. "There was always trouble with the bank when you recorded at De Lane Lea," says Chandler. "There was a bank above the studio and it was at the time when computers were just coming in. Every time we went in, we would play so loud that it would foul up the computers upstairs. As a result, we would always have trouble getting in there when we wanted." Another R&B-influenced song cut at De Lane Lea perfectly illustrated how loud Hendrix would be playing while laying down a song's basic rhythm track: in the opening notes of "Remember," Mitchell's drum kit resonating from the volume of Hendrix's Marshall 4 × 12 speaker cabinets can be heard.

Although Hendrix would record his guitar parts, both rhythm and lead, at a volume level he chose, he would only briefly run through each song before recording began to ensure that Redding knew the chords and changes and Mitchell the tempo. Sometimes well-rehearsed, stage-proven songs couldn't be reproduced in the studio. "I always wanted to do a studio version of 'Like a Rolling Stone,'" explains Chandler. "We did it a few times, but for some reason, Mitch could never keep the time right. It used to drive them nuts because Mitch would be either winding up or slowing down. The thing that bugged me about that one was that the first time I saw Hendrix, at the Cafe Wha? in Greenwich Village, the first thing he did was 'Hey Joe' and the second was 'Like a Rolling Stone,' and for the first time, hearing Jimi sing it, I understood what the lyrics were trying to say. I was a Dylan fan, but I had started cooling on him at the time he wrote 'Like a Rolling Stone.' It was the first Dylan song I was struggling with. So we both wanted to record it but we were never successful. I tried over and over to get it."

The band next joined the new Animals tour of England as their opening act. Ever industrious, as Gerry Stickells recalls, the Experience would play a gig as headline act at London's Flamingo Club during the afternoon before moving on to the Ram Jam Club later the same evening to open the new Animals show. This series of gigs was the new Animals' first venture into the heart of England, and – because the original

Animals had enjoyed a large British following – the Experience were exposed to packed clubs on a nightly basis. With "Hey Joe" still selling and climbing up the British charts, these gigs, no matter how small, were crucial to the group's success. Playing almost every night eased their cash flow crisis and, more importantly, perhaps through having to play the same set each night, triggered a burst of creativity in Jimi that took its form in songwriting. Three of the new songs, "Love or Confusion," "Fire" and "Foxey Lady," would be included in the Experience's debut on BBC radio's *Saturday Club* program, part of an in-studio performance that also featured "Hey Joe," "Stone Free," "Killing Floor" and "Purple Haze."

"Foxey Lady" was another Hendrix original that perfectly suited the image the Experience loved to flaunt, and London's Fleet Street press loved to devour. Once again, as Hendrix described in a 1968 interview, preparation for these recordings was spartan. "On 'Foxey Lady' we just started playing, set up a microphone, and I had these words …" "Foxey Lady" was indicative of Chandler's directness as a producer. He would look for riffs as Hendrix would jam, either alone or with Mitchell and Redding, and stop Jimi when he heard something that caught his ear. Hendrix's lyrics, on the other hand, were often passages from his poetry, committed to paper almost as soon as they arrived in his head. "Sometimes it all depends," he would say. "A lot of times I write words all over the place, on matchboxes or on napkins, and then sometimes music comes across to me just when I am sitting around doing nothing, and then the music makes me think of a few words I might have written. So I go back to those few words if I can find them and just get it together. Sometimes it all happens at the same time."

Another song still in development during the "Foxey Lady" sessions was "Red House." Unlike the former, "Red House" was not a spontaneous attempt to record a blues song. As has been seen, Hendrix had composed "Red House," at least its chord sequences, well before Chandler took him to England. At that time, however, he had not found lyrics that matched the emotion of the music – they would undergo the same process of trial and error that he would also employ for such blues-influenced songs as "Hear My Train A Comin'" and "Bleeding Heart," experimenting with them on the concert stage, then adding and subtracting lyrics until he felt comfortable.

While this process extended to the great majority of Hendrix's compositions, "Red House" was a very special and important song. This was his original blues composition. Throughout most of his life he had loved to listen and play the blues, either alone or with Faye Pridgeon at her apartment in Harlem. There they would listen and sing, as he strummed his unplugged electric guitar, to songs such as Guitar Slim's "Things I Used to Do" and Muddy Waters's "Rollin' Stone." He had learned an endless number of blues classics traveling the "chitlin circuit," rearranging and reproducing current and classic B.B. King, Howlin' Wolf and Muddy Waters material for patrons every night. His sets with the Experience featured versions of B.B. King's "Rock Me Baby," first done as almost a straight cover version; then gradually he raised its tempo, transforming the song by the time he took it to Monterey into an incredibly powerful showcase not only for his guitar acrobatics but for the completely original marriage of his unique sound within the standard blues format. "Catfish Blues," on the other hand, was a reworking of Muddy Waters's "Still a Fool." Unlike the turbo-charged arrangements given to "Killing Floor" and "Rock Me Baby," "Catfish Blues," so called by Hendrix because of the song's opening lyric, stuck closely to Muddy's version. It was here, though, that Hendrix updated Muddy's sound, respecting his arrangement yet adding his own personal touch, phrasing his guitar passages as forcefully as Waters had vocally injected his emotions.

The blues music Hendrix loved had begun undergoing a steady decline in popularity, at least as much as that can be proven by the dwindling U.S. record sales of its top stars.

There had been few second-level stars developed by cash-poor American independent blues labels such as Chess and Vee Jay. Minor chart hits by Sonny Boy Williamson, Jimmy Reed, John Lee Hooker and Howlin' Wolf kept such labels alive, but overwhelmed by Motown's crossover success, artists like Howlin' Wolf, who rarely profited from his records regardless of their success, returned to the road, playing to faithful audiences, whose ranks now included a growing number of whites. Hendrix, like a great number of musicians who had endured the chitlin circuit, still loved the blues and harbored strong feelings about Motown, as he described to West German interviewer W.H.K. Schmid: "This may bring you down, but to me [the Motown Sound] is artificial and very commercial, and very, very electronically made ... a synthetic soul sound. It isn't the real sound of Negro artists. It's so commercial, and put together beautifully that I don't feel anything from it. Except for the Isley Brothers, they are the only ones, and maybe the Four Tops. All they do is put a very, very hard beat to it – you know, about a thousand people on tambourines, bells, a thousand horns, a thousand violins – and a singer overdubs his voice about a million times, or he'll sing in an echo chamber full of this and that, and to me it comes out so artificial. It has a very good beat, it sounds good and it's very commercial for the younger people. But it's synthetic soul – that's what I call Motown."

With "Red House" Hendrix wanted to create an updated blues song, full of the same emotion, power and clarity that his idols had incorporated into their work, yet remain within the accepted musical framework of the blues idiom. While later compositions would stretch, blend or blur many musical styles, "Red House" would still be traditional in its form. Hendrix's guitar, the song's most prominent characteristic, starkly floats over Mitchell and Redding's accompaniment. Working first at CBS, then later at De Lane Lea, Chandler recorded several different versions until deciding on an acceptable take. Hendrix tried recording the song a number of ways, singing and playing live, as well as laying down the rhythm and one of the lead guitar tracks. Not perfected at this stage, "Red House" would be completed only in early April; until then, Hendrix would continue to make further refinements.

With little available cash, but hot to capitalize on Hendrix's creative burst, Chandler called in a favor promised to him by an engineer who worked at CBS Studios in London. The Experience were allowed to come in one evening after midnight for a few hours. With John Mayall and Fleetwood Mac guitarist Peter Green in attendance, the Experience laid down basic tracks for a new song Hendrix was calling "Third Stone From the Sun." While they lacked the time to fully complete the song, Hendrix's latest composition was a quantum leap from songs such as "Remember." The rate of Hendrix's progress had become almost impossible to fathom. For Chandler, it didn't seem possible that this was the same man he had had to force to write a song just three months ago, or even the same man content to issue a cover version of "Land of 1000 Dances" as the B side of his first single.

While only Chandler was originally certain that "Hey Joe" would be a success, Chris Stamp and Kit Lambert were confident that "Purple Haze" would be the record that established Jimi and the Experience as major artists in Britain. While Track readied the single for release in March, Hendrix, Chandler, Jeffery and PR expert Les Perrin began priming the British press for the onslaught of "England's latest sensation."

After an appearance on the television program *Beat Club*, the Experience returned to Paris for the first time since their appearance at the Olympia the previous October. On this occasion, however, without Johnny Hallyday on the bill, it wasn't exactly a triumphant return. Instead of a packed house at the capital's premier venue, the Experience were booked to liven up the Faculté de Droit D'Assas graduation ball. Back in England on March 10, the group sold out the

Club A Go Go in Newcastle-upon-Tyne, a venue owned by none other than their manager Michael Jeffery. The next night found the band at the International Club in Leeds, where, after witnessing the Experience's sound check, and fearing the group was too loud for his venue, the club owner paid Gerry Stickells and told them to go home. From there, the Experience traveled to Ilkley to play at the Gyro Club. Here, much to the surprise of the owners, fans packed the small club, so much so, in fact, that the performance was stopped because the overcrowding violated fire regulations.

As the band left England once again, this time for a whirlwind seven-day tour of Amsterdam and Hamburg – where the Experience packed the latter city's Star-Club, made famous by the Beatles' outrageous shows there – Michael Jeffery left for New York to confirm a deal Johanan Vigoda had struck for the Experience with Warner Bros. Records.

# 4 THE BIG SCORE

*"Britain had been Jeffery and Chandler's laboratory. When they signed with Warner Bros., Hendrix was ready to break it wide open."*

—Chris Stamp

In January, before Jeffery left New York, he had informed Johanan Vigoda that there might be interest in Hendrix with Warner Bros.–Seven Arts' subsidiary label Reprise. It had primarily been a hunch, but Jeffery briefed Vigoda about Yameta's basic concerns, should he be able to cut a deal for the group. As further insurance, Leon Dicker would approve any contracts that Yameta would enter into upon the group's behalf. As Vigoda recalls, Jeffery was very enthusiastic about Hendrix, and this sense of excitement spilled over into the negotiations. "I was making a deal for a star I had never met. The deal I did with Warner Bros. was tremendous for that time. First, there was a $20,000 promotion budget – immense for an unknown artist's first album – and that money was just to start this thing in the works. The second part was that I threw in something, which, at the time, was completely unheard of: a soundtrack exclusion."

While obtaining such an exclusion – prohibiting Warner Bros. from using or licensing Yameta soundtrack recordings featuring Jimi Hendrix or the Jimi Hendrix Experience – seemed to be a relatively minor triumph at the time, Warner would come to bitterly regret granting it so easily. In addition to securing a major-label recording contract for Hendrix, Jeffery – working with Yameta's John Hillman in London and Leon Dicker in New York – also obtained what was known in the business as a "production deal." Warner Bros. had not signed Jimi Hendrix to Reprise Records, they had signed Yameta Co. to provide "master recordings, embodying the performance of Jimi Hendrix and or the Jimi Hendrix Experience." Neither Hendrix, Mitchell nor Redding ever signed the contract. They didn't have to, since they were already signed to exclusive recording, management and publishing contracts with Yameta.

Warner Bros. did try to ensure that Mitchell and Redding were further bound by the terms of the contract, however; Leon Dicker, the only person who did sign the actual contract, requested in a handwritten rider: "Producer warrants and represents that to the extent that it owns or controls, or that any firm owned by Michael Jeffery owns and controls the recording services of Noel Redding and or Mitch Mitchell in connection with recordings other than with Jimi Hendrix or the Jimi Hendrix Experience, that they will be offered to [Warner Bros.] in the U.S. and Canada upon a first refusal basis." Jeffery was obviously taking no chances. By signing Yameta to Warner Bros., not Hendrix himself, he reserved the ability to fire Mitchell and Redding without any future consideration, thus also leaving the door open to record Hendrix performing either alone or with a new band, live or in the studio. Financially, Yameta received a nonreturnable advance against royalties of $40,000. Their royalty breakdown gave them 10 percent of the retail list price of all records sold in the United States and 50 percent of Warner Bros.' net receipts to all such records and tapes sold in Canada. Yameta also retained "the exclusive and perpetual ownership of all masters recorded" under the agreement. Rank amateurs they were not: without the

Experience ever having issued a disc or performed as a unit in America, Jeffery and Chandler owned their artist's master recordings – something neither the Beatles nor the Rolling Stones could claim.

The ramifications of the Warner Bros. deal were immediate. Not only would the advance allow Chandler to continue recording, it gave the band a cash infusion at a critical time. Of the $40,000 received from Warner, Hendrix was given $8,000. With the remaining $32,000, Jeffery and especially Chandler – who had borne a great many expenses for Hendrix out of his own pocket – recouped their initial expenses.

Both Chandler and Jeffery were savvy enough to realize that such a unique and dynamic talent as Hendrix had to be seen as well as heard. Therefore, the promotional budget that Warner Bros. had allotted was crucial to breaking the artist in America. While they could rely on the good name of the Animals to help open doors in London, Chandler realized they lacked the marketing muscle necessary to break the Experience in the U.S. "I got Warner Bros. to pay because I convinced them that the marketing was just as important as the A&R [artist & repertoire] department, and made Mo Ostin, who was then a vice president, agree that the marketing department had to contribute to the budget. In real terms, it meant in-store displays, that was marketing; not airplay, which was A&R. For the first time, marketing was brought into promotion meetings. Before this it was ridiculous: the A&R department would deal with the artist and then deal with everyone else themselves. I used to argue that it was absurd that I, manager of the artist, wasn't even allowed to become involved in the marketing of my artist."

Obtaining the Warner Bros. contract had been a pivotal achievement for Jeffery. The contract seemed to justify his role as deal maker. There was no doubting his belief in the act, and that Hendrix was a genuine talent, but up until now Jeffery had not yet delivered. Outside of securing a distribution deal with Barclay Records covering France and the

Benelux countries, Jeffery's exact role had been blurred by his dual responsibility to Eric Burdon and the Animals and to the Experience. But ideas such as owning and controlling the services of Mitchell and Redding, and signing Yameta rather than Hendrix directly to all of the group's recording contracts, had been his.

If Jeffery had developed anything during his brief career in the entertainment industry, it was an acute skill for manipulating people to serve his wishes. A brilliant negotiator, he was not a blustering, physically overpowering figure. He was charming, well educated, slight and usually soft-spoken. Beneath his effete veneer, though, was a supremely cunning and inventive mind. Like Chandler, he too had grown up in the North. Jeffery was an ex-MI5 member with combat experience, serving in Britain's Suez operation during 1957-58. While in Egypt, Jeffery displayed the first glimmer of his notorious business acumen.

"At the very beginning of his military career," recalls John Hillman, "Jeffery was a ranking nothing [he would later rise to the rank of captain]; he was, however, a shrewd business-man in the making. While serving in Egypt, Jeffery discovered that newspapers were like gold to the soldiers. Everyone was craving for news about home. English news-papers, three days old, were selling for two dollars apiece. Jeffery decided that the sensible thing would be to find a source for the newspapers and go into business. He found out that in Cairo there was a news agent who sold papers from abroad that were only two days old. It was against regulations for British soldiers to venture into Cairo without permission. Regardless, Jeffery hired one of his squaddies to drive him to the news agent every week with a truck. They collected the newspapers, and Jeffery began selling them to the British army in Suez at two dollars each. The practice was highly illegal, but Jeffery was earning wads of money.

"He continued to make a number of trips into Cairo until he was finally caught. He was brought up and scolded before his commanding officer: 'Jeffery, you were caught in an out-of-bounds area – in a war zone no less! Do you realize how serious an offense this is? Do you know you are risking imprisonment?' 'Yes sir, yes sir,' Jeffery replied. Astounded, the officer asked, 'How could you do it? What could be worth this?' 'Well sir,' Jeffery replied, 'I went to collect newspapers.' 'Newspapers!' the commander exclaimed. 'What were you doing with newspapers?' 'Well sir,' Jeffery replied, 'I was selling them.' Now totally exasperated, the officer asked him, 'Could it really be worth it, Jeffery? For you to risk what you've risked for a few newspapers? How much could you have possibly been making?' Still at attention, Jeffery calmly said, '$8,000 a week.' Hearing this, the commander, looking painfully pensive, turned to the Sergeant Major standing guard and says, 'Sergeant Major, I wonder if you might leave the room ...' Jeffery was back in business again – in partnership! He made a fortune. That's how he financed his club, the Club A Go Go in Newcastle, with the profits from his newspaper sales."

After leaving the service, Jeffery entered the nightclub business in Newcastle-upon-Tyne and began a career as a club owner. After befriending a local group often performing at the Club A Go Go, he became their manager. They were the Animals. As Chandler recalls, Jeffery seemed a trifle out of the ordinary right from the get go. "Jeffery had a fetish for weaponry. When we first went to London, Alan Price and I made Jeffery share his London flat. We had never seen much money in our lives! The flat had a colossal rent bill, twenty-five pounds a week, an enormous amount of money in those days. My mother's rent was only one pound fifty a week in those days. In Jeffery's room, all the walls had knife holes in them. He was throwing knives through clothes into the wall. When we left the place, we actually had a thousand pounds damage from Jeffery throwing knives. He was a barbarian at times. This was a guy, upper middle class, highly educated, destroying a room and three fitted wardrobes by throwing knives through them. The band got the blame. It was in the press as 'The Animals destroy ...' but it was our manager!'"

Throughout the Animals' career, Jeffery constantly created or came upon ideas to help stash, extend or generate income for the group. Off-shore tax shelters, hidden investments and cash transactions captivated Jeffery's fertile mind. The Animals had been his guinea pig. He expanded his business, managing a host of girl groups including Goldie & the Gingerbreads and the Girls as well as purchasing nightclubs in Majorca, Spain. Yameta had been his brainchild, and John Hillman had developed the means by which it would work. Hillman was an authority on taxation, and Jeffery sought to create a shelter that could defer taxation on the vast sums of money artists generated in their short careers. Too often, Jeffery complained to Hillman, an artist's peak earning period was as little as two years. In such a short span, taxes often decimated the amount of money an artist could save or invest. Yameta, Jeffery explained, could be the agency that linked the various components of his management company together. Yameta, with Hillman as its director and Jeffery its talent scout, would sign artists, plan tours and negotiate recording and publishing agreements, all while deferring profits from excessive taxation.

Jeffery was, as well, a student of Machiavellian tactics, and employed such techniques as divide and conquer. As Chas Chandler recalls: "Jeffery used to use anything he could to keep people off balance. You didn't realize how much you had been manipulated until you were out of his circle. Suddenly it was like you woke up. Because he couldn't get close to Jimi, he would drive a wall between myself and Jimi."

"Jeffery was a lovable rogue," recalls John Hillman. "I often felt I played the role of father confessor with him. His actions could be reprehensible at times, but when I confronted him, he would throw up his hands and say, 'Okay, you (or they) caught me. Now help me get off it.'"

Jeffery's ventures to America had also introduced him to the world of the American "attorney," who, especially at that time, was much unlike its counterpart, the British "solicitor." Jeffery was seeking a young, open-minded attorney willing to try new ideas. Johanan Vigoda had met those criteria, but, shortly after securing the Warner Bros. deal, Jeffery left Marshall & Vigoda. He had found another aggressive attorney willing to listen and execute his ideas, Stevens H. Weiss.

Steve Weiss was the junior partner and entertainment lawyer for the firm of Steingarten, Wedeen & Weiss. At the time, Weiss had a handful of prominent clients, including Jeff Beck, Jimmy Page, Sid Bernstein and the Young Rascals, ex-wrestler Peter Grant, a protégé of Michael Jeffery's who managed the new Yardbirds, and Management Three, Jerry Weintraub's production company. Totally unlike any solicitor Jeffery had known in Britain, Weiss understood the business of rock n' roll, its volatility, its power struggles, its cash flow and the need for organization. The walls of his office were filled with stereo equipment, not law books. Though Jeffery placed great faith in Weiss's opinions, his new mentor was relatively a rookie within the field of entertainment law, having been ushered into the business in the early 1960s while representing television personality Jack Paar.

There were many similarities between the two. Like Jeffery, Steve Weiss would come to be both feared and respected by many in the record business. "He was disliked by a lot of people in the industry, but he was a killer for his clients," recalls Howard Krantz, a former fellow Steingarten, Wedeen & Weiss attorney. "An 'ardent advocate' as we lawyers like to say. He had no respect for other lawyers and didn't try to create relationships with them. He was a loner who cut his teeth with Hendrix and it paid off for him." Henry Kalow, who replaced Krantz at the firm in 1968, echoed a similar sentiment. "Steve was very, very good at what he did, but apparently he rubbed a lot of people the wrong way. He did not know how to be gracious when he won."

Back in London, Track Records released the Experience's second single, "Purple Haze"/"51st Anniversary," on March 27. It entered *Record Mirror's* music charts at 39 and *Melody Maker's* at 43. To help promote the A side, the band again appeared on the BBC television show *Top of the Pops*. The group's advance from Warner Bros. finally afforded Chandler the time to capture Hendrix's growing backlog of material on tape. Unsatisfied with De Lane Lea and the other studios the band had tried, Chandler was now in a position to step up a grade. Bill Wyman and Brian Jones had long been after Chandler and Hendrix to try Olympic Sound Studios in southwest London, but it was too expensive at the time for the fledgling group. But Eric Burdon, who, with manager Michael Jeffery in attendance, had recently been working at Olympic cutting "When I Was Young," a hit for the new Animals, and its producer, Tom Wilson, had been impressed with their young, enthusiastic, hardworking engineer, one Edwin H. Kramer.

Born in South Africa, Eddie Kramer had studied piano, violin and cello from childhood, and classical piano at the South African College of Music before his family relocated to England. Eager to expand his skills, he landed a job as "tea boy" in 1963 at Advision Studios in London, where he learned the basic principles of engineering, disc cutting and film dubbing. Then in 1964 and early 1965, Kramer moved on to Pye Studios, working with such diverse artists as Sammy Davis, Jr., and the Kinks. Later in 1965, he and two partners established their own two-track demo facility, KPS Studios, attracting clients such as John Mayall's Bluesbreakers, the Kinks and Zoot Money. It was here that Kramer's reputation for quality work began to spread. In 1966, Regent Sound bought out KPS and enlisted Kramer to oversee construction of its new four-track studio. From Regent, Kramer had moved on to work at London's hottest independent studio, Olympic Sound, in Barnes. Here, under the tutelege of Keith Grant and Glyn Johns, Kramer immediately began to establish himself. As fellow Olympic engineer Terry Brown recalls, Kramer would get most of the "weird" assignments that would come into the studio, and his love of sound and experimentation, regardless of the musical style, made him the obvious choice to work with a "raggedy" group Chas Chandler was bringing to record.

Kramer's first recollection of working with the Experience was seeing Gerry Stickells stagger up the Olympic stairs with a Marshall 4 × 12 amplifier on his back, bellowing, "Where do I put this!" After Stickells had carried up a seemingly endless number of Marshalls, Kramer was introduced to Chas and the Experience.

As Noel Redding recalls, Olympic was a step up for the group, a sign they had arrived. "It was quite intriguing to me," he says. "I was in awe of its size. We had recorded in a few studios, but none were this big. Someone told us that the Rolling Stones were recording in Studio B and then in came Mick Jagger with a lump of hash, with which I got well spaced out."

With an American recording contract now secured, the Experience embraced Kramer's unchecked enthusiasm. In fact, Kramer's spirit seemed to embody the general atmosphere found at Olympic. Locked in a battle against EMI's Abbey Road Studios for not only clients but prestige, George Martin would soon legitimize Olympic by bringing the Beatles there to record "Baby You're a Rich Man" and "All You Need Is Love," the former being the first Beatles song to be recorded and mixed for record entirely outside of Abbey Road. The lines of distinction between the studios were blurring. Jimmy Miller, Glyn Johns and Kramer were recording some of England's best artists on a daily basis.

Moving to Olympic would have a pronounced effect upon Hendrix, for while it was Chandler who had provided him with an outlet for his talent, Hendrix sensed almost immediately that Kramer could help capture on tape the sounds he heard in his head. To his credit, Chandler was not intimidated by Kramer, for he realized that Kramer would not only improve the band's sound, but Kramer's ideas and suggestions would help him become a better producer. There would be no doubting that Chas was in charge of the group; however, as tape operator George Chkiantz recalls: "Chas was quite receptive to suggestions. It was quite important that tapings didn't take too much time though."

Kramer arrived just at the right time in Hendrix's career. Hendrix had bided his time during sessions at Pye, CBS, Regent and De Lane Lea, quietly observing Chandler, who had assumed complete control of production duties. At Olympic, though, while always avoiding confrontations, Hendrix began voicing his thoughts through Kramer. Chandler hated endless retakes; he never minded hearing alternate guitar overdubs or replacing lead or backing vocal tracks, but recutting basic tracks was a double negative, since the song often lost its spontaneity and the process was too costly. Kramer immediately changed the way the band recorded basic tracks. The pre-Olympic recording featured the drums and bass in stereo on two of the recording tape's four available tracks. As George Chkiantz recalls: "Kramer adopted a strategy with Hendrix of getting the original live sound down on four tracks, which, at the time, other engineers, including me, thought was crazy."

Kramer filled the four basic tracks with stereo drums on two tracks, strengthening Mitchell's sound, bass on a separate track, and finally Hendrix's rhythm guitar on the last open track. Kramer and Chandler would then take this down to another four-track recorder, premixing the four tracks down to two and thereby creating an opening for two more tracks, which perhaps could include Hendrix's lead guitar, lead vocal, backing vocals or additional percussion.

Premixing was standard practice at studios throughout England, but, as George Chkiantz remembers, its success often depended on the creative style of the artist. "The problem with premixing was that you invariably got it wrong. As the snare and vocal sounds cover each other, it's practically impossible to get the snare drum balance right until the vocal is on and you can't guess this when the guy hasn't even written the lyrics yet! You just don't know where the breaks are. It's an almost impossible task, and this was where four-track recording was so very inadequate."

Hendrix would often record all of the backing tracks, leaving only his lead vocal to come, thus allowing him the opportunity to fine-tune lines and verses. Sensing Hendrix's growing adeptness in the studio and Chandler's dislike for excessive retakes, Kramer's strategy of committing the basic music recordings to all four tracks gave Hendrix and Chandler the security of having a solid basis on which to build. As Chkiantz recalls, it further cemented the rapport between Kramer and Hendrix. "Hendrix was a lot happier. He felt the track was never lost, and that his stuff was always down on tape. He and Eddie could just sit there and mix or listen." For Kramer, the idea had partly come from conversations with Hendrix. "Jimi had been exposed to eight-track recording in America," explains Kramer. "He liked hearing the basic tracks across on all four tracks. Hearing it this way, four-track recording did not seem like the step backward it really was."

For Chandler, the first priority at Olympic was to complete a B side to accompany the group's third Track single, "The Wind Cries Mary." In addition, he and the group decided that their as yet untitled debut album would not contain any of the material issued as Track singles. The advance against artist royalties in the group's Warner Bros. contract allowed Chas enough financial freedom to record day or night, and while the contract did not provide any additional monies for recording costs, perfecting the group's debut album release was of paramount importance.

A number of strong contenders for the album were completed during a flurry of sessions at Olympic. While some, such as "Midnight Lightning," "Gypsy Blood" and an early version of "Lover Man," called here "Here He Comes," remained unfinished, "Highway Chile," "Manic Depression," "Love or Confusion" and "I Don't Live Today" were recorded and mixed for inclusion. The majority of these songs had been tested live by the band. In the studio, however, Hendrix would often build a song's more intricate features by requesting Mitchell to play a certain tempo, and – while his chord structures were already determined – he would also make suggestions to Redding about bass lines that might interlock or follow his riff on the guitar. Although Hendrix had a definite sound picture developed in his mind, Redding and especially Mitchell remained free to create within the parameters of this structure. In fact, Hendrix seemed to thrive on being pushed creatively. While Kramer's ability to create and enhance sounds had impressed the band, his openness had also drawn both Hendrix and Mitchell together into the control room, a process that would further cement their own relationship.

On March 31, the group played at the Finsbury Park Astoria Theatre in London as part of a bill that also featured Englebert Humperdinck, Cat Stevens and the Walker Brothers. Before the gig Chandler had been shrewd enough to sign up the Experience as a support act on the tour, reasoning that the Walker Brothers, its headlining act, were breaking up and that their hearts would not entirely be on the task at hand. The tour would also allow the band to further push "Purple Haze," surviving by dint of the group's irregular appearances on such British TV shows such as *Top of the Pops*. (In its then form, BBC radio would continue to be of little help to the group.) So while the Walker Brothers tour may not have been the best thing, critically, for the group to undertake, Chandler knew that if the Experience were to succeed in England, Hendrix would have to be accepted by the country's teenagers and rock n' roll aficionados alike. Chandler had seen the initial reaction that fans of Johnny Hallyday had afforded Hendrix, and the same thing had happened in West Germany. Hendrix struck his German audiences as unique and outrageous yet his sense of humor and timing, not discounting his considerable talents, had made it work.

Still, while the group had been winning audiences at clubs

all over England, the Experience had yet to transcend their cult status in London, and Chandler needed something to catapult Hendrix into the mainstream. That something would come from music reporter Keith Altham, who casually suggested to Chas that Jimi should set his guitar alight to accompany "Fire." That was it! Chandler discussed with Hendrix how he could ignite one of his guitars during the group's performance at the Astoria. With the exception of Chas and Gerry Stickells, no one knew that Hendrix was planning to torch his guitar. Mitchell and Redding only vaguely heard something about lighter fluid amid the backstage clamor, but more important, neither the audience nor any of the other artists on the bill were prepared for Hendrix's axe melting.

Following a charged forty-five-minute set that featured Hendrix at his most outrageous, playing guitar behind his back, through his legs, lying on the stage floor and with his teeth, Jimi doused his Stratocaster with lighter fluid and set it on fire. The crowd erupted, and – in turn – its fervor overwhelmed Hendrix. He had seen such a reaction only once before when, after falling off a stage in Germany, he had thrown his guitar back up on stage, breaking it in the process. Now the Astoria crowd howled with excitement, clearly overwhelmed by the fury that Hendrix had somehow channeled into his stage act.

As Hendrix left the stage, waving to the screaming crowd, press agent Les Perrin was quick to corral the press, informing them that something technical had malfunctioned. A "short circuit in the guitar" was all Perrin could muster. The press then chased down Gerry Stickells hoping to clarify the incident. Perpetuating the hype, Stickells feigned ignorance about the root cause of the blaze. "The press were talking to me and the can of lighter fluid was lying in the orchestra pit, just where he had thrown it. I was trying to stand in front of it while they were looking at me! After that night he didn't try to hide it."

The Fleet Street press had a field day and, almost immediately, "Purple Haze" began climbing up the British charts as reporters tracked down the man they quickly dubbed "The Wild Man of Borneo" and "The Black Elvis." Chandler and Jeffery now began to exploit the generation gap between Hendrix and the British press. As Chandler recalls: "We used to sit at our apartment in the evenings and work out who we were going to offend tomorrow. We did nothing but sit home, play Risk, and talk about his career."

Reveling in the furor, the band reentered Olympic to continue their work. Comfortable within its cathedral-like Studio A, the Experience cut demo versions of "Go My Own Way" and a comical remake of "Hound Dog," recorded "Are You Experienced?," "May This Be Love" (first known as "Waterfall") as well as overdubbing and remixing "Third Stone From the Sun" and "Red House." As tape operator George Chkiantz recalls, a pattern had developed inside the control room. "Jimi would sit on the edge of a coffee table on Kramer's left, whispering things to him. Chas would sit on Eddie's right and field Kramer's and Hendrix's requests." Hendrix's incredible ability to know exactly where he was in a solo, backwards or forwards, astounded them. Hendrix had in fact told Kramer that he would purposely listen to tapes on his home reel-to-reel machine backwards just to study the possibilities of the technique. Hendrix's backwards rhythm guitar line (as well as Redding's bass part) for "Are You Experienced?," which almost doubles as percussion, was laid down as part of the basic track, a remarkable feat. Whereas the success rate for other artists inserting backwards guitar parts was often hit or miss, Hendrix used his as a rhythm guitar guide track not just for straight leads, but additional backwards lead guitar overdubs.

"Third Stone From the Sun" was yet another example of the group's growing sophistication. While the song had begun life at CBS Studios some time back, Hendrix, Chandler and Kramer changed the feel by adding and over-dubbing effects. Mitchell's jazz-influenced percussion now became a prominent element within the track. Kramer mixed Mitch's cymbals very high to give it an airy sound amidst the panning. The song's signature riff had been its main feature at CBS, but Hendrix's absorbtion of Chandler's science fiction books clearly became its most obvious new influence. Slowed down to create an eerie background sound, Hendrix's voice wafted in and out of his panning guitar leads and Mitch's crashing cymbals.

As advanced as final mixes for songs such as "Are You Experienced?" and "Third Stone From the Sun" were, a mistake would sometimes be left in because it worked. A close listen to "May This Be Love" will reveal Hendrix turning over a page of his lyrics. In the case of "Red House," meanwhile, the version heard on the British pressings of *Are You Experienced?* is the one cut at De Lane Lea and mixed at Olympic, while the version that graces the American *Smash Hits*, though also recorded at De Lane Lea, additionally features premix guitar overdubs taped by Hendrix at Olympic.

The final mixing sessions for *Are You Experienced?* took place through the evening of April 9 and the morning of the 10th. Chandler was very much in charge, working with Kramer, while Mitchell and Redding were essentially excluded from the process. It was decided that "Highway Chile" would become the B side for the "The Wind Cries Mary" and thus be omitted from the album. While Chandler was set against tampering with the spontaneity of "The Wind Cries Mary," he and Kramer did attempt to improve the final take, in particular by trying to doctor Mitchell's drum sound. In the end, however, the song was not rerecorded at Olympic and was deemed suitable for release in its present form. After Kramer had banded the master tape for disc cutting, Chandler and Hendrix personally delivered it to Chris Stamp at Track Records.

The Walker Brothers tour took the Experience throughout Britain, playing two shows, usually no longer than thirty-five minutes, every night. The tour did not play clubs; rather, it stuck to larger-capacity theater halls, filled with rabid young fans of Engelbert, Cat Stevens or the Walker Brothers. Soon enough, though, as electronics whiz Roger Mayer recalls, the girls fell in love with Hendrix. "We were at the Speakeasy Club in London one Friday [April 28] until about six or seven in the morning. As I was leaving, I asked Hendrix where he was going to be playing that night. He replied Bournemouth and asked if I was going to come along. I said no, I was going to miss it and that I would see him again at the Speakeasy later. About four that afternoon, I got a phone call from Jimi. 'Where the hell are you?' I asked. 'At the flat in London!' 'What the hell are you doing there?' He said, 'I'm a bit late for the gig tonight.' So I drove him to Bournemouth in my white midget MG hardtop sports car. There was a crowd of people by the backstage door; I drove through them so that the passenger door was about six feet from the backstage entrance. Security came over and got Hendrix inside. I didn't park my car far enough away though – being white it was pretty distinctive – and after the gig, though Mitch was taking Jimi back, there was 'I love Jimi' in red lipstick all over it. The windshield wipers were stolen, the gas cap, the little nuts off the windows, all of this type of nonsense. I started her up and drove to the stage door, where Jimi asked me what happened. I said, 'I don't know. They're your fans!' We had to drive a few miles to a gas station, without wipers to clear the lipstick-smeared windshield, and while we filled up, Hendrix and I cleaned the lipstick off and drove on to the Speakeasy."

Hendrix's fiery debut had not sat well with the other artists. The Walker Brothers had not taken kindly to being upstaged. In their minds, they had granted Chas a favor by letting the Experience join the tour. "There was plenty of tension backstage," recalls Chandler. "John Walker would walk into our dressing room and say, 'Who do you think you are!'" Hendrix voiced his frustration during a 1967 interview. "The bosses of the tour are giving us hell," he said. "The organizers don't give us a chance to tune up before we go on stage. They say we are vulgar and obscene, but we play our act as we have always done everywhere else, and there have never been complaints before. We refuse to change our act and the result is that my amplifier sometimes gets cut off at the funniest times. I wonder why? But I don't let them hang me up. I play to the people and I don't think our actions are obscene. It's really funny playing for this tour. I don't know if it's like this on all tours but just before I go on, I turn around and find a guitar string is broken or my guitar is all out of tune after I just tuned it up. But they are not getting rid of us unless we're officially thrown off the tour."

Despite the squabbles, the Experience survived the tour. In fact, Noel, ever the opportunist, had made some extra money by playing guitar for Engelbert Humperdinck from the orchestra pit or the wings during his performances.

May 1967 saw the band return to Olympic Sound Studios to continue recording. As with those for *Are You Experienced?*, there was no real outline to these sessions. When Hendrix had material, Chandler would bring in the group to record. Once again, Chandler was very much the man in charge. "Mitchell was late for a session once," recalls Redding, "and Chas didn't pay him his wages for that week. He was never late again."

While waiting to be videotaped for a *Top of the Pops* appearance, Redding composed "She's So Fine." After he showed it to Hendrix and Chandler, the band went straight over to Olympic for what both Kramer and Chandler recall was a hilarious session. "Jimi was laughing when Noel was singing," recalls Chas. "Nobody could keep a straight face – every time Noel opened his mouth, Hendrix would burst out laughing." "I clearly remember Jimi, Mitch and Noel all laughing in the studio trying to put on the backing vocals," Kramer recalls with a smile. The whole track was fun and very loose."

The contributions by Hendrix and Mitchell, perhaps with their guard down, being that it was Redding's song, were superb. As Chandler further recalls, Hendrix actively encouraged contributions from the band. "Jimi insisted that Noel's song be allowed on the album. He wanted Mitch to put one on as well, because he felt he would get more commitment from them. It was being generous really, just as simple as that."

The Experience also returned to a song that had not been completed in time for *Are You Experienced?*, "If Six Was Nine." Here again, though, the group failed to complete the recording, but basic tracks were committed to tape and the master was set back upon the shelf. Hendrix also dug into his past, recording a version of "Mr. Bad Luck" – better known as "Look Over Yonder" – as well as a medium-tempo blues, "Taking Care of No Business." Both remain unreleased. Chandler was familiar with "Mr. Bad Luck," as it was a staple of Jimmy James & the Blue Flames' live set. He had in fact seen Jimi perform the number at the Cafe Wha? the night he first encountered him. Ironically, "Taking Care of No Business" was a derivative of an old number Hendrix had performed with Curtis Knight & the Squires. While the Experience would never return to the song after this session (the version Hendrix recorded as a member of the Squires in October 1965 would ultimately grace Capitol Records' December 1967 album *Get That Feeling*), the song *was* considered for inclusion on 1972's *War Heroes* LP. Electric Lady engineer John Jansen, dispatched in 1971 by Kramer and Michael Jeffery to research tapes still stored at Olympic Studios, located the master, and as a precaution, the song was copywritten February 1, 1971, by Yameta and Sea-Lark Enterprises. In spite of the effort, "Taking Care of No Business" ultimately remained unissued.

Just as Kramer had once been Glyn Johns's assistant, so now Glyn's younger brother Andy had recently been hired to assist Kramer as his tape operator. By now, Hendrix had grown comfortable with Kramer and indeed all of the staff at Olympic. Johns recalls Kramer challenging Hendrix to a hearing test. "Jimi was just about deaf in one ear. Eddie did an ear test on him, he put on the oscillator and he couldn't hear past 6K in one ear. The other ear was fine."

During the sessions for what would become *Axis: Bold as Love*, Hendrix, and to a lesser degree Mitchell, began to voice more concise ideas about particular sounds or effects and so, in a subtle way, Hendrix began to challenge Chandler. Contrary to their first sessions at Olympic, where the band had recorded either staples from their live set or more sophisticated studio ideas such as "Third Stone From the Sun," the songs Hendrix had recently written had not yet been tested on the road. For the first time, Olympic became the group's creative base, Hendrix now entering the studio with ideas rather than an established outline for a song. "During sessions for *Axis: Bold as Love*, Hendrix never really came in with the tunes finished," says Andy Johns. "Chas would pick out a riff for a line and go 'That's good. Work on that.' Or he would put two things together for him and Hendrix would go off and muck about with it, but when Hendrix wanted a particular sound or effect he would just ask Eddie."

As "Purple Haze" climbed to number 3 on the British music charts, Track Records released "The Wind Cries Mary" backed with "Highway Chile." With a laugh, Chandler remembers having to continually correct critics and Polydor executives that it was pronounced "Highway Chile" not "Highway Chili," perhaps a ballad about bad roadside food. At the same time, Reprise Records in America released "Hey Joe" (backed with "51st Anniversary"), the Experience's debut U.S. single. And just before Hendrix left for a two-week tour of West Germany and Sweden on May 14, 1967, Track released the group's first album. Issued almost three weeks before the Beatles' *Sgt. Pepper*, *Are You Experienced?* burst onto the British music charts, entering both *New Musical Express* and *Disc and Music Echo* at number 3.

Interviewed at this time on West German radio by W.H.K. Schmid, Hendrix was asked what his greatest wish was. "I wish you could send me home, so I could see my parents for a few days," he replied. "I haven't been home for about five and a half years. They don't know what is happening at all, except I called them two times – once when I first came to England, about seven months ago, and then again a few days ago when we were in London. I told [my Dad], we have three records out. He said, 'Oh yeah!' He didn't even know that I was singing, because I was [always] too scared to sing. Chas has made me sing *serious*." As was the case with most European interviewers at the time, Schmid wanted to know if dressing up and having long hair was truly necessary. "I don't consider it necessary," Hendrix replied. "For instance, pop stars like Engelbert Humperdinck and Cat Stevens and all the beautiful people don't necessarily have to have long hair. Myself, and I believe this goes for other cats too, I dig it. I think it's very nice, especially in your own style. Regarding my clothes, anything I see that I like, regardless of what it costs, even if it is only two shillings, I will get it."

For the first time, in this interview, Hendrix revealed his love of classical music. Later, in 1968, after stopping by Hendrix's room at the Hotel Drake in New York, Eddie Kramer was afforded a firsthand view at the depth of Hendrix's appreciation for such composers as Bach, Beethoven and Handel, noticing a number of classical records mixed in with his many blues albums, and they had gone on to discuss their admiration for particular composers. To Schmid, Hendrix spoke of music in general. "Classical music is very beautiful but I don't like to listen to it all the time, [just] at the most relaxing time. You see, different music is supposed to be used in different ways. You are supposed to appreciate music. A bright day with a lot of noise is not the right time to listen to classical music. But anytime when it is very quiet and your mind is very relaxed and you feel like daydreaming, turn on the stereo."

Confident of his sound, yet never satisfied, he tried to point out the deeper messages behind his music, believing it could help remove stress, or relieve tensions welling up among his fans. Above all, the Experience were sincere, and Hendrix wanted people to know that their music should be believed in, and that the power for productive change could be found within his amplified message. He strove to point out that the blues, then undergoing a revival in both Britain and America, was not necessarily restricted to poor American blacks. "You can have your own blues. It doesn't necessarily mean that folk blues is the only type of blues in the world. I heard some Irish folk songs that were so funky; the words and feel were so together – that was great. We have our own scene. We don't even try to give it a name. Everybody has some kind of blues to offer."

For Jeffery and Chandler, the blues would take form in one Edward Chalpin, president of PPX Industries. On May 22, Chalpin began notifying anyone he felt was involved with "Jimmy Hendrix" that the musician was under "exclusive artist, production and writing contract with PPX Industries, October 1965 through October 1968." Only by chance had Chalpin learned of Hendrix's amazing overseas success, noticing U.S. trade paper reporting of the strong sales in Britain, Scandinavia and elsewhere. The shockwaves were both immediate and tremendous. Chalpin had cabled Polydor, Pye and Warner Bros., looking for an explanation regarding the Jimi Hendrix Experience's three hit singles in England and abroad. Jeffery and Chandler were taken completely by surprise. For Jeffery, Chalpin's allegations were especially painful. He had tried to settle all of Hendrix's prior commitments back in January. Now someone was threatening Yameta's management contract – and to hand Hendrix (not Mitchell and Redding, who were irrefutably exclusive Yameta artists) back to PPX Industries, without compensation, would destroy Jeffery's reputation.

Jeffery and especially Chandler had sacrificed a great deal to ensure the group's success, and committing seven solid months to breaking Hendrix *was* worth something. To make matters even more frustrating, Hendrix seemed vague about Chalpin and the nature of their relationship. Naturally, he had no copies of any agreements with PPX, nor tape copies of any of the material to which he had contributed. Indeed, outside of admitting to playing guitar for Curtis Knight on a few sessions, Hendrix could offer little information. He hadn't even seen Chalpin for over a year.

While Hendrix may have been unsure about Ed Chalpin and PPX Industries, Jeffery immediately set about obtaining a profile of the man and his business. Working at his own studio in New York, Chalpin had achieved success by recording cover versions of Top 40 hits for worldwide release – he would tape the backing tracks and foreign singers could overdub translated lyrics. These records were very successful and Chalpin had fast established a large clientele licensing his recordings on a regular basis. In addition, Chalpin would try his hand with various original recordings for the American charts. His primary recording artist was Curtis Knight, a former member of the Ink Spots. The single that Hendrix had heard in a London disco, and whose release had so alarmed Jeffery, had been originally issued by Jerry Simon's RSVP lable. Still, Chalpin had produced the recording, as well as a number of others featuring Jimi's accompaniment. While Jeffery had secured Simon's rights vis-a-vis RSVP Records, Chalpin now loomed as a major threat. Jeffery needed sight of the contract Hendrix had signed before a damage assessment could be calculated.

Chalpin had first met Hendrix and Curtis Knight in September 1965 through a friend who thought he would be interested in recording Knight's group, the Squires. To Chalpin, Hendrix was an unknown, unrecorded and unemployed musician. He agreed to audition the Squires at Studio 76, his recording studio located inside PPX Industries' headquarters. After recording a number of finished songs, Chalpin signed both Knight and Hendrix to separate artist royalty recording contracts, one-page agreements signed at Studio 76 on or about October 15, 1965. Hendrix asked for money before he would sign, and after accepting approximately $200 in cash did so. At no time did Hendrix ever mention to Chalpin any other existing agreements to which he was party, such as the Sue Records contract he had signed on July 27, 1965, only three months earlier.

After recording another series of songs with the Squires at Studio 76, Hendrix seemed to disappear. Chalpin tried to reach him at the Hotel America, the address Hendrix had provided when he signed the contract, but he had moved on without leaving a forwarding address. His hasty exit from the Squires had been nothing more than a quiet declaration of independence.

As far as Hendrix was concerned, his contract with PPX dealt only with Knight and the Squires. Clearly, Ed Chalpin did not share this opinion. As the producer later recalled: "I was heartbroken. You finally make it and then they steal you blind." Having notified the various companies he felt were trying to take Hendrix away from him, Chalpin sat back to await their response.

# 5 MONTEREY

*"Monterey was great. I was scared to go up there and play in front of all those people outside. It was like 'Wow! What am I going to do!' But once you hit the first note, then it's [time] to get to those people's butts!"*

— Jimi Hendrix

With the release of *Sgt. Pepper* on June 1, 1967, the Beatles legitimized a new sound and movement coming to be known as psychedelia. Although Track Records had been surreptitiously shipping British copies of *Are You Experienced?* to the growing American underground market, *Sgt. Pepper* had a tremendous impact all over the world. On Sunday, June 4, the Experience performed at the Saville Theatre with Paul McCartney and George Harrison in attendance.

Most of the Saville's audience had only just begun to absorb *Sgt. Pepper's* incredible new sounds, so when Hendrix and the Experience opened their set with their own version of the album's title track it brought the audience to their feet. As Chris Stamp notes: "Hendrix had this instinctive sort of magic in that he could suddenly play the right music at absolutely the right time. This hip, London, big-time, show-yourself audience was wondering, 'Who is this black guy?'"

Graham Nash was another of the many other British pop stars in attendance that Sunday night. "Hendrix came out in this flame orange velvet suit playing 'Sgt. Pepper' and we were just blown away," he says. Paul McCartney was impressed by the Experience's version, describing the show and Hendrix's rendition as "simply incredible, perhaps the best I had ever seen him play." McCartney's only disappointment is that the show, unlike a number of other Saville concerts, wasn't professionally recorded.

The show was a smash success, capped by a massive party thrown for the group back at McCartney's house. McCartney had recently agreed to sit on the board of directors for an American pop music festival in Monterey, California. During a phone conversation with John Phillips, leader of the Mamas & the Papas and co-organizer of the event with Lou Adler, McCartney mentioned that the Jimi Hendrix Experience would be a great addition to the lineup. On faith, backed by the great power the Beatles wielded, the Experience were booked to make their American debut at the festival on June 18.

Their first American engagement secured, Chandler and the Experience returned to Olympic Studios to continue recording. "If Six Was Nine" was pulled off the shelf and completed in what Eddie Kramer recalls was a festive session. "Because Olympic recorded a lot of classical sessions, we had these different platforms. We pulled one forward and put Mitch's drums on it and on another we put microphones on top and underneath to record a foot-stomping track. Jimi was the gang leader, and people were laughing and falling all over each other." Graham Nash was also in the studio and was recruited by Hendrix to contribute. "Jimi said, 'Can you walk?' I said that I had been known to in the past. He then said to Gary Leeds of the Walker Brothers, 'Hey Leeds, can you walk as well? I need the sound of people walking.' So Jimi, Chas, Gary Leeds and I stomped on the platform."

"I compressed the foot stomps so much that you can hear

the compression kick in and out," explains Eddie Kramer. Hendrix then added another offbeat touch by playing a recorder, heard at the end of the song. Not formally trained on the instrument – he had in fact purchased the battered device from a London street vendor for two shillings – its addition was the result of a last-minute inspiration, most likely a sound Hendrix felt he could not achieve with his guitar.

Also in June, Hendrix, this time with permission from Chandler and Jeffery, contributed to Roger McGough and Mike McGear's eponymous album, adding guitar to "Ex-Art Student" and "So Much." Mike McGear, alias Mike McCartney, Paul's brother, was a close friend of Noel Redding and it was through him that the invitation to play was made. The sessions, which mostly took place at De Lane Lea Studios, also featured Paul, Graham Nash and a number of other British rock luminaries.

Before leaving for America, the group completed a number of interviews and photo sessions, most notably working with photographer Karl Ferris on shots that would grace the U.S. cover of their debut album *Are You Experienced?* Although Warner Bros. had yet to set a date for the album's release, they were willing to try another single. "Purple Haze" had been the obvious choice, Warner hoping that the song might capture at least some of the success it had enjoyed in Britain. As a label, Reprise lacked the widespread contacts needed to break an underground artist at that time. In the States, "Hey Joe" was too hard for Top 40 AM radio, and with virtually no AM stations supporting the single, only a handful of the country's few rock FM stations would give the song a chance. As polarized then as it is today, radio was split by color, and at this stage – though admittedly, matters were to change – neither black nor white AM Top 40 picked up on the group's unique interracial appeal. Furthermore, although the Experience had filmed a promo of the song ("One of the first groups to create a music video," states Chandler proudly) no TV station would air it, and without any personal concert appearances yet, no one knew about the band. Reprise would need to mount a sustained effort if the Jimi Hendrix Experience were to succeed in its leader's homeland.

The Reprise label had enjoyed sporadic success as an outlet for such friends and associates of Frank Sinatra as Dean Martin and Sammy Davis, Jr., and under the leadership of Morris "Mo" Ostin, it looked set to become a major player of the future by developing a roster of talented new acts such as the Experience, even though as a debut release "Hey Joe" was a total failure.

The Experience were coming to America with one booking, the Monterey Pop Festival, a visit perceived by Michael Jeffery as an opportunity to gain the high ground as manager of the Experience. Hendrix's success in Britain owed much to Chandler's tireless campaigning. There was no denying Jimi's talent, but Hendrix would never have come this far without Chandler. He was a musician, something Hendrix respected. He was also a man of strong convictions, with a firm sense of purpose, something Hendrix desperately needed. But as devoted as Chandler was to Hendrix, Jeffery was a realist, who, unlike Chandler, never had or never would be an artist. He realized that the music industry was a short game, where winners and losers were decided almost immediately. Record royalties, especially in the 1960s, could never generate the kind of income required to justify the endless hours of work it took to establish an artist. Touring was the key to that door, and creating a mystique and establishing an image were two prominent initiatives of Jeffery's outline for financial success.

On June 14, the band flew to New York and while there Jeffery took Hendrix to the office of Premier Talent, a burgeoning booking agency, and Teen Mail Ltd., a fan club organization, where Jimi was introduced to Frank Barselona, Bob Levine and Kathy Eberth. Toting a copy of "Hey Joe," Jeffery asked Barselona to find some bookings for the group, and at the same time asked Levine to work for

Hendrix. Jeffery had met Bob Levine in 1964 when he first brought the Animals over to the U.S. Levine was then stage manager at the Paramount Theater in Times Square, and he helped snare a booking for the band at the Apollo, making the Animals the first British group to play the legendary Harlem venue. Following that stint, he had worked with Sound Directions, show business veteran Walter Hyman's publicity firm whose clients included Barbra Streisand, Alan King and Dustin Hoffman. Levine was loyal, a credo crucially important to an inexperienced British nightclub owner managing a hot new group trying to break in America. He had brought Jeffery the demos to "We Gotta Get Out of This Place" and "Don't Let Me Be Understood," which in the hands of British producer Micky Most resulted in two top 20 hits for the Animals in America.

Barselona was an aggressive independent amidst fierce and sometimes hostile competition. He had scored a coup by booking U.S. dates for fellow Track artists The Who and other British groups such as the Hollies and Herman's Hermits.

Levine, meanwhile, ran Teen Mail Ltd., which handled fan club licensing and merchandising for all artists in the Premier stable. In addition, Levine had acted as tour manager for the Beatles' North American excursions. In fact, Premier Talent acted as a conduit for such influential pop mentors as Peter Grant (Led Zeppelin), Ron Terry (Cream, then Hendrix), Don Arden (Peter Frampton and Rod Stewart), Kit Lambert and Robert Stigwood, as well as Steve Weiss and Michael Jeffery. Unlike the great majority of other booking agencies, Premier opened its arms to British groups by creating tour packages and finding venues for them to play, and would, for example, combine Cream with The Who, or the Animals with Herman's Hermits. This helped ensure that the financial gains in touring the U.S. were not drowned by excessive expenses. Premier also booked all of disc jockey Murray the K's concerts at the Brooklyn Fox Theater, an act for which the DJ would reciprocate with ample AM airplay and exposure – a crucial asset for these fledgling groups. Jeffery would be dependent on this network to help preserve his hold on the Experience after Monterey.

Having arrived in San Francisco on June 15, the band drove down to Monterey to get settled in and rehearse for their appearance. As Chandler recalls, while no strangers to mayhem themselves, the Experience were somewhat taken aback by the full-tilt partying already underway. "We stayed at a little motel – us, Eric Burdon and the Animals, and the Buffalo Springfield. That was all they had room for. I had never seen anything like the Buffalo Springfield. It was like oil and water, that band. We had some great times with them!"

At rehearsals, Hendrix ran into an old acquaintance, Buddy Miles. Miles was now the drummer for the Electric Flag but the two had first met when Miles was sixteen, playing with Ruby & the Romantics in Montreal. Hendrix had come through town as a member of the I.B. Specials, the Isley Brothers' support band. There the two had fast struck up a friendship. As Miles recalls: "Jimi was from Seattle, a city that had not only American but Canadian blacks, so he could fit into the mainstream much easier than rural blacks. I was from Omaha, Nebraska, where you also had a good racial mix of people." Here at Monterey, Miles had his first glimpse of the Jimi Hendrix Experience, and came away stunned.

Despite the wealth of talent set to perform at the three-day festival, Gerry Stickells sensed a quiet confidence among the band. "Hendrix usually lived for the challenge, and he was very happy to be back in America." For all of the band, Monterey was an opportunity to meet new people, jam, exchange ideas and party. Indeed, for Jeffery, it was a golden opportunity to stimulate interest in the group, or risk returning to England with little accomplished.

Publicity for psychedelic rock artists barely existed when Michael Goldstein arrived in Monterey. Goldstein, at the festival on behalf of the Temporary Tattoo Company, had experience as a publicist, covering such mainstream events as the 1964 New York World's Fair. Eschewing his hippie garb for a suit, Goldstein was hired as a publicity agent for a number of artists, including Big Brother featuring Janis Joplin & the Holding Company, the Association, and Eric Burdon and the Animals. On the strength of his pitch for Eric Burdon, Goldstein became publicist for the Experience. Although Beatles (and Monterey Pop Festival) publicist Derek Taylor had fast developed his reputation, he was not an American, something Jeffery was specifically seeking. Jeffery wanted someone who had had direct experience with various levels of American media. Jeffery had been impressed that Goldstein had handled events as wide ranging as circus shows and Broadway musicals. By employing Goldstein, Jeffery hoped that the group's performance at the festival could be maximized, and as a result more U.S. gigs would be forthcoming. As with his British press agent Les Perrin, Jeffery was not looking for someone hip, rather, a veteran of the legitimate show business circuit.

The festival opened the night of Friday the 16th, the Association greeting some 20,000 of Northern California's burgeoning hippie culture. Each group had been specifically instructed to restrict their set times to not less than thirty minutes and no more than forty-five, owing to the fact that many of the San Francisco-based psychedelic bands might stretch their set out to seventy-five or even ninety minutes at more familiar venues such as the Fillmore West or Avalon Ballroom. The aim at Monterey was to present as wide a range of performers as possible. The Experience represented a commitment to new talent, as did The Who, Big Brother & the Holding Company and the Electric Flag.

By Sunday, the pace in the performers' tent was finally calm. Two days and nights of all-out partying had tested the stamina of even the most durable artist. After three hours of Ravi Shankar during the afternoon, the Grateful Dead opened Sunday evening's show with a forty-minute set, after which the Blues Project returned for a short encore performance. The next band to perform would be The Who. Both the Experience and The Who were familiar with each other's stage show. More importantly, after a weekend of great music, each band recognized the opportunity to establish themselves. The Who went on first, holding nothing back and energizing the crowd with charged versions of "Pictures of Lily," "Substitute," "Summertime Blues" and, ultimately, "My Generation."

Thanks to "Happy Jack," the group's minor U.S. chart hit that spring, some of the Monterey audience had at least heard of The Who. But none were prepared for the destructive climax of "My Generation" when the group seemed suddenly to explode. Mostly obscured by smoke, Roger Daltrey swung his microphone through the air, Pete Townshend began smashing his guitar, soon joined by Keith Moon, kicking and destroying his drum kit. Amid the smoke and bleating noises emitting from the group's battered amplifier stacks, The Who strode defiantly off stage to wild cheers from Monterey's startled peace, love and flowers audience. No other artist or group had ever concluded their set in such a fashion and The Who had given the Monterey crowd a brief glimpse of the power and emotion that rock, especially their brand, was capable of delivering.

The Who's manic stage show did not escape the attention of Jimi Hendrix. Watching from sidestage, publicist Michael Goldstein observed a transformation in Hendrix's mood, from nervous fidgeting to complete commitment. He hadn't intended to burn his guitar. According to Chandler, the Experience had planned to perform their regular set and had rehearsed at the festival site to do just that. But after witnessing The Who's final acts of destruction, Hendrix had immediately decided to sacrifice a hand-painted Stratocaster. Just before the group took to the stage, Chandler left the performer's tent to join engineer Wally Heider, recording the performance in his eight-track remote truck. After a short introduction by the Rolling Stones' own Brian Jones, for which the Experience would be forever grateful, Hendrix, Mitchell and Redding strode on stage together to make their American debut.

It would be pure fiction to say that the Experience hit the Monterey stage running and never stopped. As the Reprise *Jimi Plays Monterey* proves, they came out on stage, tuned up and waited for Jones to alert the crowd to their presence. (His introduction, though partly muffled on the recording, rang loud and clear in the audience, as McKuen's and Heider's sound feeds were split. Heider had simply turned down Hendrix's vocal microphone until the group was ready to start.) After the crowd's polite applause, the Experience launched into Howlin' Wolf's "Killing Floor." The stage lights remained down throughout Hendrix's frenzied chord-laden introduction until Mitchell crashed in on his snares, allowing the crowd their first glimpse.

Sporting the eye vest of the still unreleased Reprise *Are You Experienced?* LP, and a bright pink feathery scarf, Hendrix unleashed a torrent of one-handed hammer-on notes, as his other swung wildly in the air. Mitchell and Redding were relentless behind him – Mitch especially, whose performance at Monterey ranked among his very best work with the Experience. The pace of the music had been cranked up a notch, principally because of sheer nerves. Neither The Who nor the Experience had wanted to follow each other. Monterey was too important to both bands and it had required a coin flip by festival producer John Phillips to finally decide the matter. Having lost, Hendrix jumped up onto a chair and announced that if he had to follow The Who, he was going to pull out all the stops. He did. "Foxey Lady" followed "Killing Floor" and Hendrix began his stage routine in earnest. Unlike concert performances of the song in later years, this live version of "Foxey Lady" remained very close to its studio counterpart, though it was also somewhat ragged, as exploding with nervous energy, Hendrix struggled to maintain tempo. Despite his audacious between-the-legs solo, Jimi's playing lacked fluidity, pressing – almost squeezing – the notes too hard.

As "Foxey Lady" crashed to a close, Hendrix stepped up to the microphone and audaciously asked the crowd to give him one second to "get right down to business." As he stripped off his vest and scarf, Hendrix further disarmed the audience, quipping as he held the pink scarf, "I don't want anybody to think I'm ... you know. You've got to keep people honest." As he had learned by watching both Johnny Hallyday and the classic R&B performers he had backed, a crowd could be set at ease with some self-deprecating humor.

Hendrix's aside perfectly set up his next song, a masterful version of Dylan's "Like a Rolling Stone." Once again, Hendrix had chosen to play the right song at the right time. As with the Beatles', and to a lesser degree the Rolling Stones', Dylan's influence hung over the Monterey audience. Hendrix's emotionally charged rendition surprised the crowd, while its length allowed them a chance to settle down and listen to the musician Brian Jones had described as "their fellow countryman." "Like a Rolling Stone" won the Experience a warm ovation and with "Rock Me Baby" it was time to ratchet things up again. The band, especially Hendrix, seemed to sense that the crowd was now with them, and as Redding's bass lines pushed him ever onward Hendrix responded, playing the main solo with his teeth and ending the song with a dramatic tremolo finish.

With electric tuning devices unavailable then, Hendrix's constant tremolo bar assault forced him to tune up between almost every song during a live performance. Monterey was no exception. "Hey Joe" – "the song that really brought us here," as Jimi described it – followed next. Injected with the same passion and enthusiasm afforded "Like a Rolling Stone," this Monterey rendition was far more powerful than the studio single. Singing with conviction, Hendrix stayed within the song's tempo, playing the first solo with his teeth and the second one behind his head. The Experience would never perform the song, with this arrangement, as brilliantly again.

As Hendrix stopped to tune up once again, he slyly noted the band's desire to visit New York to see the "golden streets of the Village. The reason why they are golden is because of all of the banana peels." After this quick dig at his former home, Hendrix launched into "Can You See Me" at breakneck speed, forcing Mitchell, with varying success, to keep up. This track was not captured by D.A. Pennebaker's film crew in its entirety for they were reloading film during the performance. (The same fate almost befell "Purple Haze," but one camera did manage to maintain complete coverage throughout.) Hendrix quickly introduced "The Wind Cries Mary" as "the next single here" and again settled down the audience with a ballad, this time his own. Although he battled through a slight tuning problem after the song's solo, it remains a mystery why this version was kept off Reprise's August 1970 *Otis Redding–Jimi Hendrix Experience Live at Monterey* LP in favor of "Can You See Me," a decision in which neither Hendrix, Kramer nor Chandler were involved.

"Purple Haze" came next, and once again Hendrix invoked his sense of humor by pointing to Redding and singing "Excuse me, while I kiss this guy." As with "Foxey Lady," "Purple Haze" would later become little more than a showcase for Jimi's stage routines, but here the Experience stayed within themselves, presenting the song as carefully as they had "Hey Joe" and "The Wind Cries Mary." In Britain, and as it would become in America, these were the group's first three singles, and considering the chart failure of "Hey Joe" it was essential that "The Wind Cries Mary" and "Purple Haze" be well received, and both enjoyed warm, sustained applause.

Prefacing the group's final number, Hendrix took time to thank the Monterey audience, then teased them, cryptically declaring his intent to "sacrifice something I really love."

Calling it the "English and American anthem combined" he launched into a feedback-drenched rendition of the Troggs' "Wild Thing."

As he had promised in the dressing room before the show, Hendrix pulled out all the stops, incorporating all of his fabled stage moves, including a wonderfully fitting, one-handed version of Frank Sinatra's "Strangers in the Night" inside his solo. Hendrix rolled on the floor, cranked his amps as high as he could and ran toward his bank of amplifiers to begin a vicious frontal assault. As Mitch – "Queen Bee" as Hendrix introduced him to the Monterey crowd – continued to maniacally pound out fills, Hendrix squatted over his guitar and began to pull on the tremolo bar. Incredibly, the sounds still retained an eerie musical quality missing when The Who's Pete Townshend had smashed his guitar. With Townshend, the act seemed violent: his lips pursed, and face contorted with anger, destroying his instrument was his final contribution to the performance. With Hendrix, the act seemed overtly sexual, and his relentless grinding, tongue wagging and showboating left the Monterey audience staggered.

As Redding and Mitchell frantically continued their playing, Hendrix walked back to his amplifier, grabbed a can of Ronson lighter fluid and, for better or worse, created one of the most striking images in rock n' roll history.

Whereas most bands would have appeared feeble after The Who's set, the Experience firmly established themselves as the single most dynamic act in rock. The looks of astonishment on the faces of the crowd as Hendrix threw pieces of his battered, charred Stratocaster to them, captured by Pennebaker's film crew, were precious. Abe Jacob, sound engineer for the Mamas & the Papas, was mixing the house sound during the Experience's performance. His thoughts reflect the general feeling of the festival participants. "The first thing that went through all of our minds, at least through mine, was that, at last, someone was doing a theatrical show. As far as rock music was concerned, everybody at that point was very laid back, giving a kind of nonshow performance. T-shirts, torn jeans, hair in your eyes, and you looked down at your guitar and played. Hendrix was someone who really was an entertainer. Actually, my most vivid memory is of Wally Heider running up to get his Sony overhead microphones from the drum kit as they were being knocked over."

As Chandler recalled, one of Heider's microphones was broken as Hendrix wildly swung his smoldering Stratocaster. "I was in the control room of [Heider's] remote truck doing the sound. When I got to the dressing room there was a blazing row going on between Jeffery and Hendrix because Jimi had broken a microphone on stage. I yelled to Jeffrey, 'What the fuck are you going on about! This guy has destroyed America and the industry is at his feet and you're giving him hell for breaking a microphone! Piss off!' I threw Jeffery out of the dressing room that night. 'Let the lad enjoy his triumph,' I said. 'He is an American and this is his first gig in America.'"

With no other U.S. concerts booked, Jeffery and Chandler needed to keep the band working in order to stay financially afloat. Jeffery was leaving for New York to meet with Steve Weiss to try to confirm some bookings with Frank Barselona when Bill Graham came to the band's rescue, offering them the opportunity to open for the Jefferson Airplane and Big Brother & the Holding Company. While the pay – $500 a night – certainly didn't overwhelm the Experience, the chance to play at the Fillmore West, in front of a sophisticated San Francisco audience, and to maintain their Monterey momentum made the effort worthwhile.

San Francisco fell in love with the Jimi Hendrix Experience. "Hendrix murdered the Jefferson Airplane," recalls Chas Chandler. "After one night they gave top of the bill to Jimi. It was Big Brother & the Holding Company on first, the Airplane as the middle act, and the Experience at the top." From Tuesday night, June 20, through to Sunday night the 25th, the band performed two shows a night at the Fillmore, jamming and partying the rest of the time. The Experience were being given the royal treatment in San Francisco. The Fillmore West concerts created so much excitement around the city that on Sunday afternoon the Experience performed at an impromptu free concert in Golden Gate Park.

Now the rage of Northern California, their two weeks in America promised the Jimi Hendrix Experience inconceivable success.

# 6 OLD DEMONS AND NEW HEADACHES

*"Jeffery couldn't understand why Jimi and I were so angry. He thought pairing Hendrix with the Monkees was no different than having Herman's Hermits touring with the Animals."*

—Chas Chandler

Exhausted by their free concert and two evening sets at the Fillmore West that Sunday, the band planned to fly down to Los Angeles within a day or so. Northwest-based promoter Tom Hulett, another key contact Jeffery had made at Monterey, booked the band into the Earl Warren Showgrounds in Santa Barbara on July 1 and the Whiskey a Go Go in Los Angeles on the 2nd. The band was also waiting to hear back from Jeffery about dates he was trying to secure in New York. No one could have ever guessed what Jeffery had arranged.

"We had just walked in, and Hendrix and I were sitting in my room," recalls Chandler. "Jeffery got me on the phone and said he had great news. 'I have just got them on the hottest tour in America as a support act,' he said. I said, 'That's great, who is it?' 'The Monkees.' I dropped the fucking phone. I couldn't believe it. While Jeffery was talking, I said to Hendrix, 'Do you fancy playing with the Monkees?' He went, 'What's Jeffery doing!' I had a flaming

95

row with him on the telephone. I went berserk. The tour was opening in Florida: I said, 'You can go on those fucking dates because I ain't going. I am totally disassociating myself from it. It's your fuck-up. You take care of it!'"

The Jimi Hendrix Experience would join the Monkees Northeast U.S. tour within two weeks. Michael Jeffery's decision to make the Experience join the Monkees tour was perhaps rooted in the phenomenal success the band had enjoyed while supporting British teen favorites the Walker Brothers. That tour, Chandler's idea all the way, had come to be seen as something of a masterstroke. But in trying to copy a winning formula, Jeffery had overlooked the size of the playing field in America. Britain could not compete with the number of bands and venues available to U.S. promoters. Considering Hendrix's triumphs at Monterey and now the Fillmore West, it would have been wiser to package the Experience, perhaps even with Eric Burdon and the Animals, and send the tour out to clubs and small halls.

Jeffery had secured the Experience a slot on the tour through Dick Clark. There was no questioning Clark's power with promoters, radio and television. Jeffery took the deal and turned to Chandler and Hendrix looking for their gratitude. Their violent rebuff rubbed him raw. As was the case with the clearing of Hendrix's old contracts and commitments, the perception was that again Jeffery had not come through.

Having arrived in Los Angeles, Chandler and Hendrix were eager to check out the city's best studios. Hendrix, according to Chandler, had only one or two songs deemed worthy of recording, and work commenced on "The Stars That Play With Laughing Sam's Dice." Chandler initially planned to use a three-girl vocal group on the track, the original arrangement being less bombastic than the version eventually issued. The first girls chosen, with little success, were former groupies of the original Animals. Undaunted, Chandler vowed to find the proper female backing vocals to suit Hendrix.

After checking out a number of different studios, they settled on a small eight-track facility that according to Chandler was "like a rehearsal studio compared to Olympic – it was dire." As rough as the finished master sounded, "The Stars That Play With Laughing Sam's Dice" was a telling example of just how difficult it could be to correctly capture Hendrix's live guitar sound. Jimi was clearly too loud for the small studio, his distortion-drenched lead guitar screaming incessantly before being squashed by Redding's bouncing bass and Hendrix's shout "Don't open that door!" "The Stars That Play With Laughing Sam's Dice" also marked Hendrix's recording debut with the wahwah pedal – used quite tastefully considering the sheer insanity of the overall session – and the Experience's first eight-track studio recording.

Arriving in New York on July 3, the Experience jammed at the Scene Club, a new venue run by Steve Paul. With only one more gig scheduled before the band had to leave and join the Monkees tour, Chandler agreed to have the Experience come back the next night to perform their regular show. For the 5th, publicist Michael Goldstein had arranged a number of interviews, and also a photo session, to take advantage of the group's much talked about Monterey performance.

While most of the legitimate press simply yawned at the Experience's Monterey debut, not all of their reviews were as low-key; in fact *Billboard*, the industry's trade magazine, drubbed the band and Hendrix specifically. "The Jimi Hendrix Experience proved to be more experience than *music*, pop or otherwise. Accompanied by overmodulated squeals and bombastic drumming, the Hendrix performance is quite a crowd rouser but its sensationalism is not music, and unlike Chuck Berry (who was doing some of this stuff fifteen years ago), when Hendrix sings he has trouble phrasing, and his modal turned chicken choke handling of the guitar doesn't indicate a strong talent, either." Goldstein had his work cut out for him, and Jeffery counted on his publicist's contacts with such popular New York writers as Al Aronowitz to help make inroads. Although the group had seen some of the film footage from the show at Monterey, none of it was made available to the band or to Goldstein for any type of promotional use. There was no point: outside of the sheer shock value of Hendrix burning his guitar, there was no outlet for rock n' roll on television. The producers of the movie *Monterey Pop* were having enough trouble trying to finalize their own television deal.

That night (July 5, 1967), the Experience had been added as a support act to the Young Rascals, who were playing in Central Park. Hamstrung by the impending Monkees tour, Jeffery had turned to Sid Bernstein, manager of the Young Rascals, who were also represented by Steve Weiss, and at the last minute the Experience were added to the bill. Stopping just shy of burning his guitar, Hendrix once again packed his dynamic stage show into the Experience's thirty-five-minute set. Every gig, regardless of its size, was important. But to finally be back in New York – playing in Central Park no less – while hardly a homécoming concert, primed Hendrix to play well.

Most important, even before the concert, Hendrix couldn't wait to drive up to Harlem and tell Faye Pridgeon all about his success in Britain. From the Buckingham Hotel, Hendrix had called his close friends, twin brothers Arthur and Albert Allen, reaching Arthur, who accompanied Hendrix to Faye's apartment. As Faye fondly remembers, Hendrix was bursting with pride. "He was bragging and waving this album cover, and Jimi was always ashamed to brag. I said, 'Oh, give me a break! I don't believe a word of it.' He said, 'This is my picture! This is me!' but I replied, 'You can have that stuff printed downtown on Broadway.' He kept saying, 'Why don't you believe me?' until finally I said, 'Okay, okay, I believe you!' Then he said, 'But you're just saying that, you don't really believe me!' I responded, 'Look, you come here with an empty damn jacket sleeve and you tell me that's your record? Yeah, sure.' He said, 'Oh no, the record is back at the hotel.'"

Painfully self-conscious, Hendrix most likely left the record back at the hotel on purpose: Faye was too honest, she would have told Hendrix what she thought right up front. Alone with her, though, he would have time to explain the new directions his music had taken. With the twins present, he would be too uncomfortable to debut his new music. It was not that Faye and the twins would have been completely taken aback by his new music; they had seen Hendrix study, not just listen, to the roots of the blues. Hendrix used his extensive record collection to open his ears to as many different influences as he could. When Hendrix arrived upon the Harlem scene, he was, as the twins described, "a hobo," with his guitar under one arm and his record collection under the other.

Hendrix took nothing more seriously than music. "Jimi had really known hard times," remembers Arthur Allen. "So for him to be famous, it was like, 'Oh come on, Jimi ...' Out of all of us, I believed it, because we had lived together. I remember Jimi with all of his records, stacks of Elmore James, Lightnin' Hopkins and all of the blues greats. In those days, most black entertainers were not getting into the depths of black music, its roots. Most performers thought, 'It's me,' totally an ego thing. Hendrix, even though he couldn't read music, would still study it and take you into areas that nobody really knew. He would even get into white music, and when you found a black entertainer who would *study* white music – you knew the guy was serious. Before we started the Ghetto Fighters, my brother Albert and I were in an R&B combo named the GTO's and, like the great majority of black musicians, we couldn't have been bothered with the Beatles, let alone Bob Dylan."

To both Pridgeon and the twins, Hendrix's openness to all styles of music was another example of his universal attitude toward life. Emerging as the leader of an interracial rock group seemed a quantum leap from singing and playing an unplugged electric guitar to Bob Dylan records alone in the cramped apartment he and Faye had shared. It was also much more organized than his struggles in Village clubs, fronting and supporting pickup bands for marginal money or encouragement. As surprising as his rapid ascension to stardom had been to him, he now had to explain that the Jimi Hendrix Experience actually had a *following*, let alone a recording contract.

Owing to his uncertainty of their feelings about his music, Hendrix had invited them down to see the Experience perform in Central Park so that they could see that the crowds were enthusiastic about his music. For Faye, what she saw barely resembled the "Jimmy" Hendrix she had seen perform a countless number of times in the past. "I mean, it was nice, and I guess I liked it, but it just wasn't black music," says Pridgeon of this show. "I was a funky person. I came from Jimmy Reed, Guitar Slim, Muddy Waters and Lightnin' Hopkins. This is what had blown me away about Jimi – he wasn't your average John Q. African American. He was a real blues fanatic. I sensed it right from the first time he sat on my mother's living room floor and played his guitar. When he went into rock n' roll, it kind of knocked me for a loop."

For Hendrix, this subtle struggle for artistic acceptance would never subside. In fact, as his success grew, so did the pressure to address the issue. But for now, certainly as far as Faye could tell, Hendrix was at least eating regularly and making a living playing his beloved guitar. That, as she knew better than anyone, was an achievement worth celebrating.

Hendrix's return to Harlem was also cause for celebration. "Jimi pulled my brother and me aside," recalls Albert Allen. "He said, 'Let's have a party.' We decided to go over Faye's house. Jimi said, 'I got some new stuff here you all gonna love!' When we got there, we all took this new drug – acid Jimi called it. I took more than I should have and he warned me, saying, 'Hey man, watch what you are doing.' After we got high, Faye started bugging out. She was looking at Jimi saying, 'Doesn't Jimi look funny over there? We should hang him.' In a complete trance, I said okay. Jimi was sitting in the corner whimpering, 'No, no, you can't do that!' Then Faye flipped out, she bolted out into her apartment building's hallway, running up and down yelling, 'There are men in my house!' She didn't recognize any of us. It's 3 A.M. and both Jimi and I were undressed. We ran into the bathroom and hid behind the shower curtain. We turned the water on when Faye started yelling, 'They're in there!' It was crazy!"

While in New York, Chas had been doing some visiting as well, running into Tom Wilson, who had produced a number of Animals' sessions. Wilson suggested to Chas that the Experience try recording at Mayfair Studios, a small eight-track facility he regularly used. With "The Stars That Play With Laughing Sam's Dice," Redding's "She's So Fine" and "If Six Was Nine" in the can, Chandler brought the band into Mayfair to record a new song that Hendrix had written, "The Burning of the Midnight Lamp." Track was looking to release another single in Britain and Europe, fresh on the heels of "The Wind Cries Mary."

A black American, best known for producing some of Bob Dylan's finest work, Wilson loved Hendrix's playing and wanted, as had Lambert and Stamp, to be involved in some way with the Experience. Working with Wilson was an excellent young engineer from Iowa, Gary Kellgren. Kellgren, the "American Eddie Kramer" as Gerry Stickells described him, impressed the band with his facility and creativity. As he had been with Kramer at Olympic, Chandler was receptive and appreciative of Kellgren's contributions. "The Burning of the Midnight Lamp" saw the debut of another new instrument on Hendrix recordings, the harpsichord. In addition, Hendrix tastefully incorporated a wah-wah sound, effectively doubling the harpsichord's introduction.

Although vastly different from anything on *Are You*

*Experienced?* or the track "If Six Was Nine," "The Burning of the Midnight Lamp" clearly demonstrated that Hendrix had total freedom to create and record whatever he desired. There was no plan by Chandler to create soundalike sequels to ensure the success of the group's second and still untitled album. If anything, Hendrix needed something stronger than "The Stars That Play With Laughing Sam's Dice" because they were following "The Wind Cries Mary," one of their finest efforts. After recording the song's basic tracks, Chandler still wanted to incorporate female backing vocals onto a Hendrix record. Gary Kellgren's wife Marta, who doubled as Mayfair's secretary, tracked down the Sweet Inspirations, Aretha Franklin's backing vocalists. The Sweet Inspirations' lilting, gospel-inflected background vocals were recorded by Chandler and Kellgren, filling the tape's eight tracks. The long session was finally concluded by mixing the song down to half-inch four-track tape (Olympic's standard format). Clearly pleased with their work, it was decided that "The Burning of the Midnight Lamp" would become the band's next single.

The next morning, the Experience – without Chas, who stayed behind in Manhattan – left for Jacksonville, Florida, to begin their tour with the Monkees. Unlike their first gig on the Walker Brothers tour, however, when a spotlight-stealing Hendrix had set his guitar on fire and the audience loved it, the Monkees' subteen devotees gave the Experience a lesson in just how bad a tour could be. The Experience were not even halfway through their opening number before the first wave of "We want the Monkees!" rang out from the crowd. Although the Monkees themselves tried to make light of the situation, their fans clearly hated the Experience. Concerts in Miami, and Charlotte and Greensboro, North Carolina, were the same. Michael Jeffery felt pressure from the band and especially from Chandler for subjecting the group to such a fiasco. From Charlotte, seeking to rectify the situation, Jeffery contacted Ron Terry, an enterprising young booking agent who had recently left

Premier Talent, and was now orchestrating Cream's North American engagements for CMA.

When the tour reached Forest Hills in New York, a seething Chandler, who forced himself to attend, saw the Experience struggle through a thirty-minute set in which Hendrix split his pants on stage. He had seen enough, this was too embarrassing. Meanwhile, Jeffery had called Bob Levine, influential New York promoter and Vanilla Fudge manager Phil Basile, Ron Terry, as well as his own mentor, Albert Grossman – manager of Bob Dylan and Big Brother & the Holding Company – to meet at Steve Weiss's Long Island home. From the outset of the meeting, the biggest issue was damage control. How could they pull the Experience off the tour without hurting the group's fragile image? Jeffery and Levine threw out such potential ideas as Hendrix telling the press, "They couldn't make a Monkee out of me."

Chandler, on the other hand, had lost all patience. "I had this flaming row with Jeffery. I told him I was pulling them off the tour, no matter how I had to do it. He said that we would get sued by Dick Clark, so I rang Dick there and then – he was staying at the Americana in Manhattan – and I arranged to meet him the next day. I had toured for Dick in the Animals days and we had always gotten on well. In the meantime, we sat and cooked up the Daughters of the American Revolution story that afternoon. I had to tell all these lies that [the DAR thought that] Hendrix was too outrageous and obscene to be seen by the Monkees' pre-pubescent admirers. All it was was a device to get off the tour without losing face but it actually became this massive public relations story overnight. We never expected that, though we did expect to get sued by the Daughters of the American Revolution and we never were. As far as we were concerned, it was just a story for the trade magazines so it would not look as if we had been jerked off the tour. Dick Clark agreed with me, it was the worst match he had ever seen."

As abruptly as they had joined the tour, the Experience – courtesy of the unknowing Daughters of the American Revolution – had been afforded a graceful exit. Whereas burning his guitar at Monterey had garnered Hendrix notice in underground papers such as *Rolling Stone*, the mainstream media, with the exception of Pete Johnson in the *Los Angeles Times*, had ignored the whole festival. Now, being asked to leave the Monkees tour by the DAR attracted the attention of rock n' roll fans across the country. One of the most interesting things about the story is that nobody bothered to even look into the matter. To the established media, the Hendrix-DAR episode marked another signpost in the growing "us versus them" cultural battle with America's youth.

The Experience returned to Mayfair to attend final mixing sessions for "The Burning of the Midnight Lamp." At the same time, Gary Kellgren was given a chance at remixing "The Stars That Play With Laughing Sam's Dice" because it had now been chosen as the B side. Additional overdubs were attempted, but in its final form the song changed little from the previous mix completed in Los Angeles.

Having dodged one bullet in their escape from the Monkees, another came in the form of a lawsuit filed by PPX Industries against Jimi Hendrix, Polydor Records and Track Records in the Queen's Bench Division of the High Court of Great Britain. Ed Chalpin, PPX's president, was asking that his claim for an injunction be heard at the earliest opportunity and, in the meantime, that the three defendants be restrained from issuing any more recordings featuring Jimi Hendrix. Chalpin had filed suit in late June while the band was in California and Jeffery in New York. Track was incensed that Jeffery had not dealt with Chalpin back in January.

The PPX case began to border on the bizarre. On July 17, 1967, after completing a press conference held at the Warwick Hotel in Manhattan, Hendrix met Roselyn Morris and Toni Gregory, who was married to Ed "Bugs" Gregory, an old friend from his days with the Squires. Inquiring as to Bugs's whereabouts, Hendrix was told they were recording with Curtis Knight. Anxious to see his old friends, Hendrix took along his wah-wah pedal and an eight-string bass, in addition to his guitar, should there be a chance to jam. When he arrived with Morris and Gregory at Studio 76, PPX's recording studio, the session was already in progress, so Jimi waited until its conclusion before making the rounds, greeting everybody. To session producer Ed Chalpin, it seemed as if Hendrix had finally responded to the repeated messages he had left for him at his hotel, or even to the letter he had sent Hendrix care of Chris Stamp and Track Records. Also in attendance at the session were engineer Mickey Lane and Decca Records executive Dick Rowe – the same Dick Rowe who had earlier turned down the Jimi Hendrix Experience and "Hey Joe." According to a 1967 deposition, Rowe had gone to PPX to arrange for the acquisition of past Hendrix recordings.

Out in the studio, Hendrix began jamming with Gregory, playing the eight-string bass he'd brought along, while Ray Lucas soon joined in on drums. It was Lucas who led the group into a jam, later to be christened "Flashing." With Hendrix still playing eight-string bass, Ed Gregory played rhythm guitar, Ray Lucas was on drums and Knight handled tambourine. According to Chalpin in a 1967 deposition, he then recorded Hendrix (on tape machines he had customized to record ten tracks, predating the arrival of twelve-track recording by more than a year) overdubbing a wah-wah electric guitar part "in order to achieve a fuller sound and obtain a final product." Chalpin also asserted that Hendrix knew he was being recorded: "It is not possible that Hendrix did not know he was recording. In addition, we interrupted the session frequently to make balance tests [of] microphone volume. During these pauses at Hendrix's request, we would play back the material recorded to hear the previous sound, and after each number, Hendrix personally entered the control room to hear the results in order to judge whether they had been recorded correctly."

Curtis Knight, also speaking in a 1967 deposition, agreed: "There was no question in my mind that we were recording and it would have been impossible for Hendrix not to be aware of that fact. During the time I sang the vocal part, in the case of 'Hush Now,' we frequently interrupted the session and listened to what had been recorded to be sure that there was a proper balance [between] Hendrix's guitar and my voice." For this track, Knight also played tambourine while Lucas remained on drums and Hendrix, once again, according to Chalpin, recorded the basic track on bass and overdubbed the guitar.

Hendrix, on the other hand, was quite adamant that while he had participated in the "practice session," Knight and Chalpin had violated his trust. According to Hendrix, after the session had ended, he told Knight that he had participated as a personal favor, and that while he had no objection to the recording, under no circumstances was his name to be used in connection with it. In his deposition, Hendrix stated that Knight agreed, though – crucially – Chalpin would later state that at the conclusion of the session he offered Hendrix a check, which Jimi refused, but that he gave him cash: "I don't recall the exact amount. It could have been anywhere from $50 to $200."

As illogical as Hendrix's action appeared, he was a trusting person who considered the lawsuit in Britain to be of no real significance to him, something that Jeffery and Chalpin would solve between them. It was Yameta that he had chosen to work with now, but Curtis Knight had helped him out in the past – what better way to show that gratitude existed among musicians? Lending his talents to Chalpin and Knight, so long as they did not use his name, demonstrated a sincere gesture on his part, and a consistent one too: Hendrix would make a point of helping old friends throughout his career, whether it be lending money to Faye Pridgeon to help defray moving expenses or reaching back to Billy Cox and Larry Lee. Hendrix would never forget where he had come from.

What Hendrix did not take into account was the unassailable fact that Chalpin and PPX were not interested in his occasional tokens of generosity. Chalpin felt that he had signed Hendrix to a valid contract in 1965, and that he had given Hendrix the opportunity to develop his unique sound. While Hendrix may not have been happy backing Curtis Knight as a member of the Squires, he had also signed as a solo artist with Chalpin. Hendrix's notoriously cavalier attitude toward contracts had come to haunt him, with a vengeance. Previously, it had not mattered what Hendrix signed. His value was so minuscule then that fighting for his rights would have been pointless. But Chalpin had been shrewd enough to sign Hendrix to a legal, albeit severe, contract. Now that Yameta, a company whose executives he could not identify let alone contact, had enjoyed great success with releases by Hendrix, Chalpin felt he had to resort to legal action if he wanted to regain his artist – and enjoy the financial reward which he considered himself due.

Chalpin had now amassed a number of recordings that featured Knight on vocals and Hendrix on guitar. If the courts in Britain enjoined Hendrix's foreign releases on Track, he would have enough finished masters available to lease or license an album, should he be granted the opportunity. On or about July 27, 1967, Chalpin and Knight met Jerry Simon of RSVP Records, as recalled by Simon in his deposition: "I was approached with the request that my company sell them the seven master tapes ('The UFO,' 'I'm a Fool for You Baby,' 'Ballad of Jimmy,' 'They Gotta Have a New Dress,' 'Hornet's Nest,' 'Knock Yourself Out' and 'Your Love') which I had previously acquired from PPX. They informed me that the purpose of the proposed acquisition of the tapes by them was that Knight was about to enter into an exclusive recording agreement, and both of them desired that there be no competing recordings of Curtis Knight issued." Simon responded positively, and for the princely sum of $400, Chalpin and Knight reclaimed seven additional songs that featured Hendrix with the Squires.

Amid almost daily press interviews arranged by Michael Goldstein, agent Frank Barselona had secured a number of club and theater dates for the Experience, first at the Salvation and Cafe Au Go Go venues in New York, then on to the Ambassador Theater in Washington, D.C., for a five-day engagement. While at the Salvation Club on August 4, Hendrix was personally served with a notice that Warner Bros. had been added as a co-defendant to this new action by PPX Industries, because it had just released *Are You Experienced?* in the U.S. and Canada. While its version also featured eleven tracks, Reprise – much to Hendrix's dismay – chose to include the three British singles (successful there and elsewhere too, they had barely dented the *Billboard* Hot 100) while deleting "Red House," "Remember" and "Can You See Me" from the album. The exclusion of "Red House" was a particularly sore point for Hendrix, and he often preceded live performances of the song on 1968 U.S. tours with a dig at the label's reluctance to include a blues number on the album.

Incomprehensibly, on August 8, a mere four days after being served notice, Hendrix again returned to PPX's Studio 76 to continue recording with Knight. It was during this 4 A.M. session that "Gloomy Monday" and other Knight songs were taped. In 1973, while working for Studio 76, engineer Mark Linett – later, ironically, to work for Reprise, mixing and mastering such posthumous Hendrix albums as *The Jimi Hendrix Concerts* – found a fascinating section of studio chatter that preceded a take of "Gloomy Monday." Chalpin was in the control room speaking through the talkback microphone, Knight and Hendrix were out in the studio, and the tape started with Chalpin announcing "Gloomy Monday" over the talkback.

> HENDRIX (talking to Chalpin): Okay, look, you can't, you know ... like, when we do this thing, you can't put my name on the single.

KNIGHT (agreeing): No, no, hell no.
HENDRIX (laughing, indicating to Knight that Chalpin cannot hear him): Okay?
KNIGHT (To Hendrix): You got it.
CHALPIN: Rolling!
HENDRIX: Edward, can you hear me?
CHALPIN: I hear you.
HENDRIX: In other words, you can't, you know, you can't use my name for none of this stuff though, right?
CHALPIN: I can hear you now that I'm rolling.
KNIGHT: You can't use his name for any of this.
CHALPIN: Oh, don't worry about it.
HENDRIX: No, but ... (laughs)
CHALPIN: (laughs)
HENDRIX: No. Serious though, serious though, you know?
CHALPIN: Like I said, don't worry about it.
HENDRIX: Huh?
CHALPIN: I won't use it, don't worry!

Immediately after this exchange Hendrix launched into the first take of "Gloomy Monday." Though it broke down midway through, the second take was complete, featuring his infectious rhythm guitar mixed to the fore, with only Ray Lucas's drumming and Knight's occasional vocals otherwise audible.

This taped conversation was not presented in either the British or American court actions. This was just as well, since, while it would have clarified Hendrix's actual intent, it would also have flown in the face of his assertion that he did not realize Chalpin was recording the jam session. Chalpin states that he first became aware of the tape many years later and puts little faith in the recording – feeling that it had been doctored. He states that he first became aware of the tape during a separate lawsuit against Audio Fidelity Enterprises, the same company that released the egregious Hendrix album *High, Live & Dirty*.

Considering now that there were two lawsuits pending, filed against him personally as well as his record companies, Hendrix's actions seem childishly irresponsible. He most certainly knew that a lawsuit had been begun, and as PPX attorney Elliot Hoffman stated: "It is incredible that after having been sued in London and New York for enforcement of the recording agreement with PPX, Hendrix can now say that he didn't realize that he was being recorded. Both of the suits pending against him were entitled 'PPX Enterprises, Inc. against Jimi Hendrix.' PPX Enterprises, Inc. has its offices at 1650 Broadway in its own professional recording studios. They were reached through a single door on which, in large letters, the words 'PPX Enterprises, Inc.' appear. It is, to say the least, enterprising of Mr. Hendrix to suggest that he walked from that door, into the recording studio of PPX, in front of PPX microphones, watching PPX's sound engineers twirl dials, listened to playbacks of various tracks, overdubbed himself on his tracks, rearranged and adjusted the microphones for his performances and selections for the best recording effect, and still did not know that he was recording masters for PPX."

Clearly, Hendrix's returning a second time to Studio 76 wrecked claims by Jeffery on Yameta's behalf that Chalpin and PPX were trying to market his old recordings. In fact, Chalpin now had new material, albeit sung by Curtis Knight with Hendrix on guitar, from sometime after *Are You Experienced?*!

Despite legal troubles at home and abroad, the Experience roared into Washington. Performing two forty-minute sets each night, Hendrix topped off the group's run at the Ambassador Theater by burning another guitar. From Washington, the band then flew to Detroit for a one-night stand before returning to Los Angeles for their first big show there, appearing with Scott McKenzie and the Mamas & the Papas at the Hollywood Bowl. "The Experience followed McKenzie," recalls Abe Jacob, who engineered the band's sound on tour. "The Mamas & the Papas were the headliners. At the end of the Experience's set – after the mayhem and the total destruction of the stage – out came a classical string quartet, booked by promoter Lou Adler. They walked over the rubble, positioned their chairs and performed Beethoven while the crew changed equipment during intermission."

# 7 AXIS:BOLD AS LOVE

*"I feel guilty when people say I'm the greatest guitarist on the scene. If only people would take more of a true view and think in terms of feeling. Your name doesn't mean a damn, it's your talent and feeling that matters. You've got to know more than the technicalities of notes, you've got to know what goes between the notes."*

—Jimi Hendrix

Before the Experience left for London on August 20, Track Records there released the group's fourth British single, "The Burning of The Midnight Lamp"/"The Stars That Play With Laughing Sam's Dice." Not all of the British press were Fleet Street veterans only too eager to call Hendrix the Black Elvis or the Wild Man of Borneo. Chandler and Hendrix cultivated strong relationships with the weekly pop papers *New Musical Express* and *Melody Maker* and with writers such as Keith Altham. Jeffery and Chandler had been quick to realise how important hype could be. They had carefully chosen PR agents Les Perrin in England and Michael Goldstein in the U.S., who could direct publicity not only to *Melody Maker* and *Rolling Stone* but to the London *Times* and *Newsweek*. As dynamic as Hendrix and the Experience were, they were jockeying for position in the era of flower power, Carnaby Street and considerable musical competition. Cream, The Who and Traffic were also frequenting such clubs as the Marquee, the Flamingo and the Speakeasy. These new groups were far removed from the era of the British Invasion of the mid-1960s, where a number of groups climbed high onto the *Billboard* Top 40 chart. Psychedelia and flower power had changed all of this. Groups such as Cream and the Experience struggled to place chart hits in America, as they were album artists, whose songs were not intended to be stripped off for Top 40 AM radio. In America, the competition was far more diverse: not only did Hendrix have to contend with the likes of Motown artists such as the Temptations and Supremes for airplay, sales and recognition, but also Atlantic and Stax artists such as Aretha Franklin and Sam & Dave who were crossing over from black radio to Top 40, further reducing programming options for DJs across the U.S. Through this situation evolved "progressive" or "underground" radio. Stations such as WNEW-FM in New York and WBCN-FM in Boston opted to tap into an older audience, weaned on the Beatles and now interested in psychedelia and the new wave of artists from Britain and San Francisco. When visiting cities such as San Francisco and Boston, Cream, the Jimi Hendrix Experience and others reaped the benefits of FM radio, at last receiving regular airplay and tour support for local appearances. For those artists savvy enough to foresee the advantages, working with FM radio – granting interviews, voicing advertisements, acting as DJs – was an invaluable promotional tool. Eschewing the tour support of a local underground radio station and newspaper often meant the difference between success and failure, a fact not lost on Michael Jeffery and Steve Weiss.

Their debut album a smash in Britain and Europe, the Experience completed a number of press engagements and television appearances before their show at the Saville Theatre in London on August 27, coinciding with the entry of "The Burning of the Midnight Lamp" at number 29 on the *New Musical Express* chart. For Chandler, the return to the Saville brought with it news that the Experience, especially Hendrix, had been consuming alarming amounts of LSD. "I didn't even know they were on acid. It was Tony Bramwell who told me – he was from Liverpool and was the youngest member of the Beatles' entourage, helping Brian Epstein to run the Saville. He was giving me hell in the Speakeasy for letting them do so much LSD. 'Don't you know how much acid they're doing?' I said, 'What the hell are you talking about?' 'Hendrix's with Lennon and McCartney and they're all pouring acid down their throats!' I said, 'What?' I was living in the same flat as Jimi and I had no idea!"

Their first exposure to Owsley LSD had been in San Francisco, and the "experience," according to Gerry Stickells, was "grim." At this point in their career, the Experience – while certainly not babes in the woods – did not come close to the levels of overindulgence that Lennon and Brian Jones seemed to reach on a regular basis. But the seeds for trouble had been planted.

The Experience played only one of the two scheduled performances this evening at the Saville, for late during the first set word came through that Brian Epstein had been found dead. Out of deference to Epstein's memory, the second show was canceled.

September saw the band perform in West Germany and Sweden. On the 2nd, the Experience were invited to appear as part of West Germany's unveiling of color television. As Gerry Stickells recalls, the fact that it was lip-synch, rather than live, allowed the Experience to have some fun. "Traffic was on the show too and everybody was swapping around in the bands because the German producers wouldn't know better."

As rudimentary as promoting rock n' roll was in the U.S., every show in Europe was an adventure. Performing on September 9 in Karlstad, Sweden, the Experience were preceded on stage by performing seals. "It's true," remarks

Gerry Stickells. "We had performing seals as an opening act! The show took place at a fairground and I said to the promoter, 'Who's going on first?' He couldn't even explain. Then I went out and saw this ramp and the performing seals went on. They weren't even any good. They couldn't keep the balls on their noses! Hendrix thought it was hilarious."

Back in London, on September 25, the Experience were included as part of the "Guitar-In" concert at the Royal Festival Hall, featuring acknowledged virtuosos from rock, jazz, and classical music. The event drew a decidedly upmarket London crowd, many of whom were not prepared for Hendrix's sonic onslaught. Midway through the Experience's opening number, a woman sitting in the front decided that she had heard enough, got up and started to walk out. Hendrix spotted her and stopped playing to say "Good night!" The woman was mortified and the audience delighted. Once again, Hendrix's delicate touch had perfectly handled the situation and turned it in his favor.

The band's coffers replenished from their recent spate of touring, Chandler brought them back into Olympic Sound Studios to mine Hendrix's backlog of material. Bursting with confidence, Hendrix seemed eager to become further involved in the recording process, first by verbalizing to Kramer sounds he was trying to create, then by exhibiting a surprising dexterity behind the control room console. Founded on the success and trust they had developed during sessions for *Are You Experienced?*, Chandler, Kramer and Hendrix felt free to openly exchange ideas or suggestions. But while Kramer was infinitely patient with Hendrix, Chandler grew increasingly irritated with Hendrix's ceaseless quest for perfection. As before, he had no problem with overdubs, changing tempos or arrangements, redoing vocals or other modifications, but to Chandler, Hendrix was wasting too much time on endless retakes of backing tracks. Spontaneity had been proven to work, at least in Chandler's mind: while there had been some thirty-odd takes of "Hey Joe," the basic track chosen was one of the first laid down by the band. Hendrix was creating a number of brilliant guitar tracks but spotting flaws only he could hear. Chandler's objections stemmed from his role as producer-manager. His best "production" took place outside the studio, by providing Hendrix with whatever resources he needed to create and by becoming involved during the very early stages of each song's creation.

One obvious difference between the new and earlier sessions was in atmosphere. Whereas the spring 1967 sessions were, for the most part, closed to outsiders, now, other musicians and a small but steady collection of hangers-on began to appear. Gerry Stickells and Noel Redding were sharing an apartment at the time with Viv Prince of the Pretty Things. When the Move were recording in Olympic's Studio B, the Experience were working on "You Got Me Floatin'," and Redding and Hendrix asked Roy Wood and Trevor Burton from the Move as well as Graham Nash from the Hollies to contribute to the song's backing vocals. Spontaneity was not always so successful, however, as Chandler recalls. "Dave Mason [of Traffic] came to a lot of our sessions. One time he brought his sitar, but after trying a song, Hendrix put it down and said, 'That's the last goddamn time I play that instrument.' He was awful." A tape of this session has surfaced in recent years, clearly confirming Hendrix's struggle with the Indian instrument.

More successful was "Spanish Castle Magic." As the session evolved in the studio, Kramer translated the song's chord progression on the piano suggesting, as he had done with "Are You Experienced?," the use of piano to accentuate Hendrix's rhythm guitar. Hendrix also played bass, the same Hagstrom eight-string used on the recent Curtis Knight sessions, further enhanced here by feeding the sound through the octave-boosting Octavia.

Mitch stepped up his contribution at this time too. "Ain't No Telling" would rank among his best Experience work, pushing Hendrix's lead guitar during the solo and doubling his rhythm guitar throughout. With input from Mitch,

Kramer helped improve his drum sound, creating different textures to fit certain songs, dramatic in the case of "Little Wing" or delicate in "Up From the Skies," where Mitchell's brush strokes wonderfully complemented Hendrix's muted wah-wah playing. Hendrix gave Mitchell complete freedom to create: outside of indicating the desired tempo or perhaps a particular effect he wanted to hear, Mitch was on his own.

Not all of the material on *Axis: Bold as Love* was as spontaneous. "EXP" – with sonic blasts, "like dinosaurs fighting during nuclear war" as David Crosby described them – was the result of a lengthy session that stretched through the night. Unable to attend on this occasion, Kramer had asked fellow Olympic engineer Terry Brown to sit in with the band. "I was sort of dropped into the middle of it," he says. "It was Eddie's gig and he knew everybody. I remember it all being very intense with quite a few people sitting around listening. We were working so hard for Jimi. He was such a soft, gentle person, it seemed like he knew something we didn't know."

"EXP" gave Hendrix a chance to utilize some of the custom devices designed for him by Roger Mayer. Brown recalls Hendrix playing through a bizarre speaker system that included a small stack and a sixfoot horn mounted at the side of his amp. Hendrix's guitar part was recorded first, with Mitch and Jimi's "interview" added after. In fact, on a close listen, the hand-cranked VSO (vari-speed device) slowing down Hendrix's voice can be heard. The "Paul Corusoe" character was based upon one Paul Caruso, an American Jimi and Linda Keith had been friends with in New York during Hendrix's short stint as Jimmy James & the Blue Flames.

Hendrix told reporter Jules Freemond that another new recording, "Little Wing," had come from an idea he had while playing in the Village. "I dig writing slow songs because I find it easier to get more blues and feeling into them," he said. "Most of the ballads come across in different ways. Sometimes you see things in different ways than other people see it. So then you write it in a song. It could represent anything. Some songs I come up with the music first, then I put the words that fit. It all depends. There is no certain pattern that I go by because I don't consider myself a songwriter. Not yet anyway. I just keep music in my head. It doesn't even come out to the other guys until we go into the studio."

Hendrix could use effects with delicacy and restraint. On "Little Wing," it was the use of a glockenspiel; with "One Rainy Wish" it was the Octavia; with the title track, it was phasing. For Hendrix, the separation between live performance and recording was both intentional and important. "On a record we might emphasize a certain point or a certain passage. We might have the drums or the guitar swing around to the other side with the echo going the opposite way. Some people say this is a gimmick. We don't need that. We don't do it in person. In person, we play it a different way. So for the record's benefit, we just try to take you somewhere as far as the record can go. On records, you can do almost anything that you want. But in person, like with the three-piece or four-piece, with a small group, you are not actually trying to get that same sound, because that has been done on a record. You can leave the concert and go home and play the record if you want to hear it just like that. We give you another side of it." Indeed they did.

As the rapport between Kramer and Hendrix deepened, Jimi began to describe his sound in colors, primarily when discussing subtle shadings of his sound. Colors, as Hendrix described, could also describe emotions. "Some feelings make you think of different colors. Jealousy is purple; I'm purple with rage or purple with anger, and green is envy. This is how you explain your different emotions in colors toward this certain girl who has all the colors in the world. In other words, you don't think you have to part [with these emotions] but you are willing to try." Certainly "One Rainy Wish" and "Bold as Love" are two fine examples. Hendrix would speak to Kramer of sounds playing in his head or sounds that he had heard in a dream. These were the sounds he wanted to include on disc, these were sounds that frustrated him – he could hear them clearly, but he could not translate the idea to the guitar.

At Olympic, especially during these fall 1967 sessions, Hendrix clearly illuminated the dividing line between studio recordings that would not be reproduced on stage, and recorded versions of the Experience's live staples. Unlike "Hey Joe," "Purple Haze" or even "Can You See Me," Hendrix's new songs had not been developed on the road. They were studio compositions from front to back. In fact, only "Spanish Castle Magic" and occasionally "Little Wing" would be added to the group's future live repertoire. For the first time, the sessions were full of experimentation, only a percentage of which made the final mix of a song. But the transition from the group's strict early sessions to the openness of Olympic was a complex one, though *Axis: Bold as Love* – the Experience's Rubber Soul as some observers describe it – was still recorded and mixed quite quickly. In retrospect, one might even say too quickly, though both Chandler and Kramer would disagree. It can be argued that Chandler should have brought in different singers to add backing vocals to songs such as "Wait Until Tomorrow," or that he should have forced Hendrix to fully develop and complete "You Got Me Floatin'."

The sessions for *Axis: Bold as Love* ranked among the band's happiest times. Even then, however, there were differences in philosophy between Hendrix and Noel Redding. Like Chandler, Redding thought Hendrix had become far too precise, especially since it resulted in far less time and attention for his own compositions. As Olympic tape operator George Chkiantz recalls: "Redding was bored stiff. When his songs were done, and they were done under extreme duress and extremely rapidly, it must have hurt. A lot of my grumbles about the Hendrix sessions concern Redding's backing vocals. It was the kind of sloppiness that Chandler should have stopped before they got on. There were plenty of other people around he could have used."

When the Beatles and George Martin had come to Olympic to record "Baby You're a Rich Man" and "All You Need Is Love," Eddie Kramer – who worked on both the recordings – discussed phasing sound with Martin as well as a new technique EMI had been utilizing on Beatles recordings, artificial double-tracking, or ADT for short. Martin had remarked that its secrets could be found in the handbook of the BBC Radiophonic workshop. Phasing sound had actually been discovered by accident when, in 1959, an American disc jockey tried to fatten the sound of "The Big Hurt," a recent single by Toni Fisher. To make the song's sound seem bigger, the DJ cued two dubs of the song to begin play simultaneously, and soon thereafter phase cancellation ensued, and a new technique was born. Hendrix had been trying to describe an underwater sound that had come to him in a dream, in the hopes that Kramer, as he had in the past, could dial up the effect on the recording board. This particular sound, however, had proven to be more of a challenge to create.

For George Chkiantz, ADT was close but it was still not exactly what *he* wanted to hear. "I had been bugged for ages by the fact that tape loops and tape delay echo always gave an even number of beats," remarked Chkiantz. "I was always trying to work a system that gave an odd number of beats."

Eddie Kramer and Andy Johns clearly remember Chkiantz's big breakthough. "One night, while we were working on *Axis: Bold As Love*," remembers Johns, "George had taken a Small Faces tape ["Green Circles"] and locked himself in Studio B. He burst into Studio A with a mad expression and said, 'Come and listen to this!' So we all went in, Jimi too, and George had created sound from a stereo mix, depending on the dynamics of the song, coming from behind your head. It wasn't phasing, but it was the first big step. Even still, we couldn't get it on disc."

Further refinements of Chkiantz's discovery were difficult, because he was using up every available machine at Olympic in an effort to capture the sound on tape. Chkiantz appealed to Kramer and Glyn Johns for assistance. Johns wanted to use this new sound, a combination of phasing and flanging – yet another EMI variation of ADT – as part of a new recording by the Small Faces, "Itchycoo Park." Via this record, the process, applied during the mono mixing, had made a debut of sorts, but Chkiantz still hadn't made the breakthrough in stereo.

Kramer had been thinking about phasing and its possible applications for Hendrix, and it was decided that they would try to utilize the process on "Bold as Love." Kramer asked Hendrix to listen to a sound he wanted to introduce. Upon hearing phasing, Hendrix exclaimed, "That's it! That's the sound I've been hearing in my dreams!" Kramer, Chkiantz and Johns then set about organizing what was still a complicated process, and overdubs – complete with phasing – began. A careful listen to the finished master will indicate exactly where the process kicked in. At 2:46 into the song, Mitch's phased drums are audible, and just as his roll is rushing from left to right, Kramer pans the drum sound through the speakers, effectively canceling the phasing just a split second before Hendrix's guitar dramatically reappears, now awash in this new sound. For the first time, phasing had been recorded in stereo.

As for the nimble bass lines featured throughout "Bold as Love," they were overdubbed by Hendrix. Redding had cut the basic track, but during all of the experimentation, Hendrix had decided to rerecord the bass line, especially during the song's phased outro. Once again, Kramer's dexterity with keyboards came in handy: dancing amid Hendrix's phased guitar notes are the jangling sounds of a harpsichord. So pleased were they with the results that "Bold as Love" became the title track for the next album, which both Track and Reprise hoped would come before Christmas.

Phasing was also applied to another *Axis: Bold as Love* cut,

"Little Wing." After the basic track had been completed, Kramer half phased Hendrix's vocal and put it through a revolving, electronic Leslie speaker. Also added at this time was a glockenspiel, recorded "dry," without any effects, to accompany Hendrix's guitar.

Of all of the tracks that found their way onto to the final album, one of the hardest for Hendrix to complete was "Wait Until Tomorrow." "For no apparent reason," recalls Kramer, "Jimi just could not play the opening notes to his satisfaction." Eventually, however, the track jelled, and as Hendrix put on his lead vocal, the tape caught him laughing as he listened to Mitchell and Redding finish their vocals.

Also cut during these October 1967 *Axis: Bold as Love* sessions were a number of unreleased four-track demos and instrumentals that Hendrix and Redding wanted to commit to tape. One of the most promising was Noel's uptempo rocker "Crying Blue Rain." Hendrix was taken by the song's title, and would later use the phrase as part of his own 1970 composition "In From the Storm" (as well as crafting his own, entirely original, version of "Crying Blue Rain" on the backside of a Red Carpet Inn laundry ticket; Hendrix had previously pinched another Redding song title – "Midnight Lightning" – to christen a promising original blues composition he first recorded in February 1967 at Olympic). Another was an untitled "party" recording, which featured Experience roadie H voicing the role of a smarmy host, something not dissimilar in style to the Beatles' own lunatic number of this time, "You Know My Name (Look Up the Number)." Another demo was of an instrumental, "South Saturn Delta." Unable yet to set lyrics to this tune, Hendrix would return to it a number of times over the next year and incorporating a host of different ideas, including horns, keyboards and multiple guitars, with varying degrees of success (one scrapped version of the song was recorded at the Record Plant in 1968 with the Brecker Brothers on horns). Considerable work, Eddie Kramer recalls, was also devoted to "Little One," an attempt to add a distinctive Eastern

Late 1965: Hendrix is a full-fledged member of Curtis Knight and the Squires. (*Michael Ochs Archives*)

Slipping on the headphones, Olympic Studios, London, April 1967. (*Eddie Kramer*)

December 1965: Hendrix, Knight and an unidentified session musician overdubbing vocals at Ed Chalpin's PPX studios. (*Michael Ochs Archives*)

★ ★ ★ ★ ★
Mitch Mitchell
listens to playback during
session for *Are You
Experienced?* April 1967.
(*Eddie Kramer*)

★ ★ ★ ★ ★
Eddie Kramer:
engineering *Are You
Experienced?* Olympic
Studios, April 1967.
(*Eddie Kramer*)

★ ★ ★ ★ ★
Michael Jeffery, Hendrix's
notorious manager, together with
Chas Chandler, directed one of
the most profitable rock n' roll
careers ever documented.
(*Linda McCartney*)

July 5, 1967, Central Park, N.Y.
(*Linda McCartney*)

Chas Chandler: ".Jimi
walked out with one hand
in the air, still playing, when
the audience suddenly
realized that all this great
guitar was being played
one-handed."
(*Linda McCartney*)

July 5, 1967, Central Park, N.Y.
(*Linda McCartney*)

Sporting his new hairdo, Mitch Mitchell cuts basic tracks for *Axis: Bold as Love*, the Experience's second album. (*Eddie Kramer*)

Record Plant, April 18,1968: sessions for "Long Hot Summer Night." *FROM LEFT TO RIGHT:* publicist Michael Goldstein, Chas Chandler (*HEAD TURNED*) unidentified man (*STANDING*), and Gary Kellgren. (*Eddie Kramer*)

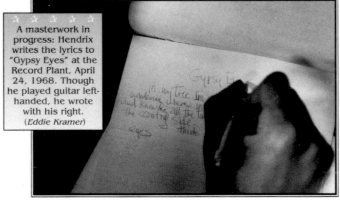

A masterwork in progress: Hendrix writes the lyrics to "Gypsy Eyes" at the Record Plant, April 24, 1968. Though he played guitar left-handed, he wrote with his right. (*Eddie Kramer*)

☆ ☆ ☆ ☆ ☆
Record Plant, May 1,
1968: sessions for
"Electric Ladyland."
Hendrix frames the
song's chords on
the organ.
(*Linda McCartney*)

☆ ☆ ☆ ☆ ☆
Record Plant, May 1,
1968: Jimi illustrates
a point behind Mitch
Mitchell's drum kit.
(*Linda McCartney*)

☆ ☆ ☆ ☆
Record Plant,
May 1, 1968:
sessions for
"Electric
Ladyland." Mitch
Mitchell cutting
basic tracks.
(*Linda McCartney*)

☆ ☆ ☆ ☆ ☆
Record Plant, May 1, 1968:
sessions for
"Electric Ladyland." Hendrix
cuts one of his many intricate
guitar overdubs.
(*Linda McCartney*)

Record Plant, May 1968: sessions for "Electric Ladyland." Eddie Kramer and Hendrix discussing the mixing process. Kramer: "Hendrix was intuitive, learning the concepts of mixing quickly. He was a wonderful man and a pleasure to work with."
(*Linda McCartney*)

Record Plant, May 1968. Buddy Miles: "Jimi really felt he had an ally in Eddie because he would always listen to his ideas."
(*Linda McCartney*)

Record Plant, May 1968.
(*Linda McCartney*)

Deep in thought, Hendrix
listens to a playback.
(*Linda McCartney*)

flavor to the Experience repertoire. Featuring Dave Mason on sitar, two different versions of this promising uptempo rocker were recorded, one with slide guitar tastefully added by Mason to his own sitar and Hendrix's wah-wah lead. Although Hendrix and Mitchell would later overdub additional guitar and percussion, neither Hendrix nor Mason had composed lyrics, and, as a result, the song's progress stalled.

"Driving South," an even stronger contender for inclusion on *Axis: Bold as Love*, was also recorded at this time. One of Hendrix's earliest known compositions, "Driving South" was often his showcase number as a member of Curtis Knight & the Squires. Similar in style to the versions found on Stateside's *Jimi Hendrix Live in New Jersey (1965)* and Rykodisc's BBC sessions album *Radio One*, one can only speculate that the Olympic demo was left off the 1967 album because Chandler and the Experience were hesistant to include an instrumental.

It had been decided that thirteen songs, including "EXP," would make the final cut. For four days, Hendrix, Chandler and Kramer labored over the tapes before finally finishing during the early hours of the 31st – Halloween. Somehow, and – even now – no one is exactly sure how, Hendrix proceeded to lose the mixes for what was to become side one. Still living together, Hendrix and Chandler had taken the final masters home to their apartment. As Chandler surmises, Hendrix was eager to audition the Experience's new album and had taken the masters before any safety copies had been made. "He went off to a party and took the masters with him. Coming back, he left one of the boxes in a taxi. It was all scheduled for release! So we rang up Eddie and went into Olympic the next night and mixed the entire A side of the album again, all in one night." For Kramer, the news was painful. The mixes that they had labored on, deriving from only fourtrack tapes, were almost performances in themselves. Ideas and sounds, "flying by the seat of our pants," as Kramer described it, were gone.

under my name or at all." In a deposition, Hendrix described the circumstances that led to the recording of the single. "In July or August 1967, in America, I was engaged in a practice session in New York and just three notes that I played during that practice session are to be found at the beginning of the record 'Flashing'; no part of the remainder of the record has any connection with me or my music. At the same practice session I demonstrated the use of a tone control device (known commercially as a wah-wah pedal). The musical figure I used in this demonstration was the main guitar figure in a song I had written and recorded called 'The Stars That Play With Laughing Sam's Dice.' I verily believe that without my knowledge, consent or approval, the said practice session or a part of it was recorded at the time and I verily believe that the defendants have incorporated or caused it to be incorporated in the recording, which they now intend to release for sale under the name 'Hush Now'/'Flashing.' At no time during the said practice session did I sing a song as such and from the beginning of such session I was under the impression that I was 'jamming' with old acquaintances."

In *his* deposition, Chalpin, naturally, disagreed. "In the process of mixing, only the performances from the session on 17 July 1967 were used by me. Specifically, I included no guitar part other than those recorded by Hendrix." Chalpin also produced a number of photos taken at the sessions, featuring a jovial Hendrix posing, guitar in hand, with Chalpin, Dick Rowe, and Curtis Knight & the Squires, which clearly sustained his claim that Hendrix had entered the studio by his own decision. Chalpin also denied Hendrix's allegation that he merely wished to jam and show off his wah-wah pedal. "In the course of this recording session [July 17, 1967] there was no demonstration as such of the use of a 'wah-wah' pedal, and there was no mention made of a song entitled 'The Stars That Play With Laughing Sam's Dice.'"

Hendrix also tried to voice his displeasure with the single by submitting "a copy of the *New Musical Express* for the week ending 21 October 1967, wherein at page 10 is an adverse and highly damaging review of 'Hush Now'/ 'Flashing.'" The musical paper, along with others that had been supportive of Hendrix, took his offended tack and applied it throughout their reviews. Quite apart from the legality of the single, the recordings were certainly inferior – particularly in the construction of the songs. While the production techniques employed by Chalpin were comparable to those used by Chandler in London, Curtis Knight, as "Hush Now" would emphatically demonstrate, was simply not on Hendrix's level as an artist.

Knight was, without dispute, a PPX artist. Hendrix, however, despite his contract with PPX, was caught in the middle. He would neither have included Knight in the Experience nor rejoined the Squires at this point. Working on Curtis Knight material no longer interested him. Chalpin's solicitors sought the professional opinion of Dick Rowe, who had refuted Hendrix's claim that he was unaware of the session being recorded and that its results were inferior. "I have listened to several published records made by Hendrix," Rowe stated. "In my opinion, the performances on the record 'Hush Now'/'Flashing' published by PPX are not below the general level of the other records and certainly do not injure his reputation. Hendrix's guitar playing technique and sound is distinctive and immediately recognizable by those addicted." Indeed. Rowe also noted that Hendrix took the time to pose with both him and Chalpin for pictures and was "very pleasantly disposed" throughout his stay at the studio.

With their final British theater tour having ended in Glasgow on December 5, 1967, the Experience immediately returned to Olympic for more recording. *Axis: Bold as Love* had enjoyed positive reviews from the British music press, and the album entered the *New Musical Express* chart at an impressive number 8. For the first time, however, these new sessions at Olympic saw Hendrix and Chandler drifting apart musically, and the seeds of the problems that would unseat Chas as producer were sown. Hendrix's social life had noticeably accelerated, and more and more hangers-on now accompanied him to Olympic, as well as other artists who were genuinely interested in playing with Hendrix or, at the very least, would want to watch him create. As polite and shy as Hendrix was, he would never ask anyone to leave. George Chkiantz had to continually make sure the door to the street remained closed to keep out those unwanted.

Suddenly the use of studios extended beyond recording. Andy Johns recalls stumbling upon Mitch Mitchell at an untimely moment. "I walked in on Mitch when he was duffing some bird in Studio 2 with the lights out. There was all this scuffling going about in front of the mixing board." Clearly, Mitchell had found a novel way to bide his time while Hendrix recorded his overdubs. For Redding, it was only a short walk over to the pub, where he would await word that he was needed to add or rerecord a part.

Despite Chandler's stern lectures about the dangers of LSD, Hendrix had not curbed his use of the drug, and as Hendrix became more famous, Chandler seemed to be hanging on to a rocket, furiously trying to direct and protect it. Chandler had divined right away that LSD possessed no hidden powers of self-discovery. He had no problems with marijuana – he wasn't a prude, rather a hard-drinking Northerner – but LSD was far too disruptive. It should be noted, though, that recording sessions were treated seriously by Hendrix: Chandler and Kramer were straight, and both vouch for Hendrix's behavior in the studio.

Unlike Kramer, who placed no restraints upon Hendrix, Chandler's approach, perhaps even unconsciously, was tempered by the role of parent that Hendrix's actions had forced him to play. Kramer and Hendrix had developed an unspoken bond. Kramer respected Jimi's ability to grasp the essentials of the mixing process, and seemed to understand what Hendrix could not verbalize. Kramer was just as aggressive as Chas, perhaps even more so, but his role was always clearly defined. With Kramer, at the end of a session, Hendrix could leave Olympic, party, sleep and meet girls, but when he returned Kramer would be ready to help him realize his ideas. With Chandler, though, Hendrix felt both guilty and cramped. They didn't fight – Hendrix loathed confrontations – but neither did Hendrix curtail his desire for LSD. But as time passed, despite the love they felt for each other, the two began to separate. Chandler yearned to produce, not baby-sit.

Despite the cracks, some of the Experience's strongest work was done during these December 1967-January 1968 sessions. The band addressed their full attention to such new songs as "Have You Ever Been (To Electric Ladyland)," first attempted in October. With Redding's "She's So Fine" having secured a position on the *Axis: Bold as Love* LP, Hendrix renewed his invitation for Mitchell to include a song too. In a benevolent mood, Redding offered Mitchell "Dance," another of his new songs. A version with Mitchell on lead vocals was recorded and an acetate struck from a Kramer rough mix was cut. But, as Chandler explains, the song evolved into "Cat Talking to You." "That's what it ended up being called. Even though, in the end, Mitchell never got a song onto the album, Hendrix and I sat at home and doctored Noel's lyrics to improve them." While "Cat Talking to You" never materialized, Hendrix lifted Redding's lead guitar line, and would later develop the riff as "Ezy Ryder."

"Dance" or "Cat Talking to You" was the last time anyone tried to find a vocal vehicle for Mitch Mitchell. The whole concept lost steam and was forgotten entirely by the time the band reached the Record Plant studio in April 1968.

Aside from "Dance," Redding had written another fine new song, "Dream," his second effort as lead vocalist. The song demonstrated the progress he had made over the past five months as a composer, and even in demo form it had potential.

A number of other new demos were cut, including early

versions of "Long Hot Summer Night," "Angel" and "1983." Hendrix had also composed another compact classic in "Crosstown Traffic." Eddie Kramer declined Hendrix's invitation to contribute piano, instead showing Jimi the correct chords to play while Dave Mason contributed background vocals.

Interrupting their recording schedule was the "Christmas on Earth" concert, held on December 22 at the London Olympia, a huge, cold indoor exhibition venue, also featuring The Who, Pink Floyd and an array of other top British bands. The Experience roared through a set that now included "Spanish Castle Magic." As intense as their performance was on stage, the Christmas party backstage, for all involved, seemed almost as ferocious. A splendid time was guaranteed for all, including the BBC film crew that had been dispatched to document the event for posterity. Chandler recalls viewing the performance footage sometime after. "I saw the first cut of it, but it was lousy. The cameras were jumping around as if the crew was on acid."

In the U.S., Reprise had set a release date of January 10, 1968, for *Axis: Bold as Love*. But much to their surprise, Capitol Records issued *Get That Feeling: Curtis Knight Sings, Jimi Hendrix Plays* in December. Chalpin had escalated the fight by going to Capitol and leasing them some thirty-three masters of material featuring Hendrix playing with Curtis Knight, a bold stroke that he could not have timed better had he tried. Michael Jeffery had been busily making elaborate plans for the Experience to tour America in support of the new album. Chalpin's release not only dulled Christmas season sales of *Are You Experienced?*, but it was accepted by many of Hendrix's new fans as the group's latest album. Equally infuriating was the album's advertisement in *Cashbox* featuring a shot of Hendrix from Monterey (not only playing but, very misleadingly, clearly singing too), with no liner notes detailing the recordings, and no photo of Curtis Knight.

While many unassuming fans snapped up the record,

several major newspapers, now aware of the Hendrix phenomenon, realized that not all was as it should be. The *Los Angeles Times* of December 24, 1967, wrote, "Beware when an album shrinks the featured vocalist's name into small type beneath the twice-as-large name of a back-up musician. Hendrix records for Warner Bros. but last July he backed up Knight for what sounds suspiciously like no more than a demonstration record with some after-the-fact engineering tricks."

Not only was Michael Jeffery livid that a picture of Hendrix singing was chosen for the album's cover, he was particularly incensed by Capitol's subsequent advertising campaign that implied that Hendrix did actually sing on the record. "The album cover itself contains the word 'plays' alongside of Hendrix's name, but this is deliberately omitted from the album reproduction used in the *Cash Box* magazine advertisement because of the adverse effect it would obviously have on sales."

*Rolling Stone* was quick to condemn the album too, stating that "the record is barely representative of what Hendrix is now doing and is an embarrassment to him as a musician. Moreover, while it does show the early elements of the style he has now developed, it is so badly recorded as to be of little historical value." *Rolling Stone* reporter Michael Lydon also contacted Nick Venet, Capitol's A&R man, who prepared the album from the masters that Chalpin had given him. Venet told Lydon, "I didn't trust what Chalpin had told me, so I didn't put any liner notes on the cover." Venet was also unsure of exactly when the material had been recorded. While he thought that most of the tracks were "several years" old, Venet figured that two songs, "Get That Feeling" and "Hush Now," had been recorded recently. Venet told Lydon that Chalpin hoped four albums could be made from his masters. However, only eight tracks seemed to be immediately salvageable, as "we had to remix and re-record Chalpin's tapes," owing to PPX's outmoded recording equipment. "We lost some fidelity along the way," Venet explained.

Despite the almost unanimously negative reviews, Chalpin secured the services of attorney Elliot Hoffman and was committed to seeing the fight through. He felt that he had an enforceable contract, and wanted the opportunity to share in Hendrix's success. Even today, Chalpin still bristles at the sustained slagging he and his recordings have received. In the opposing camp, recognizing that his signature was on the Chalpin contract, Hendrix assumed the stance of offended artist. Speaking through his January 2, 1968, deposition, Hendrix assailed the Capitol recordings as "malicious," and clarified the differences between the recordings in question and his work with the Experience. "The [Capitol] label creates the impression that Knight and I recorded as at least equal performers, which is untrue. My involvement was completely subordinated and accommodated to Knight's musical personality and ability, which are the obligations of a 'session man.' The record therefore conveys a completely erroneous, unflattering and unfavorable impression of my talents and abilities."

Hendrix also wanted the court to know that his recording sessions were now conducted with great care. "The Capitol recording is greatly inferior in quality in comparison with my recordings today. At PPX we spent, on the average, about an hour recording a song. Today, I spend at least 12 hours on each song. The difference in time is a measure of the care now being taken to obtain the highest technical quality, which is totally lacking in the Capitol record." To further illustrate how important his Experience recordings were to his career, Hendrix offered a news article that he considered most appropriate. "I submit that a most suitable description of my talents is contained in the *Financial Times* (London), 28 December 1967 issue, in which it is said: 'Hendrix, with a wild untamed guitar and only another guitarist and drummer for accompaniment, filled the role vacated by the Rolling Stones. There was a hint of voodoo about the group's music as "Hey Joe," "Purple Haze," "The Wind Cries Mary," and "The Burning of the Midnight

Lamp" soared up the charts, rather bizarrely, because the Hendrix tunes had no fixed shape and certainly no commercial sound. Probably with the general acceptance by the adult population of all their heroes from the Monkees to the Beatles, young people needed a point of musical revolt, and try as hard as the Rolling Stones did, it was Hendrix who provided it in 1967.'"

Although Capital had selected eight tracks it deemed worthy of issue, the British version of *Get That Feeling*, issued in March 1968 by London Records, featured ten tracks, including "Happy Birthday," "Ballad of Jimmy," "Hornet's Nest," "Flashing" and "Future Trip" – tracks Chalpin would include on his second Capitol album, Flashing. Hendrix listed "How Would You Feel," "Simon Says," "Welcome Home" and "Strange Things" as "songs [of] which I recall recording solely as a 'session man' for Knight. The song 'Gotta Have a New Dress' was recorded by Knight for RSVP Records, with me as a 'session man.' As for the remaining songs: 'Get That Feeling,' 'Hush Now,' and 'No Business,' I have no distinct recollection of those songs by their names, but for commercial reasons song names are often changed. I can state most definitely that they were recorded under the same circumstances and conditions as the first four songs referred to above."

But no matter how eloquently Hendrix voiced his disapproval of these recordings, he had no one to blame but himself. While some may argue, with merit, that Chalpin had simply seen an opportunity for a fast buck, Hendrix *had* signed the contract. From the start, he seemed to give the entire matter little consideration. It was only the release of *Get That Feeling*, with its poor-quality material, that the situation struck him personally. What, in his mind, should have been Michael Jeffery's problem now seemed poised to rear its ugly head within every article and interview about him. The very success and acceptance he had dreamed about all his life and worked so hard for over the last twenty months seemed threatened and, worse, perhaps even cheapened.

Arriving in Sweden on January 3, 1968, the Experience checked into the Hotel Opalean in Gothenburg. The rigors of the band's breakneck schedule were something Hendrix had always seemed to manage, but the added weight of the PPX case had frazzled his nerves. Contrary to his legendary reputation for excess, Hendrix had an unusually low tolerance for alcohol, hardly surprising considering his irregular diet and low body weight. Later that evening, Mitchell, Redding, Gerry Stickells and a handful of groupies returned after a long night of reveling to check in on Hendrix. Having lost a battle with the bottle that evening, Hendrix overreacted when a groupie began to annoy him. All hell then broke loose: punches were thrown and furniture began to fly. The three men took turns grappling with Hendrix in an effort to calm him down, only achieved when Mitch sat on top of his lead guitarist. But by this time the hotel management had already sent for the police, who promptly arrested Hendrix and Stickells, who had had nothing to do with the destruction but was trying to straighten out the situation when the police arrived. The two were booked and ordered to remain in Sweden until their case came up later that month.

The Experience performed their concerts on January 4, 5, 7 and 8 before Hendrix and Stickells returned to Gothenburg to await their punishment. "We were not allowed to go out," recalls Stickells of the boring two-week wait, "except that once a day we had to report to the police station. We had to stay in our room at the Esso Motel, right behind the gas station, the only place that would take us, though the manager was a fan so he would even lend us his car to go to the police station. Hendrix used to put rollers in his hair to get his look and in our boredom, he would put them in my hair too! I'll never forget that motel because we had bunk beds and every night two girls used to come around with a joint: we would eat and get laid in the bunk beds, which was quite a struggle."

Fortunately for all concerned, Chas Chandler's father-in-law was the chief of Swedish Customs and Excise. With some strings gently tugged, Hendrix and Stickells were merely fined and released. Reunited in London, the Experience fielded press interviews on a daily basis and booked into Olympic to continue recording. While in Sweden, Hendrix had been introduced to fellow pop artists Hansson & Carlsson, and came away impressed by one of their songs, "Tax Free." At Olympic, the Experience recorded a number of different interpretations. As Chandler recalls, the song had stuck in Hendrix's mind, and he wanted to complete a definitive version. "We must have done that eight times, all instrumentals, but he wanted to find a vocal and a melody for it." Eddie Kramer would later remix the best instrumental take, completed on January 26, 1968, for inclusion on the posthumous *War Heroes* album in 1972. Despite these eight complete versions, Hendrix made one further attempt at recording the definitive version on May 1, 1968, during one of Chandler's final sessions as producer. But though the song would figure frequently in Experience concerts of 1968 and 1969, it did not make the *Electric Ladyland* album.

With Traffic also working at Olympic, guitarist Dave Mason was on hand to contribute to another series of Experience recordings. Having already provided backing vocals for "Crosstown Traffic" in late December, Mason added sitar to a lovely instrumental track which, according to the tape box, labored under the working title "Mushy Name." This was a structured attempt to add a distinctive Eastern flavor to the Experience repertoire. Two versions have come to light, one with slide guitar tastefully added by Mason to his own sitar and Hendrix's wah-wah lead.

Dave Mason also contributed to another classic Hendrix track, "All Along the Watchtower." Andy Johns remembers that Hendrix had come to Olympic armed with tapes of Bob Dylan's latest songs, received courtesy of publicist Michael Goldstein, who also worked for Dylan's manager, Albert Grossman. With the recent U.S. chart failure of "Up From the Skies," Michael Jeffery hoped that a Dylan interpretation could help Hendrix crack what seemed to be impenetrable AM radio playlists. On this Sunday afternoon, January 21, Hendrix had arrived at Olympic early. "That was the first time any of us had heard any of those Dylan tapes," recalls Andy Johns. "He came in with these Dylan reels and we played them in the studio." Burning with inspiration, Hendrix decided to record "All Along the Watchtower," full of the wonderful imagery he loved in Dylan's best work, and for just the right touch it was decided that a twelve-string guitar was needed, fetched by Andy Johns from his flat in South London, courtesy of Dave Mason, who acted as chauffeur.

Hendrix knew exactly what he wanted, remembers Eddie Kramer, and would yell at Mason, playing guitar in the studio's vocal booth, as he struggled with the song's chord changes. As a result, Hendrix cut a staggering number of basic tracks, so much so that midway through the session Redding decided that enough was enough and bolted from the studio. His exodus was a clear sign that all was not right within the group. Mason took over bass in Redding's absence, but Hendrix would later overdub the part himself, using a small, custom bass guitar that Bill Wyman had given to Andy Johns. Kramer and Chandler mixed "All Along the Watchtower" five days later on January 26, thinking the recording complete. But many months and three tape generations later, at the Record Plant in New York, Hendrix would record a number of additional overdubs.

Despite the high quality of material recorded, the sessions at Olympic were fraught with petty arguments, and these didn't only stem from the number of hangers-on Hendrix attracted, for they were far more manageable here than the hordes that would accompany him at the Record Plant. These January 1968 sessions simply pitted Hendrix against Chandler. Hendrix had felt pressured to complete *Axis: Bold as Love*. At odds as well with his managers over his plan to release a double album as the group's next release, Hendrix felt strongly that any money the group made should be poured back into recording costs, enabling him greater if not complete artistic freedom. Hendrix felt that *Axis: Bold as Love* could have been stronger and was also stung by criticism of "The Burning of the Midnight Lamp." Many critics, elated by the group's first three singles, thought the song weak. Taking the slings and arrows to heart, Hendrix was adamant that the song, after it was remixed, be included as part of the next Experience album.

While Chandler in no way wanted to impose any restraints upon Hendrix's creativity, he was clearly in a bind. Hendrix had become far more difficult to direct in the studio. If Hendrix could correctly channel his energies, as he had done so successfully during sessions for *Are You Experienced?*, Chandler had no problem with the double album concept, but the very success that had driven Chandler so tirelessly had complicated his simple premise – to produce recordings by Jimi Hendrix. Certainly, Hendrix was under an increasing degree of strain, but Chandler hadn't signed that PPX agreement, nor had he taken LSD with such frightening regularity. Hendrix, perhaps unknowingly, was kicking down the wrong door. He could not seem to realize that the bevy of revelers who flocked to his side were also slowing his progress. It was time to address these problems and regroup, but Hendrix would do no such thing.

Michael Jeffery was even less sympathetic. On the heels of the impending PPX lawsuit and the release of *Get That Feeling*, *Axis: Bold as Love* had come out of the box slower than anticipated. Jeffery had organized a massive tour of the United States, and was confident that all of America would soon know about the Jimi Hendrix Experience. Touring was his specialty, not Chandler's. Indeed, Jeffery was not only insensitive to his managerial partner's concerns, he also fostered the infighting and stoked the fires of division. Jeffery, who always had a tendency to paranoia, resented Chandler's close ties with Hendrix. Jeffery was not an artist and felt left out, especially in the studio where he did not speak the requisite language. Jeffery even grew wary of Hendrix's relationship with Eddie Kramer. Kramer and

Chandler, each headstrong in his own right, were a double strength when together.

Hendrix felt comfortable when he knew what roles people were to play within his organization. Jeffery was to have no creative input; merely exercise his acumen in business dealings. Hendrix became physically jittery whenever Jeffery stepped into the creative circle. When Hendrix was first brought to England, he had accepted Jeffery gratefully and carried a fierce loyalty as a result. Jeffery had been the difference between starvation and success. An even greater sense of loyalty prevailed toward Chandler. But Hendrix wanted Chandler to recognize his growth as an artist and allow him more freedom in the studio. The problem for Chandler – who had never denied Hendrix studio time, had graciously accepted Kramer as an equal who could improve the band's sound, and had imposed little, if any, restraint upon Hendrix's creativity – was Hendrix's escalating use of drugs and his growing, almost selfish, disregard for the direction of his career. He would stress, during long conversations with Chandler, that he did not approve of the ceaseless partying now dominating the group's time. But then, completely at odds with this opinion, and possessed by an almost complete inability to say no to anybody, Hendrix would jump at the chance to party.

Before leaving for another visit to America, the Experience performed two shows in one evening at the Paris Olympia. Grateful to Parisians for the warm reception afforded them as a support act, the Experience's Olympia concerts were always special. Slightly ragged from almost three weeks off the road, the atmosphere was loose and fun again, much like their early club dates. Hendrix and Redding had a surprise in store for the audience, a switch of roles that saw Redding play guitar on "Red House" while Hendrix took over on bass, driving the song as he had always wanted Redding to do. But Redding proved no slouch on guitar either; he had often declared the guitar his first love and his performance on "Red House" confirmed a genuine talent for the instrument.

On January 30, 1968, the Experience flew to New York amid a gaggle of fellow British rockers as part of the publicity campaign "The British Are Coming!," taking part in a reception at the Pan Am Building. Although they had successfully debuted in America some nine months before, the Experience were about to embark on the biggest and most demanding tour of their young career. Promotion of the first shows was given to Bill Graham, a thank-you for his establishing the band in San Francisco following Monterey.

But this tour was going to be different from the previous one. Just as Hendrix had set new standards for guitarists, and his recordings in the studio had broken into uncharted territory with stunning success, Michael Jeffery had elaborate plans for lifting the personal appearance business out of what he considered the "Elvis Presley era." The idea had been developing for some time. He recalled that in Albuquerque, on an earlier Animals–Herman's Hermits package tour, Jeffery's tour manager Bob Levine and assistant Kathy Eberth had been held backstage, guns behind their heads, and told, in no uncertain terms, that neither band would be getting paid. British bands were often exposed to harassment such as this. There was no network, no communication, no support from record labels, and they took their chances when they ventured too far outside of the established touring circuit. Jeffery privately vowed that this would never happen to him again. As delicate as he may have appeared, he was a brilliant organizer of talent, and when he stayed firm with a particular idea, his impressive support network, directed by attorney Steve Weiss, enjoyed great success. Jeffery knew that he possessed the most dynamic act rock n' roll had witnessed since Elvis. Beatlemania had been one thing, but Hendrix drew *adults* and was the first artist to tap into America's burgeoning base of maturing rock fans.

Working with booking agent Ron Terry, Weiss had convinced Jeffery of a concept he wanted to implement –

self-promotion. "Before we started to self-promote Jimi's concerts, there was a lot of difficulty in his obtaining dates in America because at that time, although it seems ludicrous by today's standards, he was considered to be a very erotic act," remembers Weiss. "Most of the deals available then were 60 percent artist 40 percent promoter. We hired a promoter and paid him a small [10 percent] percentage for promoting the concert. That way, if you did very well, the artist made a lot more of the money. You could only do this with an artist of Jimi's stature, because if you guessed wrong, the artist wouldn't make as much or might even lose money." Another advantage of this concept was that it reduced the number of promoters: instead of having 100 in 100 cities, Terry would employ a small number of key people who could handle much larger territories. Weiss and Terry wanted to break the theater-package-tour mentality, bringing large-scale rock concerts to minor markets on a regular basis. Terry could not give Phoenix or another small city to a local promoter while giving, say, the lucrative San Francisco market to Bill Graham. There had to be a compromise. If a promoter lost money in a city such as Tucson, he had to be given the chance to make it up in a bigger city.

To fund the concept, Ron Terry turned to comedian Danny Kaye and his partner Les Smith, owners of Smith-Kaye Studios and the SP&S Radio chain. Terry asked for $500,000, explaining that his promoters would need close to $20,000 for each date. Without the money, the concept – self-promotion – could not work. Les Smith introduced Terry to Pat O'Day, who ran KGR Radio in Seattle, one of SP&S's powerhouse stations. O'Day was also involved in a promotion company with Tom Hulett and Terry Bassett, operating dances and concerts throughout Washington state. Jeffery had been impressed with Hulett's work after Monterey, and had no quarrel with his involvement. O'Day also had friends in Texas, because he had been cutting jingles for various SP&S stations throughout the Southwest. Terry had Les Smith call his stations to get Hendrix played on the radio. For the first time, some form of coordination had been set in place. For additional support, O'Day created radio spots promoting Hendrix's appearances. Some stations ran the advertisements nearly forty times a day prior to the group's appearances.

Every advertisement aired (until well into 1969) featured "Purple Haze," Hulett and his company, Concerts West, selling the act on that song and the image of the first album. The response was incredible: *Are You Experienced?* remained on *Billboard*'s album chart for an astounding 106 weeks, for 77 of which it was lodged in the top 40. (No other song had the dramatic effect that "Purple Haze" seemed to have. "Hey Joe" was tried, but it failed to stir people's interest. When "All Along the Watchtower," the Experience's only top 20 hit broke, it was added to the advertisements but did not replace "Purple Haze." By inundating fans and potential followers, Hulett helped ensure that Hendrix had a signature song, something that would trigger the interest of potential customers every time he came to town – regardless of the success of his most recent work.) When the Experience went on the road, their music, even via an advertisement, would be featured on the local AM (and FM if available) outlet. Just as well, for there was little help in this direction from Reprise. The $20,000 advertising budget Jeffery and Chandler had won was spent primarily on print advertising, the more proven form for selling an artist.

For the first time, the band was met at the airport, food and drinks were made available backstage and their needs were met. To Hulett, this type of reception seemed to be nothing more than common sense. And to the beleaguered Experience, who had endured both opening for the Monkees and having performing seals open for them, Concerts West was a blessing. For Ron Terry, self-promotion would finally address nagging equipment and acoustic problems. He had grown tired of local promoters ill-equipped to handle sound requirements for the bands he booked, artists like Cream whose innovative sound was a vital component of their attraction.

Gerry Stickells is quick to point out the conditions one had to endure amid the infancy of rock n' roll touring. "It was so different then. We never used to get to the venue until two in the afternoon at the earliest, and I laugh when people tell me how loud those shows were. They couldn't have been loud, what did we have for sound? For the first tour of America, everything, including the PA, fit into the back of a Chevrolet station wagon. Even when we flew, all of our equipment was checked luggage or excess baggage. There was no air freight in those days. The amplifiers didn't even have cases, the speakers didn't have cases, the drums had just a fiber case. Our stuff just came rolling out as luggage."

As part of a bill that included Albert King and John Mayall's Bluesbreakers, the Experience triumphantly returned to San Francisco. Peppering their sets were charged versions of "Sgt. Pepper," which caught the audience by surprise, while as a paean to Albert King, Hendrix performed "Rock Me Baby," using the arrangement B.B. King had popularized. In San Francisco for four days, the Experience jammed and partied with total abandon. Musicians from the Bay Area flocked to the Fillmore and Winterland to check them out. From San Francisco, they then played a string of colleges and auditoriums booked by Concerts West. At each of these shows, Eric Burdon and the Animals and Soft Machine would take turns as support act. Even as headliners, the Experience rarely exceeded sixty minutes on stage. Some nights were still only forty-five minutes, depending on the mood and condition of the band. After Tempe, Tucson, Sacramento and Anaheim, the Experience, with Buddy Miles and the Electric Flag on the same bill, were masterful at the Shrine Auditorium in Los Angeles.

Arriving at the Shrine, the band had been presented with new amplifiers from Sunn. For Gerry Stickells and road sound engineer Abe Jacob, the new amps provided a much needed respite from the cranky, battered Marshalls. On February 12, the Experience traveled to Seattle, giving Hendrix an opportunity to see his family. Tom Hulett was also from Seattle, and had, like Hendrix and Quincy Jones before him, also attended Garfield High School. With help of KGR Radio's Pat O'Day, Hulett helped arrange a special day for Hendrix: he would be given an honorary diploma from Garfield High and the key to the city. Hendrix, says Hulett, was clearly uncomfortable with the process. After short speeches from Garfield's principal and Pat O'Day, Hendrix froze at the microphone, his shyness clearly evident. After a brief thank-you, and a futile attempt at a question and answer session with the students, Hendrix was whisked from the auditorium.

While in Seattle, Jimi and his dad had the opportunity to catch up with each other. Al had remarried and Jimi had a new stepsister. Hendrix's homecoming would be brief, however, as the Experience still had another six straight days in six different cities before they would have another day off. Concerts West booked the band through the Southwest and into Texas. To a man, all of those within the Hendrix organization list Texas, especially Dallas, as the worst stop on any Experience tour. In San Francisco, crowds were stoned and rowdy, but rarely, if ever, were there problems. In Texas, the Experience seemed to be a lightning rod for confrontation between police and angry, stoned fans. Though the audience was nearly all white, deep-rooted and thinly veiled racist feelings fueled the us versus them mentality between police – forced to protect an interracial band, whom they would have rather run out of town – and rebellious kids. On stage at least, Hendrix handled the tension with aplomb. Abruptly ending the newly added Dylan composition, "Can You Please Crawl Out Your Window?," Hendrix slyly laughed, and remarked in a lame Texan drawl, "Yes indeed, how you all doing out there in Texas land? I got my pointy-toed shoes on, I'm really cool baby." Before the crowd could react, Hendrix, in mock disgust, added, "Pointy-toed shoes? Well I am the biggest square in the whole building!" to the delight of the packed house. Despite Hendrix's humor, however, the tension had merely subsided, not dissipated. Later in the set, the crowd rushed the stage, stopping the show. Hendrix spoke to those invading the podium, asking, "Do you want to play in the band?"

"Can You Please Crawl Out Your Window?" was one of a number of songs both inserted into and deleted from the Experience's repertoire in 1968. "Are You Experienced?, "Catfish Blues," "Tax Free," "Sgt. Pepper's Lonely Hearts Club Band," "Manic Depression" and "Like a Rolling Stone" were featured regularly. But outside of "Spanish Castle Magic" and "Little Wing," there are no known live versions of other *Axis: Bold as Love* compositions. Despite the growing variety of material available for the Experience to perform, Hendrix seemed to be growing bored. Set lists were usually drawn up minutes before a show – if they were drawn up at all. Outside of including at least one blues number, a tradition he would rarely, if ever, stray from throughout his career, Hendrix's desire to replicate the guitar smashing and burning had waned. In fact, he had begun to introduce older numbers such as "The Wind Cries Mary" and "Fire" as having been recorded in 1776, or as he did in Fort Worth, noting that "1776 was a good year for recording, this next number was done in 1932 with the Everly Brothers..."

Though their schedule was grueling enough, constant partying made matters worse. The atmosphere at each gig seemed out of control and each seemed to be a clone of the previous one, with waves of women throwing themselves at the band amid countless hangers-on desperate to get high with the Experience. In Philadelphia to play two nights at the Electric Factory, a clutch of beautiful girls came to the Experience's hotel naked, with clothes painted on their bodies. The lunacy appeared to know no boundaries.

February 1968 also brought Hendrix a partial victory in the PPX litigation. District Judge Charles Metzner granted

Yameta's motion for a preliminary injunction but only insofar as PPX's albums violated the Lanham Act. "Do the words and symbols on the jacket of *Get That Feeling* and in the advertising therefor tend falsely to describe its contents? I think that they do," Metzner wrote in his decision. In essence, Metzner dictated that Capitol should change the album's jacket cover. However, he did not extend the injunction to the album's contents, the legality of which was still to be determined. On February 14, Metzner issued an order, pending the trial, blocking Capitol from selling *Get That Feeling*. He also ordered Yameta to file a surety company bond in the sum of $25,000, should Capitol be found to have been wrongfully enjoined or restrained.

Efforts to discredit *Get That Feeling* had apparently begun to work, the LP peaking at only number 75 on the *Billboard* chart. Hendrix's attorney Henry Steingarten had included a deposition from Robert Plotnick, owner of the Manhattan record store Village Oldies, in which Plotnick stated that Hendrix, by virtue of *Are You Experienced?*, was the largest-selling artist in his store. Plotnick spoke of the disappointment his customers felt after purchasing *Get That Feeling*, so much so that he began to discourage potential customers from buying it. In another deposition, Mo Ostin, general manager of Reprise Records, attacked *Get That Feeling* artistically, stating that the album: "In my opinion [has] damaged Hendrix irreparably in that the recordings technically and artistically are inferior." Ostin also spoke of the incredible success *Are You Experienced?* had achieved in less than six months. "The sales of Hendrix's first album have been extraordinarily successful, and up until 31 December 1967 aggregated in excess of 287,000 albums, and are anticipated to continue at a very satisfactory rate. Although it is impossible to state with any specificity the number of Capitol albums sold, based upon my conversations with distributors throughout the country, I believe that such sales have exceeded 50,000 in number."

Quietly troubling Michael Jeffery was the fact that *Axis:*

*Bold as Love,* while it was enjoying accelerating sales, still seemed hurt by *Get That Feeling.* It was as if consumers, especially those who had purchased the Capitol album, were a trifle gunshy. Regardless of the artistic value of *Get That Feeling,* however, Chalpin dug in his heels, determined that the court would recognize his contract as enforceable. The Metzner injunction had been a minor setback for Chalpin; in fact, he would later testify that he had nothing to do with the album's artwork or advertising campaign. The photo, however misleading, was not even supplied by him, and he had no input to the final banding of the LP.

After a brief vacation in the Bahamas, the Experience returned to Manhattan and became the toast of the local club scene. Hendrix had taken to hanging out at the Scene Club, especially after hours, when manager Jim Marron would instruct doorman Danny Blumenauer (both of whom would later work for Hendrix at Electric Lady Studios) to allow a select number of musicians inside for after-hours jamming that would often last until four or five in the morning. Those patrons lucky enough to get inside the Scene witnessed some fabulous jam sessions that paired Hendrix with Larry Coryell, Buddy Miles, Steve Stills, Johnny Winter and a number of other top-notch musicians, though many were nothing more than disjointed, twelve-bar blues meanderings. On March 7, the Experience and friends were jamming and partying at the Scene when, midway through a set – while thrashing about in a vain attempt to perform a version of Jimi's "Bleeding Heart," a blues song he had written but not yet recorded – Jim Morrison ambled on stage and, pathetically, began screaming obscenities and subjecting the stunned audience to ceaseless torrents of "Suck My Woman," among other unprintable epithets. Ever the voyeur, Hendrix took great pleasure in Morrison's condition, even instructing him on which microphone to sing into – "That's the recording mike. Sing in that one right there, that's the recording mike." Later, while Hendrix was playing the riff to the Beatles' "Tomorrow Never Knows,"

Morrison fell to the floor and began moaning into the microphone, oblivious to the accompaniment. Hendrix stepped up to his own microphone and for the benefit of those who would be listening later, tried to explain Morrison's behavior. "In case anybody wants to know what's happening, that's Jim Morrison on the ... Jim Morrison on the, the ah..."

After Hendrix died, his tapes of this jam fell into the hands of bootleggers who, in 1972, issued *Sky High*, a collection of perhaps the best, if that word can be used here, of this night's Scene festivities. While its liner notes incorrectly listed the source of the material as the Record Plant 1970, at least this particular album never made it into mainstream record shops. The same cannot be said for 1980's *High, Live & Dirty* and the subsequent *Woke Up This Morning and Found Myself Dead* albums. (The title of the latter had been adapted from a lyric Hendrix sang during one of the jams, and even though Hendrix was singing about a woman, the "producers" obviously saw some dark humor in the title.) Somehow *High, Live & Dirty* was sold in stores, and unsuspecting consumers, without the benefit of liner notes, were duped into buying what they thought was a legitimate release.

In Cleveland on March 26, Hendrix chose to reward himself, and, after touring an area dealership with Noel Redding, became the proud owner of a new 1968 Corvette. "Hendrix called me from Cleveland," recalls Leon Dicker. "He said that he wanted to buy a Corvette and asked that I wire $5,000 from his Yameta account to the dealer. Now I knew he didn't have a driver's license and couldn't see to save his life. Five thousand dollars was a considerable amount of money in those days. 'C'mon Jimi!' I said. 'Whose money is it?' he admonished. So, I did as he asked. He drove it once – down a one-way street. He was cited for that, as well as not having a license. The next day, Hendrix left for Indiana, and Jeffery had the car shipped to New York."

On April 5, the Experience were booked to perform two

shows at the Symphony Hall in Newark, New Jersey. The city had been simmering with racial tension for some time and when news of Martin Luther King's assassination hit the city the downtown area exploded. Even though tickets for both Experience shows were sold out, only one-fifth of the crowd bothered to come. The Experience's following was predominantly white and many fans forfeited their tickets for the safety of their homes. Indeed, the rioting became so bad that the second show was canceled, not out of deference to Dr. King, but for the safety of the audience and musicians.

Huddled nervously backstage were Hendrix and five anxious Britons eager to return to Manhattan alive. Roger Mayer broke the ice by teasing Hendrix that they were going to strap him to the front of the limo just to get out of there. Having finally made their escape, Hendrix later turned up at the Generation Club, where Buddy Guy was performing. Filmmaker D.A. Pennebaker was also in attendance, scurrying to the club with all of the equipment he could carry. In capturing Guy's set, Pennebaker's single camera also caught Hendrix himself monitoring Pennebaker's Nagra tape recorder. Ever the recording enthusiast, Hendrix volunteered to act as soundman for Pennebaker, sitting virtually at Guy's feet, before the guitarist summoned him to the stage to play.

While it has been reported that Hendrix gave a $5,000 check to the Southern Christian Leadership Conference or another related agency in Dr. King's memory, no documentation exists to support the story. Hendrix *did*, however, make an appearance at Madison Square Garden together with Sam & Dave, Joe Tex and Aretha Franklin as part of "Soul Together," a benefit concert which raised more than $50,000 for the Martin Luther King Memorial Fund. (Sometime after Dr. King's death and before his own assassination, Robert Kennedy had his press secretary contact Hendrix's management trying to garner his support in reducing the racial tension that seemed set to explode in the coming summer months. Bob Levine recalls taking the call and forwarding the message to Michael Jeffery, but there the request stopped: Jeffery dismissed the idea without consulting Hendrix.)

# 8 CIRCUS OF AMBITION

---

*"A couple of years ago, all I wanted was to be heard. 'Let me in!' was the thing. Now, I'm trying to figure out the wisest way to be heard."*

– Jimi Hendrix

ollowing a week's vacation in London, the Experience returned to New York, receiving word that Judge Metzner's temporary injunction had been reversed. This was a clear setback, since Capitol had been furiously preparing alternate album sleeves for a rerelease of *Get That Feeling* and was now being shown a green light. With a trial date set for late May, there was a real fear in the Hendrix camp that if something was not arranged with Chalpin, and swiftly too, further albums made from the masters he had leased to Capitol would be issued. Chalpin's original contract, if found enforceable, carried until October 15, 1968, and with only a handful of tunes completed, Hendrix was far from finishing the Experience's third album.

The terrifying thought of a second album of Chalpin-produced material distributed by Capitol forced Chandler and Jeffery into confrontation. Through their attorney, Henry Steingarten, they offered Chalpin a cash settlement. "They offered me $70,000 to buy me out," recalls Chalpin. "I wouldn't take it. My lawyer insisted that I take it, but I said no. They were stealing my artist. I was the producer and the original sound was mine." Chalpin had resolved to have his day in court. He was no fool: the more popular the Jimi Hendrix Experience became, the more valuable his potential settlement became.

Partly because of the PPX proceedings, as well as his own desires, Jeffery had reconciled himself to the fact that New York, not London, was now the natural base for the Experience. This further strained his relationship with Chas Chandler, since, as well he knew, Chandler did not like New York (and neither did Mitch Mitchell or Noel Redding, initially). Jeffery thrived upon power. While Chandler had cultivated his musical contacts in London, Jeffery had built his organization in the U.S. For Hendrix, Manhattan was home, and he moved into a basement apartment below Jeffery's 37th Street power base at which Hendrix also installed Bob Levine, Kathy Eberth, Gerry Stickells and Trixie Sullivan.

With business pressures mounting, Chandler felt that he could at least look forward to new recording sessions at the Record Plant, to where Tom Wilson and Gary Kellgren had shifted from Mayfair Studios. Record Plant had been the brainchild of ex-Revlon employee Chris Stone, who, backed with an investment of some $300,000 by Revlon magnate Charles Revson, opened the facility in late 1967. Kellgren had become a minority partner in the studio, buying for it one of only two twelve-track tape machines in America. With the company keen to expand the operation, the New York studio needed a top-drawer recruit to handle engineering chores. Tom Wilson had been steadily lobbying Eddie Kramer to relocate. His reputation was growing and the Record Plant wanted to assure clients like Jimi Hendrix that moving to their facility was in no way a sacrifice. With an endorsement from Hendrix and Chandler, Kramer joined the staff at the Record Plant.

Arriving at his new workplace April 18, 1968, Kramer was ushered down to the studio by Kellgren, where Hendrix greeted him with the welcoming message "Where the hell have you been?" Obviously, it was time to get to work. Despite the potential for power struggles between Kramer and Kellgren, none ever materialized. In fact, they became fast friends, respectful of each other's ability, and though it was clear that Chandler, Kramer and Hendrix were a team, Kellgren and Kramer did work on some sessions together.

For Chandler, meanwhile, having Kramer in New York was a relief. Hendrix now had his own apartment, so they were no longer living together, and Jimi had been partying at a frightening pace. In fact, Mitchell, Redding and Chandler had taken to hanging out each on his own, apart from the others. The breakdown in communications was evident from the first Record Plant session. Whereas the concert stage had specifically defined their roles, success in the recording studio was dependent upon a frail, unspoken sense of unity among players, producer and engineer. As a result of the January sessions at Olympic, Hendrix decided to exert more control over the recording of his music, while Mitchell also began to verbalize an interest in the process. The first track started at the Record Plant was "Long Hot Summer Night." Unlike the solo Hendrix demos cut at Olympic, this version, engineered by Gary Kellgren, featured a contribution from Al Kooper on piano in addition to Mitchell and Redding. While Hendrix would return to overdub and remix the song, the basic track was produced by Chandler and completed on April 18, 1968.

For a number of reasons, the recording of *Electric Ladyland* was almost entirely different from the sessions that had made up the group's first two albums. There was little concern for schedule and no concern for cost. Hendrix felt that *Axis: Bold as Love* had been rushed and that it was up to him to ensure that this album had no discernible flaws. The problem was, Jimi would also pack the control room with hangers-on and be caught between entertaining them and recording music.

For Chandler, his inability to communicate with Hendrix

was further strained when Michael Jeffery began taking LSD. For Jeffery, acid was a sole link, the *only* link he now had to Hendrix's attention, for unlike his mentor, Bob Dylan's manager Albert Grossman, Jeffery was not naturally close to his artists. Chandler was rightfully aggrieved: LSD had dulled Hendrix's focus and was beginning to change his disposition, but as fast as he could speak with Hendrix about the perils of the drug, Jeffery would turn up with something for them both to try. Because he wasn't dropping acid, the two of them felt Chandler just wasn't connecting with them, and if he couldn't, then there was no need for the old all-for-one and one-for-all attitude.

On April 20 and 21, Noel Redding finished taping the basic tracks for "Little Miss Strange." It was a tune he had composed some while before, biding his time for the chance to record it. In the past, Hendrix had made a point of contributing to Redding's songs, even at the demo stages. At the Record Plant, matters were far less structured: even though time had been booked, Jimi did not appear, and with Chandler otherwise engaged, Redding turned to Eddie Kramer for production help. With Mitchell on drums, a "test session," as the box was marked, was undertaken. Redding would tinker with the track again on April 29, this time with Chandler and Hendrix in attendance, and a final mix was completed on May 5, insuring Noel a spot on the projected double album.

"Gypsy Eyes" was the next track to be started, though its complicated rhythm pattern bogged down its recording and frayed nerves between Chandler and Hendrix. The basic tracks were cut on April 24 and 29, but the seemingly endless remakes that filled the days in between pushed Chandler to the brink.

On May 1, playing rhythm guitar and with Mitchell and Redding accompanying, Hendrix cut "House Burning Down," another track that had begun as a demo in London, while, for the third time, basic tracks for "Gypsy Eyes" were recorded. Now it was finally deemed finished, although, even so, Hendrix would overdub and remix the song no fewer than five times in order to achieve the effect he desired. The Experience also tried to complete "Tax Free," choosing not to transfer and work on the best take recorded on four-track at Olympic in January but to recut the title entirely. Once again, the sound or feel Hendrix sought from the song eluded him.

Michael Jeffery had planted the seed of the idea of owning a nightclub in Jimi's head amid the parties and jams held at the Scene, or as Faye Pridgeon called it, the "Champagne Colony." The concept seemed so perfect. A safe haven, just for Jimi and his friends. Chandler would have none of these utopian visions. "Hendrix came to me and said that he wanted to buy the Generation Club. We spent weeks talking about it. I said, 'What the hell do you want a nightclub for?'" Chas guessed immediately that Jeffery was behind Jimi's latest passion. He tried to explain to Hendrix that owning a nightclub in Greenwich Village would mean butting heads with the Mafia, and that the ramifications of such a policy would be dangerous. Hendrix didn't need these kinds of connections. Chandler seethed. Jeffery had done almost the same thing to the Animals. Through Yameta the Animals had helped establish Jeffery's clubs in Spain and were promised shares in them though the deal was never committed to paper.

Soon after Hendrix's initial request to buy the Generation, Jeffery approached Chandler and told him about his great new idea – adding to it a small recording studio. Chandler bridled at the idea of owning and operating such a facility inside a club. Quite apart from the protection money needed to operate in Greenwich Village, how many groups had live albums in the charts at the time? How many were queueing up to make them? Jeffery suddenly turned around and said, "Yes, but what you don't realize is that we have to get involved in business with Jimi to tie him more to us." "I said that the only way you tie Hendrix to you is by doing the fucking job right," says Chandler today. "He couldn't see that. He couldn't understand that it was that simple. All you had to do was do your job to get Jimi's respect. Jeffery wanted to put invisible chains around you, he was totally paranoid about everything. I had seen this paranoia right from the early days of the Animals. A lot of people tried to get pieces of the Animals when we first came down to London but they were all screwed by Jeffery."

By placing Hendrix between them, Jeffery successfully shifted the balance of power away from Chandler. Not so subtly, Jeffery made the purchase of the Generation Club a personal, not a business issue. Always the pragmatist, Chandler knew Jeffery's true motivation but still had to try to direct Hendrix honestly. The original concept – "Jimi's Place" – would be a challenge in itself to operate. Jeffery owned nightclubs, not Hendrix, and the addition of a small studio to accommodate artists looking to record live performances further clouded the concept. To Chas, Jimi's business was music and recording. That's where the money was coming from. He had seen the effect that Hendrix's "friends" had been having on him lately. If the success of Jimi's Place relied upon Hendrix to at least appear there regularly, when would he concentrate on writing and recording? When he came back from one of Jeffery's exhausting tours? It was hard enough for Hendrix to ask people to leave the Record Plant while he was working let alone establish and maintain a successful nightclub.

In an effort to appease Jeffery and Hendrix, Chandler suggested that, as part of a settlement agreement with PPX, they buy Ed Chalpin's Studio 76 and refit it. It was a shrewd idea. The machines themselves were not that good, but the room was and machines could always be replaced. Buying Studio 76 might help rid themselves of Chalpin. They could also at least get some long-term value out of any potential cash payout to Chalpin. And just as Eddie Kramer was lured to the Record Plant, would it not make sense to house their artist Jimi Hendrix, their producer Chas Chandler, their engineer Eddie Kramer and Yameta's self-described talent agent Michael Jeffery in one facility? At least Hendrix could own a productive work space that, while he was out on the road, might even earn some money. In buying a club, Chandler argued, you paid nightclub prices; considering the moribund goodwill of the Generation, you were purchasing a lease agreement. It would be cheaper to add an "artists' lounge" to Studio 76 than redo the Generation to accommodate live recording.

Jeffrey and Hendrix dismissed the idea. For Chandler, their refusal to, at the very least, consider reason, further alienated him. Back at the Record Plant too, he had reached the end of his tether. Recording had continued with the Experience cutting basic tracks for "Voodoo Child (Slight Return)," "Three Little Bears" – which would later be included as part of 1972's *War Heroes* – "Little, Little, Girl," which Noel recalls as one of his compositions, and "How Can I Live," a Redding number later to appear on his group, Fat Mattress's, debut album. Shortly thereafter, Chandler decided that he was leaving the project. He would stay on, managing with Jeffrey, but for now he would not continue producing for Hendrix.

Buoyed by the lifting of Judge Metzner's temporary injunction, PPX took the offensive and struck back at Hendrix and company with an order of attachment. Elliot Hoffman, attorney for PPX, wanted to exert some pressure on Yameta. All of Hendrix's record royalties from Warner Bros., his tour money from General Artists Corporation, and for dramatic effect, all his receipts from the concert at the Fillmore East on May 10, 1968, were frozen by the court order. There, both Hendrix and promoter Bill Graham were promptly served with writs before the show, which, despite nagging feedback problems, won Jimi raves from the press. Double billed with Sly & the Family Stone, whose music Hendrix loved, the Experience roared through two sets. During one of the several technical delays, Hendrix announced that it was nice to be in "Miami Beach, Florida" and launched into the Beach Boys' "Surfin' U.S.A" before abruptly stopping. In mock shock, he then apologized for the slip. "I'm sorry. I had a big flash. Oh my head. Something just told me to play that." He then played a snatch of Eddie Cochran's "Summertime Blues" before Redding requested, "Do that bit again, it was lovely; do that for me, whatever it was." As Noel tried to hum "Surfin' U.S.A.," Hendrix laughed to the crowd, "Oh yeah, 'Summertime Blues,' do you remember that?" Jimi then tried to explain reasons for the impromptu comedy: "We are doing this because we don't know what we are going to play next." When a fan then let loose with an indecipherable yelp, Hendrix picked up on it without missing a beat, "Yeah, we'll play that next!"

Versions of "Hear My Train A Comin'," with Hendrix playing some of the solo with his teeth, and "Lover Man" (simply "Rock Me Baby" reinvented with different lyrics) rocked the sold-out auditorium. Cryptically, Hendrix instructed the crowd to "Please crawl out your window or else I'll put a curse on you and all your children will be born butt-naked." The Experience put the final touch on this magnificent Dylan interpretation with a sudden, surprise ending. Despite the recurring amplifier problems, the Experience were all their PR promised they would be: loud, brash, cocky and marvelously talented. The frequent delays had made the Fillmore crowd especially rowdy: replying to a fan who asked if Jimi was better than Clapton, Hendrix stopped and – to the delight of the audience – said, "You say, 'Am I better than Clapton,' right? Are you better than my girlfriend?" To another, who yelled for Hendrix to take off his hat, he replied, "I'll take it off if you take off your pants!"

Clearly, live, the Experience were playing at their best, and now the focus was to capture it on tape. An earlier effort to record the band in Ottawa, Canada, had failed, dogged by technical snafus that disrupted not only Hendrix's concentration but his sound. The Experience had been booked to play at the Miami Pop Festival, held at Gulfstream Park on May 18 and 19, and a decision was made to tape the performances. Recording of *Electric Ladyland* was halted and

Eddie Kramer flown down – along with New York photographer Linda Eastman, hired by Michael Goldstein to document the event – to supervise.

In Miami, the Experience had been booked on a bill which also featured Frank Zappa, NRBQ, Chuck Berry and a number of other top stars. As had been the case with most other festivals, however, the real action took place elsewhere. The Experience jammed through the night at their hotel, the Castaways. In time for Saturday's performance, just for fun, Linda Eastman tinted blond streaks throughout Hendrix's hair. Sunday's performance was washed out by torrential rainstorms, and there was a mad dash back to the gaggle of limousines. (Linda Eastman climbed into the wrong one, finding herself alone with Chuck Berry. True to character, Berry told Eastman that he didn't mind if the festival was canceled as long as he got paid.) While Eddie Kramer and Hendrix were stuck in traffic, Jimi wrote the lyrics for "Rainy Day, Dream Away" in the limousine.

Taking full advantage of the Experience's sudden change of schedule, Jeffery organized a short European jaunt to infuse the band with cash immediately following their stop in Miami. That night the Experience flew from Florida to Italy. After stops in Milan, Rome and Bologna, the Experience traveled on to Zurich where they were featured with Traffic and the Move as part of a "Beat Monster Concert." Hendrix jammed with Traffic during their set on the May 30. After their show on the 31st, the group had to quickly skip town because the promoter had gone bankrupt and had not paid their hotel bill.

Back in New York, the PPX trial had begun before District Judge Dudley Bonsal. With Hendrix in attendance, Henry Steingarten's opening argument stressed that PPX was exploiting the success that Yameta had helped create for Jimi. Steingarten spoke of Yameta's commitment to Hendrix, resulting in sales of almost 500,000 copies of *Are You Experienced?*, his debut album. Steingarten also pointed out that Chalpin could produce only two checks ever written out to

Hendrix. Both, dated October 1965, were compensation for Curtis Knight & the Squires sessions. Despite recording a number of so-called masters between October 5 and December 31, 1965, Jimi received the munificent sum of $10 and $25 for his work, and while Chalpin stated that he often paid Hendrix in cash for sessions, he could not present any receipts. Steingarten also struck at Capitol's "misrepresentation" of Hendrix, illustrating that in 1966 RSVP Records, when issuing PPX-licensed recordings, featured Hendrix's name only as an arranger, using 1/64 type to credit him. Knight's name however was boldly featured in 1/4 type. Clearly, Hendrix's name had become the focus of the Capitol release.

Speaking for PPX, Elliot Hoffman said that Yameta "wooed" Hendrix to England, enticing him to abandon PPX in favor of Yameta. He also argued that PPX's contract with Hendrix was in fact equitable and discredited Jimi's contract with and Yameta's assignment from Sue Records, citing that this assignment had been backdated to May 31, 1966. Compounding the confusion, Juggy Murray swore that it had been completed on August 15, 1966, while Jeffery put the date at January 20, 1967.

Irked by Hoffman's request that witnesses be excluded, Steingarten had Judge Bonsal order Curtis Knight to leave the courtroom, after which the two lawyers proceeded to battle.

Warner Bros. maintained a low profile throughout the trial's initial stages, which rankled Chas Chandler. "Mo Ostin [a Reprise executive] came to New York to see how the case was going, and he, Henry Steingarten and I went out to eat that evening. In the middle of the meal, I turned to Mo – who I got on great with – out of sheer frustration and said, 'What the fuck is going on here? We have writs against us, we can't get any cash and we're not getting a bit of help from Warner Bros. You're not lifting a finger.' Mo threw up his hands and sighed, 'Chas, it's business. What can I say? At the end of the day, no matter who wins the case – you or Chalpin – Warner Bros. will be left with Hendrix.' Surprised, I said, 'How do you work that out?' 'It doesn't matter to the business affairs office whether you have Hendrix or Chalpin does,' Ostin replied, 'we have the artist.' 'What do you mean, you have the artist?' When he mentioned Hendrix's March 21, 1967, contract with the label, I blurted, 'You have a contract with Yameta! And Yameta is me!' 'What do you mean?' Ostin asked. 'You haven't got Hendrix's signature on a contract!' 'Of course we have,' Ostin interjected. I told him, 'You better go back to California and check the fucking contract, because the only contract you have with Jimi Hendrix was signed by Yameta. If I lose, you lose!'

"The very next day," continues Chandler, "I sat down with fourteen lawyers from Warner Bros. and told them where they could shove the settlement agreement they had first proposed we sign. I walked out, went straight to Steingarten's office, broke into his desk, pulled out a big bottle of Four Roses from its hiding place and sat there drinking until Steingarten came back from the meeting – some five hours later – with the settlement. Warner picked up the bills, and gave Hendrix a three-point hike in his royalty rate."

"Warner was always bugging us to have Hendrix's direct signature on their contract," recalls Yameta's John Hillman. "I always refused – but not for the same reason Jeffery did. Jeffery wanted to keep Hendrix cordoned off from everybody. I gave him the opportunity to do that by saying Hendrix couldn't sign the March 21, 1967, agreement for tax reasons. If he did, it would bust the tax shelter. Naturally, Jeffery used this as his shield."

On Chalpin's behalf, PPX received 2 percent of the suggested retail selling price of all Hendrix recordings sold in the U.S. by Warner until 1972 (less packaging costs of up to 54 percent per $4.79 recording). PPX would also receive a 1 percent royalty on tapes, cartridges and all Canadian sales by Warner. This settlement was also made retroactive, including royalties from *Are You Experienced?* and *Axis: Bold as Love.* PPX further received an immediate payout of $50,000 as an advance against these royalties and was guaranteed an additional $200,000, due in full by December 31, 1969. Incorporated into the settlement were provisions clearly defining PPX's rights regarding future Knight-Hendrix releases, stipulating that artwork for Capitol's second Knight-Hendrix album had to be approved by Yameta. Both PPX and Chalpin were restrained from "directly or indirectly [covering] any Hendrix recording to utilize such recordings in any manner for recording purposes without consent of Hendrix or Yameta." In simple terms, Hendrix fans were spared from hearing versions of "Purple Haze" and "Foxey Lady" by Curtis Knight.

Another interesting clause within the agreement forbade Chandler, Jeffery, Chalpin, Yameta or PPX from receiving credit on the final album due Capitol. Following the issue of a second Knight-Hendrix album, Capitol was granted an album featuring recordings by the "Jimi Hendrix Experience." That album, which ultimately became *Band of Gypsys,* would list "Heaven Research" as its producer (a name coined by Hendrix) since by the time of the album's release, Yameta had long since severed its ties with Hendrix.

As far as Hendrix was concerned, the impending PPX settlement signaled the phasing out of Yameta. For Hendrix, a U.S. citizen, Yameta had not been the great tax dodge John Hillman promised. Hillman, Yameta's creator, defended the scheme. "U.S. taxation," he recalls, "is based upon citizenship rather than residency. The U.K. was a very good tax haven for Americans in those days because there was a very old U.S.-U.K. double taxation convention which could be used advantageously. Yameta couldn't avoid Hendrix's taxes but these offset principals reduced his tax burden considerably."

Jeffery himself was growing disillusioned with Yameta. When he became short of funds an associate would be sent down to Nassau, to the Bank of Nova Scotia, to surreptitiously withdraw cash and smuggle it back to New York.

Leon Dicker, Yameta's American representative, fondly recalls Trixie Sullivan, Jeffery's secretary, returning from such a mission, unbuttoning her shirt in his office and subtracting bundles of cash from her bra. "Michael always knew how to beat the system," recalls Jeffery associate Linda Sharlin. "Even when Electric Lady Studios was up and running, he would send [studio receptionist] Iris to the Bahamas to stuff wads of cash into the long boots she used to wear." Such intrigue, says Bob Levine, was an essential part of Jeffery's makeup. "I don't know how many times he came back from abroad with a paper bag full of money – English currency, West German marks – from wherever he went traveling, and would ask me to take it down to the currency exchange on Broadway. I never questioned it, but where the hell did those bags of money come from? We aren't talking about $1,000 here."

Warner Bros. wasn't the only source Jeffery would ask for an advance when his cash flow dwindled. "I remember going to Harold Davison's office, looking for money due Jimi," recalls Chandler. "Davison was a very powerful promoter and agent, the biggest in England. The accounts department there politely said, 'Sorry, there is no money. It's all owed to Harold.' So I went to see Harold and said, 'What the fuck is going on here?' He said, 'Oh, I lent Jeffery 50,000 pounds against Hendrix's earnings.' 'I'm sorry, Harold. I've got a band here panting for cash. You'd better give us the money now or you don't have the act anymore. Show me a bit of paper that proves Michael Jeffery has anything to do with this act.' This was my only recourse, as I knew Davison only had an agreement with Yameta, not Jeffery directly. It was absurd."

In business, Jeffery trusted few, while trusted by even fewer himself, but he was far from the tyrant thief many writers have painted him. More cunning than given credit for, Jeffery was a master negotiator, who, unlike his famous client, *never* backed away from confrontation. His callous disregard of Hendrix's friends and sidemen – from Noel

Redding to Buddy Miles – made him few friends. "Jeffery made it very clear that Hendrix was the only 'artiste' Yameta was to sign and receive a share," recalls John Hillman. "In his mind, other musicians were simply 'employees.' What people like Noel Redding couldn't understand was that he was not a partner. Jeffery wasn't the only one who had signed the contracts. Hendrix knew perfectly well who was getting what, but he could finger Jeffery as the bad guy, just as Jeffery could point to Yameta."

Ever an entrepreneur, Jeffery fought to suppress a notorious inability to refuse a scam. He longed for the respect accorded his American mentors, Allen Klein and Albert Grossman, privately admiring Klein's ferocity and Grossman's paternal aura. Arguably, he deserved a place among them, orchestrating one of the most profitable careers in rock history, but the accolades never followed. "Jeffery was a lovable rogue," recalls John Hillman. "He begged, borrowed and stole just to keep his artists going, but his return was only financial. They were his investments and he was entitled to recoup."

"He would stop at nothing to ensure the success of his artists," explains Michael Goldstein, "but he couldn't relate to them personally."

"Jeffery was a brilliant visionary," recalls Bob Levine. "He was a great person for spotting an artist's potential, literally saying, 'I can see us doing this ...' The problem was that, while he had an eye for raw talent, he couldn't be bothered to follow through on their careers. Hendrix was always his foremost concern, and, after he'd secured his latest discovery a fantastic advance from a record company, the group would be dumped in my lap and sent out to open for the Experience." For someone who didn't comfortably fit in, Jeffery had a knack for anticipating trends. He signed Amanda Tree, who was the original female Pee-wee Herman; Third World, one of, if not the first heavy metal groups to dress in costumes as well as featuring a drummer who painted his face; and Cat Mother & the All Night Newsboys, before the "1950s Get Back" revival got started in 1969.

Steve Weiss continued to press Jeffery about the practicality of Yameta. Weiss and partner Henry Steingarten hired accountant Michael Hecht to address the Yameta issue. Hecht was not, as was John Hillman, an expert on U.K. tax laws as they related to U.S. citizens, but he knew Yameta was not structured to address Hendrix's taxes properly. Hecht suggested that Hendrix, as a U.S. citizen, create a company in the U.S. to collect and control his earnings, as well as pay his taxes and expenses – instead of utilizing an offshore arrangement. Weiss implemented Hecht's instructions, and flew with Steingarten to Nassau to settle with Yameta. Hendrix, Mitchell and Redding signed an agreement under which they would be released from their previous obligations and began to contract in their own names. This new corporation – Are You Experienced? Ltd. – began to operate.

As part of the PPX settlement, Jeffery arranged for Warner Bros. to buy out Yameta's management contract with Hendrix for $250,000 upon the execution of the agreement and the delivery of a master recording equivalent of an album. This provision allowed *Electric Ladyland* to be issued on Reprise and not Capitol. Warner also agreed to pay Yameta $200,000 over the next four years, at the rate of approximately $50,000 a year. In exchange, Hendrix would be signed to an exclusive artist's agreement directly with Warner.

In addition to the 3 percent hike in his royalties starting with *Electric Ladyland,* Hendrix was given a 1 percent raise on future sales of the Experience's first two Reprise releases and a $100,000 advance paid to Sea Lark Music, the administrators of his publishing company. Jeffery also won a clause Warner would soon regret. Unlike their original agreement, Warner would now pay half of the costs incurred creating future Hendrix albums, the remainder to be borne by Hendrix or whoever Jeffery could dispose foreign rights to, such as Polydor. The recording costs, not to exceed $20,000, were advances against future Hendrix royalties, effectively creating an additional source of credit for Jeffery.

Though Hendrix was signed to a new four-year deal, Jeffery and Chandler were not out of the picture. While no longer receiving the producer's fee accorded them in their original agreement, they were "jointly responsible with Mr. Hendrix for the delivery of future product to Warners," as well as parties to this agreement. A host of books and articles have cited October 1970 as the time when Jeffery's "contract" was to expire, freeing Hendrix from his clutches. Simply put, this was not true. Jeffery's agreement would expire on December 1, 1970, and although Jeffery later bought out Chandler's interests, Hendrix and Jeffery were tied together to Warner through 1972 and perhaps even longer since Jeffery later negotiated a separate contract for the soundtrack album accompanying the film *Rainbow Bridge*.

By leaving as producer some months before, Chandler had clearly weakened his position. The move to 37th Street signaled Jeffery's ascension to power. Jeffery knew Chandler wished only to produce, not to involve himself in the myriad details of management. In the interim, Chandler had grown homesick, especially as his wife Lotta was expecting their first child. He would soon have to decide his fate: stay in New York with Hendrix or return to England and begin producing another act.

Meanwhile, Jeffery attempted to address the one trait associates universally felt he lacked most: trust. Meeting with Michael Hecht, Jeffery explained that Hendrix, Mitchell and Redding would never be satisfied about their financial situation. Specifically, they spent like crazy, did what they wanted and suffered from "artist paranoia." Sensing that the trio would never be happy, Jeffery asked Hecht to completely remove him from their finances. As he had tried to do with Yameta, Jeffery did not want to sign any checks or pay any of their bills. Hecht complied, and Jeffery was never again involved with their day-to-day finances. (He was, however, still firmly in charge of negotiating their contracts, managing their careers, their publishing arrangements and their personal services. His 40 percent compensation for these services – "I remember his share being on the high side of what was considered a normal business relationship," recalls Michael Hecht – was paid directly to him.)

As money poured into Are You Experienced? Ltd., Jeffery was paid, just as were the expenses. The net profit was then allocated to Hendrix. At this time, Abby and Aaron Schroeder set up Bella Godiva (so named by Jimi), a new publishing company separate from Jeffery to replace Yameta–Sea Lark. "Bella Godiva was a much cleaner corporation for Hendrix," recalls Michael Hecht. "Abby and Aaron Schroeder signed him up directly, and their company, Arch Music, continued to administer his catalogue. Mitchell and Redding did not share in Hendrix's publishing revenues."

Absolving himself from the group's finances temporarily strengthened Jeffery's position with Hendrix. On the surface, the maneuver appeared to be a sincere effort to quell fears about his fiscal accountability. In actuality, Jeffery's move was both shrewd and cleverly timed, an attempt to prove to Hendrix that life without Chandler was not only possible – it was inevitable. The action was an unspoken, subtle strike at the strong bond between Hendrix and Chandler.

At the Record Plant on June 10, 1968, Hendrix busied himself recording a number of new tracks, including "Rainy Day, Dream Away" and "Still Raining, Still Dreaming." "Tom Wilson had discovered and produced my little R&B band," remembers Mike Finnigan, organist on the session. "He introduced us to Hendrix, and Jimi asked me, Larry Faucette [congas] and Freddie Smith [saxophone] to jam on this tune he had in mind. In the early 1960s, Jimmy Smith had made these great, obscure organ quintet albums, which featured organ, congas, guitar, tenor saxophone and drums. Before we started the session, Hendrix reminded me of this and joked, 'We're going to do a slow shuffle in D. You be like Jimmy Smith and I'll be Kenny Burrell.' Having heard his first two albums, I thought he'd be using stacks and stacks of amplifiers and electronic toys to get his sound. To get the right guitar tone for 'Rainy Day, Dream Away'/'Still Raining, Still Dreaming' [these two tracks were recorded as one, then split by Hendrix and Kramer during later mixing sessions], he was using this small, blond, thirty-watt Fender Showman amplifier. We couldn't believe it."

Two of the wonderfully exotic compositions that fill *Electric Ladyland*, "Rainy Day, Dream Away" and "Still Raining, Still Dreaming" mark drummer Buddy Miles's first contribution to the Hendrix canon. Much to the usurped Mitch Mitchell's credit, Miles had become a regular visitor to the Record Plant and was accepted gracefully. Then all of twenty years of age, Miles admired Hendrix. "I had a deep fascination for the man and I wanted to learn," he says. "We kidded around a lot, but there was a real harmony between us. He had a charm and a grace about him. When I first met him in 1965 at the Grand National in Montreal, he had his hair in a pony tail with long sideburns. Even though he was shy, I could tell this guy was different." Miles openly emulated Hendrix, joining his tight-knit social circle and befriending Faye Pridgeon and the Allen twins.

Miles wasn't the only musician now jamming regularly with the Experience at the Record Plant. By June, with Chandler out of the picture, Hendrix had settled into a pattern. Daytime sessions – work – were for cutting tracks with Eddie Kramer, while evening sessions soon became Hendrix's after-hours retreat – a place where he and his friends could jam and capture their ideas on tape. Jamming was Hendrix's principal source of inspiration. Unfortunately, unlike "Voodoo Chile," where Eddie Kramer was able to properly direct and therefore record the session, most of the jams were either poorly recorded or too sloppy to be seriously considered worthy of release. While Chandler would bristle at the idea of wasting expensive studio time, Hendrix had no such concern. Recalls engineer Tony Bongiovi, "Hendrix would be booked for a 7 A.M. session and 7 P.M. would come and go. I'd sit there and doze off until he and his entourage would come back from the Scene. Then they'd usually be totally ripped, gone, out the window with drink. One of Jimi's favorite things to do, if I was asleep, was to turn on all of his stuff and play it as loud as he could."

Having recently transferred from Apostolic Studios, Bongiovi was a keen but green eighteen-year-old from New Jersey, the self-described "clean-up guy" for Kellgren and Kramer. Totally straight, Bongiovi was often the victim of Hendrix's late-night pranks. "Gary Kellgren had given Hendrix a huge bag of pot," recalls Bongiovi. "Kellgren was a daytime guy, but at night he would get pretty ripped with Hendrix. The first experience I had around people and dope was at Apostolic. I was in the building when a guy jumped out the window on an LSD trip. Drugs were not cool. I was like this little kid. I remember Hendrix's girlfriend Devon Wilson in the control room blowing smoke in my face, trying to get me to smoke a joint, while Hendrix held me down."

Night sessions gave Hendrix an opportunity to stretch out, a safe haven where ideas could be developed in a relaxed atmosphere. Regardless, Hendrix expected Bongiovi to understand and adhere to his many idiosyncrasies. "He was one of the few artists who would just put the tape on and let it run," recalls Bongiovi. "I remember him yelling at me for stopping the tape. He said, 'What did you stop the tape for?' 'Because you weren't doing anything!' 'No,' he demanded, 'leave it running.' So I put reel after reel after reel through the machine. At the start of sessions, I would ask Hendrix what he wanted to work on. You would start and he would say, 'No, I don't want to do this, let's go to this,' and you would have to go to that. He would stop in the middle of that and want something else entirely. We would start out with a couple of tapes and end up with a pile."

For Eddie Kramer, one of the secrets of keeping Hendrix

focused was by challenging him to do something differently, be it immediately following a take, or later in a session when – after Hendrix might create a sound or style – Kramer would suggest adding it to a previous recording. Their many sessions at Olympic had created a strong, unspoken bond between them. A host of different ideas were tried, including small and large horn sections as well as the spacious sound painting created for "1983 (A Merman I Should Turn to Be)."

Recalls Kramer, "'1983' came together during the mixing process, where overdubs as simple as the sounds of crying seagulls were improvised on the spot." By cupping earphones over the microphone during the playback of an overdub, Hendrix and Kramer were struck by the short peal of feedback. Within minutes, with delay added to dramatize the squeal, the effect became part of the collage. The final mixing session for "1983" was a performance in itself, the panning, fading and additional sound effects stemming from a continuous flow of ideas and a joint decision to make the song free from edits. One of *Electric Ladyland*'s most memorable performances, this gentle, ethereal ballad best exemplified Hendrix's abstract vision.

As the Beatles had displayed with *Sgt. Pepper* and later the White Album, *Electric Ladyland* featured an amazing array of influences, each boasting Hendrix's own personal stamp, touching upon – in one double album – rock, pop, blues and jazz, creating perhaps the first fusion album, brilliantly marrying his trademark sound to a host of different musical influences.

Through his music, Hendrix attempted to break barriers between styles and, ultimately, between races. His personal vision seemed oblique, marbled within his poetic compositions. He neither claimed nor envisioned himself as someone to whom young African Americans (or native Americans for that matter) could look to as a leader. Chandler, Redding, Kramer, Stickells, Levine and a number of close associates all testify that Hendrix didn't have a political bone in his body. In private conversations, he would articulate universal, rather than specific solutions. He could, for example, relate to the Black Panthers' attempts to improve the quality of life for black people, yet he abhorred their violent tactics. While a great number of his fans opposed the war in Vietnam, Hendrix struggled with the human toll of war, casting the politics aside. In his own, often obtuse way, Hendrix would dedicate versions of "I Don't Live Today" and, later, "Machine Gun" not only to the soldiers in Vietnam, but to "all the soldiers fighting in Chicago, Milwaukee, New York ..." Chandler recalls the rapport Hendrix had with fellow servicemen he would meet on his travels. With those who had shared his personal experience in the military, he could express his relief at having served before Vietnam, yet he remained a realist who recognized that, for blacks, the various branches of the military represented one of the few opportunities available to them to better their lives.

The colorful prose Hendrix invoked to stymie straight journalists fostered a perception that he was either completely out of touch with reality or perhaps thoroughly manipulated by his all-white management. In actuality, the situation was far more intricate. The paucity of black faces at his concerts *was* distressing, but so were the demands by fans to see him smash and burn his instrument. Far more sensitive and insightful than his audience ever knew, Hendrix possessed a grand design for his music, stressing its positive potential to help change society. Deeply spiritual, Hendrix felt music could heal and bring races together. Through interviews, Hendrix, in his own inimitable fashion, expressed concepts, such as his preference for performing outdoors, where he felt his music best combatted the tension and strife between people of all races. As Chas Chandler testifies, Hendrix was far from naive, understanding that music and politics were a very tricky mix, where one continually ran the risk of being used and having the message cheapened.

The most significant stumbling block that Hendrix faced

in trying to "cross over" to a black audience was that of radio airplay. Virtually ignored by black radio (an absurd term when one considers that most were owned by white corporations), Hendrix was thus locked out from black audiences. (In his 1986 autobiography, James Brown wrote, "While there were around 500 black-oriented radio stations in the country, only five of them were owned by black people – and three of those were mine.") With his music deemed too white for black radio and too hard for white AM airplay, Hendrix became a staple of the country's growing number of FM stations.

Though predominantly shunned by radio, Hendrix's fame was a classic combination of talent and hype. His management team controlled the marketing of the artist while Concerts West, essentially his own touring company, ensured – via their radio advertisements – that the faithful knew his songs. The Hendrix image – the "experience" one had at his performances – was a savvy sales tool, unique among his contemporaries.

Tom Hulett of Concerts West remembers the impact this self-promotion had on other artists. "We had purchased some Creedence Clearwater Revival dates from ABC Booking. John Fogerty came to me at Vancouver Airport and said, 'I hear you're doing something with Jimi Hendrix. How do you do it? I'm really unhappy with our situation. Hell, we were playing in Fresno last night and the guy didn't even rent a PA!' So from Jimi Hendrix, we ended up with Creedence Clearwater Revival. I sat down with John and his accountants in Oakland and showed them how our concept worked."

"There were no rules," further recalls Hulett. "I give Hendrix credit for introducing a whole new way of doing business, where the artist made most of the money. The booking agencies didn't like it because the time had come when Michael Jeffery and Steve Weiss no longer needed a booking agent to get to a Tom Hulett or a Phil Basile. All of a sudden the middle man was cut out and Hendrix made more money."

These radical changes within the business structure of rock n' roll enabled Hendrix's explosion of popularity to continue unabated, creating a machine that smashed barriers in radio and personal appearances that had long stunted the growth of other artists – especially blacks. Hendrix, Hulett states, was far more than the black marionette, as some have intimated, pushed on the stage night after night for the benefit of his tyrant-like manager. The needs of the Experience – outlaws on the main streets and back roads of middle America – were made first priority.

Concerts West, and later Concerts East, were "four-walling" Experience appearances all across the country, that is, booking the band into venues without using a middleman, thus giving the local promoters a higher percentage of the take. Jimi Hendrix was not only putting up the money to stage his own concerts, but he was making more than any other artist in the business. The communication network, as Hulett describes, was very efficient. "I would call up and clear the dates with Steve Weiss, who would clear them with Gerry Stickells, who in turn would let Hendrix know where we were going to play. I knew what Hendrix wanted. I knew about his security requests backstage and that he loved 'festival seating' where, unlike reserved seating, kids could move around. We made the tours as comfortable as we could for him."

The success of the self-promotion concept was the source of great pride for Hendrix's team. The Experience tours were phenomenally profitable, consistently outgrossing Hendrix's contemporaries, who struggled to fill 60 percent of the venues they played. Hendrix handily outearned artists such as the Doors and Janis Joplin – all while earning eighty-five cents on the dollar. The process of self-promotion propelled the Experience to the forefront of the rock scene, making them, outside of the Beatles, the most sought after attraction in the business.

# 9 ELECTRIC LADYLAND

*"I have plans that are unbelievable, but then wanting to be a guitar player seemed unbelievable at one time."*

—Jimi Hendrix

The withering relationship between Jimi Hendrix and Noel Redding threatened to throw a wrench into Jeffery's well-oiled money machine. Effective communication between Hendrix and Redding had begun to erode on their spring 1968 tour. Despite Buddy Miles's presence on the scene, Mitch Mitchell was in no danger of losing his gig, and his work on *Electric Ladyland* was nothing short of brilliant. Mitchell and Hendrix had developed a quiet trust between them and shared a deep sense of mutual respect. Mitch did not infringe upon Jimi socially: if they were going out together, fine; if not, that was fine too. Hendrix enjoyed the challenge Mitchell presented him musically. While willing to change or adapt his style, Mitch was not one to grow complacent. With Chandler out of the picture, Mitchell expanded his relationship with Eddie Kramer, becoming more interested and involved in the group's sound.

Noel Redding, on the other hand, simply did not share the same philosophies about recording. He grew increasingly irritated with Hendrix's lack of interest in his work and longed to get back on the guitar, his real love. Experience sessions had become a chore, fraught with petty arguments. "To get back at Hendrix," Redding says, "I would purposely play out of tune." His frustration barely concealed, Redding would simply not turn up at sessions, tersely remarking to Bob Levine that "Hendrix was going to play over it anyway." This attitude grew darker as their relationship worsened, and getting stoned seemed to be the best way to mask problems within the band. "I remember Noel being so stoned on a couple of sessions that he couldn't even stand up to play," says Tony Bongiovi.

Redding had also taken to recording apart from Hendrix, asking Eddie Kramer to engineer sessions for "How Can I Live" and "Walking Through the Garden," both of which would later appear on Fat Mattress's debut release. Made up of Noel's old friends, this band had become his artistic diversion, and soon after Chas Chandler expressed an interest in producing them.

While Hendrix's relationship with Redding disintegrated, a nagging sense of self-doubt began to permeate Jimi's fragile psyche. As June slipped into July and July into August, Hendrix attempted countless numbers of overdubs and remixes, trying to perfectly capture the vision so clear in his mind. "All Along the Watchtower" best exemplified this obsession. "I remember setting up for a mix of that record at 3 A.M.," recalls Tony Bongiovi. "We mixed from an Ampex MM1000 sixteen-track down to a two-track Scully machine running at fifteen ips. The song had begun on four-track, progressed to twelve-track and finally sixteen-track. In the transfer process, the tape got lost and we ended up doing more than fifteen different mixes. Hendrix would stop the tape, pick up his guitar or the bass and go back out and start re-overdubbing stuff. Recording these new ideas meant that he would have to erase something. In the weeks prior to the mixing, we had already recorded a number of overdubs; wiping track after track – and I don't mean once or twice – he would overdub the bass and guitar parts all over, until he was satisfied. He would say, 'I think I hear it a bit differently.'"

At the end of July, the Experience began a lengthy three-month American tour, assured of ever larger audiences. An upgrade of their road equipment was therefore in order, though all of their guitar equipment, drum set, PA, floor lights, wardrobe and posters could still fit into a nineteen-foot U-Haul truck, driven by Eric Barrett. Redding was satisfied with his Sunn amplifiers but Hendrix preferred Marshalls; the problem, states Abe Jacob, the Experience's road sound engineer, was that the speakers – rather than the amplifiers – were breaking down, burning out as a result of the constant sound barrage pushed through them.

For the Experience's live sound, neither Hendrix's nor Redding's amplifiers were miked. Jacob mixed Mitchell's drums plus all lead and backing vocals through a primitive eight-channel, rotary knob mixer. Of the eight possible microphone inputs, one was reserved for Jacob himself, as he often doubled as MC, introducing the band from his position in the audience. The group's PA system was made up of six Altec A-7 cabinets, three on each side of the stage. For stage monitoring, four small Altec 604s were utilized.

In spite of the rudimentary equipment available, Hendrix was sensitive about the quality of his live sound. "It was much more complicated than plugging in, cranking the Marshalls to ten and jumping on stage," recalls Jacob. "He was very aware of the dynamics of his sound. Our sound level coming off stage was 102dB at the peaks. With just 300 watts of power, we could get his lead vocal over. The real problem was getting enough monitor level for Mitch, so he could hear both Jimi's vocals and his drums. We were able to put together a special monitoring unit for him, made of four Altec cabinets that stood right behind his drum kit. Mitch could finally hear his own playing over the din of the Marshalls."

The "entourage" that traveled with the band was as spartan as the equipment, as Gerry Stickells and Eric Barrett were true yeomen, attending to the band's every need on the road until November 1968, when Gene McFadden was recruited as their assistant.

Opening in Baton Rouge on July 30, 1968, the new U.S. tour got off to a roaring start. After the Experience's show at Independence Hall, the local promoter drove Hendrix, Gerry Stickells and Abe Jacob to a small blues club, hidden some forty miles deep into the bayou. "Hendrix was sitting there listening to these old guys play," recalls Jacob. "The youngest man on the stage must have been fifty-five or sixty. He got up and played guitar with them. It was a wonderful evening." Though never one to pass up a chance to jam, this respite was a special opportunity for Hendrix to reaffirm his love for the blues.

They moved on to New Orleans, where, after a particularly outrageous performance, local police were furious with the Experience, charging that Hendrix was trying to incite a riot. Tempers frayed backstage as defiant police officers confronted both Stickells and Hendrix, who were growing visibly agitated. In an attempt to defuse the situation, publicist Michael Goldstein redirected the police assault onto himself. "Better to sacrifice the New York Jew than the black superstar," Goldstein says today with a laugh. "I wasn't worried. Touring with Hendrix taught me to carry at least $10,000 in case of situations like these." Barely escaping the wrath of the local police, Soft Machine road manager Tom Edmontson huddled with Stickells in his hotel room, having safely transported nearly $50,000 inside a duffle bag and briefcase. "No security, no Wells Fargo, nothing," recalls Edmontson. "We had to convert the cash to a bank check the next day. Stickells had a little .38, I had nothing. Hiding behind a locked door, we had to order food and beer up to our room."

In Texas, the Experience were relentlessly harassed. "Every time we set up," recalls Abe Jacob, "the fire department, police department and mayor's office were all there saying, 'You can't do this, we don't allow *that* kind of stuff

[Hendrix's pyrotechnic stage show] in our town. They all thought Hendrix was going to burn the building down."

While few civic leaders had actually seen the Monterey film clip, the rumor – the threat of Hendrix burning and smashing his guitar – was enough. Actual news coverage of Hendrix's concerts was rare, because U.S. television stations were still utilizing film for news retrieval. Due in part to the time needed for processing, most news divisions turned in their exposed film for developing at approximately 9 P.M. to ensure making the 11 P.M. newscast. These established deadlines forced them to bypass Experience concerts. Remembers Abe Jacob, "News crews were not given audio feeds because we didn't know how to do that with the equipment we had." Outside of the notorious Monterey clip and the various promotional films for songs such as "Hey Joe" and "Foxey Lady" that Chandler and Jeffery had made in London and Los Angeles, local media outlets had little ammunition to debunk the outlaw image that preceded the Experience – the same image that drove fans to see the group in person.

As Gerry Stickells explains, although the tour started out strong, Hendrix had grown bored of the routine, lacking the discipline needed to churn out the same songs night after night. "He used to always say that people were only coming to see him burn his guitar, and he was bored with that. Playing seven days a week instead of two no doubt made it worse."

Chandler echoes this view. "With Jeffery, it was gigs, gigs, gigs. He couldn't even see to plan the tour in advance so, at least, we could sensibly route the cities. He did the same thing with the Animals."

"There was stress," agrees Stickells. "But the circumstances were entirely different. The Experience didn't play a structured show as groups do today. There were neither lighting cues nor preprepared set lists. After the first few shows of a tour, we rarely bothered to do sound checks. Most nights it took forty-five minutes just to convince

Hendrix to go on, then when you got him on, he didn't want to come off. Every night he'd say, 'Give them their money back. I don't feel like playing tonight. We'll do it tomorrow,' then he would go on and we would have to scream at him to stop at eleven P.M. [because of the local curfew]."

Just as the Experience were among the first rock artists to self-promote their own personal appearances, and one of the first groups to travel with their own PA system as well as hanging speakers throughout an auditorium to improve sound quality, so Hendrix was the first artist to fully control his merchandising – from its concept directly through to the consumer. Michael Jeffery was the first to recognize Hendrix's marketing potential, especially as it so obviously translated into ticket sales. At first glance, Track Records' Chris Stamp had known that an artist as visually compelling as Hendrix had dynamic sales potential. Just four years before, a naive Brian Epstein had given away millions of dollars by taking only a minor holding in a company called Selteab, formed to administer the Beatles' lucrative merchandising rights: in exchange for an up-front cash payout, the group had retained only a paltry 10 percent interest. Jeffery, on the other hand, was far too shrewd to let dollars slip through his fingers.

Of the many contacts Jeffery and Chandler had made at the Monterey festival one was Jerry Goldstein, whose company, the Visual Thing, secured the rights from Jeffery to market posters (and, afterward, tour books) of both Hendrix and the Experience. Later to produce a long string of chart hits for the seminal funk group War, Goldstein understood the potential of marrying merchandising techniques of the teen idol era with psychedelic artists – especially one as exotic as Hendrix. Utilizing such photographers as Ron Raffaelli, Goldstein dramatically captured the essence of the Experience's image, never failing to present rock's interracial, intercontinental combo in a typically striking pose. Sales of memorabilia, right from the outset, were strong.

Citing his experience with Teen Mail Limited, the organization set up to handle merchandising for a number of top British acts, including the Animals, Hollies and Herman's Hermits, Jeffery tapped Bob Levine to supervise Hendrix's merchandising. Design ideas were cleared in advance through Hendrix and his management. The system worked effortlessly, as Goldstein and Levine would settle up regularly, maintaining a strong and open line of communication. Remembers Bob Levine: "Hendrix continually called me for accountings on merchandising sales. Even out on the road he'd take time to call me and ask about the poster money and what his share was. Don't think for a second that this guy didn't realize how profitable merchandising was."

On August 23, the Experience appeared with Janis Joplin, Soft Machine and the Chambers Brothers before a sold-out crowd of 18,000 at the Singer Bowl in Flushing Meadows, New York. Backstage, PPX attorney Elliot Hoffman made a surprise appearance. Along with his pregnant wife and elderly mother, he had come by to see the concert. "Two of my clients were staging the show, and one of them whispered into my ear that the security force had not shown. He and his partner had closed the box office – as the concert had sold out – and they were leaving. I had to do something, so I went downstairs to Hendrix's dressing room. Steve Weiss and Albert Grossman were there, and Steve, unlike Jimi, could be antagonistic. I told them straight out that, outside of a handful of uniformed police officers, we had no security personnel on site. I didn't know who to blame, but I told them that we could either be responsible for a lot of people getting hurt or we could do something about the situation. I appealed directly to Hendrix, asking him not to incite the crowd in any way, as people were sure to get hurt, and requested that the house lights remain on all evening."

After Weiss and Grossman huddled briefly, a compromise on the lighting issue was agreed to. Much to the delight of the crowd, which packed the former site of the 1964 World's Fairs, the event was a resounding success. "It was a great show," recalls Hoffman proudly. "No one noticed that there weren't any security guards; there were no fights or injuries." Outside of one minor incident during "Hey Joe," when, as the crowd became unruly, the house lights were brought up full, the Experience capped off a brilliant evening of music. Their performance brought raves from area critics, including a writer from *Billboard*, who informed the trade. "Hendrix's bluesy singing was first rate; his guitar playing superb, and his stage presence, electric. From the opening 'Are You Experienced?,' every number hit the mark."

After the show, Hendrix returned to the Record Plant, where he and Kramer completed mixing for "House Burning Down." Warner Bros. had been clamoring for the group to finish the album, and finally on August 27, 1968, after remixing "Gypsy Eyes" one final time – fittingly, since it was Hendrix's inability to concentrate on this song's basic tracks that had so frustrated Chas Chandler – Eddie Kramer prepared a tape of the album's four sides and sent it off to be mastered. The marathon final mixing session continued all through the night, well into the morning of the 28th.

Having completed their third album, and sensing Hendrix's keen interest in production, Jeffery looked to bolster his standing with Hendrix by inviting him to produce the debut album by Eire Apparent, another of the many groups in the Jeffery stable. Just as Chandler was slated to work with Fat Mattress, Hendrix would be given Eire Apparent, and Tom Wilson, shut out of the running for producing Hendrix, was given Soft Machine.

Jeffery's reputation as a negotiator grew with each new record deal he secured. For Soft Machine, he obtained a $50,000 advance from ABC/Paramount Records; for Goldie & the Gingerbreads it was a sizable sum wrought from Atlantic. Despite Yameta's self-imposed dissolution, Jeffery continued to develop new bands and look for record deals, usually taking a minimum of 20 percent of each advance he could procure, as well as sharing in potential publishing and record royalties. Each band taken under his wing would also be exposed to the growing audiences who came to see the Experience or Vanilla Fudge, the second half of Concerts West's one-two punch.

Jeffery's ability to self-promote concerts by his artists was nothing to take lightly; in fact, it would play a major role in securing a staggering advance for Fat Mattress – reportedly then the largest ever given to a band that had only a handful of songs completed and had never before played in public. Just knowing that Fat Mattress would open each show for the Experience was insurance enough for Atco/Polydor. The problem facing Jeffery was that, like his most famous client, he grew quickly bored with the day-to-day details. Without Chandler to direct and produce these bands, each struggled to develop a following, despite the benefits the Experience and Jeffery's extended management team provided. Jeffery had no artistic ability; he was a deal maker, and dealing with Hendrix on a day-to-day basis was quite enough. Jeffery had Bob Levine deal with the various road managers such as Tom Edmonston for Soft Machine and John Gardiner for Cat Mother & the All Night Newsboys, asking only to be keep abreast of their progress and problems.

Alienating Chas Chandler had been a shortsighted decision. What better addition to a production team than a producer interested only in producing? By undermining Chandler's relationship with Hendrix, Jeffery had won a Pyrrhic victory. Severing ties with Chandler limited his options with developing bands.

At the Record Plant, Hendrix asked Eddie Kramer to engineer the Eire Apparent sessions. Although Hendrix had helped produce his own recordings in the past, the process had been dictated to and from the studio and the control room. Kramer had assumed a larger role than most engineers while Hendrix immersed himself in all facets of the recording process, accepting more responsibility than many of his contemporaries. Now, for the first time, Hendrix remained exclusively in "the big chair," working at Kramer's side.

Their many sessions together had fostered a warm, productive relationship and Kramer prided himself upon his engineering work for Hendrix. "I watched those two guys work," recalls Buddy Miles. "Jimi really felt he had an ally in Eddie, because he would always listen to his ideas. Nothing was more important to Jimi than his music and Eddie was always pushing him."

"Hendrix couldn't mix a song properly," recalls Stephen Stills. "We would walk in and Eddie Kramer would have everything set up, playing back a really good mix. You could hear everything. Then Jimi would start fiddling and there was this wall of sound that hit you in the face. I would tell him, 'That sucked.' He would look surprised and say, 'Oh really?'"

Buddy Miles remembers a similar incident during the mixing sessions for "Rainy Day, Dream Away" and "Still Raining, Still Dreaming," when Hendrix squashed his voice, masking it between his guitar and drums. (The origins of this are easily recognized. Since his very first sessions with Chas Chandler, Hendrix had strong reservations about his voice. Sensing his discomfort, Kramer adopted the strategy of surrounding Hendrix with partitions during his lead vocal overdubs. In addition, at Hendrix's request, Kramer would dim the studio lights to make him feel more comfortable. This strategy originated at Olympic Studios. Explains Kramer, "After taping a lead vocal, Hendrix would poke his head around the screen with this bemused look on his face, asking, 'How was that? Was that okay? Was it all right?' Jimi needed every bit of encouragement because he lacked confidence in his voice. I would say, 'Yes Jimi, it was great, but if you want to do another one, go ahead.'")

The Eire Apparent sessions were difficult. Unlike Experience sessions, where the roles of everyone involved, albeit unspoken, were defined, Hendrix began to dominate both engineering and producing chores. Linda Eastman, on hand to take photographs, can talk of the tension caused by Hendrix's encroachment upon Kramer's duties. The two started bickering, something they had never done in the past, and she couldn't help wondering why they were involved with the project in the first place. Having disposed of Chandler, why would Jeffery now risk harming Hendrix's key relationship with Kramer, especially over a project of such relative unimportance?

On August 30, 1968, the Experience embarked upon Concerts West's most ambitious tour to date. Beginning in Salt Lake City, each concert was to feature Eire Apparent and Vanilla Fudge as support acts. Once again, every show was self-promoted, buttressed by Concerts West's custom radio advertising campaigns. Most importantly, gate receipts continued to be split 90-10 in favor of Hendrix. After deducting expenses, Concerts West received their 10 percent, 5 percent of Hendrix's share covered expenses incurred by Steingarten, Wedeen & Weiss, who negotiated and approved the performance and building contracts, and Jimi's remaining 85 percent was sent back to Michael Hecht to be deposited in Are You Experienced? Ltd. The success of this tour was crucial and both Michael Jeffery and Chas Chandler were frequently in evidence, as well as Vanilla Fudge manager Phil Basile, booking agent Ron Terry and Concerts West's Tom Hulett.

Immediately after the Salt Lake City show, Hendrix returned to the Newhouse Hotel to begin outlining his ideas for the *Electric Ladyland* cover and sleeve design and layout. From Utah, the tour headed to Denver. Once again, the Experience were seeing their audiences double, and at times triple in size, along the tour. In Denver, they packed Red Rocks Park. Despite the great financial success the tour was enjoying, however, Hendrix, recalls Ron Terry, wanted Vanilla Fudge thrown off the tour. "Jimi had a bad night in Denver, Vanilla Fudge had one of their best. On the plane, Hendrix threw into my lap the paper he was reading and told me to 'send those fuckers home.' Back at the hotel, I got a call from Michael Jeffery telling me that Jimi didn't want the Fudge on the bill. I asked Jeffery to let me speak to

Hendrix personally: I wanted to try to appeal to his competitive sense. 'Look,' I said, 'you're being a pussy about this whole thing! They had a good night, you had a bad night. Just do your thing!' He first told me to go fuck myself but then offered me a warning: 'Okay, we'll see what happens tonight.' That night we were in Phoenix and the Vanilla Fudge's set went over well. Hendrix came out on stage and the fire was coming out of his ears. He was smoking. He showed everybody in the house who Jimi Hendrix was, and as he came off the stage he looked right at me and said, '*That's* the way it's supposed to be.'"

It was in Denver, at the Cosmopolitan Hotel, between "4:30 to 6:00 A.M." that Hendrix finished his *Electric Ladyland* cover sleeve designs as well as a poem entitled "Letter to the Room Full of Mirrors," that would ultimately grace the album's inside sleeve. Hendrix wrote to Warner Bros. apologizing for the delay, citing the group's busy schedule, and closing with a request that the label not stray too far from the concept he had outlined.

In his rough sketches, Hendrix requested Warner, "Please use color picture with us and the kids on the statue for front or back cover – OUTSIDE COVER." One potential cover photo was of particular importance to Hendrix, as he had specifically asked Linda Eastman to photograph the group with both white and black children surrounding them. It was to be a quiet statement rather than a bleating rave to improve race relations, a subtle touch he wanted to project. A different photo from the same Central Park session graces the inside sleeve of the U.S. release. Hendrix had also collected a number of color and black-and-white photographs for the inner sleeve. These photos were taken by Eastman, although some other photos by Eddie Kramer and David Sygall were included too. Hendrix requested this inner sleeve feature both color and black-and-white, going as far as to illustrate how to intersperse the pictures. For some reason, though one can only surmise cost, his requests were rejected. Instead of the photo of the Experience with the children, a blurred, solarized shot of Hendrix was substituted. Inside the sleeve, though the photos Hendrix submitted were almost all used, none were printed in color. Hendrix was not informed of any of these decisions. But while these changes were sure to disappoint him, he had no idea what Track Records had in store for their British cover of *Electric Ladyland* ...

In San Diego on September 3, the Experience packed Balboa Stadium, enjoying tremendous financial success. Even in smaller cities such as Phoenix, where the Experience had never before performed, fans were tearing the doors down trying to get in. But in the eye of this hurricane of acceptance and popularity, the Experience had begun to unravel. "We started to grow apart but nobody wanted to own up to it," is how Mitch Mitchell describes the situation. Even as pressure welled within Hendrix, he had no close friends on the road with him to vent his frustration. Most discomforting to Hendrix seemed to be the grind of touring, which, when coupled with drug use, effectively diluted his message and sapped the strength he needed to call upon to deliver it. Blurred by the pace of his own success, Hendrix vacillated between bouts of exuberance and depression. He was, says Mitchell, "a loner, a recluse; a lot of people like to think they were his friend but I don't think he needed them."

Mitchell describes even his own relationship with Hendrix as "pretty distant," refusing to overstate the friendship. "We had to get off on stage. The friendship came for me from the musical trade-off. We did not hang out together, except in Europe. We would go our separate ways; but 75 percent of the time we would all end up at the same party. It was a close band but in a very abstract way. Everyone had very firm ideas about what they wanted; unfortunately, only two-thirds of the band were aiming for the same thing, and having been on the road so long before forming the Experience, Hendrix had very firm ideas about what he wanted."

Even a stop home in Seattle didn't provide Hendrix with a chance to unwind and refocus his energies; he was there for only one day, playing that same evening before moving on to Vancouver. "This time," he instructed Tom Hulett, "don't make a fuss. Let's get in and get out and don't tell anybody where we're staying." Hendrix wished to see his family, but he wanted no part of the hoopla that had dominated his previous recent visits.

Physically and mentally exhausted by their ceaseless touring, the trio's nerves were now frazzled. In Spokane on September 8, the normally reserved and even-tempered Mitch exploded with rage. "It was an early Sunday morning," recalls Ron Terry. "The hotel didn't have our rooms ready so we all sat in the coffee shop. We were sitting quietly when a businessman in a suit and tie said to Mitch, 'Oh young lady, would you pass me the cream?' Mitch flipped, screaming, 'I'll tell you who's a fucking woman!' He was ready to start whaling on the guy with his travel bag and we were saying, 'Mitch, cool it!' The guy caught him at the worst possible time because he was tired and bitchy from the road and wasn't about to take shit from anyone."

Previously, slights such as these – intentional or not – had been brushed aside without incident. Dating back to their first trip to America as members of the Experience, Mitchell and Redding had been struck by the oddities that separated their culture from that of Middle America. For Redding, the absurdity was encapsulated in various vignettes, such as the "fat balding man in Bermuda shorts pointing at me and laughing at the way I looked." Mitchell seemed to view America with a cautious sense of optimism, home of the jazz idols he revered but also with a massive contingent hostile to the lifestyle he had adopted. "America is fabulous," Mitchell told Chris Welch, a writer for *Melody Maker*. "But I still couldn't live anywhere else but England. In London, if they see you with long hair on the street, people just laugh and say: 'Oh, he must be in a group,' then forget it. In America they'll shout: 'Are you a boy or a girl?' The younger generation in America are very nice, but in New York you get the really ignorant and violent people, and they are mostly tourists from the Midwest. There are junkies who come up and paw at your girl when you're walking along the street. We were told not to go in Central Park after dark or go in the subway after 9 P.M. or walk down 42nd Street because we might get shot. We saw cops using nightsticks to club Negroes to the ground and Noel saw five cops kicking a Negro on the pavement. I was staggered."

Such pressures further weakened the fragile coalition of Hendrix, Mitchell and Redding. Despite the astonishing success of both *Are You Experienced?* and *Axis: Bold as Love*, the Experience had not, as Hendrix had wanted, cleared their schedule to make the recording of *Electric Ladyland* their sole concentration. Having spent close to $60,000 at the Record Plant alone (another $10,000 went to pay for the December 1967–January 1968 sessions at Olympic Sound Studios), Hendrix had felt pressured by both Jeffery and Warner Bros. to complete the project. He had been infuriated that final mixing sessions had to be squeezed into off days from touring. Hendrix had no qualms regarding recording costs; recording was his top priority and gate receipts, he reasoned, were *meant* to pay for recording costs. "The money doesn't make any difference to me," Hendrix would explain, "because that's what I make the money for, to make better things."

Arriving in Los Angeles on September 10, the Experience settled into a mansion rented for a vacation of sorts. On September 14, they packed the Hollywood Bowl. During their set, a number of frenzied fans jumped into the pool that separated the band from the audience. As they roared through their set, fans continued to dash by police and leap into the pool, creating utter chaos. The unruly crowd interrupted the beginning of "Little Wing," causing Redding to reprimand those flailing in the water. "If you get near all this electricity, you'll get electrocuted. So stand back!" Bemused, Hendrix slyly added, "Y'all up on the hill, don't think you can fly, because you can't." Still somewhat astonished, yet wanting to continue, Hendrix again began the delicate introduction to "Little Wing," asking the crowd, "Just let us play, okay?"

Back at their rented mansion, the Experience were free to terrorize Southern California. Vacationing in Los Angeles gave Hendrix the chance to hang out with Buddy Miles. "We were staying up at this house," recalls Miles. "This house was *bad.* It was on Benedict Canyon Road and our next-door neighbor was [actor] Buddy Ebsen. On the other side was Marlene Dietrich's daughter. We partied for days doing some crazy shit. One night, I was taking a shower when I heard a knock on the door. And there was Jimi, with a blond wig and a brassiere. He says, in a female voice, 'Buddy?' I said, 'Come on in, James.' He said, 'Can we go out to the pool?' So we went out to the pool, and I jumped in, and the splash knocked off his wig. He would just do funny shit like that."

Hendrix had extended an invitation for Buddy to stay with him, especially, recalls Miles with a laugh, after he saw his new Corvette. "I had a beautiful Corvette with pipes and cheetah slicks and I let the fool drive it. He pleaded with me, 'Buddy, Buddy, stay over at the house, man. I don't want to let that car out of my sight.' I said, 'Look James. You can't keep my car, but I *will* stay overnight.'"

Hendrix was a diehard Corvette fan and, just like his trademark Stratocasters, there were, in his opinion, no other sports cars worth owning. Just as he could dress outlandishly, Hendrix seemed to gravitate toward the gaudiest of motors. While he loved to race down the road with his rag top down, his eyesight was miserable. Too vain for glasses, Hendrix was content to squint and hope for the best. Stories of his attempts at driving are legion. Bob Levine vividly remembers one incident when he and Jimi were driving to Harlem. Without a driver's license, Hendrix was frantically weaving through traffic up Park Avenue. Knowing full well that Hendrix couldn't see to save his soul, Levine was terrified, screaming at him to pull over. Eventually he did and Levine wasted no time in continuing his journey by cab. Eddie Kramer survived a similar experience: after a session at Record Plant, Hendrix and Kramer were roaring up Eighth Avenue in a rainbow-colored Corvette. Perhaps sensing Eddie's terror, Hendrix asked Kramer to reach behind his seat for his glasses. Kramer handed them to him, relieved that Jimi had had the sense to obtain some optically prescribed sunglasses, only to find out later that the sunglasses were exactly that, and nothing more. This combination of high speed and poor vision finally caught up with Hendrix, nearly claiming his life on the high, winding roads of Benedict Canyon. He completely demolished his Corvette, walking away from the accident dazed, with only cuts and bruises. He could have easily been killed; in fact, had he not crashed into rocks, he might well have vaulted over the side of the canyon wall. The accident didn't seem to faze him, however. After a day or so he walked into a dealership, bought another Corvette for cash and was back on the road. Hendrix had as many as six Corvettes although no one remembers exactly how many. Over time he traded in some and got new ones.

Hendrix was fast becoming destructive in many ways. While in Los Angeles, he had fought with a groupie, hitting her in the face with a brick, her cuts requiring stitches. The incident cost Hendrix dearly in an out-of-court settlement but money was easy. He would spend a small fortune on stereo equipment or televisions or on shopping sprees for girlfriends. In one weekend, he contrived to buy nine guitars. His expenses were staggering, and, as guitars were treated as a group expense, Mitchell and Redding were responsible for half of the cost. They too were not exactly maintaining a low profile at this time, wholeheartedly enjoying the various fruits of their hard labor.

The Experience and their army of friends were regulars at the Whiskey A Go Go, checking out bands, hanging out, jamming through the night and generally having a good time. For Chas Chandler, this stop in Los Angeles would be his last: he informed Jeffery of his decision to leave and soon after returned to London, making it clear that he would settle his interest in Hendrix without incident. These few weeks in Los Angeles had cemented his opinion that Jeffery was not working in Hendrix's best interests. How could he remain behind in New York, content to let Trixie Sullivan, his secretary, deal with this insanity?

Having already stepped aside as producer, Chandler was not interested in fighting Jeffery over every facet of Hendrix's career. Even though the PPX lawsuit had been settled, the issue of Jimi's Place, the proposed New York nightclub-studio, was still simmering below the surface. Despite his love and respect for Hendrix, the real conflict ultimately, just as it had always been, was between Jeffery and Chandler. "I respect Chas a lot," explains Bob Levine, "because he knew there would be destruction if he continued with Jeffery. He specifically requested John Hillman to make some kind of settlement that would not interfere with or hurt Jimi. Chas earned a great deal of respect for that, because a lot of people would have said, 'Never mind Jimi, I'm going to get what's mine.'"

"I had to referee that split," explains John Hillman. "I tried to do what was fair financially, but there was no way I could settle it emotionally. That would never be settled, and Chas remained very bitter."

"Jeffery was the big obstacle for Chas," recalls Levine. "Chas was interested in the career of Jimi Hendrix, the welfare of Jimi Hendrix and the growth of Jimi Hendrix. He was interested in working with Eddie Kramer to make the recordings sound good. I mean, how many sessions did Jeffery ever sit through?"

Almost two years from the day he had brought Hendrix to London, Chandler returned home alone. And although Hendrix refused to acknowledge it immediately, he had lost more than a manager. He had lost his staunchest supporter.

# 10 TOO MUCH DAMAGE TO CONTROL

*"Jimi would say, 'Buddy, let's take the 'Vette down to the beach and check out the surfer girls.' I'd say, 'Surfer girls? Aren't you the silly ass singing 'You'll never hear surf music again'?"*

—Buddy Miles

The first firestorm after Chandler's departure was Track Records' release of *Electric Ladyland*, in a sleeve featuring nineteen naked women, a concept dreamed up by Chris Stamp and Kit Lambert. Track had always fostered Hendrix's image brilliantly, first in Britain and then through Europe, issuing wonderfully exotic picture sleeves, posters and publicity photos. Because of this, Michael Jeffery had placed complete faith in their judgment. Track designed their own artwork, usually without any feedback from Hendrix, Chandler or Jeffery, though Hendrix had voiced some reservations about the sleeve design for *Axis: Bold as Love.* "The three of us have nothing to do with what's on that *Axis* cover," he later said. "When I first saw that design I thought it was great, but maybe we should have used an American Indian." Now, with the Experience no longer based in London, nor the center of British press attention, Track was keen to vault the band back into Fleet Street headlines.

That goal was certainly achieved, but controversy was the last thing Jimi Hendrix needed at this time. Now that the group had achieved more fame and success than it seemed it could handle, stunts such as the nude cover crossed an imaginary line with both the band and the legitimate press. Having to preface nearly every interview with a disclaimer about an album cover over which he had not been consulted was yet another in a ceaseless series of nagging problems diverting Hendrix's focus. "People have been asking me about the English cover and I don't know anything about it," he would explain. "I didn't know it was going to be used. It's not my fault. I don't even know what the B side to 'All Along the Watchtower' is!"

Hendrix had been disappointed with Reprise's U.S. version too. Not only were his instructions about the album's artwork compromised, but the mixes he and Kramer had labored countless hours over had been altered. "We wanted a particular sound," explained Hendrix, "and it got lost in the cutting room. [This is] because we went on tour right before we finished. I think the sound is cloudy." This dissatisfaction formed a theme Hendrix would run in countless interviews throughout his lifetime. He had been unable to convince Jeffery to push back or reschedule concerts. Their priorities were diametrically opposed and, as a result, Hendrix took the argument to the press. "*Electric Ladyland* was really expensive because we were recording and playing at the same time, which is a whole lot of strain on you. Therefore, you have to go back into the studio and redo what you might have done two nights ago. That's twice as much strain on you."

In another interview, Hendrix barely concealed his disdain for the cutting and mastering done by the record company. "We were recording while we were touring and it's very hard to concentrate on both. Some of the mix came out muddy, with too much bass. We mixed it and produced it, but when it came time for them to press it, quite naturally they screwed up, because they didn't know what we wanted. There's 3-D sound being used on there that you can't even appreciate because they didn't know how to cut it properly. They thought it was out of phase."

Fans ignored Hendrix's complaints, snapping up *Electric Ladyland* in droves. For the first time, the Experience had broken a single into the *Billboard* Top 40 chart, as "All Along the Watchtower" debuted at number 31.

Hendrix set out to inform critics and fans alike that *Electric Ladyland* was a serious statement. "All the tracks are very personal," he stated that same year. "It's different to what we have ever done before." Hendrix was specific in addressing his vulnerability to criticism. "[The album] starts with a ninety-second sound painting of the heavens. I know it's the thing people will jump on to criticize so we're putting it right at the beginning to get it over with. When it all comes down to it, albums are nothing but personal diaries. When you hear someone making music, they are baring a naked part of their soul to you."

Hendrix obviously wanted to shatter the very image that had propelled him to stardom. If *Time* and *Newsweek* had been interested in the "Black Elvis," he now wanted them to inform their readers that there was more to Jimi Hendrix than burning guitars. Just as the Experience's wild stage exploits had garnered them press in 1967, so Hendrix took advantage of *Electric Ladyland*'s success to try to reclassify both his and his band's image. "I don't want to be a clown anymore, I don't want to be a rock n' roll star," were statements intended to prove that he took his work seriously. The Experience had provided him with both a platform for his unique talents and financial reward for their acceptance, but, if he was to be forever known as an amplifier-smashing, guitar-burning novelty act, then perhaps it was time to re-evaluate the concept of the Jimi Hendrix Experience. "This pop business is much harder than people think," Hendrix would complain. "It's nerve-wracking and mindbending. The people who dig ditches for a living don't know how lucky they are."

The sheer volume of his business transactions was an additional burden. It has been suggested that Hendrix, like many black artists of the 1950s and 60s, was overwhelmed by financial issues. However, while Hendrix was neither lawyer nor simpleton, he understood the outlines of his major contracts and commitments. While perhaps he could not tell you how his publishing agreements were worded, he certainly knew what his percentage was. As a result of the Experience's explosion of popularity and the subsequent demands on their schedule, Bob Levine admits that many of Hendrix's performance contracts were signed for him. But Levine is quick to add that disinterest did not mean lack of knowledge. Michael Jeffery directed all negotiating for Hendrix and did not seek his artist's input on such decisions.

Hendrix's notorious reputation for signing anything thrust in front of him still lingered, but Barry Reiss – another of Jimi's attorneys at Steingarten, Wedeen & Weiss – insists that the PPX debacle *had* taught Hendrix something. "I was one of the people who used to go over contracts and explain them to him. He was never handed a piece of paper and told to sign. I vividly remember having to go see Jimi in a hotel room and there were five ladies lined up outside. There would be a knock on the door and one lady would answer while another remained in the bedroom. I would interrupt him to say that I had tour contracts that needed his signature. We would sit down at the table in his hotel room and I would explain it page by page, asking if he understood what he was signing. I remember the first couple of times that I did it I was very impressed by how bright he was, how aware he was. When we had to talk to him about the PPX case, he was very articulate. He knew exactly what was going down."

Jeffery's singular brilliance had propelled the Experience financially far in front of such contemporaries as the Doors, Janis Joplin and even the Rolling Stones. In Jeffery's mind, the very concept of the Experience was much like a successful patent, in that while one can tinker with the elements, they cannot be changed. The public had accepted the Jimi Hendrix Experience and to enjoy that success one also had to endure the costs associated with it. The public had not, Jeffery pointed out to Redding one day, supported him, Mitchell and Hendrix as solo artists. There had been a growing feeling within the band that each member would form his own group. For Mitch it might be Mind Octopus. For Noel, Fat Mattress. For Jimi, Band of Gypsys. Redding had taken the lead with Fat Mattress and was the most vocal supporter of the concept. One plan suggested that all three bands might precede the Experience on stage before the three members reunited as the Experience. While the concept was buffeted by the fact that the Experience self-promoted their own concerts – thereby allowing them complete control of each evening's entertainment – it was evidence, poorly masked evidence, of the Experience's crumbling frame. The concept of a wild caravan cavorting across the U.S., allowing the Experience to spend only as much time as necessary with each other, was dropped. Even if they had tried the idea, wouldn't potential customers want only the hits, having endured nearly two hours of Fat Mattress and Mind Octopus?

At some point in 1968, Hendrix clearly recognized that there would indeed be life for him after the Experience. It can be argued, supported by hindsight, that the release of *Electric Ladyland* demarcated the end of the group as a functioning unit. Hendrix seemed to have stretched the trio's potential close to its limits, perhaps even beyond the simple three-man concept with the inventive addition of horns, keyboards and additional percussion. Even when *Electric Ladyland* claimed the top spot on the *Billboard* album chart, *Are You Experienced?* continued to thrive in the top 10.

In celebration of the band's second birthday, the Experience were booked for a three-night stand at Winterland in San Francisco, performing two shows a night. Considering the occasion, Jeffery arranged to have the performances recorded, contracting Wally Heider, the noted West Coast live music engineer, to oversee the exercise. Apart from a concert in Honolulu on October 5, necessary to justify the Experience's retreat there as a business expense, the group had not performed live for a month. With the Buddy Miles Express as one of the opening acts, jamming replaced rehearsing. The Jefferson Airplane's Jack Casady was among those who dropped by to jam and later join the Experience on stage.

In the light of the 1987 issue of *Live at Winterland*, these San Francisco performances have recently come under a great deal of scrutiny. While a number of critics cite the recordings captured by Heider on his two eight-track machines as "definitive," they also represent the Experience at perhaps their most fragmented. There were a number of exceptional peaks, most notably "Fire" (included on the *Jimi Hendrix Concerts* LP), though even an untrained ear can't help but hear the rust that's evident, brought about by the group's lack of touring and rehearsing. While many of the songs featured on these two discs are highly charged, their sheer ferocity cannot mask the tuning problems, missed notes and generally sloppy play. The Winterland renditions of "Manic Depression," "Spanish Castle Magic" and "Sunshine of Your Love" were almost brutish in their delivery, with Hendrix trying to combat his defeated sound system by overplaying through its deficiencies. Though Redding's bass, jacked to maximum volume, throbbed incessantly, Hendrix was dogged by tuning problems and struggled to keep time with Mitchell. No amount of added echo or effects could mask Hendrix's tuning dip some three minutes into "Are You Experienced?" While the overall sonic qualities of the master recordings are laudable, it was Hendrix's Winterland performances themselves that were below par.

Digging deep into their stage repertoire, the Experience also performed "Like a Rolling Stone," as well as an early rendition of "Hear My Train A Comin'." When Casady joined the band, he added a second bass to "Killing Floor."

Virgil Gonsalves added flute to a wild and lengthy rendition of "Are You Experienced?"; Herbie Rich contributed organ to four songs – "Fire," "Lover Man," "Foxey Lady" and "Hey Joe" – offering a tantalizing insight into what role keyboards could have played within the Experience.

Following the Winterland concerts, the band returned to Los Angeles with recording time booked at TTG Studios. Chas had tipped off Hendrix about TTG, as the Animals had worked there some years before. These sessions formed the first attempt at recording the Experience's fourth album. With Chandler in London, and Kramer back working at the Record Plant in New York, Hendrix was now in complete control. Inevitably, therefore, the sessions were often chaotic, memorable more for the many parties than for creation of music. But the band did find time to complete a batch of new songs. On October 18,1968, the first version of "Izabella" (later a staple of Hendrix's *Band of Gypsys*) was recorded with Mitchell and Redding accompanying. A new composition with a strong R&B feel, this particular version was never released and Hendrix would continue work on "Izabella" throughout 1969 and into 1970, recording and remixing new versions with different musicians and engineers until finally satisfied.

On October 20, the basic tracks were completed for a tune that carried the working title "Messenger." Utilizing TTG's eight tracks efficiently, fifteen takes were attempted before the final one, complete with piano accompaniment by Lee Michaels, was deemed acceptable. On the 21st, the studio packed with friends, the Experience recorded "Calling All the Devil's Children," a tongue-in-cheek "party" recording that could have easily felt at home on *Axis: Bold as Love* or *Electric Ladyland*. Twenty-seven takes were attempted before the final version, complete with Hendrix's narration, was finished. On the 22nd Hendrix revived "Mr. Lost Soul," deciding, by the second reel and the seventeenth take, to rename it "Look Over Yonder." On the following day the Experience recorded an early version of another strong new

Hendrix composition, "Hey Baby," known at this time as "The New Rising Sun." Although he would also rearrange and record this track a number of times, take two of five full complete takes was the one chosen as the song's master.

After a concert in Bakersfield on October 26, the Experience returned to TTG to continue recording. Sessions on the 27th were fruitless, as only one untitled take was even considered finished. On October 29, however, the Experience were augmented by Buddy Miles and Lee Michaels. Having carted along a bevy of friends and groupies from the Experience Club in Los Angeles, Hendrix deemed them fit to contribute to the session. With both Mitchell and Miles on drums, Redding on bass and Michaels on organ, the Experience recorded "Electric Church – Red House," a remake of "Red House" in the style of "Voodoo Chile," complete with Hendrix's spoken introduction of the players.

Perhaps the strongest of all the material taped at TTG to date, "Electric Church – Red House" was a recording of considerable interest. Hendrix had regularly voiced his displeasure at Reprise's decision to siphon "Red House" off the U.S. version of *Are You Experienced?* Determined to release the song in America, this version might have been part of the Experience's fourth U.S. release had *Smash Hits* – with the original "Red House" – not been released in July 1969. First scheduled for release on Reprise's unissued 1985 album *Bootleg,* "Electric Church – Red House" has since surfaced on *Variations on a Theme,* a collection featuring no fewer than seven different versions of the song.

While these new songs, most notably "Electric Church – Red House," showed flashes of brilliance, none were considered a worthy successor to "All Along the Watchtower," which had broken into the British top 5 and reached number 20 on the *Billboard* chart – the highest U.S. position ever for an Experience single. As a result, neither Track nor Reprise received new material to release as a follow-up. Little did they know, but they wouldn't receive anything from Hendrix for a long time to come.

November's itinerary brought relief, Jeffery modifying the Experience's tour schedule so that instead of traveling across the country for weeks at a time, they now, with only an occasional exception, played three-day weekends. Concerts West, under the Jeffery-Weiss umbrella, had become so skillful that, with thorough precision, the Experience could remain in New York until the day of the show, fly in and, after one or two local bands had warmed up the crowd, play their set.

With the exception of a jam session at the Record Plant on November 6, the impetus to finish, or at the very least continue working on the group's fourth album, had dulled, the Experience struggling to direct their energies and concentration back into recording. As Mitchell would later describe, they were not three men heading for the same goal.

Regardless of the group's private troubles, the Experience's popularity continued to soar and Michael Jeffery looked straight ahead to new projects. One of the more interesting proposals centered around Hendrix's U.S. television debut, and negotiations began for the Experience to perform on the *Ed Sullivan Show*. "Bob Precht, Ed Sullivan's son-in-law, produced the *Ed Sullivan Show*," recalls Bob Levine. "Sullivan Productions really wanted to have Jimi on. Ed Sullivan had to get him one way or another, so Sullivan, Precht, Jeffery and I sat down to talk. Sullivan wanted to have the Vienna Ballet dance to his music, with Hendrix in front of a big orchestra, done on location in Europe. Jeffery figured out the money he would need and agreed to the concept verbally. He left the meeting to speak to somebody – I don't know who – and when, a day or so later, I told him he was supposed to follow up with Bob Precht he replied, 'We aren't going to do it.' I asked if he had spoken to Jimi and he said, 'No, I am not going to let Hendrix do that. I've got my reasons.' Jimi would have loved to have done it."

One interesting project Jeffery did accept at this time was an invitation from promoter Ron Delsener to speak with

Leonard Bernstein. Delsener wanted to promote "An Electric Thanksgiving" featuring the Experience at the New York Philharmonic on November 28. This was a prestigious offer, as no rock band had ever performed there. With Fernando Valenti and the New York Brass Quintet also engaged, it was agreed that one member of the Experience would perform with them, playing classical music. While Hendrix may have been flattered by the offer, he soured on the idea, recalls Bob Levine, upon learning that Jeffery had helped set it up. Redding simply refused, so it fell to Mitchell, always on the lookout for an interesting musical collaboration, to don a tuxedo and join the New York Brass Quintet for the night.

Although this performance was not professionally recorded, Hendrix was keen to take advantage of the Philharmonic's famed acoustics. Hanley Sound, later to equip Woodstock, was hired in from Boston, bringing huge loudspeakers, normally used in movie theaters, that were four times the size of the Experience's PA.

The concert itself was anticlimactic, but backstage before the show friends threw a small twenty-sixth birthday party for Hendrix. Twenty-four hours earlier – before Hendrix had left for a performance in Providence – there had been a private party for Jimi at the 37th Street office. "We baked a cake for Jimi and everything known to mankind went into it," remembers Kathy Eberth. "The remains of the birthday cake were left on the desk of this very, very straight secretary; when we came back to the office she was typing away and eating the cake, and though acting a little bit strange, was handling it very well. When Joe Head, the chauffeur, came in and said, 'Oh, you're having Jimi's cake! Is this your first trip?' she freaked out, running around the office covering her eyes yelling, 'Kathy, I can't see! I can't see! I'm blind!' Then she ran out of the office into the street, screaming up and down Park Avenue."

After Hendrix had moved into the apartment underneath Jeffery's office apartment on 37th Street, he grew ever closer to Bob Levine and Kathy Eberth, finding in their friendship an effective shield from Jeffery. Hendrix's relationship with Levine and Eberth blurred the line between professional and personal. As close as Levine was to Jeffery, Hendrix felt more comfortable taking Jeffery's directions from Levine, just as he felt more comfortable with Henry Steingarten, considering him his advisor, rather than Steve Weiss, his attorney and de facto business manager. With Eberth, Hendrix had someone inside his management team who seemed sensitive to his creative needs, someone he could articulate things to that he couldn't to Jeffery or even Levine. Eberth's evolving role as a conduit between the two provided Jeffery with one small, yet crucial insight into Hendrix that Chandler had formerly provided: when to push Hendrix, and when to lie back.

Completing their tour in Chicago on December 1, the Experience splintered, with Hendrix remaining in New York and Mitchell and Redding returning to London, spending the weeks before Christmas jamming in the Speakeasy and recording at Olympic. However, things had changed. Just one year after gathering at Olympic to record some of their finest work, Olympic's Studio A was now booked, but this time for Noel Redding's Fat Mattress.

Fat Mattress had received its astounding advance of $150,000 from Atco/Polydor based purely upon Redding's association with Jimi Hendrix. Made up of friends and associates from England, Fat Mattress carried over many of the demos Noel had cut at the Record Plant during the *Electric Ladyland* sessions. The Experience's bassist was committed to Fat Mattress and rallied his new band to complete their debut album.

During December, final negotiations for the purchase of the Generation Club had been completed. With Chandler no longer involved, the acrimonious debate that had shrouded Hendrix's foray into the nightclub business had all but vanished. Attorney Howard Krantz obtained the club's lease from Steve Friedman, a businessman friend. Jeffery was so pleased that Krantz had been able to obtain the lease without incident that he handed him $5,000, an impressive fee at that time, for securing it. Henry Kalow, also from Steingarten, Wedeen & Weiss, drew up the new corporation that confirmed Jeffery and Hendrix as 50-50 partners in the venture.

With the lease secured, the partners were eager to move forward. "At that time, there was a plan to serve drinks in the studio," recalls Henry Kalow. "Although they later abandoned the idea, we made out the application for the liquor license, which required that applicants be finger-printed. The closest precinct house was on 22nd Street. So we caught a cab, Hendrix wearing a red outfit with a bandana, Jeffery dressed in a mod suit and little sunglasses, and me in a Brooks Brothers three-piece suit. We went into the precinct house and the officers looked up at Hendrix as if he had been arrested. I walked up to the desk and asked to have my clients fingerprinted. The officer said, 'What do you want to have them fingerprinted for?' I said that they wanted to obtain a license, the State Liquor Authority had told us to come here and that we had all of the necessary forms. He looked at them, and then at me, and said, 'These guys get a liquor license? Do you really think they have the financial ability?' I said, 'Yes, I think they do.' He looked at me and said, sarcastically, 'Well, counselor, what makes you so sure?' I said, 'Have you ever heard of Jimi Hendrix?' Without looking up he replied, 'Sure.' 'Well, that's him over there.' The officer flipped out. 'That's Jimi Hendrix! Who's the other guy?' 'That's his manager.' In exchange for auto-graphs for his kids I asked if he could get us out of there quickly and so four cops lined up to help him. They couldn't believe that Jimi Hendrix had walked into their precinct house. From treating him like a semibum, he was now a VIP."

Hendrix sailed through the Christmas holidays eager with anticipation, only to be struck down by the news that the Experience would embark on a month-long European tour in January. Just as his batteries had been recharged by the excitement of the nightclub, Jeffery was forcing him to take what could only be described as a backwards step. In Jeffery's mind, the need for additional touring was obvious: the club would need cash, and lots of it. *Electric Ladyland* had been a smash throughout Europe, and in countries such as West Germany, which the Experience had not visited in sixteen months, ticket sales were guaranteed to be brisk. However, touring Europe was nowhere near as profitable as touring the U.S., principally because Jeffery and Weiss were unable to self-promote concerts there, the task falling to Harold Davison. Hendrix's projected nightclub studio gave Jeffery a thinly veiled opportunity to get the band back out on the road, earning money necessary for the studio, a tactic not lost on Gerry Stickells. "It wasn't as if you planned to tour in support of your album," says Stickells. "You just strung together dates to maintain your cash flow. They obviously wanted him to work all the time. Remember, record deals weren't what they are today. Percentages were very small."

Returning to London in January, Hendrix reunited with Mitchell and Redding for an appearance on the *Lulu Show*, a popular BBC entertainment program. Slated to perform two songs, the Experience opened with a spirited, if slightly rusty version of "Voodoo Chile," full of Hendrix's trademark stage exuberance, including a short solo played with his teeth. At its conclusion the camera cut to Lulu, who uttered a blissfully stilted, "That was really nice." Lulu then continued, mentioning *Billboard*'s recognition of the Experience as the top rock band of 1968, before introducing their next song, "The one that really made them in this country and I love to hear them sing it, 'Hey Joe.'" After admonishing the audience to "block your ears," Hendrix launched into a magnificent feedback-drenched introduction before heading into the first verse, after which, his guitar dreadfully out of tune, he looked back to Mitchell with a laugh, moaned, "woah," and tuned up without missing a beat.

Mumbling through the second verse Hendrix suddenly burst out, "I forgot the words," before beginning his solo. It was midway through this that he stepped back to the microphone and brought the Experience to an abrupt halt. "We'd like to stop playing this rubbish and dedicate a song to the Cream, regardless of what group they might be in." All of one mind, the Experience immediately leapt into a muscular rendition of "Sunshine of Your Love." Ignoring the pleas of a desperate floor manager, who was imploring them to stop playing, the Experience continued until, after Jimi announced, "We're getting put off the air!" they finally wound down to a rousing cheer from Lulu's audience.

Back in their dressing room, Chas Chandler, who had stopped by to visit the band, wound up holding furious BBC personnel at bay. The *Lulu Show* appearance had been a tour de force, a rallying of otherwise disparate musicians. No matter how fleeting it may have been, the Experience seemed unified, with all of the verve and irreverence intact that had elevated the group from their contemporaries. While there are musically superior versions of the songs performed that evening, the *Lulu Show* had been a group effort, Hendrix, Mitchell and Redding setting aside personal differences to channel their talents in unison. To their still growing army of followers, the Experience, their beloved outlaws, had done it again, jabbing their thumb into the eye of the staid and pompous BBC. Within the band, the *Lulu Show* appearance had been an attempt to rekindle the former passion between the players. And if their performance perpetuated the outlaw myth, so be it.

It was in Gothenburg, Sweden, on January 8, 1969, only the first date in the European tour, that the briefly renewed unity, already little more than a distant memory, collapsed. In Stockholm on the 9th, the Experience were lifeless and Hendrix openly bored, greeting the crowd by walking on stage and casually tuning up. "We're going to play nothing but oldies-but-baddies tonight because we haven't played for about six weeks," he fibbed. "Hope you don't mind:

we're going to mess around and jam. You won't know the difference anyway." As cold and unemotional as this introduction was, Hendrix then half heartedly tackled "Fire" and "Spanish Castle Magic." After finishing the former he sarcastically remarked, "Thanks for waiting this long"; before lurching into the latter he spoke of its recording, "In 1733, at Benjamin Franklin Studios."

In just two years the group had come full circle and were now three individuals playing alone. Mitch Mitchell seemed the least affected by the turmoil; Redding was also performing well, but without passion. The rejuvenation that Fat Mattress had provided him vanished amid the tension. "Noel was getting frustrated because he wanted to play guitar," recalls Gerry Stickells. "Since there were only a handful of us out on the road, he could only talk to so many people. It isn't like now, where you may have thirty guys traveling with you."

Redding wasn't the only one feeling pressured. In an interview before the concert, Hendrix tried to downplay rumors that the Experience would be breaking up. "It's no definite breakup thing like that. We might work a little less but our records will be better. I get very bored, regardless of how good anyone else is. I'm sure other people might get bored too. I get tired and I can't play the guitar anymore like I want to. I get very frustrated sometimes on stage when we play and I think it's because we are only three pieces. I would like to work with other people too, but that doesn't necessarily mean we have to break the group up." Speaking of his plans for the immediate future, Hendrix grew optimistic. "We are going to settle down and record some nice things, like a single and an album. I plan to have two albums really quick, together, maybe two months apart. The second of these LPs will be called *First Rays of the New Rising Sun*. Every time we come into a town, people come to us looking for answers to tell them, which is a good feeling, but it is very hard to tell them that I have to live the life, witness all the bad scenes and good scenes, so I can say what I found out. Therefore, I am going to get all these words together in nice, heavy songs. Very straightforward songs. Properly."

Back in New York, Michael Jeffery was just as ambitious. Although he had bypassed Ed Sullivan, Jeffery had been surprised by the strength of his offer. If such an interest existed, why not own and produce your own special? Instead of receiving a percentage, why not offer the likes of Sullivan Productions a financial interest in a television special produced independently while retaining ownership of all master recordings associated with the project? Jeffery had long harbored an interest in films and filmmaking. Perhaps the strength of a Jimi Hendrix special would allow him to lobby additional funds necessary to develop non-Hendrix projects. In a burst of shortsighted energy, he arranged for Gold & Goldstein to produce a television special.

Steve Gold, who now managed Eric Burdon, and Jerry Goldstein, whom Jeffery had known through the Visual Thing, his lucrative merchandising company, were funded and dispatched to West Germany to begin filming the Experience on tour. At the very least, Jeffery reasoned, a live album could be realized from the project, and plans to record the group's concert at the Royal Albert Hall in London on February 18 were set in motion. A second concert at the venue was also added, allowing the production crew an additional opportunity to capture the group at their best. Having a live album in tow would also give Jeffery the opportunity to honor the PPX settlement. According to the terms of that agreement, the Experience's next album would be issued by Capitol Records. If a live album could be culled from the February Albert Hall concerts, and released perhaps in early June, Hendrix would have enough time to ready an Experience album of new studio material for Christmas, the industry's peak selling time.

But Jeffery's optimism was premature, as the Experience swayed between good performances and bad. Even the best shows on this European tour paled against the Experience of old. The premise that something, outside of any mercenary intentions, was to come of this tour briefly brightened the morale in the band. However, Hendrix was irked that a creative decision had been made without any consultation. He was bitterly angry because he could not reach Jeffery to discuss his ideas for the production. He had no problem with doing a television special, but he loathed the prospect of another situation where he would be forced to make creative sacrifices due to financial or schedule limitations. Moreover, what was the focus of this special? Where was it going to air? Hendrix had pressing questions regarding basic production matters that would need to be addressed. In a memo to management, he stated that he wanted to choose the engineer who would record the Albert Hall shows. This, Hendrix stressed, was "very important." He also wanted details about the film crew, the expenses they were likely to incur, and how the financial aspects of the TV deal would be broken down. Jeffery may have succeeded in getting the band out on the road earning money again, but the television special, at least in Hendrix's mind, was to be treated just as preciously as the recording of an album. He vowed not to stand for any more creative compromises: as a result, and in this Mitchell and Redding agreed, he treated the project with caution, dubious of Jeffery's intentions.

Gold & Goldstein's cameras filmed a number of concerts, shooting some 90,000 feet of 16mm film; however, the best material seemed to come when off stage. Amid the mass of unreleased footage there are wonderful vignettes of Hendrix playing alone in his hotel room, Hendrix backstage, as well as interviews and impromptu comments.

On stage, the Experience seemed maddeningly lethargic; these concerts were far from today's multimedia events, organized right down to the number of encores. (Hendrix did not believe in encores and rarely gave them. Abe Jacob, who handled live sound engineering for the Experience, once questioned Hendrix about the unspoken policy. "Somebody said to him that when fans want to hear an

encore, they will go out and buy the record. So he remembered that and rarely gave them.") There were *some* musical
highlights on this tour: ferocious renditions of "Come On
(Part 1)" that were even more powerful than the studio cut.
Versions of "I Don't Live Today," which Hendrix would
routinely dedicate to the "American Indian," were especially lively.

Hendrix loathed requests shouted from the audience and,
not unnaturally, the success of "All Along the Watchtower"
made fans expect the Experience to perform the song in
concert. But despite its chart success, it had not been added
to the Experience's live set, a decision that had caused a mild
dispute between Hendrix and Jeffery. In Frankfurt on
January 17, during one of their better performances of the
tour, Hendrix, in an attempt to pacify steady calls for the
song, finally addressed the issue. "There is something we
would like to tell you about that 'Watchtower' scene," he
drawled. At the mention of "Watchtower" the predominantly German-speaking audience roared with approval.
"Wait a minute," he asked them. "We recorded that a year
ago and if you've heard it, we are very glad. But tonight,
we're trying to do a musical thing, okay? That's a single, and
we released it as a single, thank you very much for thinking
about it but I forgot the words, that's what I am trying to
say..." Considering the language barrier, his appeal must
have left the crowd puzzled. There was some truth to his
statement: Hendrix really did have trouble remembering
the song's lyrics and he more or less ignored it until it began
to appear on a semiregular basis as part of the 1970 tour
repertoire.

In West Berlin on January 23, almost a month before their
Albert Hall concerts, the Experience concluded their fifteen-
day European tour. Previous rock concerts held at the city's
Sportspalast had been blighted by random incidents of
violence and the Experience's show was no exception. "Our
agent Dick Katz was there," recalls Gerry Stickells, "and we
were told that if there was any trouble, there would be no

more rock concerts. Frank Zappa, among others, had seen his gear smashed and people that night were trying to do the same to us."

"We were escorted by armed troops with Dobermans to the stage from the dressing room," recalls Abe Jacob. After a lackluster performance, getting out of the venue proved difficult. Brawls erupted and Gerry Stickells and Eric Barrett dodged between fistfights to save the group's gear, and Dick Katz held back the police and attack dogs amid scenes of pure mayhem. It was a fitting finish to a disastrous mini-tour.

As soon as he could, Hendrix returned to New York and busied himself attending to the many details his new enterprise required. Hendrix and Jeffery had agreed on one thing, that Steve Paul's Scene Club was the true model for their nightclub and if their new facility was to become successful they would have to replicate the Scene Club's atmosphere. Their facility had to be one where artists would want to stop by, jam and record – albeit for a fee. And what better way was there to ensure the feel of the Scene Club than to steal its manager?

Jim Marron had managed the Scene Club since 1967, steering it through times of great success, with the Experience, the Doors and other major acts frequently performing showcase gigs and participating in regular late-night jam sessions. The Scene Club was "artist friendly": doorman Danny Blumenauer (who would later follow Marron to Electric Lady Studios, becoming its night manager) would close the door anytime after 2 A.M. if artists such as Hendrix, Stephen Stills or Larry Coryell wished to jam or perform exclusively for friends. Its bathrooms were legendary, the 1960s Webster's definition of decadence.

Fascinated with the success of the Scene, Jeffery had often discussed with Jim Marron his own clubs in Newcastle and Spain. As their friendship had deepened, Jeffery found himself asking Marron to conduct a feasibility study for the once bankrupt nightclub he and Hendrix had purchased. As

Chas Chandler had done before him, Marron injected some cold realism into their visions. "With Jimi being black, he couldn't go into the nightclub business on 8th Street," says Marron. "Eighth Street was mob governed and there were four Italian clubs already there." Jim Marron seized on the studio aspect of the project, suggesting that the feasibility study be based upon the studio, as it now loomed larger than originally conceived. Meeting with Hendrix and Jeffery, Marron was instructed to put together a team of people he could work with. "We are not going to tell you who to use," Jeffery instructed him. "You put the team together. You search the market."

Further dampening the chances of reopening the facility as a nightclub was Hendrix's own exotic reputation. Despite adhering to the bureaucratic procedures, his chances of obtaining a liquor license appeared slim – Hendrix music had come to be associated with burgeoning drug use in America. To many, he was the high priest of the counter-culture, a defiant symbol whose music and style set him apart from his contemporaries. The release of *Electric Lady-land*, the phenomenal success of *Are You Experienced?* and the Experience's extensive U.S. tours had generated a broad base of support and adulation. In addition to the countless letters proposing dates, sex and even marriage, many of his fans mailed him drugs. First addressed care of Reprise Records in California, which sent them on to Jeffery's office on 37th Street in Manhattan, these could contain bizarre assortments of controlled substances. There would be LSD from a fan in Northern California, complete with a short note describing the trip Hendrix would enjoy; peyote from an Indian in Arizona, with elaborate instructions on how to extract the strychnine. Most, with their return addresses written on the envelopes, simply wanted Hendrix to share in their "experiences." Marron was correct in guessing that the prospect of being able to serve drinks was dim.

Because of Marron's background in psychology, Jeffery considered him an intellectual equal, a status he rarely afforded his associates. Marron's circumstances struck a chord: most important, he too had been seduced by the nightclub business, despite many other diverse opportunities for success. These circumstances saw him secure the post over two other competitors, the Record Plant's Gary Kellgren and Chris Stone having lobbied Jeffery intensely. Their facility had become Hendrix's de facto recording base. Jeffery knew that the two had access to financing from Revlon Cosmetics, as well as two Record Plant studios, to which in time, after Hendrix's career had waned, he could laterally transfer from personal management to an executive position within the Record Plant's organization. But Jeffery was also troubled by Hendrix's friendship with Kellgren and paranoid that Kellgren might pull Hendrix to him, forcing a power play. Without the nightclub portion of the facility, what would Hendrix need Jeffery for? What would stop Kellgren and/or Stone from advising Hendrix to sell the lease from the Generation Club and become a partner in an existing Record Plant, or perhaps even a third studio facility? These were troubling questions. Jeffery had seen the relationships that Chas Chandler and then Eddie Kramer had developed with Hendrix – friendships from which he was thoroughly excluded.

Kellgren had remained close to Jimi; in fact, he occasionally dated Faye Pridgeon, one of Hendrix's closest friends. As a result, Kellgren's net worth, despite his immediate access to development money, plummeted in Jeffery's eyes. The manager's tenuous grasp on his star would not allow Kellgren or Stone to become involved.

The only other challenge to Jim Marron's role was short-lived: the trendy downtown venue Max's Kansas City made a pitch to Jeffery that echoed his original concept. By utilizing Max's Kansas City's existing liquor license, a small recording facility could be constructed within the club. As alluring as the offer sounded, Jeffery wanted to retain his club's own liquor license. If Max's were to retain the majority interest in both the liquor license and lease,

Jeffery's power would be severely limited. As a result, this proposal was dismissed quickly.

Marron had come to know Eddie Kramer through the engineer's visits to the Scene Club and was aware that Kramer had left the Record Plant to work independently. Marron invited Kramer to the hollowed shell of the Generation Club where the two discussed the advantages and difficulties of building a full-scale, world-class in-house recording facility. Having decided that Kramer was the man for the job, Marron returned to 37th Street to inform Jeffery of his decision. By chance, Hendrix happened to be in the office. Owing to the European tour in January, Hendrix had been left out of much of the decision making regarding the facility. In his absence, a shift from planning a nightclub with a recording capability to one with a full-fledged studio had taken place. On hearing Marron's decision to hire Eddie Kramer, Jeffery drew pale and huddled with Hendrix. "'We didn't tell you, but we know Eddie Kramer,'" Marron recalls Hendrix telling him. "I asked innocently, 'How do you know him?' He then told me that Kramer had been his engineer since London. I said, 'Oh my God, I had no idea.' They hadn't told me and he hadn't told me. I liked the guy and thought he was the best available for the job. Hendrix was blown away that I came up with Kramer, with whom he had already worked."

Jeffery was not so pleased, speaking of the difficulties that had arisen during the Eire Apparent sessions. But, recalls Marron, "Hendrix gave the matter thought and decided there hadn't been anything he couldn't overcome." With that, Hendrix pushed the ball back to Jeffery, clearly putting him into a bind. Not wanting to deny Marron, and especially Hendrix, the right to hire Kramer, Jeffery was stymied.

By smashing such coalitions, Jeffery had always been able to keep at bay moves to impinge upon his position with Hendrix. It was a strategy he had perfected with the Animals. Mitch Mitchell and Noel Redding, while essential to the musical success of the Experience, were powerless against Jeffery. Chas Chandler had been a real obstacle but, though it had taken some time, Jeffery had been able to dispose of him too. Now that the facility was to become a first-rate recording studio, Hendrix's interest was piqued. By shunting Kellgren and Stone, Jeffery had dodged a further bullet, hoping that any audio considerations be handled by consultants like Phil Ramone, whom both Jeffery and Marron had interviewed. By keeping such people, as Jeffery described, "out of the family, the inner circle," no serious threat could be mounted against him.

Until Marron submitted his decision to hire Kramer, Hendrix had exhibited only a detached enthusiasm about the entire project. His own experiences with Jeffery had fostered a wait and see attitude, regardless how ambitious the project be. But with Kramer now on board, the project became more personal. He now had an ally.

Another conflict arose in that, while Kramer had been a salaried staffer at both Olympic and at the Record Plant, now Jeffery would have to directly compensate him as a Hendrix employee. "I always had the feeling," recalls Jim Marron, "that half of the problem between the two men was chemistry." Jeffery was vehemently against granting any royalty points to Kramer, vowing to Marron that he "would fight Kramer to his grave on points." "And they did," says Marron. "Jeffery died and Kramer never got his points." Anyway, Kramer knew Hendrix wanted to produce his own recordings and harbored no reservations about it. Having been close to both Hendrix and Chandler, he knew how important it was for Jimi to direct his own sessions and their relationship had thrived on the free exchange of ideas, with mutual respect their only guideline.

One of the clubs that had impressed both Hendrix and Jeffery was Cerebrum, a popular new venue in SoHo. Designed by young architect John Storyk, Cerebrum soon became the rage, its layout and who's who list of patrons seizing the attention of both *Time* and *Life* magazines.

Remembers Storyk, "Cerebrum was a club for the senses. It was a three-dimension, multimedia show that you walked into." But in spite of the raves, Cerebrum was destined for failure. "It had a short life because of the Mob," recalls Storyk. "They couldn't figure out how to get money from us, because we weren't selling liquor or cigarettes, so one day they broke the windows and thoroughly trashed the place. Without adequate insurance, that just did us in."

Jeffery instructed Jim Marron to find the architect who had designed Cerebrum, and after a brief meeting with Jeffery, Marron and Hendrix, Storyk was hired to design a club that would incorporate recording capabilities. Over the next few weeks, as Storyk went about his work, he was struck by Hendrix's low-key demeanor. "I think Michael Jeffery was really building the club with very little input from Jimi," he says. "If Hendrix cared about any of this stuff, he really didn't say it to too many people. He was an intuitive type of guy and made decisions about people like he played his guitar. He'd say, 'I'm sure it will be just fine...'"

The night of Sunday, February 23, 1969, the day before Storyk was to present his final drawings, he received a phone call from Jim Marron. "Marron said, 'No club, it's not going to be a club.' I was heartbroken, I thought my whole career was gone." But Marron reassured Storyk that Jeffery and Hendrix still wished to retain him, only what they now wanted was a design for a full-fledged studio. Eddie Kramer was soon assigned to Storyk to help prepare the new drawings. "Very few people realize it," remembers Storyk, "but this studio was an accident. Basically, I believe it was Kramer catching Hendrix on an off moment."

Recognizing John Storyk's absence of experience in building recording studios, Marron also hired Bob Hansen, a noted acoustical engineer, to tutor Storyk and work with Kramer during construction. After intense meetings with Kramer and Hansen, Storyk set about designing what would come to be Electric Lady Studios.

Kept abreast of his studio's progress, Hendrix left for London. Attending to the needs of his new facility had distracted him from Experience business. The trio had scattered after the January European tour and he knew they would be rusty. Only Hendrix himself had remained in New York, producing and recording tracks at the Record Plant with the Buddy Miles Express.

On February 17, Hendrix phoned Chas Chandler. "I had already parted company and come back to England," his erstwhile co-manager recalls, "when they came over for the Albert Hall concerts. I was going there to say hello but Jimi rang me up the night before and asked if I would come down, as he was thoroughly aggravated with the entire affair. When I arrived for rehearsals and sound checks, Hendrix was having trouble with feedback through his amplifiers and there was also interference in the recording equipment. It was a shambles. I ended up running both shows for him, trying to get everything right. I hadn't been 'hired,' I was there to help out friends."

Existing tapes of the February 18 rehearsal support Chandler's recollection, as technical problems certainly did plague the crew. In Jeffery's absence, a tense power struggle emerged over who was in charge of the proceedings. Jerry Goldstein, Steve Gold's partner in Far Out Productions, had designated himself producer for the two shows. Jeffery, in an effort to pacify Hendrix's repeated requests to choose his own production staff, substituted Glyn Johns, sending him to Albert Hall to supervise the engineering. Hendrix then superseded them both, installing Chandler amid the fray as "supervisor." Hendrix and Johns clashed, and Johns's involvement concluded during the February 18 afternoon sound check. On the other hand, Chandler had long known both Gold and Goldstein and had no problem working with either. He was also helped by the fact that no one wished to upset the man Hendrix had personally designated to salvage the recordings. The feedback problems were traced to poor grounding and the absence of the Experience's battered but road-tested sound systems. "We used a Charlie Wadkins/ WEM sound system in there," recalls Abe Jacob, "because we hadn't taken our stuff over to England. We used a wall of sand-filled speaker cabinets, large columns filled with sand for damping."

Despite working feverishly throughout the afternoon of the 18th, the audio technicians were unable to guarantee that the feedback that had plagued the sound checks would not reappear in the concert proper. So it was decided that a separate sound system would be installed for recording purposes, utilizing two feeds (rather than the traditional one) in which "splitters" would send the sound to both the house and also a mobile recording truck. It's for this reason that Hendrix sings into the trio of microphones seen in the film and photos of the shows.

After opening sets by Soft Machine and Traffic, the Experience strode to the stage and launched into a lengthy rendition of "Tax Free." Fifteen months had passed since the Experience's last London concerts and the sold-out audience was treated to a far more sophisticated Jimi Hendrix than that of 1967, a man now content to shun many of his trademark stage moves. While his performance showcased the progress he had made on guitar, the Experience seemed reduced to acting as support group for a virtuoso. There was to be no "Sgt. Pepper" or "Wild Thing" on this night, as the Experience stood stock-still and stone-faced, without a visible trace of emotion, almost as if unaware of one another's presence.

Hendrix developed a number of brilliant themes within "Tax Free," but his free-form playing came at the expense of Mitchell and Redding, reducing his potent sidemen to mere timekeepers. The Experience then barreled through unconvincing versions of "Fire," "Hear My Train A Comin'" and "Foxey Lady" without a trace of conviction. Midway through "Spanish Castle Magic," Hendrix happened upon the riff for "Message to Love." Much to their credit, Mitchell and Redding allowed him to develop the pattern, quickly falling in behind, but the cohesion was short-lived; indeed, on returning to the trademark riff in "Spanish Castle Magic," the three were unable to bring the number to a close effectively.

Regardless of their lack of preparation, many people, including Chas Chandler, felt that there was little excuse for such a listless performance. "That was a lousy show," he recalls, "among the worst I had ever seen Jimi play. And it wasn't his fault, it was Mitch and Noel's. They were lifeless: Mitchell's timing seemed totally off, he was coming in late so often it seemed like he was out of his brain, and Redding was just trying to show how awkward he could be. It truly was one of the worst shows I had ever seen. Up until that point I had been a supporter of the group, because I thought that they made for a good unit. Now I felt it was time they got thrown out. If I had still been in charge, they would have been sacked the next day. Mitch and Noel wouldn't have done the second show, that would have been the end of it."

Determined not to duplicate the disastrous opening night, additional Experience rehearsals were scheduled. Considering the money invested in the project to date, it was imperative that *something* be salvaged from these Albert Hall performances. Following sets by Fat Mattress and Van Der Graaf Generator, the Experience rallied once more. The second show was a great Hendrix concert but one totally unlike past triumphs such as those at Monterey or the Saville Theatre. Predominantly abandoning his traditional stage routines, Hendrix opted to perform his own three blues masterworks, "Hear My Train A Comin'," "Red House" and a stellar version of "Bleeding Heart." With the house lights turned up full at the request of the filmmakers, the Royal Albert Hall took on the presence of a recording studio, and even though there was a large live audience present, it sat quietly and offered polite applause, not the fighting or stage crashing that had marred Experience concerts from Texas to West Berlin.

This show's versions of "Little Wing" and "Voodoo Child

(Slight Return)" (both included on the 1972 Reprise album *In the West*) ranked among Hendrix's finest, as did "Foxey Lady," delivered with great gusto. "Lover Man" and "Stone Free" were given new arrangements, allowing Hendrix space to improvise brilliantly. "Fire" was a combination of the old and new Experience, Redding's bass racing at full volume while Hendrix unleashed a lightning fast solo over Mitchell's furious accompaniment.

At the conclusion of "Voodoo Chile," the Experience provided a rare treat: an encore, with percussionist Rocki Dzidzornu, along with Dave Mason and Chris Wood from Traffic, joining them for a soulful version of "Room Full of Mirrors," Hendrix convincingly singing the few verses he had written before the song disintegrated into a loose jam with Mason and Hendrix trading riffs. Before concluding the show, this temporarily expanded Experience managed a heavy-handed "Purple Haze" complete with a bit of nostalgic amp smashing by the master himself.

As brilliant as this second Albert Hall performance had been, the vitality so prevalent at Monterey now seemed cold and almost unemotional. Monterey had embodied a spirit, an energy now no longer visible. Here, the Experience were making a focused attempt to recapture their unity, whereas at Monterey the combination of talent and nervous energy had fused to create a feeling of sheer excitement – felt both by the band and by the audience. At Albert Hall, Hendrix showcased his unparalleled talent as a musician and composer, his ability now light-years ahead of the standards he himself had set at Monterey, but now, more than ever before, the triumph was his alone, a passionless victory won with as little interaction from Mitchell and Redding as necessary. Even the Winterland shows of the previous October, the first obvious sign of trouble within the ranks, were masked by a giddy, stoned exuberance. At the Royal Albert Hall – during both performances – the trio had barely acknowledged one another's existence.

# 11 INNOCENCE LOST

> *"For three years, we've been working non-stop. That's a lot of physical and emotional strain. It's the strain of the moral obligation to keep going even when you don't feel you can even manage one more show. Maybe I'll never get to take that break; all I know is that I'm thinking about it most of the time now, and that doesn't help create the right mood."*
>
> —Jimi Hendrix

**J**ust days after the final Royal Albert Hall concert, Hendrix returned to New York and continued work with the Buddy Miles Express, having agreed with Miles that he would produce the band's forthcoming album for Mercury Records. While some work had been accomplished at the Record Plant in February, most notably "I Can See," a Miles original recorded and mixed February 11, 1969, the finished master was soon due, and Hendrix and the Express feverishly resumed work, though no deadline could stop Hendrix stepping out from behind the recording console to jam with the band.

The additional components the Express offered him, chiefly horns, second guitar and Miles's own fatback drumming, made for some interesting recordings. As was often the case with Hendrix jamming – certainly sessions where tape was rolling – there was always a root or specific pattern to his playing. His guitar, be it rhythm or lead, would dictate where his accompaniment should follow.

All the while, Hendrix continued his quest to enlarge his own sound, booking a solo session at the Record Plant on March 18. Informed that the studio had now installed a twenty-four-track machine, Hendrix recorded a series of solo demos. "We had Ampex deliver us one of the first twenty-four-track machines available," recalls Tony Bongiovi. "It was really a sixteen-track unit with a separate set of electronics alongside of it."

With Bongiovi engineering, Hendrix recorded a version of "Star Spangled Banner." Working quickly, he filled all of the tape's twenty-four available tracks with overdubs of different effects. Despite its considerable promise, however, this particular arrangement of "Star Spangled Banner" never progressed past the demo stage during Hendrix's lifetime. "It was not," recalls Eddie Kramer, "among the songs we were considering part of his next album. I did mix the track at Electric Lady, but only after Jimi had died, as part of *Rainbow Bridge*." One of the more intriguing post-humously issued tracks, many of the frenetic, synthesizer-like sounds Hendrix created in the studio were vastly unlike any known live version. As with the majority of his own compositions, "Star Spangled Banner" developed over time, from its origins as a clumsy solo within "Purple Haze," often out of key and tune, through to his definitive version at Woodstock. "Star Spangled Banner" remained an integral part of Experience performances from 1968 to 1970.

As plans for a large American tour were being mounted, Hendrix concentrated on writing new material and working with the Buddy Miles Express. Hanging out with Miles and the Allen twins loosened Hendrix up a few notches. "Jimi loved to party and get laid," recalls Albert Allen. "We would go to after-hour clubs, night spots uptown, parties at hotels or just spend money shopping. He loved to do that."

Bob Levine would usually be the first to know how successful Hendrix's parties had been, as he dealt with irate hotel managers, building supervisors and the like. Despite his own apartment on 37th Street, Hendrix often stayed in hotels while in New York. The Elysee and Navarro were frequent victims of his gala celebrations; on one notable occasion, one of Hendrix's guests became unmanageable, taking an axe and trashing his room, bringing the party to an abrupt close. After accountant Michael Hecht debited his account to pay for the damages, Hendrix was once again a valued customer.

Preceded by his reputation as the wildman of pop, whose sordid offstage life was just as wild as his dynamic onstage gyrations, those who knew the man well could instantly recognize the dichotomy between Hendrix the experience and Hendrix the person. He was a fascinating study, an intensely private individual who rarely offered his closest associates even a glimpse inside the real person. "Nobody knew the real Jimi Hendrix," recalls Bob Levine, "because he wouldn't allow you to go that deep." As hard as Michael Jeffery worked to create the aura of mystique about Jimi, the part was a natural one for Hendrix. He lived his life shrouded in it.

"His philosophies were often abstruse and not easily grasped," explains Eddie Kramer. "There was a closeness between us, as I was able to understand and interpret his needs, his music and the sounds he was driving at, but I don't think anyone truly knew him."

"I had great respect for the man," recalls Leon Dicker. "Having both spent time in the military, we often swapped stories. Although the situation was always friendly and comfortable, Jimi only let you get so close before he would politely shift or change the subject altogether."

Hendrix's multifaceted personality also kept associates guessing. Although they had been introduced during the PPX trial, Mrs. Steingarten was eager to see socially her husband Henry's famous client and extended a dinner invitation. Recalls Bob Levine: "Henry arranged for the entourage to be picked up and escorted to his house. 'Let's do it,' Jimi told me. 'Why not have a nice dinner?' The Steingartens lived in a beautiful mansion with a long dinner table lit by candelabra. We were sitting having dinner, exchanging small talk, when, all of a sudden, out of the clear blue sky, Jimi's sense of humor came about him and he started giggling about something. From that moment on we lost control, having dessert in total hysterics. And what did Hendrix do? As the dessert was being cleared away, he got on the table and started to boogie, sending the silverware and plates flying. On the one hand Mrs. Steingarten was horrified; on the other hand she was acting like, 'Well, why not?' I was looking only at her – I couldn't bear to look at Jimi – and she was staring at him, mortified, her mouth gaping wide, trying to say, 'Why not?' before fainting. By this time, Jimi was playing air guitar, singing *and* dancing on the table. After we left that night, we never heard of the incident again."

Although the Record Plant's new twenty-four-track room was booked solid, Hendrix was hot to record, so instead he checked into Ohlmstead Studios, an eight-track facility. Apart from taping an alternate version of "The Train" on April 2 with Buddy and the Express, Hendrix recorded with his first all-black trio, essentially a cut-down version of the Express that featured Miles on drums and Billy Rich on bass. A number of demos were attempted with this lineup, including another attempt at "Midnight Lightning" on April 3 and "Trash Man" on the 4th.

From Ohlmstead, Hendrix returned to the Record Plant

and with April 11 – the first date of the Experience's upcoming tour – fast approaching, Mitch Mitchell and Noel Redding had returned and the line between recording with Miles and Rich, his "Band of Gypsys," and finishing his fourth Experience album blurred.

Although he had been unable to finish any tracks of late, Hendrix continued to record a torrent of demos of songs he had recently written. On April 6 and 7, early versions of "Lullaby for the Summer" and "Ships Passing in the Night" were committed to tape. But, as the tape boxes indicated, "no finals" were completed, another two compositions joining his growing pile of uncompleted work.

The lack of technical and organizational support available to Hendrix while he created in the studio no doubt limited his progress and forced him to accept creative compromises. Gary Kellgren, the one other engineer deemed capable of organizing and operating on Hendrix's level, had faded from the scene, and his fleeting romance with Faye Pridgeon didn't exactly endear him to Devon Wilson, now regularly accompanying Hendrix to sessions; indeed they had clashed on more than one occasion. Long after Kellgren and Pridgeon had parted company, he and Devon were still not close. Another problem with Kellgren was due to the fantastic success of the Record Plant. When he wasn't in California, he tended to work days, not Hendrix's preferred twelve- to sixteen-hour overnight sessions. Privately, Kellgren was also somewhat peeved that Michael Jeffery had chosen Jim Marron to oversee Jimi's new studio, and Eddie Kramer its chief engineer. With Kramer and Kellgren thus occupied, and Chandler out of the picture, Hendrix was left without the necessary creative force behind the board to execute his ideas. Over time, this would lead to a marked drop in quality opportunities to develop his exciting new compositions.

While Hendrix was preoccupied with recording, Michael Jeffery and Steve Weiss summoned their resources to ensure

that the imminent tour would be the most profitable string
of self-promoted personal appearances rock n' roll had ever
witnessed. To ensure that the large-venue successes Concerts West had enjoyed would extend right across the States,
Weiss recruited Vanilla Fudge manager Phil Basile and,
with booking agent Ron Terry, devised a new plan. "Concerts West sounded too much like California," Terry recalls.
"What I had to do was make it sound bigger. So I went back
to Les Smith [Terry's original investor] and said, 'Les, we're
going to branch out, start a second company and make the
network bigger: we're going to form a company called
Concerts East.'" The Weiss/Terry/Hulett team had been
instrumental to Concerts West's initial acceptance; now
Weiss wanted to develop an East Coast version that shared
the company's name, but little else.

While Phil Basile headed Concerts East, he was not to be
involved with Concerts West. This was a particularly sensitive matter to Les Smith, whose fortune had been predominantly built through the SP&S Radio chain. Smith praised
Terry's ingenuity, but still refused any affiliation with
either Basile or Concerts East.

Enlarging Phil Basile's role set up a power struggle with
an unsuspecting Tom Hulett and Concerts West. "We had
put this tour on sale," recalls Hulett. "L.A. Forum, Oakland
Coliseum, Dallas, Houston and a bunch of other dates, then
I got a phone call from Steve Weiss. He said, 'Tom. We've got
a problem.' Weiss told me that Michael Jeffery had not
approved the dates. Meanwhile, on good faith, we had put
up money for deposits. I think I already had 8,000 seats sold
at the Forum, and the Oakland Coliseum was already half
sold. So I got on a plane and went to New York without
announcing myself – I had never been there in my life – and
I called Steve Weiss's office and told him I wanted to meet
him. I walked in this room and there with Steve were Phil
Basile, Jeffery, Bob Levine and Ron Terry. The problem, I
was told, was that other promoters had the cities and dates

we had. Even though Concerts West had gone on sale with some of the dates, I told them that I was prepared to refund all of the money to the public and that they could do as they want. I went back to the New York Hilton and by the time I got there there was a page for me. It was them, so I went back and we sat down and had a better meeting. At that point, I think I got some respect, which I didn't have before. They probably thought we were some kids out of Seattle. We started doing our business without partners, we didn't take in partners, we did our job and we did it well. At that point, Phil Basile started calling his company Concerts East and he was going to get Boston, New York and that area of the country."

Hulett's refusal to cave in won him points but, as Bob Levine recalls, Concerts West had already proven their value to the organization. "Concerts West knew where their bread was buttered. They took care of Jimi and made sure his needs were met. Remember, those gigs were self-promoted, so Jimi usually came out with 85 percent of the money." Hulett himself admitted that making Hendrix feel at ease was top priority. "Jimi was not an easy guy to promote and I don't think he wanted to work for a lot of people, but if he felt comfortable he would work with you. He liked to see familiar faces." Ron Terry echoes that same sentiment. "He would always ask me why we needed particular people, like 'What exactly does that person do for me?'"

As hard as touring was, Hendrix did recognize that Concerts West looked after his needs, requesting them to Jeffery. Hulett's company deserved his loyalty: they had never missed the Experience at airports or forgotten to have food backstage (of special importance to a black American touring the South in the late 1960s), nor sold seats normally reserved for Abe Jacobs to mix the group's sound properly. Hulett and Concerts West had also made the 90-10 net profit split work successfully. It had been Weiss himself who, in the latter half of 1968, had asked Hulett to find more dates to promote the Experience.

With the roles of Concerts East and West now defined, Steve Weiss's function within the organization continued to expand, emerging as de facto business manager – as well as attorney – for both Hendrix and Jeffery. Considering the size of the venues on the itinerary, the profit potential was staggering; to maximize the potential return, efforts were made to unify all advertising and merchandising for the tour. Jerry Goldstein's company the Visual Thing created a lavish tour book to be sold at each venue. *Electric Church*, a title coined by Hendrix, was a stylish, thirteen-page collection of photos by noted photographer Ron Raffaelli. Posters of Hendrix and the Experience – including one of Hendrix standing with two topless female admirers – were sold at each concert, providing Are You Experienced Ltd. with a lucrative return. Sales of posters had always been strong at Hendrix's concerts but varied considerably from venue to venue, depending on the location of the vendors and the cooperation from local promoters. Now, with every date on the spring tour self-promoted, Concerts East and West had complete control over merchandising sales.

In light of the vast sums of money the Experience stood to earn, a decision was made to send Arthur Johnson, an accountant from Michael Hecht's office, on tour with the band to make sure that all funds were received and properly handled. While there had been some rumblings about financial impropriety during the 1968 tour, having an accountant on the road to help the trusted Gerry Stickells had actually come at the request of Michael Jeffery.

Gerry Stickells had fast become one of the key players in the entire organization. As with most who toiled for Jimi Hendrix, Stickells far and away exceeded his basic responsibilities, in his instance those of a road manager, and his dedication and loyalty were not lost on anyone within the extended Hendrix management team. Jeffery had total faith in Stickells, trusting him not only with the safety of his artist, but also with the enormous sums of cash the Experience generated on the road. While their relationship never strayed far from that of employee and boss, there was an unspoken bond between the two Britons. That same relationship lost him none of the trust and respect of all three members of the Experience, who came to rely on Stickells for everything from wake-up calls in hotel rooms to paying out petty cash for spending on the road. Hulett, Terry, Levine and others all vouch for Gerry Stickells as a soldier who took care of business and rarely complained.

The cash avalanche that the coming spring tour promised was to be fed into the "money network" that accountant Michael Hecht had structured following the dissolution of Yameta. "On the 1968 U.S. tour," recalls Hecht, "Stickells would settle at the box office after every Experience performance, and use that money to pay bills. On his arrival in New York he would walk into our office with suitcases and paper bags full of money. We would do the accountings and then physically take the money down to the Franklin Bank. They would have countless slips of paper for receipts but would always be close to $10,000 short. Whatever the excuse, it just wouldn't add up. It was an impossible way to work. But when we sent Arthur Johnson on the road with them, he would take each concert's receipts, buy a bank check the next day and then send the bank check back. Stickells had said that he didn't want the sole responsibility of carrying so much cash while handling all of his other duties and I don't blame him: the people on the road were crazy and had crazy demands. Their inability to settle for anything less than what *they* wanted at the moment made this new arrangement the best that could be done."

Reducing the number of different promoters further reduced Stickells's burden, recalls Concerts West's Tom Hulett. "Gerry and I would settle at the box office. That money would go straight to Steingarten, Wedeen & Weiss minus our 10 percent after expenses – and we would cut the best building rental and advertising deals we could. It was great for everybody."

As Concerts East was to promote the majority of concerts on this blockbuster tour, it too made every effort to reduce potential expenses. Larry Vaughan, who worked for Ron Terry and Phil Basile, recalls traveling to the Philadelphia Spectrum with Steingarten, Wedeen & Weiss attorney Henry Kalow just to negotiate the best possible building rental agreement. Such fastidious attention to detail became the example rather than the exception for Jeffery's fiercely independent, extended management team.

At the same time, Michael Hecht attempted to provide Hendrix, at his own request, with more accurate accountings of his expenses. While generous to a fault, Hendrix was far more aware of his finances than most give him credit for today. He had a personal checking account, did his own shopping and while he often may have spent money unwisely, it was his money – and ultimately his decision to do so. In the memos with which he peppered his management, Hendrix's mildly frustrated tone was clearly evident. "TV specials should be looked into," he instructed in one such missive. "If not now, soon. We should have details on deals that we may be able to make [if any] and soon. I would like to see [my] personal accounts on expenses [as close as possible] to the present, also on personal rough net figures. I know they should be able to take at least five or ten minutes today and reply over the phone or by messenger service in an envelope."

In an April 17, 1969, memo to his management, Hendrix requested account balances for Bella Godiva, Are You Experienced? Ltd. and current balances for Electric Lady Inc., his studio project. The cash-management system that Hecht had devised required him – or any employee Jimi requested to withdraw money for him – to sign a withdrawal sheet. But, as imposing as this formality may seem, it did not, stresses Bob Levine, keep Hendrix from his money. "I never saw a problem for Jimi to get money within reason. If he had it in the bank, Michael Hecht would give it to him. He just had to ask for it and sign a receipt. These were required because Jimi wanted to know exactly where his money was and where it went. He accepted the system because Hecht had come recommended by Henry Steingarten, whose word he trusted as honest and proper."

With all of the necessary business concerns in place, Hendrix, Mitchell and Redding again re-formed the Experience. Hendrix's relationship with Redding had worsened over time; Noel's absence had not made Jimi's heart grow fonder; indeed his own work with the Buddy Miles Express had fostered a sense of liberty. Mitch Mitchell continued unscathed, emerging as Hendrix's sole musical link to his past. Despite his ever-increasing visibility with Hendrix, Buddy Miles was not being considered as Mitchell's replacement. Miles and his Express, with considerable assistance from Hendrix, were still busy trying to establish their own following.

On April 11, the Experience's tour got off to a strong start with a sell-out show in Raleigh, North Carolina. Then after their concert at the Philadelphia Spectrum on the 12th, the Experience returned to the Record Plant as a unit. But the session was uneventful, work being restricted to improving the best take of "Ships Passing in the Night," which had been recorded April 7. Based on the full two tape reels of jamming it seems that the Experience returned to the studio to become reacquainted rather than make real progress toward finishing their fourth album. With the tour due to resume in Memphis on April 18, the Experience reentered the Record Plant on the 14th and 15th, but again, these sessions yielded only jam sessions. On the 16th, in an attempt to tighten up the band, the Experience held a formal rehearsal. The next day, with demolition of the Generation Club well under way, Hendrix stopped by his future studio with Michael Jeffery for a progress report.

Even those outside of rock n' roll couldn't help but notice Hendrix's upward-spiraling popularity and influence. Recalls Bob Levine, "Ron Ziegler, press secretary for the White House, called us up personally. He wanted to ask Jimi if he would come to the White House, not to perform but to meet with President Nixon for a fireside chat. Ziegler told me that the President wanted to hold a youth conference and felt that Hendrix would give him a better grip on the counterculture. Jeffery flatly turned him down. He didn't even tell Jimi about it."

"I was also there when the call from the White House came," recalls Kathy Eberth. "I told Jimi. He wanted to go have dinner at the White House – the conference didn't mean much to him but he did want to go to the White House and see how it looked." Jeffery, according to both Eberth and Levine, never offered the slightest reason for dismissing the invitation.

Jeffery's political leanings, though he remained only slightly less apolitical than Hendrix, were fascinating nonetheless. The only hint of any political affiliation came from his occasional relationship with radicals Jerry Rubin, Abbie Hoffman and Tom Hayden. Jeffery's friendship with Hoffman seemed motivated by status, a calculated attempt to be hip. Considering Jeffery's unflinchingly capitalist business standards, the relationship seemed curious. On the other hand, "Ignore the establishment," Jeffery would implore Leon Dicker. In the entertainment business, the "establishment" represented the status quo. Throughout his variety of schemes, Jeffery looked to buck a system he felt poised and ready to thwart his ideas. Having surrounded himself with the likes of Steve Weiss, who shared his tenacity, one can perhaps understand Jeffery's desire to align himself with those who shared his contempt and distrust of authority.

Hoffman and his crew also tapped, if unknowingly, into

Jeffery's vanity; having beaten down his competition and alienated the very artists whose careers he managed, he was lonely in his success. Aside from girlfriends, Jeffery had few close friends who shared both his fervor and respected his considerable achievements. "Hoffman felt he could tap Jeffery for money," recalls Gerry Stickells. "And as a result, Michael was on the fringes of various stunts Hoffman's crew staged. I always felt Jeffery lived with a fear of getting old and I think he believed that aligning with movements such as these would keep him young. Whether their relationship was superficial or not I don't know, but as Hoffman's star diminished, Jeffery cast him aside and had little to do with him."

In Memphis on April 18, the Experience arrived late for their appearance and gave a less than inspired performance, while the next night, in Houston, the trio were once again pitted against local authorities. Initially, officials at the Sam Houston Coliseum refused to allow the sale of the Experience's notorious nude poster, featuring the trio flanked by two topless blondes. Later, Hendrix's rendition of the "Star Spangled Banner" incited the local police. "Jimi used to do 'Star Spangled Banner' near the end of every show," recalls Ron Terry. "But when we did it in Houston – a few minutes past our 11 P.M. curfew – the cops got weird. As he was playing the anthem a cop came over and pushed me up against a wall, telling me to instruct them to stop. I said, 'Hey, he can't stop right in the middle of a song! Don't worry about it …' We got through that night but the vibes backstage after the show were terrible. We didn't know if we were going to get out of there."

Things slid from bad to worse in Dallas. Upon arrival, Hendrix's entourage were denied rooms at the Cabana Motor Hotel. Having secured reservations in advance, Gerry Stickells was stunned when a hotel clerk told him the hotel was fully booked. His written confirmation in hand, he demanded to see the manager. Informed that he did not work weekends, Stickells asked the clerk to put in writing what he had just been told. The clerk refused, claiming that he could neither read nor write. Undaunted, Stickells set off and soon found the manager, who happened to live on the premises. The Experience were finally allowed entrance to their rooms after Stickells had explained that the group had stayed at the hotel in the past, had always paid their bills and had never caused any trouble. "It was just a really shitty deal," he later complained to a local reporter. "They said that there was a convention there and they were afraid of having freaks wandering through the place."

Later that evening at the Memorial Auditorium, Hendrix and Ron Terry were confronted by five imposing Texans blocking their dressing room doorway. Recalls Ron Terry, "The leader got up in my face and said, 'You running this thing?' Jimi was standing right next to me but this guy didn't address him in any way. He just asked me again and I said, 'I guess ... I don't know.' He said, 'Well, you tell that fucking nigger if he plays "Star Spangled Banner" in this hall tonight he won't live to get out of the building.' I was stunned, replying, 'Come on, get serious!' 'Did you hear what I said? No one does that in Dallas, Texas, and lives to tell about it. We'll start a riot, and if he don't make it out of the building, that's just the way it fucking goes.'"

The confrontation scared both men. "Is this real?" Hendrix asked Terry. "I think we really had better think about this," was Terry's reply. Despite the threats, though, the Experience *did* perform "Star Spangled Banner." As they had done so often in the past, the Experience rose to the challenge and, starting the night with "Stone Free," staged a tremendous show. It had taken a personal crisis, but passion, long the mark of the band's classic performances, raged throughout their entire sixty-minute set. Each number was delivered with vitality and conviction, and none of the inertia that had dissipated the group's power over the previous few months. At least on this night, unity

– the silent yet crucial intangible of the band's chemistry – truly stood for something.

Leaving Dallas behind, the Experience returned to New York and time was booked at the Record Plant to continue recording – though, once again, these were not the structured sessions as at Olympic or even in earlier sessions at Record Plant. There had still been no official announcement that Hendrix was working with Buddy Miles, and Jimi remained hidden behind his role as producer. With Eddie Kramer now committed full-time to the construction of Electric Lady Studios, Hendrix utilized available Record Plant staff engineers at random. A number of songs were cut during the next week, including early versions of "Bleeding Heart," additional remakes of "Room Full of Mirrors," a hybrid version of "Freedom" called "Crash Landing" and a funky, uptempo remake of Muddy Waters's "Mannish Boy." Despite the considerable promise – even in their demo form – evident in songs such as "Bleeding Heart" and "Room Full of Mirrors," Hendrix seemed unable to pull the tracks together with any degree of focus. Though sessions concluded on April 24, Hendrix would return as soon as his schedule allowed.

The April 26, 1969, Los Angeles Forum concert was a watershed for both the band and its extended management team. "Hendrix really got up for the Forum and the Oakland Coliseum," recalls Tom Hulett. "I had walked into Jack Kent Cooke's office [owner of the Forum] and said, 'I would like to rent your building.' 'For who?' he replied. 'Jimi Hendrix,' I said. Perplexed, Cooke said, 'Who's Jimi Hendrix?' We made a deal, drew up a budget and sent it back to Steve Weiss. We had the Forum."

Noted live music engineer Wally Heider was again summoned to record the Experience's performance, and for the first time in a major venue the Experience performed through an elevated PA. "Hanging sound," as it is now commonly known, was the result of an effort to maintain quality standards as venue sizes increased.

One of Hendrix's suggestions to improve the show included a new opening act. One night after a concert both he and booking agent Ron Terry stopped by a club featuring the Chicago Transit Authority, a new band from Chicago. Jimi was taken with their sound and especially that of guitarist Terry Kath, instructing Ron Terry to somehow conscript them as his opening act. As a result, CTA's debut show opening for the Experience was at the highly prestigious L.A. Forum.

Despite all of the preconcert buildup conducted in their honor, the Experience were unable to follow their brilliant performance in Dallas with an even stronger effort in Los Angeles. While their exuberant performance thrilled the sold-out Forum, they were upstaged by a hostile and predominantly stoned crowd. Surprisingly, the root of the problem didn't involve the Experience, rather the Forum's security crew and hordes of fans intent upon rushing the stage. The start of the show was delayed as the crowd was ordered to be seated, but as soon as the Experience hit the stage the crowd surged to the lip of the dais in an attempt to get closer to Jimi, only to be pushed back by police and security forces. The problem peaked at the close of "I Don't Live Today," when the crowd's fury was reaching bedlam-like proportions. "Why don't you all sit down!" Redding barked to little avail. Hendrix then tried a personal appeal: "Listen, we understand how you feel. We want to do the same thing to you, rush up to you and all that, but listen to the sounds. We're trying to play." Pointing to the security officers now crowding the stage, Hendrix also remarked, "We don't want all these jokers up on stage with us." By this point, the house lights had been raised and the noise of taunts, insults and pleas to sit down were reverberating throughout the arena. Addressing one of the problem's root causes, Hendrix spoke again. "C'mon, let's act like we have some sense. It's groovy to get high, but let's act like we have some sense while we do it." Responding to a taunt of "Fuck you" Jimi replied "I wish I could" and, in a moment of sheer brilliance, evoked his guitar to somehow phrase the words "Fuck you, motherfucker" in return as the crowd now roared its approval. Hendrix then lurched into a version of "Voodoo Child (Slight Return)," complete with a drum solo by Mitch Mitchell, a broken guitar string, and a brief passage of "Sunshine of Your Love" before the trio bludgeoned the song to a close.

Fortunate to have escaped a full-scale riot, the Experience's Los Angeles Forum concert had largely been a failed exercise, their performance adversely affected by the unruly mob. Just one show removed, the unity and shared sense of purpose exhibited in Dallas seemed lost. Though the Forum concert had been a tremendous financial success, considering the effort, expense and potential live album, the Experience had let an opportunity slip. In Oakland the following evening, the Experience rebounded, buoyed by the addition of Jefferson Airplane bassist Jack Casady, who, as he had done the previous fall at Winterland, joined the band onstage for a spirited jam.

For Michael Jeffery, success could be measured by the group's impressive gross receipts, as the Experience's take for the two weekend concerts alone, after deduction of expenses, soared to over $100,000, and receipts from sales of books and posters added even more.

Such figures brought little comfort to Hendrix. A torrent of emotions, stoked by the recent events in Houston, Dallas and Los Angeles, coupled with a growing dissatisfaction with the direction of the Experience, was raging within him. His frustration was so great that he refused to rejoin the tour. While not an original tactic, Hendrix had done this in the past, but at that time – June of 1968 – the group had been a true unit, and the consensus of the three would force Jimi's hand.

Meeting with attorney Howard Krantz at Jeffery's 37th

Street headquarters, Bob Levine was completely unaware of Jimi's developments. "He had a gig that night in Detroit, at Cobo Hall. This was about 5 P.M; as far as I knew, he had left. Then in walked Gerry Stickells. I said, 'What are you doing here?' He replied, 'I've got a problem. Jimi's in the car.' 'What car! Didn't he leave at two o'clock?' Stickells said, 'I just couldn't get him to go.' I asked Stickells to bring him into the office. He agreed but said, 'I'll get him in the office but he really doesn't want to go.'

"I sat Hendrix down in my office but just as I said 'Jimi' the phone rang. When the secretary said, 'Bob, it's a promoter from Detroit,' I knew immediately that it was Bob Bageris from Cobo Hall. Bageris said, 'Listen, I checked reservations at the hotel and the two boys are there with a road manager but there's no Hendrix.' Jimi was sitting right in front of me but I assured Bageris that he had left for Detroit some time ago. I then spoke to Jimi. 'Jimi, I'll tell you *why* you have to do this. You don't have to do this for money. You have to do this because you are Jimi Hendrix and you have over 10,000 people in that hall waiting to see you. You owe it to them. You've got to be there, and you know it. I don't know what it is you're doing with this cute little shtick; I'm enjoying it, but I'm nervous as hell. I've got to be like the Pope's emissary to get you a charter to Detroit out of La Guardia in a couple of hours.' Jimi said, 'Well, I don't want to put you through all that trouble. It's not worth it.' 'It's no trouble Jimi,' I said. 'I don't want to be sitting here when they're rioting in Detroit for a promoter who has given us a lot of dates in the past.'

"After a half hour of cajoling, Jimi finally obliged, so I got straight on the phone to Butler Aviation. 'This is the Frank Sinatra office,' I said. 'Oh yes, sir,' came the response. 'We have a slight problem here. Mr. Sinatra has been delayed and must be in Detroit via Lear Jet in the next hour or so.' 'Hold on, sir, I don't know.' 'No,' I said. 'There are no ifs, ands or buts about it. If you're going to say no, you tell it to Mr.

Sinatra. Because I'm not.' He came back on the line after a minute and gave us a number and a gate. I knew Stickells would have access to a bag of cash once he arrived in Detroit so I sent them off in the limousine. Then the promoter called again: 'The first group has gone on and Hendrix isn't here.' I didn't tell him what was going on but I promised him that Hendrix wouldn't let him down."

When Hendrix finally arrived in Detroit, his presence did little to improve the poisonous atmosphere backstage. Mitch, Noel and Jimi wouldn't talk to one another, not even to devise a set list for the evening's performance. Making his way to the dressing room backstage, booking agent Ron Terry confronted Hendrix. "You'd better look real good tonight," Terry instructed him, "because this is going to be one raggedy-ass show." And, as Terry remembers (and a crude amateur recording of the performance proves), it was: "There were a few moments of brilliance; otherwise, it was terrible. But the people didn't care. They were all fucked up and they clapped and jumped up and down. It didn't make any difference."

Detroit, however, was nothing to what followed. A rumor circulated around the Detroit dressing rooms that the band was going to be, at the very least, hassled and detained at the airport in Toronto the next day. Precautions were taken, and both Gerry Stickells and Tony Ruffino, handling promotion for Cora Productions (a subsidiary of Concerts East), spoke to Hendrix to make sure he had nothing with him that could land him in trouble. No problem, he replied.

Arriving in Toronto, Ron Terry went to wake up Jimi and further remind him that they were likely to be detained. "Whatever you got in that bag, get rid of it," was his instruction. As a precaution, Terry took Hendrix to the bathroom, where Jimi dumped anything even remotely suspicious looking from his travel bag into the toilet bowl. "I thought he was clean," recalls Terry. "I truly think he's clean. *He* thinks he's clean and that's the most important thing."

The last two off the plane, Hendrix and Terry met the rest of their entourage at the baggage corral. Tony Ruffino, carrying Hendrix's bags, threw them onto the customs counter. "The customs guy said to me, 'If that's not yours, keep your hands off it,'" remembers Ruffino. "I said, 'Well, I work for him.' He insisted, 'Keep your hands off the bag!' Looking at Jimi, the officer asked, 'Is that your bag?' Hendrix said yes. He opened it up and inside were these small packets of heroin. He said to Jimi, 'What's that?' Hendrix said, 'I don't know.' That's when I knew we were in trouble."

Ron Terry, toting one of Hendrix's carry-on bags, was also detained, despite Jimi's attempt to exonerate him. "These are my bags," Hendrix stated, "you can let him go." In the meantime, one of the customs officers sent off the contraband – a small brown tube described as a crude hashish pipe, as well as the heroin, which had been hidden inside a small Alka-Seltzer bottle – to be examined. By this point, Mitch, Noel, Gerry Stickells, Eric Barrett, Abe Jacob and Larry Vaughan had sailed through customs and were waiting on the other side for the remainder of their party. They were not allowed to reenter the customs room, where Hendrix, Terry and Ruffino remained. Finally, an inspector came out, apprised Stickells of the situation, and the stunned entourage left for their hotel. Tony Ruffino was released, but Ron Terry and Hendrix were handcuffed and taken away to jail. At the hotel, Stickells immediately called Henry Steingarten informing him of the bad news.

For Jeffery, the news was especially stunning. Enraged, he opted for damage control, asking publicist Michael Goldstein to utilize his extensive contacts with the mainstream press to ensure that initial news of the incident, fed to wire services over the world, would be sketchy at best. Goldstein succeeded in burying the story in many places, ensuring that Jeffery's only complaint was with *Rolling Stone*, feeling that it gave the incident too much attention.

Jeffery also ordered the episode be downplayed in public. Under no circumstance was this to become a replay of the legal difficulties the Rolling Stones, and to a lesser degree the Beatles, had experienced in Britain. There were to be no calls for drug legalization by Hendrix or by anyone else in the organization. Jeffery himself refused to fly to Toronto, says Bob Levine, for fear he would be recognized by the media and forced to defend his client's misfortune. While many of Hendrix's fans may have been sympathetic to his plight, Jeffery's primary concern was that civic leaders would no longer permit Jimi Hendrix, convicted drug felon, to entertain their youth. Fighting mayors and fire chiefs afraid of a burning Stratocaster was one thing, marketing a star busted for heroin quite another.

Drawing on his extensive contacts and skills honed in the British Secret Service, Jeffery worked through back channels in an unsuccessful attempt to find out exactly what had happened. Even today, more than twenty years later, the motives and details of Hendrix's arrest in Toronto – even among those present that fateful morning – remain a matter of considerable debate. Some Hendrix historians have surmised – without providing proof – that Jeffery actually set up the Toronto bust in a further attempt to subjugate Hendrix. No member of Hendrix's extended management team believe the bust to have been a deliberate setup – either by enemies of Jeffery or Jeffery himself. Gerry Stickells echoes a common sentiment: "The whole drug scene was too loose in America then. You knew to never pick up anybody else's luggage." Under orders from Henry Steingarten not to discuss the subject with the media, Hendrix offered little explanation.

As Hendrix and Terry sat in jail, the Toronto police were being lobbied by the management of the concert venue Maple Leaf Gardens, who predicted a riot should the Experience's concert be canceled. With too little time to notify the sell-out crowd that the Experience would not perform and growing concern that the show would turn into a benefit concert for Hendrix – directing the audience's anger toward the police – by 8 P.M the Toronto police rescinded, escorting Hendrix and Terry to the venue and allowing him to perform. As they rode to Maple Leaf Gardens, Terry recalls a stunned Hendrix muttering, "This is not real, this is not really happening."

That night, the Experience took to the stage amid the watchful eye of the Toronto police. Hendrix greeted the audience with the short address with which he often prefaced his concerts, a statement suddenly invested with much greater meaning. "Forget about what's happening today, tomorrow, or yesterday. We'll build our own little world right here ..." Somehow, despite the considerable tension, the Experience staged a polished show and sent their adoring throng home happy. But the events of the afternoon clearly weighed on Hendrix's mind. During "Spanish Castle Magic" he added the word "naturally" at the end of the lyric "Just float your little mind," eschewing any and all drug references. (In a rare move, Hendrix included a passage from "Little Miss Lover" inside this elongated version.) During "Red House" Hendrix sang, "When I get out of jail, I'll come and see you."

Later, with his audience paying full attention, Hendrix sauntered into "Room Full of Mirrors." While its arrangement differed little from the slow, deliberate groove that Jimi had exhibited at the Royal Albert Hall, his message was supremely serious. Creating new lyrics as he went along, Hendrix sang of a girl who had overdosed before progressing into a snatch of "Crash Landing," pulling lyrics from that composition without changing melody. Within the same tempo, he sang of a girl named Mary, who was now dead and cautioned that those who refused to pay heed might some day wake up in the same condition. And, as if to reiterate his intent, he then stated, "I think you better take this tip from me." Before jumping directly into "Purple

Haze," Hendrix sang lyrics from "Gypsy Eyes," then, at the conclusion, spoke directly to the crowd: "Peace be with you and remember what I tried to say to you."

In a rare exhibition of passion, pride, shame and depression, Hendrix had bared his emotions to thousands of strangers, otherwise content just to see their idol in person. To their credit, the audience at Maple Leaf Gardens seemed to empathize with him. There were few calls for "Hey Joe" on this night, as fans were given a rare glimpse inside the real Jimi Hendrix, the one torn by conflicting emotions.

Before Hendrix could assess anything, another sold-out gig awaited him the very next night, Sunday, May 4, in Syracuse, New York. As part of their bail agreement, Hendrix and Terry were ordered to return to Toronto the next morning (Monday) at 9 A.M. Larry Vaughan of Concerts East was impressed that, though beset by his own personal problems, Hendrix still tried to communicate sincerely with the Syracuse audience. "We were playing at Memorial Auditorium and it was right around the time when black students were protesting and rioting at Cornell University. Before the band went on, the house played a recording of 'Star Spangled Banner' over the public address system. When the lights went down, a white kid in the front row screamed at the top of his lungs, 'I love you!' Hendrix paused to look at him and then the audience and said, 'The feeling's mutual man, but let's do something about those guns. It's getting frightening.' After the concert, walking back to his dressing room, he stopped me to ask, 'Do you think it will make a difference?'" Vaughan knew exactly what Hendrix had meant. Did his words carry any weight? Could he still help to bring about positive change? Had his arrest in Toronto cheapened his message? Vaughan could only hope it had not.

Following the performance, Gerry Stickells took the rest of the entourage back to Manhattan, while Hendrix and Terry remained behind. "We decided that we were not going to think about it anymore, so we just partied," says Terry. "He and I got adjoining suites at the end of a hall and partied all night with three stewardesses we had met on the flight to Syracuse. On Monday morning, a private plane came to pick us up and whisked us to Toronto." Still suffering the effects of their all-night reveling, Hendrix and Terry appeared before the judge, where Jimi repeatedly stated that Terry was not involved in any way. Charges against Terry were finally dismissed, while Hendrix himself was remanded on bail until June 19.

With the tour slated to resume on May 7 in Tuscaloosa, Alabama, Hendrix again teamed with Buddy Miles at the Record Plant, jamming through the night of the 6th and into the early hours of the 7th, as he no doubt sought out the sanctity of the studio. Touring offered little respite: Jimi met resistance, this time racism, almost as soon as he arrived in Tuscaloosa. "We had trouble checking in at the Ramada Inn," recalls Tony Ruffino. "The police did not appreciate all of the white girls crowding the lobby being so crazy about him. Nothing was going on, just some kids screaming, excited about seeing him. He had just broken through in the South and people were beginning to recognize him."

Regardless of his growing wealth and popularity, Hendrix kept to himself on this tour. "It was room service for Jimi," recalls Ron Terry. Hendrix, like all African Americans, was keenly aware of subtle racism, and as a result usually chose to eat in. The problems the Experience faced in Tuscaloosa spoke volumes about the value of self-promotion. Details as seemingly minor as improved back-stage food, accommodations and security made a marked difference in Hendrix's quality of life. "He would enter his room," recalls Michael Goldstein, "draw the drapes closed, place colored scarfs, made or given to him by Colette Mimram [a New York designer he had befriended], over the lamps and would pull his hulking, portable reel to reel out to record or play back tapes he had made.

"Hendrix was afraid too much sun would give him acne," Goldstein recalls with a laugh, and indeed Hendrix did fret about excess exposure to the sun. Recalls Ron Terry, "I called Jimi 'The Bat,' and he called me 'Sun God.' He never opened the drapes until the sun went down, always had room service and never went to restaurants. To show you what his sense of humor was, once, when we were in Charlotte, I was sitting by the pool and he came running down from his room, in his bathrobe, with the hood on so that the sun couldn't get to him, and gave me an issue of the *National Enquirer*. On the front cover was a picture of a lady whose face had been decayed by the sun. He said, 'This is what's going to happen to you, you silly ass,' and ran back to his room. While I was reading it I looked up at his window and he was peeking through the drapes to see what I was doing. It was silly, but it was just his way of showing he was really aware of what was going down all the time."

The privacy of his hotel room provided Jimi with a sanctuary to compose without distraction. As was his style, Hendrix would write lyrics or poetry on anything handy, be it hotel stationery, legal pads or envelopes. And he did not confine his writings to lyrics, often composing lengthy stream-of-consciousness works, drawings and hilarious caricatures, as well as notes for music, business and personal use. Since he had left London and his career had accelerated, Hendrix had increasingly less time for reading, but would often thumb through publications as varied as *Rolling Stone* and comic books such as *Spiderman* and *Toric*, a Native American comic book. The latter publication tapped into two deep Hendrix interests, science fiction and his own Cherokee Indian heritage. "It's about Indians who get lost in a prehistoric time," Jimi told John Marshall. "It's a completely different dimension. It isn't funny, it's drawn very beautifully. Almost every picture is a painting. It's very serious."

Although publicly he rarely addressed feelings about his

heritage, Hendrix warmed to Marshall and spoke of the empathy he felt for other Native Americans. "They never had a chance for a decent job. Negroes, they think they really have it bad, but Indians have it just as bad if not worse. There were a lot of them on the reservation, every single house was the same, not even a house, more like a hut. It's really a bad scene, but they still have retained their color and beads and things they had [in the past]. There's hardly any left anyway ... there's a few rich ones, [but] there's a lot of them around the West Coast and Northwest. Half of them are down on skid row, drinking and completely out of their minds. It's because of the way they started off, with hardly anything to work with."

Within his private works, Hendrix would allow his mind to spill out onto his pages, later putting himself through the painful process of editing. His medium was songwriting, and if he wished to express certain emotions, he took great care in crafting just the right lyric to suit his songs. "He always said that it was very important that I hear the lyrics before we did the tracks," Mitch Mitchell would later recall.

Not all of Hendrix's compositions featured such singular vision. Songs such as "I Don't Live Today" were direct statements, forcefully delivered. That song, Hendrix told John Marshall, addressed Indians in general as well as his own Indian heritage. "The words were simple, [yet] they were very personal. I had to make it [perfect]." Others were not as obvious. "May This Be Love," Hendrix also told Marshall, was "based on another type of Indian thing." Discussing "Little Wing," Hendrix acknowledged the obvious Indian influence. "That's exactly what it's about, like 'She's walking through the clouds.'" While his exposure to science fiction had come through his friendship with Chas Chandler, his fertile imagination both clashed with, and drew upon, his deeply rooted faith in God, as well as his interest in astrology. "I want to do one album [maybe] even a double album that pertains to mythology stories about the planets," Hendrix told Marshall. "We have Greek mythology, so I would like to write my own mythology."

Even with three smash-hit albums and countless tours to his credit, few knew or recognized Hendrix's capacities, as the hints were often as cryptic as his best lyrics. Unable to read music, but anxious not to lose an idea or inspiration that had come to him, he might jot chord progressions and sequences down on paper, even citing what string, what fret or what style his solo or rhythm part should be. If unable to describe on the printed page the sounds he heard in his head, Hendrix would rely on Eddie Kramer in the control room. Here, Hendrix could verbally sketch or demonstrate his wishes and ideas. He could request the sound of a guitar burning as he had with "House Burning Down," speak of sound and tones in colors and, most important, be challenged to direct his best effort into capturing his intense and increasingly personal vision.

Simmering deep within Hendrix was his inability to reach a wider black audience. Hanging out uptown in Harlem, Hendrix often stuck out like a sore thumb. "The black community was very conservative at that time," recalls Arthur Allen. "Jimi was totally different to anyone in the community. He would wear blues hats like the old masters. 'Blues master hats' we used to call them. Then he would put buttons on them to make them his style. He wore pins. My brother and I began wearing bell-bottom pants because of him. Most blacks associated bell-bottom pants with clowns."

While Hendrix outwardly may have ignored the quizzical looks and sarcastic remarks, they did take their toll. "I had friends with me in Harlem," Jimi told John Marshall. "Even in my own section, we would be walking down the street and girls, old ladies, anybody, would say, 'Look at that. What is this, a circus or something?'" Even during his formative years as an R&B sideman, Hendrix frequently fielded taunts about the length or style of his hair.

Now enjoying national fame, Hendrix was at a loss how to communicate with this stubbornly elusive audience. Part of the problem, suggests Arthur Allen, was that Hendrix's success had afforded him some respite from the day-to-day racial strife endured by most black Americans – especially those in dense urban communities such as Harlem. His success had not driven all facets of racism from his life, as his recent appearances in Texas and Alabama had certainly proven. If fame had provided any respite from racism, it took form primarily in financial terms, as Hendrix now had the money to structure his life and its path away from as many potential confrontations as possible. Having been shot in the back and left for dead by a white police officer during a riot in Harlem, Arthur often argued with Jimi and his brother Albert about the state of race relations. "I live it!" Arthur would tell Jimi. "*I* am in it. You are on the outside looking in." Yet Hendrix would try to act as mediator. "He was a very universal person with a great deal of sensitivity," recalls Albert Allen. Nevertheless, it had to be strange for Hendrix to tour Harlem, with Faye Pridgeon riding shotgun in his beloved Corvette, and have no one recognize him, while in the deep South his popularity grew unabated.

On May 16, the tour resumed in Baltimore. The Experience had become little more than a money machine: flying to gigs, rarely rehearsing and usually performing the same numbers, all while courteously side-stepping one another following the concert. There was little of the bitter feuding and sulking that had marred past appearances, but the group's energy and focus had dissipated far past the point of no return. There were no face-to-face confrontations between Hendrix and Redding – because Jimi detested such showdowns – rather an unspoken fragmentation that led Hendrix to bounce new ideas in the studio off Buddy Miles.

Since Hendrix's death, many allegations have been made fingering Redding and Mitchell as cold, unfeeling racists, implying that they both regarded Hendrix as their subordinate. Understandably, Mitchell and Redding bitterly resent the charge, noting that they had seen the racism by traveling with Hendrix. Both, but especially Mitch, were well liked by Jimi's closest black friends, Faye Pridgeon and the Allen twins. "Mitch was like part of the family," recalls Arthur Allen. "I loved Mitch and so did Hendrix. He and Jimi were very close and his personality superseded the racial thing." As for Noel, both of the Allen twins insist that, to their knowledge, no racial incident ever took place between Redding and Hendrix. Simply, Noel had formed his own friendships and was more outgoing than Mitch and, as a result, traveled in different social circles.

After shows in Baltimore and Providence on May 16 and 17, the Experience returned to New York for another important concert in the group's career. Despite the many impressive venues in which they had performed, Madison Square Garden on May 18 was truly a special occasion. Long sold out, this gig marked the end of Concerts East's first major tour. In all, this spring U.S. Tour had been a terrific financial success, easily outstripping the cost of damages the PPX fiasco had caused, as well as the start-up costs for Hendrix's new studio. Factoring in merchandising sales, the Experience grossed more than $100,000 at Madison Square Garden alone. After deduction of expenses, Michael Jeffery and the Experience were left with close to $75,000, a staggering fee for the time.

The tour firmly established Steve Weiss's role within the Hendrix management structure, insulated, as was Jeffery, from Jimi's cash flow by a separate accounting firm. Weiss earned his legal fees with a ferocity Jeffery couldn't help but admire. "He would be on us like a hawk," remembers Larry Vaughan. "We would leave deposits at buildings, usually a $1,000 or $2,000 damage bond. Tony Ruffino and I would finish the show at 2 A.M. and at 9 A.M. Steve would be on the phone. 'Did you get the money back from the damage bond?' I would say, 'Steve, they haven't assessed us yet!' He would say, 'Then go down and get the fucking money!' That used to be a dreaded phone call!" The success of Concerts East also directly affected Weiss's other clients. As Hendrix had done for Concerts West, establishing Concerts East was of vital importance, and bands such as Vanilla Fudge and Led Zeppelin would keep the network going.

With the Madison Square Garden gig behind them, the Experience once again split in three directions, Hendrix returning to the Record Plant continuing his sessions with Buddy Miles. On May 21, "Lullaby for the Summer" was reworked, but no finals completed. On the 22nd, "Message From Nine to the Universe" was cut. (This track, an early derivative of "Message to Love" was actually a long jam that also included off-key harmony vocals from Hendrix's girl-friend Devon Wilson.) A listen to the session tape offers a clear insight into the atmosphere Buddy Miles provided for Hendrix. From a business perspective, these sessions were not productive, yet they were fun, an element sorely lacking from the majority of Jimi's recent work with the Experience – either on stage or in the studio.

As Noel Redding had done during a time of personal crisis and self-examination – reaching back to old mates and forming Fat Mattress – so it was time for Jimi to repay some personal debts. Hendrix would soon replace Billy Rich with an old friend, army pal Billy Cox. No dispute existed with Rich, insists Buddy Miles; Hendrix merely wanted to inte-grate Cox into his music. "When we were struggling in Harlem, Jimi used to talk about Billy Cox and Larry Lee all the time," remembers Faye Pridgeon.

"Billy Cox was way, way, laid back, from a completely different side of Jimi Hendrix," recalls Arthur Allen. "Musi-cally, Billy could stay in the pocket and *never* created stress for Jimi. Hendrix needed that more than anything." Without a trace of pretension, Cox was amiable, unflappable and committed to helping his old friend. Hendrix was not quite ready to dislodge Redding, but Cox's presence brought him much needed stability.

Returning to the road again, the Experience embarked on a short, five-city tour beginning with a visit to Hendrix's hometown of Seattle. The Experience would also make stops in San Diego and Santa Clara, before ending with two shows in Honolulu. In San Diego, Wally Heider was again contracted to record the Experience's show for possible issue as a live album. After opening with an inspired version of "Fire," dogged sadly by tuning problems, the crowd began screaming out requests. A cry of "Hey Joe" caused Hendrix to chide a particularly overzealous fan. "I'll tell you what. We'll get into all that. Don't worry man, you don't have no program. Just relax. When I say toilet paper, *that's* when you come rolling out."

The thick humidity of the sold-out Sports Arena hampered both Noel's and Jimi's tuning. "Hey Joe" rebounded after a fair start, as Hendrix seemed to regain his concentration. While the audience roared with approval, Hendrix dedicated the next song, "Spanish Castle Magic," to the "plainclothes policemen and other goofballs." Again, Mitch Mitchell was uniformly brilliant, offering thundering accompaniment as well as an impromptu drum solo while Hendrix changed guitars following a broken string. As it had been at the Forum in Los Angeles, the atmosphere was electric. The audience roared at each crescendo Mitch would build during his solo, and when Hendrix did return, he ripped into a short passage of "Sunshine of Your Love" before returning to "Spanish Castle Magic." "That's what happens when you get bored playing the same old things," he told the crowd.

A magnificent "Red House" would follow next. This rendition, arguably Hendrix's best recorded version, would later be included as part of 1972's *In the West*. Though the Experience had performed the song innumerable times before, here in San Diego, as they had done only selectively throughout 1969, the trio once more channeled their considerable talent with a clear purpose. This was no twelve- or thirteen-minute meandering jam, rather a unified, masterful interpretation of one of Hendrix's finest compositions. The same raging intensity that the Experience had provided upon formation in London drove Jimi through the song's forte and pianissimo passages. It is in this performance that both Hendrix enthusiasts and those still uninitiated have an insight into the talent and innovation that Hendrix possessed. While the majority of his contemporaries rushed to ape such blues greats as Robert Johnson, Otis Rush and Howlin' Wolf in their compositions and performances, "Red House" was the full extension of a prior achievement, a magnificent version that bore witness to Hendrix's blues heritage as well as his unsurpassed ability to update the blues and retain his own imprint.

Before Mitch's frenzied pounding launched into "I Don't Live Today," Hendrix once again dedicated the song to the American Indian. While not as fully realized as the version taped on April 26 at the L.A. Forum – due in part to some bleating feedback during the song's latter half – this particular rendition was only slightly less inspiring. Even "Foxey Lady" and "Purple Haze," which followed, were top-flight and free of the ennui and sloppy playing that Hendrix's outrageous stage showboating would often cause. "Voodoo Chile" closed the set; while nowhere near as powerful as the definitive version captured February 24, 1969, at the Royal Albert Hall, it was, nonetheless, delivered with vigor. The Experience may have ceased to be an effective unit in the studio but, lost in their music on stage, their talent was undeniable.

The following day, the group traveled up the California coast to perform at the Santa Clara Rock Festival. One of the better-organized festivals of 1969, Hendrix and the Experience coasted through their seventy-minute performance, sending, as the *San Jose Mercury* described, "nearly 20,000 of the king of rock's subjects into stunned, delicious rapture." One memorable highlight of the Santa Clara appearance took place before "Foxey Lady" began. Hendrix had often introduced the song with a sly quip, usually dedicating the number to "somebody's girlfriend ... we'll find out after the show" or, while pointing to an unknown female fan, to "that girl over there in the yellow underwear." On this day, a gust of wind had lifted the skirt of a pretty folk singer who had completed her set earlier and was now watching Hendrix from the wings of the stage. The opportunity was too good to let pass and Hendrix wryly dedicated "Foxey Lady" to "the girl back there with the yellow underwear." "Yeah you," confirmed Hendrix, pointing out a young Stevie Nicks red with embarrassment.

The Santa Clara festival now behind them, the Experience prepared to leave for Hawaii. Honolulu had become a lucrative and frequent location for Concerts West, as Tom Hulett had developed a relationship with Tom Moffat, a leading DJ at KPOI-FM, one of Hawaii's most successful radio stations. Moffat arranged for two mansions to be rented in Diamond Head, one for Jimi and another for his entourage.

One afternoon, while he relaxed with Kathy Eberth at the Diamond Head mansion, some local Black Panther members discovered where Hendrix was staying and set out to find him. Jimi had been forewarned and was trying his best to duck a confrontation. If they were to come by, he told Eberth, she was to tell them he wasn't home. The Panthers did stop by, and the ringing of the doorbell threw both Hendrix and Eberth askew. As Jimi hid in the other room, Eberth answered the door. "I answered it," she recalls, "and said I was the maid. I heard this muffled laugh from the other room. They heard it as well and came in. They were talking to him about money, and the fact that he, like them, was a 'brother.' They were putting the guilt thing on him. He tried to quell them by telling them that 'the only colors I see are in my music.'"

Hendrix successfully sloughed off their approach for the time being, but the Honolulu incident gnawed at the emerging sense of black consciousness within him, and not for the first time either. Away from his shield-like management, Hendrix was more at ease to sit and reason with those, such as the Panthers, who looked toward him for guidance or financial support. He *was* doing his part, he tried to tell them. He had access to the hearts and minds of his young audience. His music gave him the opportunity to do more than protest; he could, as he would often say, give solutions. Hendrix in no way trivialized the growing sense of responsibility welling within him. It would, in fact, provide additional momentum for the coming changes in his music.

Following five wonderful days off in and about the islands of Hawaii, the Experience were booked for two engagements at the Waikiki Shell in Honolulu. Moffet had spared no detail in making Hendrix's stay in Honolulu nothing short of spectacular. Later that evening, before taking him to the venue, Moffat arranged for a beautiful white limousine tour of the magnificent condos that surrounded the Shell. Arriving with Gerry Stickells while Noel and Fat Mattress were on stage, a pensive Jimi Hendrix took time to speak with a local Honolulu reporter. "I attribute my success to God," he told Ben Wood. "I'm really a messenger of God." Questioned about his impending trial in Toronto, Hendrix replied, "All of that is the establishment fighting back. Eventually they will swallow themselves up. We don't want them to swallow up too many kids as they go along. Put that down," Hendrix instructed Wood. "I know what I'm talking about."

Following Fat Mattress, Hendrix strode on stage, tuned up and ripped through two numbers. "The audience was dead," recalls Tom Hulett. "They seemed stoned and gave no reaction." His next few numbers were dogged by a persistent hum in his amplifiers. "Jimi spoke to the crowd and excused himself, saying that he had to have this problem fixed. He went and got into his limousine.

"Tom Moffat got on the microphone, Eric Barrett and Gerry Stickells ran around trying to fix the problem. I was getting nervous: we were sold out and all of a sudden nothing was happening. Then Stickells came up to me and said that Jimi didn't want to go back on. 'What do you mean he doesn't want to go back on! Doesn't he know that this is his money behind this concert?' I told Stickells to keep people playing with the wires while I went out to the car and spoke with Jimi. Stickells and I must have tried for thirty minutes, but he was not going back on. Jimi said to tell everybody to come back tomorrow night. He would more than make up for it then. I tried to explain that they were all here now and we had already torn their tickets in half, but I knew him too well. He wasn't going back on. Knowing this, we got hold of the building manager, ran down to the old Honolulu arena used for wrestling matches, and picked up rolls of tickets. We made an announcement that the sound system couldn't be repaired and Jimi Hendrix wouldn't want to perform with substandard equipment – all of which was bullshit – and that if they all left quietly and picked up a ticket stub, they would be admitted to the next night's concert. Everybody was pissed off. These people were all fucked up on drugs and little more than 1,000 picked up their stubs. The rest were yelling 'Fuck you.'

"The next night, the venue was overfilled, which is why, in my opinion, there are no more rock shows at the Waikiki Shell. We were paranoid, security was paranoid – because everybody had heard what had happened, came to the gate and said that they had lost their ticket stub – so we let everybody in. The crowd spilled over into the park behind the Shell. Jimi said to let them all in free and he was brilliant on stage that night."

Although they would perform publicly twice more

during June 1969, the Experience were now dying a not-so-slow death. Although their disintegration was free of acrimonious bickering or physical confrontation, it was real all the same. Hendrix arranged for Billy Cox to be reimbursed for expenses and placed him – discreetly at first – on the payroll. Looming ahead lay two festival gigs and plenty of time for the band to regroup and complete their anticipated studio follow-up to *Electric Ladyland*. But with Hendrix's interest in the original Experience waning, Eddie Kramer immersed full-time in the construction of the new studio, and Chas Chandler back in England, nothing – after one fruitless attempt, the last known session by the original group, on June 16 – could save them now.

His appearance in court scheduled for June 19, Hendrix continued his lengthy process of self-examination. He had now moved back to the Village, securing a lease for an apartment at 59 West 12th Street. The Village, specifically 52 West 8th Street, soon to be the home of his new state-of-the-art studio, now became his home. To keep his personal affairs in order, Hendrix invited Devon Wilson to move in with him. Since his arrival in England, Hendrix had enjoyed a conspicuous number of female relationships. His first, with Kathy Etchingham, had survived his initial trip with the Experience to America.

Hendrix's relationship with Etchingham would ultimately fail, but, as with Linda Keith, Hendrix always preserved a soft spot in his heart for her. She had accepted him without conditions, when he was little more than a broke musician trying to crack the London scene. Their relationship had flourished without money or drugs, a notion Hendrix could not put to rest about Devon.

Hendrix had a penchant for beautiful women, and his entourage came to regard them politely. One never knew the length of tenure Jimi afforded each new acquaintance. On tour, Hendrix had created a series of hilarious 8mm films he titled *The Goodbye Films*. In these, Hendrix would shoot film of each girl he had slept with, waving goodbye to him from his hotel room. Hendrix filled countless such rolls and later, during private screenings, would ad-lib comic live commentary.

Devon Wilson had been introduced to Jimi during the summer of 1967 by Emeretta Marks, an R&B singer he had known. She was a tall, beautiful, out-of-work model, and their mutual attraction was immediate. Early in their relationship, Hendrix came to learn that Devon's gruff, assured exterior hid her true personality, one filled with insecurity and self-doubt, qualities Faye Pridgeon never possessed. "In her personal relationships Faye, as did Jimi, thrived on control," recalls Arthur Allen, "and that's where they clashed. He loved Faye because she never milked him. She didn't mind him going with other women. That drove Jimi mad, because he would try to make her jealous. Faye didn't stand for any bullshit, she was very organized. We all had a piece of her heart, but only Jimi had a piece of her soul."

In Devon, Jimi could see the same frustrations he had harbored during periods in 1965 and 1966. She had high aspirations and was convinced of her talent as both a model and actress, yet unlike Jimi, she diverted her energies away from her stated career to the role of supergroupie, seducing those like Arthur Lee, Brian Jones and Mick Jagger for the rush, the thrill of the conquest. Devon tore at Hendrix's private emotions, probing for his weaknesses and then exploiting them. "It was hard for Jimi to stop his relationship with Devon," explains Faye Pridgeon, "because she had such a magnetic presence." In Devon, Hendrix had, perhaps, his true counterpart, for his own sexual exploits were just as legendary. Yet Devon wanted more than physical intimacy, and fought Hendrix's attempts to limit her emotional advances. Hendrix was susceptible to temptation and Devon was his temptress, his dark fantasy. Devon was headstrong, and like Jimi, built a hard external shell to mask her delicate inner feelings. Early on she adopted the role of protective matron for him, shepherding those Hendrix felt comfortable with while keeping away those she considered undesirable. Most of Jimi's intimate associates were wary of her, yet remained enamored by her electric personality.

In a word, Devon Wilson was different, and her antics often surprised even the most jaded of Hendrix's entourage. She was bisexual, and the inside joke was that girls would have to go through her before progressing on to Jimi. While their relationship remained open, Devon burned with jealousy when Hendrix would seek other women. "Devon just couldn't stand rejection," explains Pridgeon. "She would tell lies about Jimi and that would [infuriate] him. One time, she walked around the Scene telling everyone that Jimi had beaten her up because he was jealous." Devon had no trouble walking into the Scene and selecting women for an erotic ménage à trois. That was different: relationships with groupies were a diversion, a drug to be enjoyed for a fleeting moment then forgotten. And when it came to real drugs, Devon possessed a voracious appetite, one that exceeded even Hendrix's. "Devon was greedy," remembers Pridgeon. "If we got high, she had to be higher. I must have saved her from overdosing at least three times before it got to the point where I wanted to avoid her." And, if cut off from the resources of her conquests, Devon, as cold and cunning as the hardest of streetwalkers, would think nothing of turning a trick for money. Be it cocaine, heroin or sex, her insatiable desire for instant gratification would ultimately prove to be the downfall not only of her relationship with Jimi but also of her own life.

# 12 SKY CHURCH

*"That's the trouble with this business. People see a fast buck and have you up there being a slave to the public. They keep you at it until you are exhausted and so is the public, and then they move off to other things. That's why groups break up – they just get worn out. Musicians want to pull away after a time or they'll get lost in the whirlpool."*

**– Jimi Hendrix**

In Toronto for a hearing of his trial, Hendrix once more felt the cold, painful splash of reality when his trial date was set for December 8, 1969. By a time when he would have hoped to have put the specter of the bust behind him, it had reappeared. A surly Hendrix arrived in San Fernando, California, to play with the Experience as the headline act of the Newport Pop Festival. (Apart from the moniker borrowed from original Newport guru George Wein, this event was unrelated to the celebrated jazz happening in Rhode Island.) From a financial perspective, the Experience towered over their rivals, earning nearly $100,000 for their fifty-minute set. Neither Hendrix, Mitchell nor Redding knew exactly how much they would make, but privately knew it would be thousands of dollars more than any other performer or band on the bill.

Throughout the tour, there had been rumblings in the press that greed had edged in front of the "cause," but such charges fell on deaf ears. These shows were being done with Hendrix's money, the ticket prices were set by his business associates, and the profits – 85 percent of them – were pouring into Are You Experienced? Ltd. Even in venues where ticket sales had been only 70 percent or 80 percent of capacity, both Concerts East and Concerts West operated efficiently, without losses. While Hendrix may have been fostering an aversion to touring, he certainly couldn't complain about the money.

From the outset, Newport was an unmitigated disaster. The sour mood in which Hendrix had arrived worsened when, reportedly, he drank a soft drink laced with a hallucinatory substance. Only his remarkable constitution made it possible for him to play. "Hendrix was the only person I ever knew who could play on acid," recalls David Crosby. "Whenever I tried it, the strings always melted."

Opening with a spirited "Stone Free," the Experience roared in unison for about three minutes before Mitchell and Hendrix lost each other. Shortly after, a technical gaffe halted Hendrix as Mitch began a muscular drum solo. Partway through, Hendrix halted him with a quick guitar blast before shifting gears again into "Are You Experienced?" Despite some passionate, albeit off-key vocals, as well as beautiful solo guitar, the Experience were utterly unglued. Even Mitch, rarely below par, was performing poorly, with almost total disregard for musical time. The Experience staggered through a mediocre rendition of "Sunshine of Your Love" until Jimi once more cut off Mitch midstream by launching into "Fire." Mitchell didn't seem to notice. Dogged by feedback, his back to the crowd, Hendrix was allowing events beyond his control to compromise his concentration and overwhelm his professionalism – and for the second time in three shows. After he had bludgeoned "Fire" to a close he lashed out at the unruly audience. "We hope we're not playing to a bunch of animals," he chided sarcastically. "So please don't act like some, okay? Just lay back, because you are really making us uptight and it's a bad scene trying to get us uptight when we're trying to give you some good feeling and all this other crap."

As Hendrix strummed the introduction to "Hear My Train" the crowd refused to quiet down, and Hendrix retorted, "We would like to sing about what you all should be thinking about in the meantime while you are picking your noses and your asses." A heckler interrupted him and Hendrix shot back, "Yeah I'm talking to you. I'm trying to play guitar right now, thank you." An outbreak of violence in the audience further dismayed Hendrix. "You all just choke yourselves," he spewed, disgustedly, adding also "Fuck it." Hendrix threw himself fully into the fray. "It's so bad to see people in desperation of anything," he announced, "because pretty soon you lose the whole illusion of what you're looking for in the first place. Like for instance, love. Once you find yourself, you've got it made, but I think there are too many of us here tonight to find that out. Fuck off."

During "Hear My Train," Hendrix substituted new lyrics for old, singing "Too bad you people don't love me no more; too bad you all have to act like clowns." Later, he dedicated "Foxey Lady" "to all the teenie-weenies out there," while as he began "Voodoo Child (Slight Return)" he exhorted, "It's a black militant song and don't you ever forget it!" This reference to the Black Panthers, rare in its boldness, came not as the result of a sudden change in Hendrix's personal philosophy. The Panthers were in attendance this night and had made their presence felt backstage, crowding the performers' tent and the Experience's dressing area.

"We had two caravans behind the stage and I was wandering around," recalls Noel Redding. "I went in and there was Hendrix in the middle of all these big black guys, sitting there looking very meek. You could tell he was glad to see me. 'What are you guys doing in our dressing room?' I said. 'Hey, we're talking to Jimi!' was their reply. 'Well, get out! Or do I have to call the guard?' Jimi breathed a sigh of relief. I gather they were getting at him."

The members of the Experience having split three ways following their abysmal performance, Hendrix had second thoughts. Welling within him, regardless of his own personal problems, was a sturdy sense of pride. On June 22 he returned to the festival alone, jamming with a host of musicians, including Buddy Miles, Brad Campbell of Janis Joplin's Full Tilt Boogie band and Tracy Nelson of Mother Earth. Basking in the bright summer sun, and playing through borrowed Fender amplifiers with a Stratocaster equipped with a Telecaster neck, Hendrix led this hastily assembled aggregation through such Experience numbers as "Voodoo Child (Slight Return)" and "Hear My Train A Comin'" as well as blues chestnuts like "Things I Used to Do." This impromptu set was actually longer and more spirited than the Experience's disastrous exhibition two days prior. Buddy Miles was especially enthused, driving an extended version of "We Gotta Live Together" almost maniacally.

Hendrix's presence had injected some much needed excitement into the festival, providing a temporary respite for the beleaguered audience, the great majority of whom were drug-addled and exhausted from nearly three full days of jostling and fighting. The local media raved about the jam, some even citing it as the best performance of the entire festival. A surreptitiously made stereo two-track recording of the performance, however, certainly doesn't support that claim, and it remains (as it should), tucked safely away within the confines of the Hendrix tape vault, currently administered by Alan Douglas, having been confiscated by Michael Jeffery, along with a tape of the Experience's disastrous performance.

The Denver Pop Festival seemed to be a fairly innocuous date, a quick gig, the proceeds from which – Jeffery's and Hendrix's shares, at least – could be funneled back into the studio project. This was Barry Fey's first festival on this scale, and he hoped to avoid the usual pitfalls of other such events by housing all of the patrons inside Mile High Stadium, where they could take advantage of the building's many bathrooms and concession stands. Fey had recognized the risks associated with staging festivals of this size and trusted the expertise he had garnered promoting concerts at the city's Red Rocks Amphitheater to serve him well.

Complicating matters, however, were the Black Panthers, who were trying to establish a presence at the concert site. But they were not the only radical group trying to do so. Also present was an ultra-left-wing organization, the American Liberation Front, predominantly consisting of members of the Young Socialists and Students for a Democratic Society, which had planned a march through downtown Denver on July 4. The Experience were the headline act for a bill that also featured Creedence Clearwater Revival, the Mothers of Invention, Three Dog Night, Joe Cocker, Iron Butterfly and Zephyr, a popular local band whose lead guitarist, Tommy Bolin, showed considerable promise.

During the festival's performances on Saturday afternoon, Denver police were overrun by gate-crashing fans. Though they resorted to tear gas and riot gear, the police were still unable to handle the problem. After much prodding by the authorities, Fey was forced to open the gates. Throughout the day, police fought a losing battle trying to stem rampant drug dealing, gate crashing and fighting in and about the stadium. By the early evening, their tempers frayed, they were poised to retaliate.

Before the Experience had taken to the stage, more than 3,000 people stormed through the gates without paying. The Experience gave a spirited show, punctuated by fireworks, rock throwing and general bedlam. Despite this, the majority of the audience was trying to enjoy the show, but the police, camped out on surrounding hills, had had enough. They uncorked a barrage of tear gas, delivered by a pepper fog machine. By the end of an already abbreviated set, the riot – complete with police beating and clubbing

combatants – was in full swing. The stage and field awash
with tear gas, the Experience were escorted off stage into
a U-Haul truck Gerry Stickells had somehow been able to
commandeer. In the frenzy, a number of other people had
mounted the truck from all sides in a desperate attempt to
escape the melee, buckling the vehicle's aluminum sides.
The original Experience had performed their final concert.

Noel Redding's defection was immediate, surprising both
Mitchell and Hendrix. There had been no specific incident
between Redding and Hendrix, but Noel cited Hendrix's
desire to "enlarge the group" as one of his main reasons for
leaving. "We got to this place in Denver," Redding stated in
an interview shortly thereafter, "and somebody said, 'Oh,
you're still with Hendrix?' 'What do you mean?' I said, 'I'm
playing here tonight!' I was then told all about these press
[interviews] – with Hendrix saying he was bringing more
people in. Well, he didn't tell Mitch or me at all. So I split
there and then."

Redding's departure clearly demarcated the end of the
original Experience. "There are no hard feelings at all,"
Redding would state, but, obviously to all who knew, there
were. There was talk in the air of Noel and Chas Chandler
reuniting, and shortly after making his move, Redding did
ask Gerry Stickells to join him. Stickells's refusal strained
their friendship. "Noel had an ego as well," recalls Stickells,
"an 'I can make it as well' kind of thing. I think it did him in.
The idea always sounds great – getting all your old mates
together and doing what you used to do – but doing what you
used to do didn't make you a big star before, so what makes
you think it's going to make you one now? It's an impression a
lot of people in the business still get. This notion that once you
reach a certain level, you can dish out anything to the public
and they'll buy it. They don't. The material just wasn't there. I
know it affected my relationship with Noel, because he and
Chas both wanted me to leave and go work with them. I had
made my decision that I wanted to live in America. Their
whole thing was to go back to England."

Redding's defection caused a major disruption within Hendrix's management. As was proven by their lucrative touring, the Experience had become a well-oiled money machine. Hendrix's projected studio – the $500,000 cost of which was to be shared equally by Hendrix and Jeffery – was considered affordable only as a result of the ever-escalating fees the band could realize from touring.

Jeffery's most pressing concern was Hendrix's slated July 10 appearance on the *Tonight Show*. The issue of Hendrix and the *Tonight Show* had actually been one of great debate within his management. Steve Weiss had long enjoyed a personal and professional relationship with the program's former host, Jack Paar. Both Weiss and Jeffery were well aware of the program's track record for establishing its guests as legitimate entertainers, as so few were lucky enough to garner a booking. With Hendrix now at an unprecedented level of popularity, Jeffery saw an opportunity to break Hendrix wider than ever before. Irrespective of financial concerns, there was also a certain degree of status – Lennon and McCartney had graced its fabled couch – associated with a *Tonight Show* appearance.

Nonetheless, Jeffery's decision seemed to fly in the face of his managerial style. Jeffery's flip-flop caused some friction within his team, Ron Terry being the most vocal. He was far from convinced that Hendrix could handle the assignment. "Jimi, you can't do this," he told him. But Hendrix was adamant, retorting, "I can do it. I can handle it!" Little more than sixty days after the bust for possession of heroin, Michael Jeffery was taking a risk by placing Hendrix out of his element. This was not the *Lulu Show*, this was one of mainstream America's most popular television programs. While direct questions about the bust would be off-limits, why take the chance – especially without Mitch and Noel – that Hendrix might come off poorly? What possibly could be gained from all of this?

With Noel Redding departed and Mitch Mitchell home in England, Hendrix officially conscripted Billy Cox as his bass player. Since the Experience no longer existed, Cox became an employee of Jimi Hendrix and Are You Experienced? Ltd. His expenses were paid – along with a salary – but he was not given an interest in either Hendrix or the Experience. As a result, despite his deep friendship with Hendrix, Cox was not entitled to royalties from albums on which he participated. Even today, despite the enormous revenue accumulated by the Hendrix estate, Cox receives no compensation.

The *Tonight Show* of July 10 saw comedian Flip Wilson sit in for resident host Johnny Carson. Wilson, it was deemed, would be more sympathetic to Hendrix and, as a result, perhaps be best able to delve into his character. (His manager, show business impresario Monte Kay, had become friendly with Michael Jeffery in late 1968. Hendrix and Wilson had themselves met once before, at a private birthday party thrown for Jimi on November 27, 1968.) After a few moments of cautious banter between Hendrix and Wilson, the host asked his guest if he considered his music to be a "religious experience." Not quite sure of Wilson's true intent, Hendrix opted to address the question abstrusely: "... music is my scene. My whole life is based around it, so quite naturally it becomes even more than a religion. So what I learn, through [my] experience, I try to pass on to other people through our music. It's like church actually, how you go to a gospel church. We are trying to get the same thing through modern-day music." As a veteran guest host aware of his time constraints, Wilson seemed to sense that Hendrix was enunciating his belief seriously and tried to lighten the mood by offering a quick aside about the astrological sign they both shared, Sagittarius. But Hendrix continued to illustrate his belief. "That's why you have to have some kind of eye dreams on yourself, regardless of what you are like outwardly. As long as you carry God inside yourself, you are a part of him and he is a part of you." Wilson refused to bite, drawing the conversation to a close by jesting, "Well Jim, it's my pleasure to extend to you an invitation to whip a light sermon on us."

Moving to the stage area, Hendrix introduced Billy Cox as "our new bass player." Then, with Cox and *Tonight Show* drummer Ed Shaughnessy (who played with Charlie Parker at the Royal Roost in 1948), Hendrix opened a brief set with an odd choice, "Lover Man." Halfway through the number, however, his amplifier blew. Hoping, in vain, that the problem could be quickly rectified, Cox and Shaughnessy continued. To fill the dead air time, Flip Wilson implored his technicians to hurry, winning a warm round of applause by joking that he had to keep talking, "Because the *Joey Bishop Show* is just one notch away!" After quickly reintroducing Cox, Hendrix lurched into a sloppy but spirited retake, thankfully free of further incident. There was time for just the one song.

In the aftermath of the *Tonight Show* debacle, Michael Jeffery decided that a retreat north was in order. Neither Jeffery nor Hendrix had ever expressed a specific desire to relocate, but Albert Grossman, manager of both Janis Joplin and Bob Dylan, owned a spacious retreat in Woodstock, which, in Jeffery's eyes, was sufficient reason in itself. For Jeffery, Woodstock also had status value – but only for those who could afford to invest, not just rent, so he purchased a spacious, albeit bleak, home located at One Wiley Lane. At the same time, an associate was instructed to rent a sprawling estate for Hendrix, eventually locating an appropriate retreat some twelve miles away in the town of Shokan. Here, Jeffery figured, Hendrix could stay out of trouble, rest, relax and refocus.

Aside from rest and relaxation, there had been no other objective for Hendrix's move upstate. Convinced of Billy Cox's abilities, he was confident that Cox could handle his new assignment. Since Hendrix's death, outsiders have claimed that Cox's promotion owed more to race than ability, yet many of Hendrix's associates – including Gerry Stickells, Bob Levine and Eddie Kramer – refute the charge, stressing his deep personal relationship with Hendrix. Having graduated from the Experience, unaware of what the future held in store, the time for Hendrix to reach back and insulate himself with trusted associates never seemed more appropriate. With so few intimate friends, Hendrix sought to cushion the ride with those who, like himself, had been tested by hard times. "He needed a friend," recalls Jim Marron, "somebody from the old neighborhood who could give him continuity and a sense of identity."

Though Cox was introverted, his winning personality gained him many friends. "Billy Cox was great for Jimi," states Eddie Kramer simply. "He was wonderful," recalls Marron. "He took direction and was reliable – as well as being *black* – a fact, oddly, that seems more important today." Road sound engineer Mike Neal, later to replace Abe Jacob as live sound engineer for the Experience, echoes Marron's sentiment. "Billy Cox was steady and never caused a problem. He wasn't into drugs and you could always count on him. When we had to be in the hotel lobby at 10 A.M., Billy would be there at 9:45, waiting for Stickells to drag Mitch and Jimi down."

While Hendrix never spoke, at least publicly, of any calculated attempt to include black musicians in the Experience, the switch to Cox gave him a friend who could also lessen the tension and tedium of touring. "On tour," recalls Abe Jacob, "surrounded by Englishmen, Cox gave him someone he could relate to."

Chaos ruled Hendrix's musical retreat in Shokan, as he struggled to define his new musical direction. Mitch was still in England, and though the rumor of an appearance by Buddy Miles refused to dissipate, Hendrix, Larry Lee and Cox, as well as percussionists Jerry Velez and Juma Sultan, were involved in lengthy jam sessions. In an effort to incorporate keyboards into his new music, Hendrix also recruited former Group Therapy keyboardist Gerry Guida to the Shokan house for a short stint.

Though Hendrix may have sought a quiet retreat among Woodstock's fabled wilds, he managed to stand out as much as he had in Harlem. "Jimi used to drive through town in his red Corvette," recalls Leslie Aday, an employee of Albert Grossman, who became friendly with Hendrix during his extended period upstate. "He'd have the top down and be dressed in all of his glory. Nobody in Woodstock had a red Corvette. These people were into growing organic vegetables and making their own clothes!"

The musicians Hendrix had invited to the house were no mere motley crew. Hendrix, recalls Aday, had expressed his concept of a band that comprised musicians from a variety of racial backgrounds. The timing for such a concept, he explained, couldn't be better. Aside from Jimi's own celebrated mixture of Cherokee Indian and Negro heritage, percussionist Jerry Velez was an Hispanic from New York's Lower East Side; Mitchell (who would rejoin Hendrix) a white Briton; Cox and Lee were African Americans steeped in the Delta blues tradition; and Juma Sultan an African American who had embraced Africa's vast cultural heritage.

Juma Sultan was well known within the Woodstock artistic community, a respected percussionist actively involved with the Aboriginal Music Society, which presented a broad mosaic of musical influences in semiconcert form on Sunday evenings at the Tinker Street Cinema. Sultan introduced Hendrix to the aggregation of local musicians, but when they played together, Hendrix couldn't help plowing through their delicate, polyrhythmic patterns. He had not yet integrated softer elements into his live music, volume and feedback remaining the essential ingredients of his style. Even his rhythm playing, while not as bombastic as his solo work, was still delivered with great force. It would be this simple fact, plus a lack of adequate rehearsal time, that would doom Gypsys Suns & Rainbows, the moniker he invented for his new band.

A strange dichotomy evolved from Gypsys Suns & Rainbows' lengthy jam sessions. Hendrix, Cox and Lee shared a love for the hybrid form of blues, R&B and rock n' roll on which they had not only been reared but had based their careers. With Mitchell back behind the drums, Lee's rhythm guitar provided tasteful accompaniment to "Red House" and "Hear My Train," bolstering Hendrix's blues masterworks. What hampered Gypsys Suns & Rainbows' development was the dearth of new material *composed* with the big band in mind. Congas simply had no place in "Foxey Lady" or "Purple Haze," and even if such material could be reworked to include this and other subtle instruments, that goal would only signify a regression for Hendrix. Tracks such as "Jam Back at the House" – born from incessant jamming – did more to showcase the band's deficiencies than strengths. Larry Lee was a close friend and an accomplished player, but he was not in a league to be trading solos with Jimi Hendrix.

Mitch Mitchell was becoming increasingly frustrated with Gypsys Suns & Rainbows' inabilities, and many of those present, from Leslie Aday to Gerry Stickells, sensed his frustration with the band's distinct lack of cohesion. Mitchell could see little progress and, as a result, felt that continuing within the structure was a waste of time. In his opinion, using three percussionists cluttered the Hendrix sound. At first, Jimi was not ready to accept this, hoping that over time the band could be whipped into shape. To help track their progress, Hendrix had contacted Eddie Kramer, asking him to break from the studio project and come up to install some proper recording equipment. Kramer agreed, and borrowed a four-track machine, professional microphones and an improved PA system. Up until this time, Hendrix had been utilizing his own domestic reel-to-reel tape machine. Kramer took a weekend to organize Hendrix's requests, even engineering a few jam sessions himself.

For the most part, Hendrix was enjoying his northern retreat. The house Jeffery had rented for him came with horses and a stable. Apart from Juma Sultan, a local, no one knew how to ride, yet everybody gave it a go. There were also cookouts, informal interplay between the musicians and a general sense of fun.

Drugs were certainly prevalent at Hendrix's Shokan retreat – in spite of his impending trial for possession – as well as being openly obtainable throughout the Woodstock community. Hendrix had not curbed his drug intake following the bust and still viewed drugs – predominantly marijuana – as a recreational exercise. He was not a junkie, nor was his drug use all consuming in the manner that had destroyed Billie Holiday and Charlie Parker. He was, however, troubled by the notion that his bust in Toronto carried with it very real consequences. Unable to enunciate his fears publicly, the prospect of jail time gnawed at him. "It was really frustrating to him," recalls Leslie Aday. "He was sure that he would go to jail and be made an example of. I said, 'No, no, you'll have the best lawyers and all your fans behind you,' but he shrugged and replied, 'This is international. There are a lot of people who would like nothing better than to point at me in jail as a bad example.'"

Without knowing whether Hendrix would have his new band in place, booking agent Ron Terry was negotiating for Hendrix to headline a massive music and arts festival to be held in Wallkill, New York. Woodstock Ventures – like the great majority of festival promoters – wanted Hendrix on the bill to ensure its financial success. Terry's conditions were simple. Not only would Hendrix close the festival and be advertised as its headliner, but he would also have to be the highest-paid performer. "I got with the guys from Woodstock Ventures," Terry recalls, "and instructed them to give me $18,000 immediately and place the rest in escrow. When they did, Michael Goldstein was instructed to issue a press release saying that Hendrix would perform at the festival. Weiss, Jeffery and I had a meeting with Hendrix and told him we were getting more money than anyone else and that this was an important gig to play. Hendrix said, 'If you feel it's that important, let's do it.'"

With a concert now in place, jams became rehearsals. "They would rehearse these great free-form fusion workouts," remembers Leslie Aday. "But on stage they would never have that kind of time to get to the groove. It sounded great in the house, but before an audience..."

"Rehearsals, as I remember they called them," says Gerry Stickells, "consisted of getting stoned and talking about how great it was going to be. The fact that they kept adding people to the lineup proved to me that it wasn't together. They went along because someone else was paying the bills."

That someone, recalls Jimi's accountant Michael Hecht, was Hendrix. "On his behalf, I paid the bills for the house they trashed up there. They had gouged out the floor moving their equipment about and ruined artwork by painting on it."

With costs for the studio project escalating, and available funds dwindling, Michael Jeffery was growing impatient with his famous client. Warner Bros. had been temporarily sated by the release of *Smash Hits*, a compilation that included four songs – "Can You See Me," "Remember," "Stone Free" and "Red House" – not yet released in America, a project warmly received by Hendrix fans, who purchased the album in droves (according to official figures, it remains virtually tied with *Are You Experienced?* for most copies sold). Modeled after Track Records' 1968 British version, the U.S. album oddly featured no material from *Axis: Bold as Love* as well as bypassing "The Stars That Play With Laughing Sam's Dice" and "51st Anniversary" – songs that had only appeared in the U.S. as B sides. The most notable change in the set was the inclusion of the Olympic Studio version of "Red House," the alternate take from the *Are You Experienced?* sessions that featured additional overdubs by Hendrix as well as a remix by Eddie Kramer and Chas Chandler.

The U.S. album's artwork also featured something new: a free poster. The idea, first developed by Chandler and Track's Chris Stamp, was to not only distribute quality posters of the group for fans, but also provide extras for record shops to display. There was certainly no doubting the popularity of the concept, and Jeffery could point out the enormously lucrative success of his own merchandising efforts.

For Warner Bros, the album sleeve's legend "giant poster enclosed" was less a concession to Jeffery's marketing ploys than a deliberate attempt to add value to the compilation. "When Jimi, Mitch and Noel had been in Los Angeles for the Forum show [April 26, 1969]," recalls Ed Thrasher, art director for Warner Bros. Records, "I brought them out to the Warner Films backlot for a full-day photo session. I wanted to shoot a take-off on the television show *Gunsmoke*." Thrasher is quick to defuse a rumor long believed by Hendrix enthusiasts that the session was filmed as well as photographed. "I was the only one shooting," he says. "It's too bad, because they were having fun with the horses, drawing on each other with the guns, just having a great time."

With the color Western photos planned for the front and back covers, Thrasher wanted to capture a truly exotic black-and-white shot of Hendrix for the poster. Bare-chested, Hendrix sat astride a big Harley-Davidson motorcycle, wearing an old-fashioned World War I helmet – complete with German-styled spikes. Sadly, it was deemed just too exotic and, as a result, Reprise instead utilized the front cover that Track had issued in Britain, while selecting various Western photos for the back sleeve and poster.

Having relocated in Bethel, New York, the Woodstock Music and Art Fair awaited the performance of the "Jimi Hendrix Experience" on Sunday night, August 17, 1969. Upward of 300,000 people had jammed Max Yasgur's dairy farm to be entertained by the likes of Janis Joplin, The Who, Sly & the Family Stone, Creedence Clearwater Revival and Jefferson Airplane. Eddie Kramer had been hired by the festival's promoters to engineer the field recordings, from which an album of the best performances would be shaped. Kramer eagerly anticipated recording Hendrix live. He had done so only once before, at Gulfstream Park in Miami on

May 18, 1968, but having seen the Experience perform so magnificently at Madison Square Garden on May 18, 1969, Kramer hoped the aura of the festival would inspire Hendrix to even exceed that performance.

Inside the trailer that Hanley Sound had designated for recording, a makeshift remote facility had been constructed. "I had two eight-track machines," recalls Kramer. "But, because of the pulse tone signal required for the film crew, we were only able to utilize seven tracks for recording. One machine was installed in an orange crate and the other on a wooden box. I had a small twelve-input mixer and a bunch of little Shure mixers stacked up beside it. The buzzes, crackles and hum were making me pull my hair out. Hanley's PA system barely worked – it was hung together with baling wire and chewing gum. Having not been tested prior to the festival, it was finally completed as the concert began. After three days on site, the festival seemed to be the most unprofessional happening of all time. Michael Jeffery and Albert Grossman arrived well before Jimi, and one of my most vivid memories of the festival was seeing the two of them, in a heavy rainstorm, trying to push a jeep stuck in deep mud!"

Hendrix finally arrived amid relentless rain. "No one knew if he would get to go on that night," recalls Kramer, "because the circular stage had broken during the day, and the band changeovers had been taking too long." Out of deference, Hendrix and his entourage had been directed to a more permanent shelter rather than crowd inside one of the many performer's tents.

"Hendrix was in a farm shack," recounts Leslie Aday, "but he was the only artist who didn't have to crowd into the tents backstage. Jerry Morrison [a Jeffery aide] had come to get me, and I could see that Hendrix was ill, dosed, I'm afraid, by drinking the water backstage [some water sources had indeed been laced with hallucinogens]. He seemed really sick, or really high, and was sweating bullets. I was feeding him vitamin C, fruit and having him suck on lemon slices. As we sat there, he seemed very nervous and didn't think he could pull it off. He didn't feel the band knew the songs well enough or had had enough rehearsal. He was stressed out."

As it transpired, Hendrix had no need to go on that evening, because the event's producers, following a consultation with Jeffery, pushed back his performance to Monday morning – even though the festival had been scheduled to conclude on Sunday evening. The next morning, as Hendrix strode onto the stage leading his Gypsys Suns & Rainbows, the sun had just begun to burn the dampness and its residual chill from the air. From the stage, the festival site looked devastated. Exhausted and out of food, the great majority of the audience – unaware that the festival would resume the following morning, or unable to stay over any longer – had made their way through the quagmire back to their cars or alternate transportation. The crowd remaining numbered no more than 25,000 and a great number of these were content with a glimpse at Hendrix before upping and leaving in the middle of his set.

There were some highlights marbled within Hendrix's unusually long, 140-minute performance, but they were few and quite far between. Hendrix's preconcert jitters were justified, as Gypsys Suns & Rainbows' performance distinctly lacked cohesion, many songs seeming ragged and under-rehearsed. Never in his two and a half years with the Experience had Hendrix exhibited such disregard for professionalism, not even during that band's formative weeks when, with a paucity of original material, cover versions of songs had been performed with as much enthusiasm as could be mustered. On stage at Woodstock, the same Jimi Hendrix who had refused Noel Redding the opportunity to perform "She's so Fine" – even when fans had shouted requests for the number – allowed guitarist Larry Lee to traipse off-key through two songs, "Mastermind" and the Impressions' "Gypsy Woman."

Throughout the set, Hendrix repeatedly apologized for

the band knowing only a few tunes, having to continually tune up and not playing the old songs. The same artist who, with Mitchell and Redding, had stunned an unexpecting audience at Monterey while in total control of his seemingly limitless powers, appeared lost at Woodstock. It would be oversimplistic to conclude that Hendrix was complacent and disinterested, but for Cox, Lee, Velez and Sultan, Woodstock was simply the biggest gig of their lives. They all were trying their best, and each performed with great passion and gusto throughout. Woodstock, however, was their first real test before an audience, and they weren't ready.

Early on that morning, Hendrix leaned toward material such as "Hear My Train A Comin'" that best suited the big band. For "Spanish Castle Magic," he reverted to the power trio concept, leaving Lee, Velez and Sultan behind, and with Mitchell and Cox roared through the song's first half. Hendrix then wound down and allowed Lee to come in and solo, tastefully adding muted rhythm to his own classic composition. After a warm round of applause, Hendrix's somber lead notes signified the start of "Red House," now enhanced by Larry Lee's rhythmic brush strokes on guitar. Lee followed Hendrix's solo with one of his own, yet his playing, while competent, was nowhere near as breathtaking or emotional as Hendrix's.

For Eddie Kramer, recording the performance backstage in Heider's remote soundtruck wasn't enough. "Once I had everything set in the truck I ran out, saying to the assistant engineer, 'Watch my recording levels, I'll be right back!' and took a bunch of pictures of Jimi from the side of the stage. I just had to. Then I ran back to the truck as quickly as I could. I felt a strange sense of pride when Jimi took the stage, and was rooting for him to play well."

During "Lover Man," Hendrix tried to jump-start the band single-handedly, roaring ferociously through the song as Mitchell valiantly kept pace behind him. Lee took the first solo before Hendrix overwhelmed him with a burst of lightning-fast notes that came screaming out of his Marshall stacks. While this recording was excluded from either of the *Woodstock* albums and posthumous Hendrix collections, it remains a fascinating item, and because of its flaws, perhaps a better candidate than most for dissection by Alan Douglas in his *Variations on a Theme* collections, which try to isolate various Hendrix guitar techniques. Unlike the classic Hendrix recordings, which are far more interesting and revealing in whole rather than part, elements of this particular version of "Lover Man" are ripe for examination. In a span of roughly four minutes, while not always in tune or musical time, Hendrix demonstrated his uncanny incorporation of rhythm, lead, tremolo, feedback and distortion. As a whole, the song fails, but the guitar work was nothing short of brilliant.

After the band bludgeoned their way through "Foxey Lady," Hendrix sensed his audience's confusion. "I know it's not together," he remarked from the stage, continuing in a mocking tone, "'You're tuning up between every song! This isn't together! That isn't together!' Well, you all ain't in uniform!"

After a lengthy rendition of "Jam Back at the House" (the version that graces *Woodstock Two* is much condensed), "Izabella" came next, the song that had held such great promise for the big band concept. Although it too would be heavily edited before inclusion on *Woodstock Two*, "Izabella" was one of the day's few triumphs, the sole composition performed at Woodstock that suited the entire band, Gypsys Suns & Rainbows' extra percussion and rhythm guitar parts sounding appropriate rather than forced.

Once again abandoning his fragile coalition, Hendrix next ripped into "Voodoo Child (Slight Return)," self-described here as the "new American anthem until we get another one." With Mitchell and Cox right with him, this version – at least the song's first four minutes – was as strong as any version the Experience had performed in their prime. Velez and Sultan continued playing too, but the roar from

Hendrix's amplifiers drowned them out. As he had done with "Spanish Castle Magic," Hendrix reduced the song's tempo to allow the band an opportunity to rejoin him. The tentative meandering the audience had patiently withstood was noticeably absent as Hendrix tore through the song's famous riff before turning lead guitar chores over to Lee. Lee carried the song, by now a funk-based derivative, until Hendrix, dramatically snatching back the lead, sang the first verses of "Stepping Stone" with great emotion, bringing the song to a dramatic close with a series of wah-wah notes. Without hesitation, Hendrix then launched into "Star Spangled Banner." With Mitchell drumming furiously behind him – done, he would later report, to keep his hands warm – Hendrix invoked all of the passion and emotion welled within him, wholly realizing a consummate artistic achievement.

As he had done so often in the past, Hendrix had once more played just the right music at just the right time, rising to the occasion with a performance so brilliant that, like the "Sgt. Pepper" at the Saville Theatre or the burning guitar at Monterey, it would forever be seared into Hendrix legend, crystalized as a symbol of his incredible talent.

He next tore into *his* signature song, "Purple Haze," with a blistering intensity, culminating in an amazing, frenetic barrage of notes – an arrangement never before featured. He barreled through to the song's conclusion, his band left waiting for his turbo-charged improvisation to subside for just a moment so they could rejoin him. This free-form Stratocaster assault continued unabated for nearly four minutes before Hendrix shifted into beautiful flamenco-styled progressions. "Purple Haze" was an exquisite display, exuding a fervor his overall performance at Woodstock only intermittently showcased.

The audience, which had now dwindled to some 20,000, roared in approval, and Hendrix acknowledged their cheers, leading Gypsys Suns & Rainbows back to the stage. He wanted to try a new song, "Valley of Neptune," gushing,

"Don't laugh at us, we're going to try this song called 'Valley of Neptune.' Oh no [we can't]," he then regretfully exclaimed. "I forgot the words." Though his performance had been subpar, Hendrix drew deep upon his pride and professionalism in an effort to send the crowd home with a strong finish, playing "Hey Joe," one of the songs he knew they had come to hear.

For Hendrix's management, their artist's performance at Woodstock had been cause for great concern. For Michael Jeffery, Gypsys Suns & Rainbows would become the text-book definition of why the three-man Experience concept should never be abandoned.

Out in the remote truck, Eddie Kramer was nonplussed. "Quite frankly, I never thought his performance, save for 'Star Spangled Banner' and a few other highlights, was any good. Knowing Jimi's capabilities, I never got a good feeling as I recorded the show. Later, when I saw the film rushes and listened to the recordings in Los Angeles, I distinctly remember worrying that Woodstock might be the beginning of the end for Jimi Hendrix."

Amid the crush of activity backstage, Hendrix somehow managed to evade his management, as well as a scheduled appearance on the *Dick Cavett Show* that same day. Recalls Bob Levine: "The idea was to bring Hendrix down as soon as Woodstock finished, so that viewers could get a firsthand description of the festival. But Jimi went missing, and Gerry Stickells and I had no way of reaching him. Cavett's show was live in those days, and he kept saying, 'Hendrix should be here anytime now ...' After an hour and a half, Hendrix didn't show, and though we vowed to make it up to him, Cavett never forgave us. I later found out Hendrix thought the appearance had been canceled as a result of his own delay getting on stage at Woodstock. Hendrix just left the site with a date and holed up at Grossinger's."

Hendrix's "date" was Leslie Aday. "We left by helicopter," she remembers. "Jimi was tired, cold and hungry. We had adjoining rooms at the hotel, and as soon as we'd checked in,

I volunteered to find some food. He was unhappy with his performance and just wanted to get away where no one could find him. The hotel was filled with people who had come over from the festival, and when I came back, I heard a great deal of commotion in his room and peeked through the door. There were a number of people getting high who were not there in Jimi's best interests. After they left, I went back to check on him, and he had passed out on the bed with a cigarette going. It had burned a large hole through his sheet before going out. He was fortunate he hadn't been killed."

Hendrix came away from Woodstock convinced that Gypsys Suns & Rainbows needed more rehearsing before they took to the stage again. Michael Jeffery had other thoughts, and the two were poised for confrontation. Jeffery was under a great deal of financial pressure, needing Hendrix to perform a series of concerts, the cash benefits of which were needed to keep the studio project solvent. A host of elements had converged to restrict Jeffery's financial liquidity. Hendrix's company, Are You Experienced? Ltd., had just paid out an enormous sum to the IRS, which, despite his many deductible expenses, came as a result of lucrative touring and record royalties. Further restricting cash flow was the fact that Hendrix was also between Warner Bros. royalty statements, so although *Smash Hits* was enjoying strong sales, no money would be due for some time. Noel Redding's defection in June had brought Jeffery's empire to a near halt. At that time, the studio project had seemed feasible – its $500,000 budget represented the proceeds of just eight or ten Experience concerts. Now, with the Experience scattered and Are You Experienced? Ltd.'s till nearly empty, Jeffery began to feel the heat.

The studio project had run into a number of unforeseen problems. There were numerous delays obtaining permits, and during demolition the site was flooded after a particularly heavy series of rainstorms. Then it was discovered that the studio was being constructed on a tributary of the

underground Minetta River. Hendrix had long been fascinated by water: now, his dream studio floated above it.
Sump pumps would have to be installed and, in addition to
assigning them careful hiding places – one, for example, was
installed in the ladies' room – additional soundproofing
would now be required. To further prevent sound leakage
(Studios A and B were constructed back to back and not, as
is the norm, separated by a control room), thick walls were
bolstered by pouring sand inside hollowed bricks. According to attorney Howard Krantz, Jeffery and Hendrix also
incorrectly purchased parcels of equipment. "They under-
estimated how long the entire project would take," says
Krantz. "Eddie Kramer would tell them what to buy and
Michael Hecht would arrange to pay for it. But instead of
negotiating payment plans, Jeffery would instruct Hecht to
just buy the item outright."

This lack of contingency planning crippled Jeffery. To
date, he had invested the lion's share of the cash needed for
the project. To finance his share, recalls Jim Marron, Hendrix
"would instruct Michael Hecht to throw in $20,000 at a time,
almost exclusively from his share of concert receipts."
Further depleting his cash reserves, Jeffery had also been
forced to settle a number of outstanding debts he had left
behind in London. "Jeffery burned a lot of bridges in
London," admits Marron. "He didn't pay anyone. He owed
one 'investor' $20,000, and in an effort to retrieve the sum,
they sent a guy over to kill him if he didn't pay. That won
his respect. 'This bloke wants to knock me off,' he told me.
Jeffery gave the guy the $20,000 he had 'borrowed' and sent
him back to England."

To Jeffery's ceaseless frustration, the Experience had
folded just as the group was enjoying its most lucrative pay
days. Concerts East and West – as well as the concept of self-
promotion – had been successfully established by Hendrix
and his mentors. Now, with everything working to near
perfection, Michael Jeffery was about to be left behind. "If
Hendrix wasn't going to tour," recalls Ron Terry, "we had

enough acts to survive. Jeffery was the only one who got strangled by Hendrix's decision. He was a one-horse bandit. By that point in time, Vanilla Fudge were still going, Led Zeppelin had broken, and Mountain were just coming along. We would have loved to have had Hendrix out on tour, but if he didn't go, Les Smith was still behind us. Jeffery didn't have that luxury, he planned from minute to minute. If he was broke, he reacted, and that put pressure on his artist."

With Hendrix's plans unclear, Concerts West – working closely with Steve Weiss – quickly scheduled a mini-tour across the South. The cities, all Concerts West strongholds, were spread between September 19 and 29, taking the Experience – or whomever Hendrix wished – through Jacksonville, Atlanta, Miami, New Orleans, Lubbock, Norman, Fort Worth, San Antonio and Austin, performing ten (two shows were proposed in New Orleans) concerts in eleven days, not a particularly grueling slate in comparison to earlier Experience junkets. But just before advertising and ticket sales were set in motion, Hendrix refused to comply.

Furthermore, Jeffery had booked Hendrix to play another huge outdoor concert on the Boston Common. Jeffery's handling of this gig caused particular ill will. "There was no real purpose for dates at that point," recalls Ron Terry, "except that Jeffery was overextended and needed money. A lot of weird shit was going down. Jeffery was trying to get deposits sent to him personally instead of to Hecht or Weiss. That worsened the paranoia between him and Hendrix."

On September 9, in a letter prepared by Henry Steingarten, and signed by both him and Hendrix, Jimi ruled himself out of all his tour commitments. It said: "At a meeting with Jimi Hendrix today, at which Steve Weiss was present part of the time, it developed that Jimi Hendrix is not well enough at this time to undertake the contemplated tour scheduled to begin September 18. Also, the group which Hendrix had put together has temporarily disbanded, and the date when it will be reformed is uncertain ... probably not before next spring. At Hendrix's request, I ask Steve Weiss to communicate with the promoters of the various dates and to request from them a bill for their expenses to date.

"I [Steingarten] urged Jimi Hendrix to fulfill the dates, telling him that I thought he was doing his reputation a great deal of harm and that the financial involvement might be substantial. Hendrix's response was that his reputation as a musician was paramount, and inasmuch as he did not feel himself physically and mentally capable of performing satisfactorily, he felt that overshadowed his failure to appear."

The Boston concert was canceled too, and the decision had been a bitter one that would have lasting repercussions. Rumors had begun to circulate that Hendrix was suffering from physical exhaustion or perhaps even a nervous breakdown. These charges strained Jeffery's relationship with publicity agent Michael Goldstein (although, in an effort to pare expenses, he had already planned to trim Goldstein from Hendrix's account until Jimi became active again), and Hendrix fumed when he heard about them. To spare his own tenuous relationship with Hendrix, Jeffery made Goldstein the scapegoat. "Michael's biggest problem with Jimi," recalls Bob Levine, "was that he couldn't communicate with him. He tried drugs, mysticism, intimidation and CIA–MI5 tactics, but he was unable to do it." Hendrix had begun to notice an alarming trend: Jeffery had begun to intrude upon his creative decisions. This territory was off-limits to Jeffery, and Hendrix felt he had violated a long-held, unspoken agreement.

The one and only show at which Hendrix had agreed to perform was a benefit concert for Harlem's United Block Association. The association, located on 139th Street, had long staged street fairs and block parties. The Allen twins were working with Chet Cummings, a local activist aligned with the UBA, and through them Cummings arranged for Bob Levine and Michael Jeffery to travel to Harlem for a meeting. "Chet Cummings talked Jeffery into doing that show," recalls Levine. "Jimi's [only] concern was that people in Harlem might say, 'What's he doing here?'" Not wanting to ruffle his artist further, Jeffery agreed to have Hendrix perform. A date was set for September 5, where Hendrix would precede Big Maybelle, a perennial Harlem favorite.

To publicize Hendrix's appearance at the UBA benefit, a press conference was scheduled for September 3 at Frank's Restaurant on 125th Street in Harlem. Here, flanked by the Allen twins and Chet Cummings, Hendrix announced that he hoped his appearance could help the community, and that he wished the spirit embodied at Woodstock could be extended to black Americans. "This is a crusade," Hendrix remarked. "Why be selfish? There are a lot of black people who haven't been included yet. This is all in the womb stage. POP I call it, Pilgrimage of Peace."

Crowding the restaurant, the mainstream press peppered Hendrix with questions about the "folk festival in White Lake." A reporter asked him to compare the UBA benefit in Harlem with Woodstock. "I don't know," Hendrix replied. "Forget about comparing, that's where we make our biggest mistake, trying to put our ego against other persons. That's why I can't find out who is better, B.B. King or Segovia. They're both masters. They're both kings. Why go through 'he can play that note but he's louder there'?"

Another reporter wanted to know why Hendrix performed the "Star Spangled Banner" in such a fashion. "Because we are all Americans," Hendrix replied. Scanning the room, he continued, "We are all Americans aren't we? When it was written it was very nice and beautifully inspiring. Your heart throbs and you say, 'Great, I'm American.' Nowadays we don't play it to take away any of the greatness America is supposed to have. We play it the way the air is in America today, and that air is [full of] static."

On September 5, the atmosphere on 139th Street was electric, as members of the United Block Association's crew scurried about, busily supervising the fair. With Big Maybelle on the bill, as well as local favorites Maxine Brown, Chuck-a-Luck and J.D. Bryant, a strong turnout was guaranteed. "Big Maybelle was a household word in most of Harlem," remarks WWRL's DJ Eddie O'Jay, who doubled as the evening's MC. "*She* was a Harlem artist – as well as Bedford-Stuyvesant, Brooklyn and Queens. I knew what Jimi Hendrix had been doing in the past but I wasn't too sure the general audience would understand."

Hendrix and his entourage arrived late, so, not wanting to stall the proceedings, the organisers asked Big Maybelle to take the stage first. "Hendrix wasn't on last because he was the headline act," recalls O'Jay. "To get the show underway, we reversed the star attractions. I had a small group [made up of Sam & Dave sidemen as well as future LTD frontman Jeffrey Osbourne] back up Big Maybelle. She wowed the whole community, and had people leaning out windows of apartment buildings swaying to her music.

"Jimi and his group arrived in a van with their instruments," continues O'Jay. "The makeshift stage had been placed on the street. The kids were all gathered around waiting for the entertainment to start."

"When we arrived," recalls Gerry Stickells, "there was pressure from the Black Panthers. All of the white guys had to hide in a burned-out, defunct laundry until it was time to go on. We had to put the gear up quickly because people were throwing stuff and spitting on us."

"I doubt very seriously if there were enough people in the audience – youngsters and old people alike – that really knew what Jimi Hendrix was about," remembers O'Jay. "My not being able to play the kind of records that I'd wanted to hear on the radio meant that few people had heard of Jimi Hendrix. I don't think the black masses were appreciative of Hendrix's music because we were not exposed to it that much. It's unfortunate that still, today, black people ask who Jimi Hendrix was."

Greeted by a smattering of polite applause, Hendrix's Gypsys Suns & Rainbows took the stage. As they readied themselves to play, some unruly members of the audience hurled eggs at the makeshift platform, landing harmlessly near Mitchell's drum kit. Once under way, charged with emotion, Hendrix led his expanded ensemble through "Purple Haze," "Foxey Lady," "Red House" and "Star Spangled Banner," among others, as well as "Voodoo Chile," described by Jimi as the "Harlem national anthem."

Most reviews were wildly enthusiastic. "I can say one thing for sure," recalls Eddie O'Jay. "By the evening's end, everybody [there] knew who Jimi Hendrix was. It turned out to be a fantastic show." "The show was fine," remembers Gerry Stickells. "But it wasn't what it should have been." "It was quite a shindig," says Bob Levine. "Most people didn't know who he was, but it did the Allen brothers a lot of good up there, proving that they could deliver Jimi Hendrix."

Hendrix's success at the street fair *had* been an impressive achievement for the Allen twins. "That was an unbelievable concert," recalls Albert Allen. Sadly, while both Chet Cummings and the Allen twins made elaborate plans to document the festival, their efforts went for naught. "We had hired a guy to film the whole thing. He didn't know Hendrix, so he used all of the film on Big Maybelle. The only thing he ended up shooting was Hendrix walking on stage and stringing his guitar. We could have killed him."

At odds with Michael Jeffery over the direction of his career, and indeed against his manager's wishes, Hendrix volunteered to perform at the Salvation Club's press party, set for September 10 in New York City. The tiny club was planning to feature live music on a regular basis and had sent invitations out to members of the press. In recent weeks, Hendrix had become friends with the Salvation's Bobby Woods. Woods was active in the cocaine trade and Hendrix had quietly become a customer. On the evening of the party, a long line of fans crowded the Salvation's entrance, eager to glimpse their hero's surprise set. After midnight, Hendrix sauntered onto the Salvation's cramped stage, plugged in and began. Without a functioning microphone, Hendrix led the band through such extended pieces as "Jam Back at the House." Just as they had done earlier that summer, jamming at the Tinker Street Cinema in Woodstock, Hendrix cruised, trading riffs and solos with Lee while pulling back to integrate Sultan, Velez and Mitchell's poly-rhythmic interplay.

Comfortable and informal as the jamming may have been, the audience – packed to capacity with journalists and fans who had shelled out $10 for the privilege – had perhaps been anticipating a more dramatic close to the evening's festivities. Rock music's most visually dynamic artist, Hendrix just stood on stage, barely emitting a trace of emotion. Midway through the set, many patrons, content with a glimpse of Hendrix – and sure that this exhibition was certainly not an Experience-style concert – actually left.

Just before drawing his set to a close, a working microphone was finally produced, to which Hendrix stepped forward and delivered "Izabella." One song later, he thanked those who had chosen to remain and disappeared behind his amplifiers.

The Salvation gig had been a disaster, and Gypsys Suns & Rainbows, his grand vision, had performed their final concert.

Following his performance, Hendrix left with Bobby Woods to escape the crowd and score some cocaine. Their acquaintance had been one of convenience, and on this occasion Hendrix ended up spending the better part of the early morning with him – an association that would carry repercussions. "Although he spent the night with Bobby Woods," recalls Bob Levine, "he really didn't know who he was. To Jimi he was just a nice guy who sold cocaine. The next night, Woods was found murdered, gangland-style. The 'boys' knew Hendrix had spent the night with Woods and wanted to know what he had heard from him. Hendrix hadn't heard anything about their business, but they had to make sure."

"Making sure" translated to abducting Hendrix and

taking him upstate, where he was questioned and held against his will. "It wasn't a hostile kidnapping," remembers Bob Levine. "It was a 'house arrest.' Jimi was missing and we couldn't find him. Fortunately, this happened during a lull, when we didn't have any dates scheduled. The 'boys' sent word down that he was being treated comfortably and would be released in a couple of days."

"Jeffery was incensed that someone would actually steal his artist and question his power," recalls Jim Marron. "It was a show of force against him. Though the entire affair was really about Bobby Woods and cocaine, Jeffery was determined to back them down rather than accept any of their terms."

Adds Bob Levine, "Jeffery called in a few of his own contacts to rescue Jimi. I cautioned him against the move because we had spoken to Hendrix and he had assured us that he would be back in a couple of days. I told Jeffery – to no avail – that he was risking a situation that could turn nasty or require retribution."

Jeffery was confident he could repel the challenge, and at the same time he wanted to send a strong and clear message. "Jeffery wasn't about to mediate," says Marron. "He had developed his own connections and his were much more powerful than theirs. It cost Jeffery a favor, but once his brutes arrived, the people who had been keeping Jimi under house arrest put their guns away and left."

Hendrix, the subject of this intense intrigue, found the entire episode silly. "He was kind of amused by it all," recalls Marron. Says Bob Levine, "Jeffery had backed them down, but Jimi saw right through that. Though Jeffery had flexed his muscles and proved his own power, he had no control over Hendrix."

Careening along without direction, Hendrix's only remaining engagement was an appearance on the *Dick Cavett Show* – and that a make-good for his no-show following the Woodstock festival. Even his recording sessions, once the sole bastion of sanity within his professional life, had progressively grown unruly and unproductive. "There were fifteen to eighteen people hanging all over him in the office on 37th Street," remembers Bob Levine. "Hendrix was already late for a session and the driver was outside. I cornered Jimi and forced him into the bathroom, the only quiet space available. I put the lid down on the toilet and sat down. Flustered, I said, 'Get in the tub!' So he sat in it, put his legs up and got comfortable. I tore into him, screaming at the top of my lungs. He kept saying, 'Yes Bob, I understand. I was wrong.' I told him he had to leave for the studio without all of these people, just to leave with the driver. He *had* to leave these people behind. I told him to walk out and tell them that you have a private thing to do and that you would see them later. If he didn't get to the studio without them it would be bedlam. 'What you do after,' I told him, 'is your business.'

"What we needed," Levine continues, "was to get Eddie Kramer out of the studio's construction and back with Jimi. Hendrix's sessions had become nothing more than unproductive, expensive parties. Eddie was very intimidating in those days. Jeffery may not have cared for him, but Kramer was never afraid to tell someone to go fuck themselves and get out of his studio. Hendrix respected Kramer and wouldn't have pulled that shit with him."

"Hendrix was very scattered," recalls Jim Marron. "Drugs had become the vehicle to escape his problems. He was using marijuana, hashish, cocaine – anything he could get his hands on, three to five times a week. Drugs were fast becoming a way of life."

Since Noel Redding's defection in July, Hendrix was steadily unraveling. To his legion of followers, content with *Smash Hits* and the memory of his recent public appearances, all seemed normal. But just below this thin veneer of adulation, Hendrix seemed on the fast track to self-destruction. Most distressing was his upcoming trial in Toronto, which, through any means necessary, he sought to block from his mind. However, with his judgment soon due,

Hendrix remained convinced he faced a stiff penalty.

"He truly was frustrated," remembers Gerry Stickells, "and he was going through a period where he felt he couldn't write anything. Everything sounded the same as before. He was bored and directionless." "He was hearing music in his head and seeing it in colors," says Kathy Eberth. "But he just couldn't reproduce the notes. One night, after he kept playing the same song over and over, I watched him throw one of his favorite guitars across the room."

Eberth and Hendrix maintained a close relationship, and Jeffery, desperate to keep tabs on his artist, began to communicate with Hendrix through her. "By this time, if Jeffery wanted something from Hendrix," she recalls, "he would come to me and say, 'See if he will do this.' I was aware of what he was doing; Jimi and I used to laugh about it. I'd say to him after a day at the office, 'Jimi, the word today is that Michael would like you to do this, doesn't want you to do that ...' I would ask *him* what he would feel like and if he wanted the message relayed."

Intimate with both Levine and Hendrix, Kathy Eberth triggered a wave of paranoia within Jeffery. Jeffery's grasp over Hendrix – while ironclad on paper – seemed tenuous in reality. "As much as Jeffery hated to rely on this bizarre system," remembers Jim Marron, "whenever there were problems, he would ask Kathy what Jimi was feeling or wanted to do. She was like the mouthpiece between Jeffery and Hendrix during that time. Jeffery could not get a straight answer out of Hendrix but was still desperate to know what he was thinking."

Further complicating matters, Hendrix began to avoid Jeffery, fully aware his manager needed his specific input to best address pressing business matters. He would neither return phone calls nor inform Jeffery as to his whereabouts. Hendrix relied on Eberth and Levine to stay abreast of his affairs, an activity that infuriated Jeffery.

"Jeffery would never come over to our apartment," recalls Bob Levine, "but one evening, he and his girlfriend Lynn

Bailey stopped by. I was thinking to myself, 'What's this visit about?,' but after a while, it seemed it was only a social call, probably instigated by Lynn. Michael asked me if I had seen Jimi lately and I said no – because I honestly hadn't. Just then there was a knock on the door. Kathy went to answer it and there was Jimi. She told him that Jeffery was here, but he didn't care. He fixed himself a plate of chicken and came in and sat down with us. Jeffery saw this and looked at me as if to say, 'You liar!' because I had told him that I hadn't seen him in days."

Growing increasingly paranoid, Jeffery again drew upon techniques learned as an MI5 captain, placing a hidden recording device in Levine's office and a monitor in his own – just across the parlor. "I found out that Bob's office had been bugged," recalls Kathy Eberth, "when I came into Jeffery's office and heard Bob's voice coming out of this little speaker."

Jeffery's deployment of secret surveillance devices to surreptitiously monitor his own employees had not been an isolated incident. The Animals' road manager Terry McVay recalls an incident in Spain, where employees of Jeffery's Haima nightclub were stealing and then reselling records sent over from the U.S. to maintain his lucrative jukebox business. "I didn't know what Jeffery was up to," remembers McVay, "but we were monitoring two of the club's employees plotting to steal money and records from the jukeboxes. We followed them to a bar where they had planned to meet their buyer. Before he arrived, we sat next to them and repeated *their* conversation verbatim. Jeffery knew their scheme cold and they were scared shitless, stunned that he had somehow caught them redhanded."

His relationship with Hendrix fast disintegrating and his cash flow stretched to its limits by his artist's inactivity and the studio's ceaseless expenses, Jeffery braced himself to battle with two prominent newcomers on the horizon: Buddy Miles and Alan Douglas.

# 13 A BAND OF GYPSYS

*"Jimi would ask me to come over and I would say, 'Oh, I don't want to be a nuisance.' He'd get angry and say, 'Why is it that the people you want to bother with think they will be nuisances, and the nuisances never think they are bothering you?'"*

– Faye Pridgeon

With no definitive itinerary scheduled, Mitch Mitchell soon returned to England and his new home in Sussex. Without missing a beat, Buddy Miles stepped into the open slot and the Band of Gypsys was born. In the aftermath of the Salvation Club debacle, only Mitchell and Billy Cox were spared, and although Hendrix maintained friendships with Sultan, Lee and Velez, the Sky Church ensemble had collapsed for good. Cox's position was stable; Miles, on the other hand, offered Hendrix vitality and enthusiasm, as well as his fabled fatback drumming.

Alan Douglas had come to know Jimi Hendrix through Devon Wilson's friendship with his wife Stella and with Colette Mimram, who owned a popular clothing boutique around the corner from the Fillmore East. Hendrix had an opportunity to obtain a financial interest in the business, but declined. "Jimi was kind of smitten with Colette," remembers Faye Pridgeon. "If there was anybody I thought he might be in love with, it was her."

Echoes Albert Allen: "Jimi really cared for Colette. I remember him asking us, 'Should I get her this boutique?' He really didn't know if he should do it or not." Though he chose not to buy into the company, Hendrix became its most famous client, unofficially appointing Stella and Colette his personal designers. The two crafted a host of blouses and stage outfits for him, including the long leather jacket Hendrix wore at Woodstock.

Stella Douglas's husband Alan, some fifteen years older than Hendrix, had a long history in the record industry, but little experience in rock n' roll, his forte being jazz. In the late 1950s, Douglas had been a staff producer for Barclay Records in France. There, he made a host of easy-listening sides for label chief Eddie Barclay. "Eddie Barclay was hung up on Ray Conniff," remembers Douglas. "He thought his stuff was great, so he created the Eddie Barclay Orchestra. Jimmy Mundy – who had done a lot of work with artists like Neal Hefti – did the charts, Quincy Jones conducted the orchestra and I was in the booth behind the console."

In 1962, Douglas was approached by United Artists' Art Talmadge to join UA's fledgling jazz label. Given a free hand and a reasonable cash reserve, Douglas aggressively sought artists to record. "I tried to sign all my boyhood heroes, people like Coltrane and Mingus, but they were all locked into contracts. In those days, if you paid their record companies $5,000, you could do one record with each of them, so I set about putting together an anthology of all the great artists I could sign."

In the early 1960s, during the waning days of the great American jazz era, UA issued a handful of notable releases compiled by Douglas, including John Coltrane and Cecil Taylor's *Stereo Drive* (later retitled *Coltrane Time*), as well as *Lady Love*, one of Billie Holiday's last albums. Later promoted to Director of UA Special Projects, Douglas ran the label's soundtrack division, overseeing, among other projects, the release of the Beatles' *A Hard Day's Night* and the many James Bond albums.

In 1967, Douglas looked to begin anew, leaving United Artists to start his own label, beginning with an ambitious Lenny Bruce retrospective. "I was tired of working for someone else," he says. "I knew Marvin Worth [Bruce's manager] very well and he brought Lenny's mother to see me. They had an incredible amount of tapes with them and said, 'What can you do?' The only way I could collate it into some type of library was to form the material into a book, which, after dedicating eight months to transcribe every tape in their library, ultimately became *The Essential Lenny Bruce*. The book was enormously successful and became the basis of the property; after that we started putting out records."

In creating *The Essential Lenny Bruce* Douglas developed his own strategy in creating a posthumous property that would not only be profitable, but would redirect focus and interest on the artist – a strategy he would incorporate with both Malcolm X and Jimi Hendrix. "I did basically the same thing with Malcolm X," remembers Douglas. "His wife turned over the tapes to me and I released three successful records. The process was simple; how do you take an artist and break him down to the point where people understand his value rather than his life? Most of the time, that value is obscured by the [artist's] personality. Like with Lenny, he was nuts, totally fucking crazy. If you want to think about Lenny Bruce as a person, a lot of people didn't like him and that's justifiable, because he was abrasive. That, however, has got nothing to do with his talent. What we did was to get right at his talent. What did Lenny say on divorce or marriage or blacks or Jews that was revealing? That was what was interesting. *The Essential Lenny Bruce* created a new entity that offered another perspective on Lenny and [as a concept] that worked."

Bolstered by the success of both the Lenny Bruce and

Malcolm X properties, Douglas Records, his spoken word label (funded with a paltry $25,000 annual budget – including salary), distributed by Laurie Records – the recording home of Dion and the Belmonts – looked to expand. "I went out and got financing," recalls Douglas. "And the label became Douglas Communications, a multimedia company. At that point, I signed Allen Ginsberg, the Last Poets and [Jazz guitarist] John McLaughlin, and we started to move."

Douglas was introduced to Hendrix at the boutique, first in passing and then, formally, at one of Stella's frequent dinner parties. At one such occasion in late September 1969, Douglas recalls Hendrix inviting him to one of his sessions. "I was lying in my bedroom because I was whipped," says Douglas. "There was a dinner thing going on in the front room and the gang was there, Jimi, Devon, Stella, Colette, Pete Cameron and some other friends. I was just about to fall asleep when Hendrix came in and sat on the edge of the bed. He asked if I wanted to come down to the studio tonight. I was exhausted and said, 'Well, not really,' but he wasn't about to let me go to sleep.

"It was close to midnight when we left for the Record Plant. Everyone else showed up about two hours later. I never saw such disorganization in all of my life. No one, in either the control room or the studio, was taking care of business for him. The engineer just kept putting rolls of tape on the machine and pressing the record button. I was sitting there thinking, 'What the fuck is this?' I had no idea what was going on. I had never recorded with him in a studio before and had no idea what was in his head. Billy Cox and Buddy Miles were there and the three of them jammed all night long. I sat there for four or five hours until I went out and told him I was beat and had to go. I had to be back in the studio at ten the next morning, so I left him there. On the way home, I wondered why he had asked me to come because I didn't know what he was trying or even wanted to do.

"The next day, he came over for dinner and I asked him

to explain what he wanted me to do. He said, 'Somebody has got to organize things for me.' I was very, very busy with my own projects and I needed to know how much time he needed from me – I wasn't getting paid – but he said, 'Just come down.' So I went back the next night and saw pretty much the same thing. Sitting in the control room watching all of this, I had to say something. I told the engineer, being the 'producer,' to stop running the machines. They were running off reel after reel of tape, two an hour, stacking them on the floor. It took me a while, but I started figuring out what Hendrix was doing. He was jamming, but he was trying to create a rhythm pattern for Miles and Cox to follow. Once those two were in the groove, Hendrix would break into a [structured] tune. I said, 'Okay, so *this* is how you get tracks out of the guy.' I was doing this for a friend, nobody was paying me at all. I felt that the way I could help him was to make sure there was efficiency in the control room and that they were not wasting tape."

As October 1969 dawned, Douglas involved Hendrix in two of his own projects, recordings by Timothy Leary and the Last Poets. Estranged from Jeffery and with Mitch Mitchell in England, Hendrix and Buddy Miles had further strengthened their ties. With Douglas as an unwitting shield, Miles seized control of the Band of Gypsys. "I was the leader of the Band of Gypsys," emphasizes Miles. "Having said, more or less, 'I have an idea,' Jimi looked to me to put it together. Let's get one thing straight – race was never a factor, it had nothing to do with it. Jimi and I just wanted to play together."

Miles and Douglas had worked together before, since both Miles and bassist Billy Rich, following the demise of the Buddy Miles Express, had been conscripted (along with organist Larry Young) to back John McLaughlin on his Douglas Records debut. Rich, recalls Stefan Bright, staff engineer for Douglas Records, was the consensus choice for the new group. "Buddy always had a heavy hand in these decisions, and Billy Rich had been with him in the Express.

At that point, Hendrix was open to our suggestions because he had no band and enjoyed playing with Buddy, but eventually he brought Billy Cox back into the picture."

That both Douglas and Stefan Bright had offered to help shape Hendrix's new group came as no surprise to Buddy Miles. He recalls, "Douglas was only involved with the Band of Gypsys because Hendrix was feuding with Jeffery. It was a very strange time. Hendrix couldn't communicate with Jeffery, so he made Douglas his 'spokesman.' The Band of Gypsys were put together in his office."

The first Hendrix–Douglas collaboration, recalls Stefan Bright, fell together by chance. "We had set up a jam session at the Record Plant with Buddy Miles, John Sebastian, Duane Hitchings and Stephen Stills. When we arrived at the studio, Hendrix was there. He wanted to know who was coming to the session. When he heard that Steve Stills was expected, he didn't want to play lead guitar. We thought that was strange, but he did volunteer to play bass. There wasn't a left-handed bass in the studio, only a right-handed model, so he just turned it upside down and played some of the most fantastic bass guitar I've ever heard. Stills was the last musician to arrive, and when he did, he burst into the studio saying, 'Joni [Mitchell] just wrote this song and I'd like to try and jam on it.' It was 'Woodstock' – Crosby, Nash and Young hadn't even heard it yet. Stills led the guys through a twenty-five-minute jam based on that song. As it turned out, Alan Douglas had helped get Tim Leary out of jail in Texas, where he had been busted on a marijuana charge. We held a press conference for Leary at our offices on 55th Street and decided to release his comments on an album called *You Can Be Anything This Time Around*. We used that 'Woodstock' jam for the first side of the album. Nobody knew who was playing on the album because we weren't allowed to use their names on the sleeve, but we let the word slip out. It was after this session that we really started to work with Jimi."

Douglas Records' 55th Street offices became the Band of

Gypsys' unofficial headquarters as Hendrix sought to put distance between himself and Michael Jeffery. "He used to hide in my house or at my office," Douglas recalls, "so that Jeffery couldn't find him. I put aside a soundproof rehearsal room for him on the first floor so he could practice because everyone in his apartment building was screaming at him for playing too loud."

Perhaps the strongest bind to the Douglas camp was Hendrix's deepening relationship with Stella, Colette and Devon. "They were very intriguing women," emphasizes Stefan Bright. "Especially Stella and Colette, who were so sensual. The attraction was mutual, they were both beautiful but at the same time, very sad people. Their relationship with Hendrix was intimate, it wasn't just, 'Let's go down to the Scene and listen to Jimi,' it went way beyond the club scene. Stella and Colette were more emotionally stable than Devon, who was in and out with Jimi so many times it was unbelievable, but in the end he always came back to the three girls."

The second Douglas–Band of Gypsys collaboration was also the result of an impromptu session. On this occasion, Hendrix and Miles were recruited to provide instrumentation for a Last Poets session. "Jalal from the Last Poets was in my office just hanging out," recalls Douglas. "We walked down to the Record Plant and Buddy Miles was there waiting for Hendrix. I said to Jalal, 'Why don't you do one of your poems for Buddy? Go ahead, he'll break up.' During the middle of it, Jimi arrived and got all excited about what was happening. When they finished, I went out into the studio and told Jalal to do 'Doriella Du Fontaine.' This piece was from a suite of things we were doing called *Jail Toasts*, like older black convicts would rap in prison. It started with 'Dear John' letters they would receive and in order for them to turn around and have some fun, they would create poetry out of them. We did one take, thirteen minutes straight. When it was over, everybody was amazed that it came off nonstop. Jimi was on guitar and Buddy on drums. We then overdubbed Jimi playing bass and Buddy on the organ." ("I wasn't no great organist or nothing," remembers Miles, "but I was the only thing Alan could get his hands on.")

Although the track would remain unreleased during Hendrix's lifetime, Douglas did ultimately issue a 9:37 version of "Doriella Du Fontaine" in 1984 as a twelve-inch single, backed by an edited version of the instrumental track. Largely dismissed by fans and critics alike as another in a seemingly ceaseless parade of inferior posthumous releases, "Doriella Du Fontaine" was actually a pristine example of the Hendrix-Band of Gypsys embrace of rap music during its infancy. It also provides a fascinating glimpse inside another aspect of Hendrix's unlimited potential. At that time, Hendrix had a better chance of reaching a core black audience as a nondescript Last Poets sideman than as one of rock n' roll's most profitable enterprises. While it remains the sole example of the marriage of Hendrix to rap or hip-hop, "Doriella Du Fontaine" bears an uncanny similarity to the efforts of those today – more than twenty years later – who digitally sample the classic Hendrix sound. One needs only to hear Digital Underground's inventive sampling of "Who Knows" on their best-selling *Sex Packets* album to recognize the accessibility of Hendrix music to rap.

Having incorporated the Hendrix sound to spoken word and rap, Bright and Douglas now looked toward jazz. "I wanted to push Hendrix into a jazz bag just to see what happened," remembers Douglas, "because jazz players were constantly trying to figure him out."

"To hear how Hendrix would sound," recalls Stefan Bright, "we organized an informal session over at Juggy Sound with Dave Holland on bass and Mother Hen on keyboards. We had been rehearsing for about forty-five minutes when someone walked in with a pipe. Without knowing it, Hendrix and I were smoking what turned out to be angel dust. We had just smoked a little bit, but neither Jimi nor I knew what was going on. The session had to be stopped."

As unintentional as that specific incident may have been, Hendrix's drug consumption was escalating at a frightening pace. In addition to his voracious appetite for cocaine, word got back to Michael Jeffery that, despite Hendrix's impending trial for possession, Jimi had recently snorted heroin. "The angel dust incident," recalls Bob Levine, "was all Jeffery had to hear. He was incensed."

Undaunted by Jeffery, Douglas launched his most ambitious project to date, pairing Hendrix with Tony Williams and Miles Davis. According to Douglas, Davis had often prodded him to set up an album with Hendrix when the two had met at Stella and Colette's boutique. "I talked to both of them," he relates. "Miles wanted to use [drummer] Tony Williams, which was fine with me. The deal was that we were going to split the royalties four ways – equally between the four of us – and no one would take advances. I spoke with both CBS [Davis's label] and Warner Bros. and was told that if the record was going to happen, it had to come out on Reprise. It was a fair deal and when you consider the number of albums Hendrix was selling, we each could have made a couple hundred thousand dollars.

"I set up a session at the Hit Factory," continues Douglas. "Hendrix, Tony Williams and Miles Davis were each going to do three original tunes. The session was scheduled to start at eight and Hendrix and I were in my office getting ready. At seven-thirty, the phone rang and it was Jack Whittemore, who doubled as Miles Davis's promoter and manager. He said, 'Alan, I hate to tell you this, but Miles wants $50,000 before he goes to the studio.' I looked at Hendrix in disbelief and said, 'Did you hear that?' I then put Jimi on the phone with him, but it was to no avail. Right after he hung up, I called Miles's house. His wife Betty answered the phone and told me he wasn't home. I insisted, 'Betty, that's bullshit. Let me talk to him. When Miles came on the phone I said, 'Is what I just heard from Jack true?' He said, 'Yeah. C'mon man, *you* got it!' I cursed him and slammed the phone down. I had gone through this entire process *for* Miles, because he had wanted to record with Hendrix so badly. Hendrix shrugged and said, 'Fuck it. I'm almost relieved that it didn't come off anyway.' Just before we decided to go out to eat, the phone rang again and it was Tony Williams. He said, 'I hear you're giving Miles $50,000; well, I want $50,000 too!' I laughed and said, 'Tony, the session's canceled.'"

Michael Jeffery was livid that Douglas, in his eyes, had gone behind his back to Warner Bros. Now convinced Douglas was out to steal Hendrix, Jeffery set his sights directly on him. "Douglas," recalls Bob Levine, "became the 'enemy' because Jeffery made him so. He was essentially harmless, but Douglas did have a relationship with Jimi, and that bothered him. Jeffery had the power and the contracts to back him up, but he couldn't relate to Hendrix on that level."

Adds Jim Marron: "Douglas was labeled by Jeffery as the enemy. I had met him once or twice in my whole life, and to me he seemed like a bearded Village hippie who got high with Hendrix. Jeffery described him as this guy who fed off dead artists. He told me about the Lenny Bruce thing and that his specialty was resurrecting dead artists and making money off new projects. Jeffery had just put down a Mafia takeover of Hendrix a couple months earlier and now was paranoid that Douglas was trying to steal his artist. From Jeffery's description, you expected Douglas to have fangs dripping with blood, but, in actuality, I could see why Hendrix was hanging around with his crew. Why not? Neither Douglas nor the three girls put any pressure on him. There was no day-to-day business like gigs or sessions to deal with and he could jet off to Morocco and screw his brains out."

Douglas defends his actions, insisting that his intentions were pure and always in Hendrix's best interests. Hendrix, he says, caused the tension that existed between Jeffery and himself by creating an unofficial management position for him. "I admit that there was super tension at that time," recalls Douglas, "but I didn't have any idea about Hendrix's past. When Jeffery first called and told me he was Jimi's manager, I said, 'Oh really?' I just loved the guy's records. You've got to understand, my own business was cooking. We had books and records coming out and I had just started the film *El Topo*. Jimi was just a friend in a confused state who seemed lost and had nobody to help him. I was just saying, 'I'll meet you down at the Record Plant at midnight,' never thinking about money. It was Hendrix who was telling people to talk to me instead of Jeffery. I know that really pissed Jeffery off, but Hendrix was doing this simply out of frustration, because he had gotten to the point where he just couldn't speak to him."

Douglas's associate Stefan Bright also comes to his former employer's defense. "Because Alan has always worked with packages after the fact, he has had to defend everything he's done. But the one thing the Douglas-Bright association *did* do for Jimi Hendrix was to make him feel comfortable. Hendrix was so totally fucked up by that time that I think it put a damper on his creativity. He seemed consumed by insecurity and paranoia, not knowing what Jeffery was doing for him or to him."

Using Buddy Miles and Douglas as a shield, Hendrix continued to dodge a direct confrontation with Jeffery. "Jimi had always argued with Jeffery," says Arthur Allen, "but he was very much aware of his ability as a manager. Jeffery did not like the idea of the Band of Gypsys coming together and he expressed that. Jimi was deeply offended that Jeffery would interfere with a *creative* decision. That's when he first expressed a serious desire to break away from him."

Hendrix *was* considering a split from Jeffery, emphasizes Gerry Stickells, but Jimi had yet to address the root cause of his stagnation, a maddening creative block driven in part by stress, drug abuse and exhaustion. "He was always thinking of changing management," says Stickells, "but I find that to be a generally true thing about artists. In reflection, his actions were pretty typical, whereby creatively he had run out of steam. At that point, you blame everything and everyone – except yourself – for that loss of creativity. Whether he had the best management in the world is subject to debate, but there is always someone willing to tell you, 'If you were with me ...' Douglas was obviously trying to hoist the management away as well as trying to be his producer. In my opinion, for him to say he was his producer or whatever is essentially not true. From the time Hendrix arrived back in America there were always people who weren't making *any* money, telling *him* how to make money. When everybody sits around stoned, things do tend to get blown out of proportion."

Stefan Bright acknowledges that Douglas's behavior did ultimately provoke Jeffery into action. "It was his company and I did what he asked, but I knew Jeffery was a formidable opponent to try and go against. I had a long conversation with Douglas about this, specifically saying, 'We are going to get in trouble here,' but he said that he had had a long talk with Hendrix before this had all started. That was fine, but we still had no paper on the guy. Douglas said, 'I don't care what happens, I like Hendrix and I want to help him out.'"

The problem, says Douglas, was not his involvement, but rather Buddy Miles's. "Jeffery," he recalls, "couldn't stand Buddy Miles. He was caught up in the success syndrome and thought Hendrix was fucking it up. I was recording Hendrix playing with his buddies and Jeffery felt that that was holding up the works. Hendrix wasn't touring, hadn't finished a record, wasn't making any money and Jeffery was feeling the pressure. He was doing everything he could to turn Jimi against Buddy."

"Jeffery was scared of me because of my relationship with Jimi," admits Miles. "I never tried to take advantage of Hendrix, but Jeffery still tried to victimize me as a hanger-on. Was I greedy? I was on salary – I didn't get any royalties from Hendrix's albums. I did have wants and needs and Hendrix was always there for me. On two or three occasions he gave me $5,000 cash to help keep the Buddy Miles

Express going. Douglas was no better than Jeffery. He used Devon and me as scapegoats to get to Jimi."

The Douglas–Jeffery battle intensified when Hendrix agreed – without Jeffery's authorization – to have the Band of Gypsys perform two shows at the Fillmore East on December 31, 1969, and January 1, 1970. Added to Bill Graham's standard American Federation of Musicians contract was a clause that released Hendrix from the Fillmore East dates should he be imprisoned following his upcoming trial in Toronto. "I had no contract with Hendrix and no authority to make any deals for him," recalls Douglas, "but Jimi was telling people to come to me. I remember Bill Graham coming to my office to talk about the two Fillmore East concerts. I said, 'I'm not his agent or manager. What do you want to talk to me for? I was even getting calls from Mo Ostin [then vice president at Warner Bros.] asking how Jimi's next record was coming and when would it be finished."

Concerned that Hendrix would miss the December 31, 1969, deadline to deliver a finished album to Capitol Records, Warner Bros. intensified their lobbying for Hendrix to fulfill his contractual obligation to Capitol. Mo Ostin, recalls Buddy Miles, even made a personal visit to Douglas's office to meet Hendrix and his Band of Gypsys. Clearly, Warner, which, according to Ostin's fellow vice president Joe Smith, detested Jeffery, was keeping tabs on its troubled investment.

To tighten the band's sound, Hendrix, Cox and Miles frequently booked time at Baggy Studios, a Manhattan facility opened by ex-Soft Machine road manager Tom Edmonston. While designed primarily for rehearsal purposes, Baggy's clients were able to record their sessions via a primitive two-track stereo tape machine, allowing artists to measure their progress. It was here, spread over countless hours of jamming, that the Band of Gypsys' core repertoire began to take form. Many songs, like "Izabella," grew here from fragments written more than a year before, but compositions such as "Machine Gun," "Earth Blues," "Ezy Ryder," "Message to Love" and "Power of Soul" were shaped by their steady jamming and bore the band's obvious R&B imprint.

Beginning in November, without any official designation from Hendrix or sanction from Jeffery to act as their producer, Douglas and Stefan Bright now focused their energies on the Band of Gypsys. "I didn't even know where Hendrix was going," says Douglas. "He was talking about an album, but I couldn't see it anywhere. I was just going to do some songs with him, 'Okay, you want to try this song? Let's go do it,' type of thing. Hendrix himself didn't know where he was going."

While jamming had helped formulate the Band of Gypsys' new material, Hendrix's many months of undisciplined, poorly supported recording sessions had all but shredded his ability to work efficiently in the studio. "That was my frustration with him," recalls Douglas. "That's why we got nowhere near what we should have gotten out of those sessions. Most of it was jamming because they couldn't get the tunes together. Every track I ever pulled out of those sessions was cut from a jam."

During his brief association with the Band of Gypsys, Douglas oversaw work on six specific songs, as well as a number of Hendrix demo recordings. On November 7, 1969, work at the Record Plant was restricted to two of Hendrix's most promising new compositions: "Room Full of Mirrors" and "Izabella." "'Izabella' was the last full session I did with Hendrix," recalls engineer Tony Bongiovi. "We recorded that song from start to finish, with Billy Rich and Buddy Miles backing him. We even mixed the song at the end of the session." A version of "Room Full of Mirrors" was also recorded on this night; its highlight, says Douglas, came when Hendrix, wanting to incorporate a slide guitar sound yet lacking the appropriate tool for his finger, slipped off his ring and used its stone to create the desired effect.

The Allen Twins, a last-minute addition to the session,

were shepherded to the studio by Hendrix himself, who wanted the pair to contribute background vocals. "Mountain were recording in Studio B," recalls Arthur Allen. "Leslie West was recording 'Mississippi Queen' and Hendrix was so knocked out by the riff that he invited him over for a jam."

Though the November 7 session had at least yielded a finished track – no small achievement by this time – Hendrix's Band of Gypsys, despite its obvious promise, was far from polished. Stefan Bright, who had favored bassist Billy Rich to Billy Cox, felt Hendrix never properly defined his purpose. "There was a real adjustment period that went on with that band," he asserts, "because when they first started, they weren't that good. Hendrix was looking for something that I don't think he eventually found. There was just too much pressure on him to make the next big step forward. As far as I was concerned, his best music had come before these sessions."

The problem, stresses Douglas, was that both Cox and Miles needed more seasoning if they were ever to add anything other than a basic R&B flavoring to Hendrix's new compositions. "Billy Cox was great for Hendrix personally, and as a player the more he played the better he was getting," emphasizes Douglas. "He was evolving and you could hear more variety and imagination in his playing. While he was still too cautious, he eventually would have been a great bassist. Buddy loved Hendrix and was totally devoted to him. I admired that. He did give Hendrix the R&B thump he wanted, but Buddy had to grow and expand his range as well."

Gerry Stickells, perhaps Hendrix's closest associate throughout his career, cites Jimi's own lack of commitment to the Band of Gypsys concept as its fatal flaw. "He drifted into it," says Stickells. "He felt a little bit pressured about it as well, as if it was something he *should* be doing. It was the same thing with Douglas and Stefan Bright. They were a joke, not even in the same league as Hendrix. That became evident in no time, as Hendrix's thinking was light-years ahead of those two. Nothing was ever used from those sessions with Douglas – he didn't do that many anyway. Tracks like 'Izabella'? Hendrix did those. As for Stefan Bright, that guy was supposed to be the producer and Douglas his supervisor or manager or something like that. He got heaved out and then Douglas tried to fill his shoes, but all he seemed to do was sit around the studio. Hendrix was just too nice, he just couldn't turn these people away."

Douglas defends his work with Hendrix. "We finished 'Room Full of Mirrors' in the studio. Yes, there were some flaws but those could have been fixed easily later on. 'Izabella' finally sounded as if Hendrix was off into a new place. Those tracks were working for me and were saying something different than what he had done before. Both the songs and concepts were good. I think 'Room Full of Mirrors,' from a writer's point of view, was one of his best songs. We were making progress."

Work on "Room Full of Mirrors" was indeed progressing, and Hendrix was sure he was crafting another signature song along the lines of "Purple Haze" or "Voodoo Chile." He carefully labored over the song's lyrics, inserting and deleting phrases in a quest for perfection. Kathy Eberth, whose tasks for Michael Jeffery included transcribing and submitting finished Hendrix lyrics for publishing copyrights, cites "Room Full of Mirrors" as Hendrix's most difficult composition to finish. "That song took forever," she recalls. "Hendrix didn't feel the lyrics equaled the music. He tinkered with that song for more than a year. Later, when Electric Lady Studios opened, he was struggling to try and finish the lyrics so it could be included as part of his next album."

Three subsequent November sessions supervised by Douglas yielded no finished masters, but Hendrix did record a number of demos for such songs as "Burning Desire," "Lover Man," "Power of Soul" (known alternatively at this time as "Power of God" or "Paper Airplanes"), "Lonely Avenue," "Machine Gun" and a version of Buddy

Miles's "Them Changes," as well as continuing work on both "Izabella" and "Room Full of Mirrors." Marbled within the Band of Gypsys' marathon jam sessions, embryonic versions of two exceptional new Hendrix compositions, "Dolly Dagger" and "Freedom," could also be heard.

In a mild slap at Warner Bros. for having even considered Douglas as Hendrix's spokesman, Jeffery refused to pay the Record Plant for studio time used throughout October and November, opting instead to forward the bill to the label. "Michael Hecht [Hendrix's accountant] called and told me he was having trouble with Warner Bros. over a recent bill we had submitted," recalls Bob Levine. "Accountants at Warner Bros. wanted to know what exactly 'Room Full of Mirrors' was. We had submitted Hendrix's $36,000 charge from the Record Plant and Hecht wanted to know if it represented the total costs for the album due Capitol Records. I said, 'No, that song will be a single when it's finished.' Hecht said, 'What do you mean, it hasn't been finished yet?' I said, 'No, Hendrix is still working on it.'"

These November sessions would mark the conclusion of Douglas's stint as producer for Hendrix. In a December 4, 1969, letter to Hendrix, citing his own busy schedule, constant pressure from Michael Jeffery and Hendrix's own disinterest, Douglas parted company from Jimi.

His management strapped for cash, Warner Bros. pressuring him for product and his studio still under construction, the element Hendrix needed most but could afford least was time. He needed to mold Miles's and Cox's talent into a coherent vision, a concept easily accessible to his fans. If the Band of Gypsys were to succeed, Hendrix would need to start from scratch, a daunting proposition. Desperate for direction and with his relationship with Jeffery damaged beyond repair, Hendrix needed Chas Chandler. Even Douglas, diametrically opposed to Jeffery's methods with Hendrix, concedes that Jimi "always thought of Chas Chandler as 'his' guy." It had been Chandler who had nurtured the Experience during their infancy, guiding them with passion and absolute conviction. Most important, Chandler had understood Hendrix, successfully translating his "big picture" vision into practical business and marketing decisions. Now, alone in New York, enveloped by stress, drugs and dissension, Hendrix was desperate for stability. Out of courtesy, Chandler had agreed to appear on Hendrix's behalf at his trial in Toronto, and it was in the Canadian city that Chandler – even though he was now channeling his energies to producing and managing Slade, a promising new British group – allowed Hendrix to approach him privately and seek his advice.

His trial date set for December 8 at the Old City Hall, Hendrix, with Bob Levine in tow, departed for Toronto on the 6th. Michael Jeffery chose to remain behind, asking his girlfriend Lynn Bailey to be there to monitor the trial's progress while entrusting Levine to attend to Hendrix. His personal life and professional affairs already in shambles, Hendrix then allowed the unthinkable to happen: he was busted again for possession at the airport in Toronto.

"Hendrix had a limousine pick me up at the office on 37th Street," recalls Levine. "On the way to the airport, I couldn't help but notice that he was putting a bunch of things into his guitar case. I didn't know what they were, but I had to ask. I said, 'Jimi, we *are* going to be going through customs.' 'Don't worry, Bob,' he promised, 'we're cool.' We were getting closer to the airport and I just couldn't hold it in any longer. 'Jimi, I know you have something in that guitar case. I don't know what it is and it's not normally my business to interfere but I know we will be searched at customs in Toronto.' He kept saying, 'Trust me, Bob, no one is going to recognize me.' 'Recognize you! They will be *waiting* at customs for you!' He reassured me that I had nothing to worry about. When we arrived in Toronto, he passed through customs and promptly got arrested. I had to call Henry Steingarten from a pay phone at the airport. Steingarten thought I was calling to let him know that we had arrived safely, but I cut him off with, 'Henry, sit down, you are not going to believe this. We are still at the airport and Hendrix has been busted again.' Steingarten went berserk, 'Busted!' I told him that they had found a capsule in Hendrix's guitar case and, while they could not identify it on site, he would have to remain in jail until they could classify the substance."

Hendrix spent the night in jail and was released the next morning. He went into the trial waiting for the dumbfounded Toronto police to classify the capsule's ingredients as a controlled substance, but it was of such a concoction that the charges were dropped.

Later that afternoon, Levine shepherded Hendrix on a tour of Toronto's best men's clothing stores, as Hendrix was under strict orders to abandon his normal garb for a more traditional – juror-friendly – look. "I took him to a number of stores that specialized in tailored suits," remembers Levine. "We found a conservative suit that looked great on him. It was hilarious, he was like a hick, awkwardly fidgeting around and trying to loosen his tie. I didn't care how uncomfortable he was, the suit was perfect. If you didn't know he needed it for his trial for possession of narcotics, you'd think he was off to a bar mitzvah."

Hendrix's trial progressed quickly, and Chas Chandler proved to be an effective character witness, winning the jury with his earthy sincerity. However, it was Hendrix who surprised both the judge and jury. Sitting calmly in the witness chair, he looked straight at the jury and admitted that while he had tried a litany of drugs throughout his career, this particular incident did not involve him in any way. Intrigued by this answer, the judge asked Hendrix to elaborate. "He dictated this shopping list of illegal substances that he had experimented with throughout his life – from acid to Valium – for what seemed like an eternity," recalls Bob Levine. "He admitted that he had a problem, but assured the judge and jury that someone had placed the heroin in his bag without his knowledge. I could see that his frank, honest approach impressed them. The jury expected him to be flashy and confrontational, but he was humble, and that won them over."

On December 10, the jury acquitted Hendrix of all charges. With Lynn Bailey and Jeanette Jacobs flashing the victory sign, Hendrix told the press that crowded Toronto's Old City Hall that he was "happy as a newborn baby." Ecstatic over his victory, Hendrix and Levine boarded the next flight back to Manhattan.

Reunited with Cox and Miles, Hendrix entered the Record Plant for three marathon sessions beginning December 15. On this date, as well as December 18 and 19, the Band of Gypsys once more set about shaping promising new Hendrix compositions. The versions of "Burning Desire" and "(I'm Your) Hootchie Cootchie Man" included as part of Polydor's 1973 *Loose Ends* album best exemplify this method of production. Both tracks, recorded on the 18th, were indicative of Hendrix's increasingly skittish approach to recording. Unparalleled as a player, Hendrix was struggling as a producer, and "Burning Desire," now three months old, was a prime example. Having begun as a solo demo, Hendrix had rejected versions cut with both Gypsys Suns & Rainbows and the Band of Gypsys. Despite the countless renditions of songs such as "Power of Soul" and "Burning Desire" already committed to tape, Hendrix seemed unable to pare his work down and finish them. Another stumbling block was the sameness that had gripped his most recent compositions. He did, in fact, need someone to successfully incorporate horns, keyboards and background vocals, as well as "organize things for him," as he had once told Alan Douglas. "Hendrix seemed to play better when there were certain restrictions placed upon him," recalls Eddie Kramer. "With Chas, he fought to modify his boundaries. When he had carte blanche, he would often doodle."

With each failed session, Hendrix's need for a production team grew painfully obvious, as he was beset with problems that, in the past, Chandler or Kramer had always attended to. During the rise of the Experience, pressure had manifested itself in the form of endless touring and interviews while an overwhelming itinerary had diluted his concentration. By December 1969, some six months after Noel Redding's formal departure, pressure had taken on a new dimension: creativity. While Jeffery was no longer subjecting Hendrix to absurd tests of physical stamina – the days of sixty-city tours in sixty-six days were over – the demands on Hendrix now centered around product and his failure to deliver.

Having dodged a metaphorical bullet in Toronto, Hendrix's slate had now been cleaned, yet he remained hamstrung by his inability to act decisively regarding a series of crucial decisions, specifically the future direction of his career and music. His breakdown of communication with manager Michael Jeffery had devastating consequences as Hendrix himself now struggled to assume the reins of management as well. Without Chandler's voice of reason, Hendrix paid little heed to Jeffery's direction. His personal dislike for Jeffery aside, Hendrix sorely needed a strong voice to council and ultimately guide his career. Since the breakup of the Experience, Hendrix had leaned – however briefly – to close associates who were strong and offered a managerial approach different from the one prescribed by Michael Jeffery. Irrespective of their motives, Hendrix had hoped to glean something constructive from Juma Sultan, the Allen brothers, Alan Douglas and even Buddy Miles. As he staggered from each new association, Hendrix became further confused and unsure of his direction. Returning to the methods that had created his initial success now seemed impossible. The type of relationship he had enjoyed with Chas Chandler simply could not be re-created – even when Hendrix had lived with Chandler, his best records had been cut when he had been underfunded and under pressure to produce. Where "The Wind Cries Mary" had taken twenty minutes to record, "Izabella" had taken months – and was still not finished. A paucity of organizational skills was drowning rock music's most talented virtuoso. The same artist who had smashed barriers with such songs as "Third Stone From the Sun" and "Are You Experienced?" now seemed utterly confounded by his own success.

In the more than twenty years that have passed since Hendrix's death, many have espoused that the root of his problems stemmed from "an undeniable change" in his musical direction, claiming that Jimi had "outgrown the Experience". Few will argue that such compositions as "Machine Gun" and "Room Full of Mirrors" were more mature and represented an exciting new direction for Hendrix, but each of his three albums with the Experience had documented this growth. As complicated as "Izabella" may have been, Hendrix had written and recorded far more intricate works in the past – all of which came during the time Chandler and the Experience purportedly restrained his abilities. The sly humor in many of his Experience classics – an asset of such songs as "Crosstown Traffic" and "Rainy Day, Dream Away" – had been replaced with a strident sense of self-examination. The titles alone – "Message of Love," "Power of Soul," "Burning Desire," "Earth Blues" and "Sky Blues Today" – suggest a change in theme. Hendrix addressed this change in focus and new serious tone in a 1969 interview. "*Are You Experienced?* was where I was a couple of years ago, but now I'm into different things. There is a great need for harmony between man and earth and I think by dumping garbage in the sea and polluting the air, we are screwing up that harmony. You've got to have love in your heart. A lot of people in America are looking for a leader in the music field and I am trying to use my power [responsibly]. I could buy myself a house in Beverly Hills and retire but I just want to continue trying."

Following an uneventful recording session on December 23 and time off for the Christmas holidays, the Band of Gypsys reentered Baggy Studios to begin final rehearsals for their two Fillmore East concerts. All four of the shows (two each night) were to be recorded, since – after considerable deliberation – Michael Jeffery had decided that a live album was the only feasible option, considering Hendrix's financial state and his inability to finish a studio album in time, in delivering to Capitol Records the LP to fulfill the PPX settlement.

To celebrate the beginning of the new decade, Fillmore East impresario Bill Graham went to great lengths to ensure a special evening for his patrons, dressing his ushers in special shirts and placing toy tambourines on each of the venue's 2,639 seats. Following a rousing set by the support act, Voices of East Harlem, Bill Graham strode onstage and introduced "some very old friends with a brand-new name." As the sold-out crowd roared in approval, Hendrix led his trio through a scintillating seventy-five-minute set that featured eleven songs yet to grace an Experience album.

Risking rejection and the unwelcome prospect of having to field ceaseless requests for "Wild Thing" and "All Along the Watchtower," Hendrix steadfastly omitted his most popular work, convinced and committed to such new material as "Ezy Ryder" and "Earth Blues" – which the audience, much to its credit, warmly received. Unlike such post-Experience concerts as Woodstock or even the Salvation Club, the Band of Gypsys moved from song to song quickly, adding only the merest of stage banter. The tuning and amplification problems that had so often marred his past performances – including his last Fillmore East gig in May 1968 – were infrequent and well concealed.

Then, at midnight, when the strains of the Guy Lombardo Orchestra's "Auld Lang Syne" filled the theater, the Band of Gypsys appeared back on stage, Hendrix launching into his own arrangement of the traditional year-opener, a beautiful rendition that captivated the audience immediately.

Perhaps indicative of the celebratory atmosphere filling the venerable Fillmore, the Band of Gypsys' second performance was far less intense than their first. While Hendrix was no less spectacular, his posture and disposition seemed composed and mature. Noticeably absent was the brash, haughty confidence long a hallmark of past Experience triumphs. As obvious as the change in image may have been, the change in his music was even more striking.

Unlike the first set, an unequivocal break from Hendrix's past, the Band of Gypsys now dipped freely into the Experience songbook, performing "Fire," "Stone Free," "Purple Haze," "Foxey Lady" and "Voodoo Chile." These reworked versions were superb, with "Fire" seemingly tailored to Buddy Miles's fatback, funky drumming. With Miles's insistent percussion and superb harmony vocals, the Band of Gypsys transformed the Hendrix classic into an R&B derivative Motown and Stax couldn't possibly comprehend.

"Stone Free" was especially breathtaking, as Hendrix tore furiously into his first ever Experience composition. For nearly ten minutes, he sustained an unprecedented level of improvisational genius, coming perhaps as close on stage to free-form jazz as he ever would. Having abandoned the song's traditional structure midstream, Hendrix created an impromptu musical suite, encompassing R&B, jazz and rock – including a Band of Gypsys arrangement of "Sunshine of Your Love." Far more adventurous than the vaunted jam sessions with jazz greats John McLaughlin and Larry Young or the much ballyhooed, autobiographical "Black Gold" suite (the tapes of which have never materialized), this version of "Stone Free" offered concrete proof that Hendrix could sustain long, fusion-styled songs outside of the standard twelve-bar blues tradition. In light of his lack of professional training, "Stone Free" suggests Hendrix himself was fused by his own varied influences, and that he in turn synthesized this patchwork of musical interests to create his own technique.

As he drew the evening to a close, Hendrix could barely restrain the showman in him, reaching back to "Foxey Lady," "Voodoo Child (Slight Return)" and "Purple Haze," each injected with a healthy dose of Miles's strong R&B influence – and Jimi's electrifying stage posturings and gyrations. "Hendrix made a point of being modest during those Fillmore shows," remembers Buddy Miles. "But by that time, we had been jamming for [almost] four hours and I could see it building up in him. He wanted to cut loose and have some fun."

Portions of the next two performances, on the night of January 1, 1970, would later make up the entire *Band of Gypsys* album. Unlike the two performances the previous night, especially the second show, where Hendrix was obviously enjoying himself, both concerts on this evening – save for the wild encore of "Hey Joe," "Purple Haze" and "Wild Thing" that drew the last set to a close – were tepid in comparison. It was one of these performances – the early show – that featured Hendrix performing stock-still, shunning almost all of his patented stage gymnastics. Aside from the marvelous version of "Machine Gun" – the strongest rendition of this in all four shows – each number seemed perfunctory, with Hendrix seemingly more concerned with the recording than the audience. The second show that evening was only slightly more enthusiastic. "When we hit 'Wild Thing,'" recalls Miles with a laugh, "all hell broke loose!"

In the aftermath of the Fillmore East concerts, the Band of Gypsys' sole commitment, Jeffery was convinced that the only way to save Hendrix was to mount a strong offensive and purge those he felt were detractors. Having neutralized Alan Douglas, he now set his sights on Buddy Miles. "Jeffery felt that Miles was holding up the works," recalls Alan Douglas. "He wanted to see Mitch Mitchell return and pull the Experience feel back together."

Miles felt the pressure intensify – and saw the effect it had upon Hendrix. "Jeffery was one of the people who wrote the book on artist management – no doubt about that – but he was putting pressure on Hendrix like a motherfucker. He would use whatever tactics necessary to get his way, from coercion to alienation. He simply did not want the Band of Gypsys to exist – period. After the Fillmore gigs, we were splitting time at Baggy's and the Record Plant and I would personally go and get Hendrix every day at his apartment.

Castaways Hotel, Miami, May 18, 1968. Jimi and Mitch relax before their performance at the Miami Pop Festival. (*Linda McCartney*)

Manager Michael Jeffery makes a rare appearance at the Record Plant. (*Linda McCartney*)

Record Plant, June 10, 1968: behind the console with Buddy Miles. (*Eddie Kramer*)

Record Plant, June 10, 1968: mixing sessions for "Rainy Day, Dream Away." (*Eddie Kramer*)

Record Plant,
June 1968.
(*Eddie Kramer*)

Record Plant, July
1968: recording
overdubs for *Electric
Ladyland*.
(*Eddie Kramer*)

Jamming the blues
backstage on his
hand-painted
Gibson Flying V.
(*Linda McCartney*)

★ ★ ★ ★ ★
Spring 1969: the
construction of Electric
Lady Studios begins.
(*Eddie Kramer*)

★ ★ ★ ★ ★ ★ ★ ★ ★ ★ ★ ★ ★ ★
Hendrix's power brokers (*LEFT TO RIGHT AGAINST THE WALL*):
Steve Weiss, Bob Levine, Gerry Stickells (*STANDING*),
Kathy Eberth (*BACK TO CAMERA*). Hendrix can be seen in
the mirror's reflection. From backstage at Madison
Square Garden, May 18, 1969. (*Eddie Kramer*)

☆ ☆ ☆ ☆ ☆ ☆ ☆
Jamming backstage:
Madison Square Garden,
May 18, 1969.

With Noel Redding.
(*Eddie Kramer*)

☆ ☆ ☆ ☆ ☆
Madison Square
Garden, May 18, 1969.
(*Eddie Kramer*)

Summer 1969: Jim Marron, the president of
Hendrix's dream studio at his makeshift desk during
the project's construction. (*Eddie Kramer*)

July 1969: Michael Jeffery's Woodstock retreat. Jeffery *(BEHIND THE WHEEL)* and Shimon Ron are in the Jeep. *(Eddie Kramer)*

Billy Cox onstage at the Harlem Street Fair, September 5, 1969. *(Jim Cummins, Star File)*

Fall 1969: progress on Electric
Lady Studios continues, as
Studio A begins to take shape.
(*Eddie Kramer*)

Electric Lady Studios,
August 1970: one of
the only known photos
of Hendrix working in
Electric Lady.
(*Eddie Kramer*)

Devon Wilson: Very early in their
tumultuous three-year relationship,
Hendrix came to learn that Devon's
gruff, assured, exterior demeanor hid
her true heart, one rife with insecurity
and self-doubt. Just as he did, Devon
constructed a hard external shell to
mask her delicate inner feelings.
(*Baron Wolman*)

★ ★ ★ ★ ★ ★ ★
Leading the Band of Gypsys
during one of their dynamic
Fillmore East performances.
(*Bob Oleson*)

★ ★ ★ ★ ★ ★ ★
February 4, 1970: under the watchful
eyes of manager Michael Jeffery, a
master manipulator of the press,
*Rolling Stone* reporter John Burks
interviews the Experience.
(*Baron Wolman*)

Jeffery had him so petrified he'd be spaced out."

Hendrix's problems, says Jim Marron, were compounded by his drug abuse. "I don't feel that Hendrix had peaked creatively," he says. "Drugs were not only screwing him up, they were destroying the environment he needed to create. With Electric Lady set to open, I didn't want to be the guy who procured drugs or women for him – I had seen Devon do that at the Scene. That wasn't my idea of personal management. Hendrix sat through many paternal lectures about his drug use from all of us, but I doubt it had any long-term effect."

Mired in deepening tension, Hendrix struggled with the decisions confronting him. First and foremost would be the future of the Band of Gypsys, which, in spite of Miles's unflinching dedication, seemed tenuous at best. The whispers of reserve that had plagued Hendrix's commitment to the concept from the outset had now risen in volume. "Miles and Hendrix had their times," recalls Arthur Allen, "but Buddy had an ego and that was a problem for Hendrix."

The trio needed time to develop or grow – the idea of recruiting Steve Winwood was bandied about – but in light of Hendrix's prior agreements, an additional three months on top of more than six months of relative inactivity would be impossible to accommodate. "The Band of Gypsys had a lot to do with timing," explains Albert Allen. "Hendrix was trying to find a way to get to the black audience. He felt that if he put together a band that could reach that audience, he would please them. He wanted to be liked by blacks but I don't think he knew what ingredients he needed." Not wanting to hurt either Cox or Miles, Hendrix struggled unsuccessfully throughout January to address the Band of Gypsys question.

Michael Jeffery, on the other hand, had no such difficulty. As a favor to Steve Weiss, who represented both Sid Bernstein and the Rascals, he booked Hendrix to appear at Bernstein's "Winter Festival for Peace." The concert, a nonprofit benefit to raise money for the Moratorium Fund, about him," recalls McFadden. "He said he was going to burn a guitar, and sent me off to a convenience store to buy lighter fluid for him. When I came back, Gerry Stickells stepped in my path and demanded the lighter fluid, mandating that if I didn't give it to him I would be fired. If Hendrix asked me for the fluid, I was instructed to say that I had given it to Stickells. Of course, it never got to that point in the show ..."

The concert was a fiasco. Shortly after 3 A.M., having stalled backstage for some twenty minutes, the Band of Gypsys finally took the stage. Once there, Hendrix was pelted immediately with requests. One particular fan, wrote Al Aronowitz the following day in the *New York Post*, so unnerved Hendrix with her steady shrieks of "Foxey Lady" that, in a rare display of vulgarity, he verbally assaulted her from the stage. "'Foxey Lady' is sittin' right over there," Hendrix spewed while pointing at his female adversary, "in the yellow underpants stained and dirty with blood."

In the Madison Square Garden audience, Hendrix's associates were mortified. "I was embarrassed," remembers Jim Marron. "Reacting in such a way, after dealing with hecklers throughout his career, was pathetic. This wasn't the Hendrix we knew or supported."

Hendrix's appearance would be brief, lasting only long enough for him to lurch miserably through two songs, "Who Knows" and "Earth Blues," before he sat down on stage and refused to continue. "He just plopped down on the edge of the drum riser," remembers Gerry Stickells. "He said, 'That's enough.'" As he wound "Earth Blues" down to an unscheduled early close, Hendrix stepped to the microphone and vented a thinly veiled gibe at Michael Jeffery: "That's what happens when earth fucks with space, never forget that."

Stunned, Miles addressed the audience: "Listen, it seems as though we are not quite getting it together here. Just give us a little more time because it has been hard. Give us a few minutes and we will try and get something together." Unmoved by his drummer's plea for patience, Hendrix unplugged his guitar, forcing Miles back to the microphone. "We're having trouble here," he admitted. "I don't know what's the matter but Jimi wants to go down. If you could bear with this, maybe we could try something later."

But there would be no second chance for Buddy Miles or the Band of Gypsys on this night. With Hendrix ensconced in his dressing room, Jeffery went to work, promptly firing Miles in a face-to-face showdown. In an instant, the group was finished.

Many critics cite the dismissal of Miles as a racial statement by Jeffery, a premeditated move to ensure at least one white face in the band – if not a re-formation of the original Experience. This theory, supported by Miles himself, is discounted by Jeffery's associates who cite instead Jeffery's poor relationship with the drummer. "Jeffery couldn't have cared less about the Band of Gypsys," recalls Bob Levine. "As long as Hendrix toured and met his commitments, he [Jeffery] couldn't be bothered to know what color skin his sidemen had. To him, Hendrix was and would be the only star, the other musicians were employees. If Hendrix said he was going to walk naked down Fifth Avenue and Jeffery was going to get his percentage, fine. His paranoia [about negative publicity] was still there of course, but caring is an entirely different thing."

"Jeffery," remembers Gerry Stickells, "never considered Buddy Miles in the same league as Hendrix; for that matter, neither did Jimi. Jeffery had no problem with the Buddy Miles Express opening for Hendrix on tour or Hendrix producing and playing on their albums, but as for him being part of the band and making creative decisions, forget it."

With Miles gone and Billy Cox in limbo, Jeffery immediately summoned Noel Redding, who had since been unceremoniously dumped from Fat Mattress. "I was at home in England when Jeffery called and asked if I wanted to make some money playing with Hendrix," recalls Redding. "I jumped at the chance."

# 14 ELECTRIC LADY: A RAY OF HOPE

> *"I have done great things with Electric Lady. We can record anything we like there. It has the best equipment in the world and was built with great atmosphere, lighting, seating and every comfort to make people feel as if they are recording at home."*
>
> —Jimi Hendrix

Jeffery's desire to re-form the original Experience as quickly as possible was fueled by the worst of news, that construction of Electric Lady Studios had ground to a halt and the project was out of funds. "That was a sad day for me," remembers studio president Jim Marron. "I went to Jeffery's 37th Street office to discuss our options." Troubling Marron most was Jeffery and Hendrix's method of funding the construction, specifically the siphoning of royalty money and touring revenue in $10,000 or $20,000 chunks just in time to meet payroll or other pressing expenses. At this late stage, the original $500,000 budget of January 1969 had become little more than a memory. Neither Hendrix nor Jeffery had had that amount in cash then, let alone in February 1970. The main drawback to Jeffery and Hendrix's infrequent installment method was that the project's cash flow was virtually nonexistent. Recalls Marron: "The prices for all of the work done by tradesmen kept escalating because every time the plumbers, electricians or air-conditioning men started working, we would invariably run short of cash, forcing me to shut the project down."

Jeffery had one last card to play, though: appealing to Warner Bros. for financial assistance. "I sat with Jeffery and Steve Weiss to try and figure out how we could save the studio. Jeffery wanted to know one thing: how much money was needed to finish the project? My answer was a figure between $350,000 and $500,000. Steve Weiss felt he could secure a $300,000 direct loan from Warner Bros., with payments of $50,000 every six months after the studio opened. This would be guaranteed against Hendrix's publishing and Jeffery's share of the same."

Pending Hendrix's signature on a Lloyd's of London insurance policy required by Warner Bros., Electric Lady Studios would be saved from its precarious financial position. Jeffery now looked to repair his own treacherous financial condition with another desperate maneuver: the sale of a soundtrack album to Warner Bros.

With Capitol Records due the live album of Band of Gypsys performances, Warner Bros. eagerly anticipated Hendrix's long overdue fourth studio album. Jeffery, meanwhile, had thrown himself headlong into a partnership with independent film maverick Chuck Wein. Long fascinated with the movie industry, Jeffery looked to bait Warner Bros. with the promise of an additional Hendrix release in exchange for underwriting his first film venture. During a meeting with Warner representatives, Jeffery stunned them with his latest demands. "Steve Weiss had just finished the deal to secure the loan for the studio," remembers Marron. "Jeffery thanked everyone for helping out and remarked, 'Now we're going to the studio to continue working.' One of the executives said, 'Finally, some product.' Jeffery turned to him and said, 'Yes, we're doing a soundtrack album. Would you like to buy it?' They exploded, 'What!' Jeffery said, 'Yes, if you read your contract with my artist, it excludes soundtrack recordings.' They were pissed and that's when I started worrying about Jeffery. You just don't do that to Big Brother and get away with it – but he did. When one of them called him a shrewd bastard, he sat right down and said, 'Do you want a soundtrack? Let's negotiate. We *are* making a film.' I admired him for that [risking the relationship with Warner], because that was what good negotiating was all about."

"Jeffery *was* both a clever negotiator and manipulator," echoes Bob Levine. "But he had to show Warner Bros. that he wasn't intimidated by their loan for the studio. He had to show that the relationship would remain business as usual."

As if freed from a time warp, just seven days after Hendrix's Moratorium debacle, Noel Redding returned, joining both Mitch Mitchell and Jimi Hendrix at the 37th Street headquarters for a long interview with *Rolling Stone*. There, under Jeffery's watchful eye, Hendrix dodged most of John Burks's more difficult questions, while citing the recent Madison Square Garden show as "the end of a big fairy tale." Though Hendrix was typically cautious not to expose his innermost thoughts and emotions, Burks was able to draw out some of his frustration. "I was very tired," Hendrix admitted to the journalist. "Sometimes there's a lot of [thoughts] in your head and they hit you at a very particular time, which happened to be at that peace rally. Here I am fighting the biggest war I've ever fought in my life – inside, you know? And that wasn't the place to do it." When Burks would later try to clarify Hendrix's relationship – if any existed – with the Black Panthers, Hendrix deftly replied, "Oh yeah, tell me about it. I read about that in Rolling Stone too."

Jeffery tried to make the Experience appear united to both John Burks and the readers of *Rolling Stone*, their appearance together having been staged to create some much needed positive publicity. Privately, Redding's return had made Hendrix uncomfortable, especially in light of his personal and now professional relationship with Billy Cox. And while Hendrix had no quarrel with Mitch Mitchell, their relationship had changed to a degree. "It obviously wasn't the way it was when they were younger and more enthusiastic," recalls Gerry Stickells. "Mitchell was reasonably secure because Hendrix had come to the realization that he was the only drummer who could play around him. Hendrix's only gripe had been that Mitch was a bit of a light drummer. He didn't hit the drums as hard as, say, Buddy Miles. Jimi needed to see if that style still fit his music, but after a while he realized that his music required someone who played the drums like he played the guitar. Buddy Miles was like Ringo Starr, a quality player who was rock steady, but Hendrix needed someone who could challenge him."

With Electric Lady's Studio A nearing completion, Hendrix pulled Eddie Kramer out of the project's construction to help him formulate the Band of Gypsys' live album and pore through stacks of demos Hendrix had recorded in the last few months. Hidden away from distractions while ensconced at Juggy Sound, a small eight-track facility, Kramer remixed studio versions of "Izabella" and "Stepping Stone" (known since as "Sky Blues Today") for possible issue as a Reprise single, and the best performances from the Band of Gypsys' four Fillmore East concerts.

Inexplicably, Hendrix ruled out material recorded during the two New Year's Eve performances, opting instead to cull choices from recordings of the two concerts the next night, a decision for which Eddie Kramer can only offer a possible explanation. "As great as some of those performances were," he recalls, "Hendrix wanted to wait until Electric Lady Studios opened so that he could finish the definitive version of songs like 'Izabella' and 'Ezy Ryder.'"

While "Machine Gun" would stand as one of Hendrix's supreme achievements, the remainder of *Band of Gypsys* does not match its lofty standard. With the exception of this one number, Hendrix's contributions to the album were largely underdeveloped, especially his lyrics, which, even to the untrained ear, at times sound improvised. Compositions such as "Message to Love" and "Power of Soul" represented the "earth" that Hendrix wanted to inject into his new songs, discarding the "space" that had so dominated his work with the Experience. Indeed, "Power of Soul" and "Message to Love," with its rare autobiographical references – "Well I am what I am, thank God. Some people just don't understand, help them God" – were two of his most promising compositions in this new vein.

While neither was fully realized, both these songs are engaging examples of Hendrix's new music – which, despite the Band of Gypsys' all-black lineup and the album's emphatic sales success, would continue to be ignored by black radio. Some twenty years later, though, it seems as if Hendrix's attempt to reach a wider black audience succeeded, as descendents as varied as Nile Rodgers, Living Colour's Vernon Reid, and Cameo's Larry Blackmon have repeatedly cited the album's importance and influence on their music.

*Band of Gypsys'* most glaring flaw is "Who Knows," especially considering the wealth of exciting new material available to Hendrix, including tour de force versions of "Ezy Ryder," "Earth Blues" and "Bleeding Heart" – as well as his majestic rendition of "Auld Lang Syne." It remains puzzling that he *would* choose to fill half of one side with a song that, despite its potential (most notably Hendrix's and Cox's contagious guitar-bass interplay), is obviously underdeveloped. The decision to include "Who Knows" – as well as the other tracks – says Eddie Kramer, was entirely Hendrix's.

Of the album's six songs, Miles's two contributions required the most work. "I remember when we were mixing the album," says Eddie Kramer, "Hendrix buried his head in his hands as we were listening to Miles's screaming and chanting, saying softly, 'C'mon Buddy, shut up ...' "

Recalls Kathy Eberth: "Hendrix played me a tape and prefaced it by saying it represented the new direction in his music. He had made up this long tape loop of the portions edited out of 'We Gotta Live Together.' I flipped out and he started cracking up laughing."

As the album's shortest track – and so its most radio-friendly, even by the undisciplined FM standards of 1970 – "Changes (Them Changes)," one of Miles's finest compositions, found Kramer's trimming most beneficial, as it retained all of its powerful funk while shedding most of his in concert call and response vamping that translated poorly to disc.

By comparison, crafting "We Gotta Live Together" was a chore. The group had only performed the song once during their four Fillmore shows (although Hendrix and Miles had featured a jam derivative during their June 22, 1969, Newport Pop appearance), and this rendition had been joined to the closing notes of a spirited "Voodoo Child (Slight Return)." Originally some fifteen minutes in length, Hendrix and Kramer pared the tune down to just under six, leaving not a shred of usable tape on the cutting-room floor. Still, even at 5:51, "We Gotta Live Together" lacked the power and clarity of Miles's superlative "Changes (Them Changes)," though its grand, final crescendo brought the second January 1 show to a preencore close, hence its positioning as the album's final track.

Seeking to be equitable, Hendrix wanted the album to feature two songs by Buddy Miles, ultimately choosing "Changes (Them Changes)" and "We Gotta Live Together," while excluding a fine version of Jerry Ragavoy and Mort Shuman's "Stop." In addition, as the sole composer of both songs, Buddy's own publishing company, Miles Ahead Music, was guaranteed at least some form of compensation for his participation in creating the album.

Billy Cox fared even worse. As a salaried employee, he received no financial reward for his contribution to *Band of Gypsys*. Per usual, Cox refused to complain. "I was a hired hand," he told *Guitar World*'s Gene Santoro in 1986. "My job was to support my friend in any way I possibly could. I worked for Jimi and he was the boss."

Neither Cox nor Miles (nor indeed Mitchell or Redding – even though they. had helped pay for the lawsuit against PPX) received a mechanical royalty from *Band of Gypsys*. Moreover, despite the album's exceptional sales performance, Hendrix too never lived to see a royalty check from the disc that had so complicated his life and career.

Although Jimi had finally delivered a finished album to Capitol Records, this had not placated PPX's Ed Chalpin, who felt that *Band of Gypsys* clearly violated his settlement agreement. "That was a breach of contract," argues Chalpin. "If you read the settlement agreement, PPX was supposed to receive a Jimi Hendrix Experience album and I was supposed to be the producer. I did not accept the album because it was not the Experience." Capitol *did* however, effectively ending – for the time being – PPX's dispute with Hendrix and Warner Bros. in the United States and Canada (the PPX versus Polydor-Track-Yameta trial was still pending in London).

In spite of the *Rolling Stone* article trumpeting the return of the original Experience, Billy Cox had again been assigned bass chores, replacing an understandably chagrined Noel Redding, callously squeezed out and sent home to England. With the studio's loan secured and Hendrix's signature on a number of performance contracts set to commence in April 1970, Jeffery now had room to maneuver and pursue his own interests. "Just before we moved our offices down above Electric Lady Studios, I don't think Jeffery had the same passion for managing Hendrix," remembers Bob Levine. "He wasn't as concerned about his future or creative ability as he once had been. This subject came up and it was often discussed in private between us. Jeffery was getting older, and that thought bothered him tremendously. His vanity was taking over. This was how Chuck Wein and Barry DePrendergast came into the picture. He was terrified of growing older and wanted nothing but youth surrounding him, hoping to a be part of the New Age, nonmaterialistic generation that was coming in. To fit in, he would do anything to hide his old habits. When he would be off with Lynn Bailey in Barbados spending $2,000 a day, he would call Chuck Wein and tell him he was in Chicago tending to business for Hendrix. When he would visit people in Manhattan, he would travel by limousine but have the driver stop a block or two from his destination so he could walk the rest of the way. Jeffery brought Wein and DePrendergast along, just as he had done with me, Chas Chandler and Gold and Goldstein, but they learned to manipulate him. It didn't take them long to know that if you manipulated his vanity, you could get anything you wanted from him."

While Wein and DePrendergast may have espoused the joys of the nonmaterialist age, they seemed to thrive upon the vices that shamed Michael Jeffery. John Jansen, recently hired to assist Eddie Kramer with engineering duties at Electric Lady (joining ex-Amboy Dukes drummer Dave Palmer and ex-Lothar & the Hand People guitarist Kim King), remembers the odd chemistry between Jeffery and his newfound mentors. "Jeffery was not the kind of guy you fooled around with," says Jansen. "Yet Chuck Wein knew how to press his button. He and DePrendergast played on his guilt. First of all, whenever Wein came into a room, it seemed as if he had to sit on the highest place above everyone. Then he would go into this trance and start talking about his trips to Mars and looking into a gutter and finding an Ace of Spades and a Queen of Diamonds. Only those who were cosmic could know the true meanings. Then there was his partner, DePrendergast, the producer. Before it became obvious how excessive they were, Jeffery offered to take me along with them for dinner. DePrendergast came hobbling toward me on crutches as I went to hail a cab. He stopped and said that his ankle was too bad and that he would have to travel by limousine. I was taken aback. 'I'm sorry to hear that. How bad is your foot?' 'It's really bad,' he replied. I asked, 'What do you have?' 'Oh, athlete's foot,' he said. This was typical of these guys."

Previously, Trixie Sullivan had been the only associate with whom Jeffery could enjoy a personal relationship untinged by his professional standing with Hendrix. Jeffery's own personality and business practices had alienated many, and with Sullivan entrusted to run his nightclubs in Spain and Steve Weiss and Bob Levine assuming more and more of Hendrix's daily business concerns, Jeffery grew close to Wein and DePrendergast and set about developing *Wave* (later rechristened *Rainbow Bridge*), supposedly the counterculture's continuation of *Easy Rider*, Peter Fonda's smash independent film of the previous year.

With his soundtrack deal secured – without even a written treatment, let alone a script – *Rainbow Bridge* began to take shape as director Chuck Wein's grand vision, a fact not lost on Jeffery's associates. "The money to make that movie represented Hendrix's involvement," recalls Bob Levine. "*Rainbow Bridge* was Jeffery's vanity trip. Hendrix had some ideas, but Jeffery and Wein didn't ask for his input."

"Warner Films had kicked in close to a million dollars," remembers John Jansen, "on the premise that the soundtrack album would be every bit as successful as *Electric Ladyland* or *Smash Hits*. So Chuck Wein, in his infinite wisdom – still working without a script – had money to begin shooting. With his eyes rolled up in his head, he confidently explained to me that the reason *Easy Rider* had been such a huge hit was not because of the actors or the script or anything like that. It was successful because as the motorcycles rode down the highway during the film's opening credits, they rode past the Hopi Burial Ground, and that, being a high-energy center on the planet, caused everyone to be energized. *That* was why it was a hit. So Wein's theory was that the film would be shot only in high energy centers, Maui being one of them. To make it the biggest movie ever made, he planned to weave sex, drugs and rock n' roll into the story. On that premise, shooting began."

Although Studio B remained far from complete – as did practically the entire facility – Eddie Kramer, aided by chief technical engineer Shimon Ron, readied Studio A for its initial recording session. Nearly a year late and $500,000 over budget, Electric Lady's first recorded session featured Kramer – with Jeffery, Levine, Marron and others watching anxiously – alone at a piano inside the vast expanse of Studio A. Proof that this grand experiment had finally worked, in the form of a playback, brought a collective sigh of relief that nearly drowned out Kramer's tinklings. Still, the project was far from finished: some essentials, such as the freight elevator, were not scheduled to be installed for at least another month. Gene McFadden, the self-described "low roadie on the totem pole," had the unenviable task of lugging Hendrix's and Cox's amplifiers down the studio stairs whenever necessary.

"Hendrix couldn't wait to get in and start recording," recalls Eddie Kramer. "Right up until the time Studio A was functional, Jimi would call me and ask, 'Is it done yet? When is it going to be ready?' I would simply say, 'Almost Jimi, as soon as we finish this and as soon as we finish that ...'"

Though Hendrix's sole design request had been round windows, Electric Lady Studios had been crafted with great care all over. "We were committed to creating an artist's environment at the studio," explains Jim Marron. "This would not be a facility dominated by technical types who had wires and cables all over the place. This was to be Hendrix's creative home." Echoes Eddie Kramer: "We built that studio for Jimi to work and feel comfortable in, contrary to the antiseptic boxes then in vogue."

To foster such an environment, architect John Storyk, with direct input from Hendrix, incorporated a host of ideas, including the sound-proofed, curved walls that shaped the exterior of Studio A's control room and studio. There were white carpeted walls and colored lights, complete with an instrument panel for Hendrix to control, allowing him to match his mood with the colors he so desired. These were small touches, yet they drove home the point that this facility had been tailored for him exclusively. "He loved just being in the studio," remembers Kramer. "He would say, 'Give me red lights or yellow lights tonight,' and wash the walls in a rainbow of different colors. It had always been his intent to have the studio loose and casual, yet at the same time we worked hard to maintain a high standard of professionalism."

"The studio was an accomplishment for Jimi," recalls Faye Pridgeon. "A real ego thing, I'll tell you. The exciting thing for him was that one day in 1965, my mother, Jimi and I were coming down that same street and my mom had bought him an umbrella – he couldn't afford one – because he didn't want his hair to get wet. Now, he pointed out his studio to me and said, 'Just think, I own this place. This is mine. I own it.' To him, it was incredible. He was ashamed to brag in public, but he never forgot about that umbrella and knew that I would remember and understand."

Albert Allen concurs. "He was very proud of Electric Lady, it was a very special home for all of us. Hendrix wanted to do so many things there. He was uneasy about Jeffery having his headquarters there – 'Do I really own it or does he?' type of thing – but he was happy."

With over thirty songs composed, as well as a further batch of demos and outtakes recorded at various studios during the previous year, work on Hendrix's fourth studio album finally began in earnest. "Jimi was so enthused about recording again," says Kramer, "he would arrive at sessions right on time – even early on occasion – something he rarely did. We would spend up to ten or twelve hours at a time, recording take after take. Unlike in the past, where, through jamming, he would try to develop the germ of an idea into a song, Hendrix came into Electric Lady with a distinctive idea as to how he wanted each track to sound. He would still, once satisfied with the basic track, work on his final lyrics right up until it was time to put his vocal on, sifting through pages and pages of handwritten lyrics, even lifting pieces from other songs, saying, 'Maybe that line would fit in here ...' At this point, now that we had started working together again, his sense of involvement behind the console was not as heavy as it had been before. He left it more or less up to me, and was showing more interest in what was happening out in the studio rather than the control room. However, we still mixed songs together and the old team feel came back immediately."

With a new facility came new rules and Kramer looked to break some bad habits of the past. "It had been impossible trying to get work done during those sessions at the Hit Factory and the Record Plant," he remembers. "At one point, I remember there were thirty people in the control room. That would never happen at Electric Lady. I wouldn't allow it. I knew that he enjoyed this carnival atmosphere at times, because he still occasionally would bring in a bunch of people, but if I felt they were imposing, I would turn to him and say, 'Jimi, we can't get any work done.'"

There was one observer who rarely missed a Hendrix session at Electric Lady: his girlfriend Devon Wilson. "She used to hang around a lot," recalls Dave Palmer. "She wanted to be there all the time, saying once, 'If you're going to be making music or mixing music with Jimi, I've gotta be there.' That was weird, a necessary evil for Hendrix, I guess. Kramer got along well with her, but I always sensed he would have just preferred she not be there." "Devon used to rag on Michael Jeffery," remembers John Jansen. "They would get into quite a few fights." Explains Kramer: "Devon would often try to assume the role of protector. When Hendrix would leave the room, she would often pull me aside and whisper that Jimi really liked me or thought I was doing a good job."

To his small staff of assistant engineers, Kramer issued a stern edict: no drug use would be tolerated while on duty. "That was the thing about Kramer," explains John Jansen. "He didn't do drugs. That was the rule, and when people were around him, they didn't openly consume them. We respected that, because everybody that came through the studio would try to win Hendrix's friendship with drugs."

With Electric Lady growing more functional each day, new assistant engineer John Veneble could see that a distinct pattern had begun to evolve. "The studio seemed split," he says. "Shimon Ron and Kim King worked to make Studio B operational, while Kramer and Hendrix had Studio A all to themselves. Eddie was Jimi's guy and we stayed out of their way. They had their own storage closet, tape closets, the works. As an assistant engineer, one didn't sit in on a Hendrix session. That just wasn't done."

Having opted to train musicians such as Palmer, Jansen, King and Veneble rather than hire assistant engineers from other studios, Kramer's new recruits received a firsthand view of Hendrix's unique approach to recording. "When I started there I was in fear of my life," recalls John Jansen. "It was an intense place. Kramer and Hendrix, as well as Mitch and Billy Cox, would work sixteen hours straight without thinking about it. Those sessions were weird, completely unstructured when compared with the way things are done today. Nowadays, the budget is done, the songs are done and everything is set up in advance. At that time, it was more of an open, creative process than it is now. If Hendrix wanted to drop what he was doing and jam on an idea, Kramer would encourage him and keep the tape rolling."

"Kramer was like a director," explains Kim King. "There was no telling Hendrix *what* to play, but if he was on, Kramer would channel him into something productive, because if he hadn't, Hendrix would have gone on all night long recording some marvelous jam that was simply unusable."

"On a lot of sessions, Hendrix would come to the studio without Mitch Mitchell or Billy Cox," explains Dave Palmer. "He would just use the time to write. It wasn't, 'Okay, this is *the* tune for *the* record, let's *go*.' It was mainly, 'Okay, let's do some things and see what we have.' "

Regardless of Hendrix's intent for any given session,

Kramer demanded that his assistants be absolutely prepared to accommodate Jimi at all times. "Eddie gave one hundred percent or better to Hendrix and expected nothing less of his staff," remembers Kim King. "Kramer wanted us to be on standby at all times as an extension of the equipment. If we had started at 8 P.M. and Jimi didn't show until 12 P.M., it didn't matter. Whenever Hendrix walked into the studio, we had to be at the height of readiness."

Many of Hendrix's earliest sessions in Studio A allowed Kramer and the technical staff to effectively fine-tune their state-of-the-art equipment and ready the new facility not only for Jimi, but outside clients as well.

"The hours we put in," Palmer continues, "were incredible. I remember asking someone how long they had been at the studio. When they replied, 'Two weeks,' I wouldn't believe them. It felt like six months." "We got quite a studio tan that summer," echoes John Jansen.

Palmer lived across the street from the studio, and, as a result, was often pressed into late-night service. "One night Kramer called me at 2 A.M. saying, 'Hendrix is down at the studio and we need a drummer. Get your ass over here and bang on those tubs.' When I got there, Kramer and Hendrix were showing Steve Winwood the place. Nothing was really set up, but Jimi and Stevie had the itch to play, so Eddie set up a couple of microphones and I got behind the drums and jammed with the two of them."

Interspersed within Hendrix's crowded spring and summer recording schedule was a series of large-scale U.S. concerts billed as the "Cry of Love Tour." A compromise from the outset, Jeffery had convinced Hendrix to do a continuing series of lucrative three-day weekends. Hoping to jar the monotony of visiting the same cities and impersonal arenas once more, Hendrix offered his own compromise, requesting the itinerary be spread to new countries such as Czechoslovakia – one of Mitchell's preferences – or Mexico and Japan. "Hendrix originally wanted to do a big concert at Stonehenge," explains Bob Levine, "and said that if that couldn't be arranged, he wanted to tour Mexico and the Yucatan peninsula, as well as Japan. Japan seemed the most likely, and while individual dates were never booked, John Morris and Harold Davison had set August 15, 1970, as the tentative start date."

The Cry of Love Tour featured the music of a more mature and refined Experience, Billy Cox, despite his diminutive stage presence, having a profound effect on the band's sound. Unlike Noel Redding, whose nimble bass runs continually pushed Hendrix's own playing, Cox created rhythm patterns behind both Hendrix and Mitchell. Where Redding was often bombastic, Cox was muted, confident of the delicate interplay he and Hendrix would create. And like Hendrix's own music, Mitch Mitchell's playing had also changed, now reflecting a more subtle and intricate approach rather than his previous display of power, speed and dexterity. New material, such as "Hey Baby," "Freedom" and "Straight Ahead," steeped in rhythm and blues, dictated such a shift.

Oddly, since Hendrix's death, the Experience's 1970 U.S. tour has often been cast by critics as a lackluster exercise, of only marginal musical interest, yet the majority of these spring-summer concerts showcased some of Hendrix's most sophisticated and inspired playing. Fresh material was added to the repertoire, including "Message to Love" and "Machine Gun" from the recent *Band of Gypsys* album, "Room Full of Mirrors" and an occasional "All Along the Watchtower," each presented with vigor and exuberance.

Dotted along the scattered itinerary were stops in Minnesota, Wisconsin and Oklahoma (where, performing at the University of Oklahoma, the Experience were especially brilliant). In Philadelphia, headlining a festival at Temple Stadium that also featured, among others, Steve Miller and the Grateful Dead, the Experience stole the show with a rowdy and raunchy seventy-five-minute set that began with a medley of "Sgt. Pepper" and "Johnny B. Goode." Comfortable before an audience consisting predominantly of students from the nearby university, Hendrix, Mitchell and Cox roared through eleven songs before departing some $50,000 richer for their efforts. In comparison, the Grateful Dead, second on the bill, received $7,000.

Strained for cash yet still eager to create new product, Jeffery shifted gears from his work on *Rainbow Bridge* to producing a concert film of the Experience's two May 30, 1970, performances in Berkeley, California. Considering the city's notoriety as a hotbed of political unrest, Jeffery, recalls Bob Levine, "thought he could make millions with footage of Hendrix performing there."

With Hendrix's aversion to touring growing even stronger, Jeffery hoped to stockpile enough visual material to create product for release in 1971. His interest in the film industry had made him aware of the growing number of cinemas across the country equipped to reproduce stereo sound; considering Hendrix's lucrative success on the concert circuit, Jeffery hoped to replicate that in movie theaters with filmed performances. In broad terms, the concept seemed simple, a mirror of the self-promotion strategy that had been applied with such success to the Experience's personal appearances. In the film business, self-promotion was known as four-walling, a practice whereby independent producers and distributors would book their films into individual theaters around the country, eliminating the middle man while cutting the theater owner in for a larger percentage of the profit. Tom Laughlin, star, director and producer of the wildly popular *Billy Jack* films, enjoyed enormous financial success by aggressively four-walling *Billy Jack* in city after city, before securing a lucrative distribution deal with Warner Films. Jeffery's concept was more limited in scope: he merely wanted to bicycle prints of Hendrix's concert performances to select theaters in major cities like New York, Los Angeles and San Francisco.

As innovative as his concert film concepts may have been, Jeffery, as always, had additional private motives driving him along. The December 1, 1970, expiration date on his management contract with Hendrix certainly had not escaped his notice. Should his relationship with Hendrix formally cease, products, such as the Berkeley film and *Rainbow Bridge* – as long as they were undertaken during his tenure as manager – would still garner him a 30 percent commission regardless of whatever relationship he would hold with Hendrix in 1971. Jeffery had no plans of parting ways with his troubled star, rather hoping instead that these projects would bind Jimi further to him, but it made sense for him to guard against all possibilities.

Tickets for both of the Experience's two May 30, 1970, performances at the Berkeley Community Center had long since sold out. The venue, one of the many Bay Area sites in promoter Bill Graham's stronghold, could only seat some 3,000 patrons, a paltry figure in comparison to the vast expanse of such recent tour stops as the Hemisphere in San Antonio and the Forum in Los Angeles. Outside the arena, more than a thousand empty-handed fans were turned away; most were furious, their tempers and nerves frayed. When the doors opened for the first concert, an unruly mass of gate-crashers tried to make its way in. Graham's security forces and local police were overwhelmed by the ferocity of the assault. Some scaled the building's walls, others tried to break in through the roof, while still more were lobbing rocks at those with tickets trying to gain legitimate entrance.

Inside the hall, Hendrix started slowly, his voice cracking as the trio fumbled through "Fire," the opening number. Still not quite warmed up, Hendrix launched into an electrifying version of "Johnny B. Goode," thankfully preserved on the 1972 *In the West* album. One of Hendrix's best ever concerts, Berkeley also boasted what many consider to be the definitive live rendition of "Hear My Train A Comin'," later issued as part of the *Rainbow Bridge* soundtrack album. To pacify the hostile crowd unable to gain entrance, Abe Jacob swung open the doors of the remote soundtruck, blasting the street with the sounds of the Experience in concert, affording those outside an opportunity to hear the music. Though the police were furious, the crowd surrounding the truck remained orderly. The same could not be said for those inside the overcrowded venue, however. "There was so much damage to the place," recalls Bob Levine, "that we had to release $8,000 to pay for it."

Back inside the womb-like atmosphere of Electric Lady Studios, significant progress had been made on a number of exciting new songs. On June 25, 1970, in a memo to himself, Hendrix listed the following songs as "having backing tracks completed: 'Ezy Ryder,' 'Roomfull of Mirrors,' 'Earth Blues Today,' 'Have You Heard,' 'Freedom,' 'Stepping Stone,' 'Izabella' – complete, needs new mix, 'Astro Man' and 'Nightbird Flying.'" Also listed were "Drifter's Escape" (another Dylan composition) and "Burning Desire," but Jimi had placed question marks beside them. He also made a note to "get the tape of 'Highway Chile.'"

Throughout July and August, the Experience continued recording at a frantic pace; for the first time in a long while, tracks were being completed – so much so, says Kathy Eberth, that Hendrix gave some consideration to issuing a triple album. "*People, Hell and Angels* was going to be the title," she recalls. "He couldn't settle on the songs or length of the album. In the early summer, *Straight Ahead* had emerged as a working title and then later *First Rays of the New Rising Sun* made a comeback of sorts. At the very least, he definitely wanted to release a two-record set, but was unsure of a title."

In addition to reworking and remixing demos and out-takes from earlier sessions at the Hit Factory and Record Plant, songs such as "Dolly Dagger" and "In From the Storm" were among the many new, confident Hendrix compositions recorded during July and August 1970. "Hendrix cut 'Dolly Dagger' twice," recalls Eddie Kramer. "He had recorded a rough demo at the Record Plant [in November 1969] but that was scrapped entirely. We cut the new basic track in one evening [July 1, 1970] but spent three or

four days overdubbing guitars and finishing the background vocals. Jimi would do a solo one night and everybody would be completely knocked out; then he would
come back the next day and say, 'No, that was a piece of shit,
let's redo that,' and he *would* do it better. On some of the
songs we cut, I would have nine or ten solos to choose from
and all of them were brilliant. I let him continue, because I
knew I could mix together three or four of the best ones,
keying them in and out of the mix to savor the highlights of
each one. Ultimately, 'Dolly Dagger' was a complex track
with many layers of sound. Hendrix's lead guitar somehow
floated through the whole thing and locked it all together.
We recorded his guitar in stereo, combining direct feeds
from both his guitar and amplifier. Since both Jimi and Billy
were playing basically the same riff, it kind of locked the
rhythm in. We applied the same technique to Cox's bass, and
later overdubbed a fuzz bass to capture just the right effect.
When we were cutting the basic track, Jimi put on a lead
vocal at the same time he was recording his lead guitar to get
into the mood of the vocal. Devon was in the control room
at the time, and you can hear him sing, 'Watch out Devon,
give me a little bit of that heaven.' It was a tribute to her, and
a nice touch at that."

"Dolly Dagger" was indeed a sly tribute to Devon. The
lyric "She drinks her blood from a jagged edge," explained
Devon to Arthur Lee, drew its origins from Hendrix's
November 27, 1969, birthday party, when Mick Jagger
accidentally pricked his finger. When he asked for a Band-
Aid, Devon rushed to him and told him that wouldn't be
necessary. Then, in full view of Hendrix, sucked the blood
from his finger.

Locked in a groove, the Experience, bolstered by Juma
Sultan on percussion, never broke stride, progressing into
"Pali Gap" after completing "Dolly Dagger." "As 'Dolly
Dagger' began to come apart," recalls Kramer, "Billy Cox
had started playing the bass line to 'Gimme Some Loving,'
the Spencer Davis Group song, and that developed into a

jam lasting nearly ten minutes."

"'Dolly Dagger' had broken down," explains John Jansen, "but the band continued to play. After three minutes or so, Hendrix began playing this beautiful melody and the rest of the guys fell in behind him. That was 'Pali Gap.'"

Hendrix's sustained creative burst boosted his confidence and set his bruised psyche at ease. "He was starting to get some direction again," remembers Gerry Stickells. "He realized that rock n' roll was really what he was happy doing. His enthusiasm was renewed and quite visible, especially by comparison to the fall of 1969 when he was desperately trying to write something creative and failing miserably."

Recalls Jim Marron: "Hendrix put in some long, late nights working on the *Cry of Love* album, especially 'Dolly Dagger.' Devon was giving him a real bitch of a time at home, so he'd stay at the studio and listen to playbacks. He used to let Kramer go home to catch a few hours sleep while he would just cool out. Eddie would offer to stay and keep working, but Jimi just wanted some play time. It was part of the reason we built the place for him. He would just sit in the control room and have one of Kramer's assistants thread up the tapes he wanted to hear."

Maintaining his weekly schedule of three days on the road, four days in the studio, Hendrix and the Experience had strung together a string of impressive performances in Baltimore, Boston and San Bernardino. With *Band of Gypsys* nestled among *Billboard*'s best-selling albums, crowds packed arenas and university auditoriums to catch a glimpse of their hero. In Ventura, California, the Experience performed atop a flatbed truck to a wildly enthusiastic crowd that threatened to overturn the makeshift stage. In Atlanta, on Independence Day, the band rallied once more, as a crowd in excess of 150,000 witnessed a consummate Hendrix exhibition, capped by a superb encore of "Stone Free," "Star Spangled Banner," "Straight Ahead" and "Hey Baby."

As dramatic as was their appearance at the Atlanta Pop Festival, the Experience barely made it to the site on time. "We arrived in Atlanta and couldn't rent a U-Haul truck to save our lives," explains Gene McFadden. "People had been renting and living inside of them while at the festival site. We had one reserved in advance, but some kids had torched one of the dealer's trucks and, in frustration, he closed up his shop. We finally rented an old jalopy just to get us there."

There was further aggravation when, back in New York, while the Experience were working at Electric Lady, their equipment truck was stolen. "I was staying at the Penn Gardens in Manhattan," recalls Gene McFadden. "Our truck with all the band's road gear was ripped off in broad daylight. I had come in about 5 A.M. and when I awoke the truck was gone. I got together with Eric Barrett to assess the damage, and as we were driving up Hudson Street on the way to the studio, Barrett looked over at this bar on the corner and yelled to the driver to stop. There, parked in front of the bar, was our truck. Some small things, including a couple of guitars, were missing, but the amplifiers and speaker cabinets had been too heavy to carry, so the thieves had left them behind."

Another problem at this time was the many competing Manhattan-based radical left-wing political groups besieging Hendrix with requests for benefits, guest appearances and the like, so that he had grown increasingly sensitive to being manipulated or, worse, used as a financial tool to aid causes he had little connection to or understanding of. In Harlem, Hendrix's wary and largely undefined support of the Black Panthers was used against him by the local Mafia, provoking, say Albert and Arthur Allen, what could have easily been a violent confrontation. "One particular gangster was a serious terror in Harlem and everybody knew it – including Jimi," explains Arthur Allen. "This guy ran several big-time disc jockeys, had a few bodies under his belt and nobody fucked with him. We were on 59th Street and Jimi was pissed off because this guy was advertising that

Jimi Hendrix was going to be at one of his shows. Lo and behold, there was the guy with three of his henchmen. It was confrontation time. This was the guy who had put out the ad. In his bell-bottoms, Hendrix turned around and started walking over to these guys in their gangster suits. He's waving the advertisement in one hand while carrying his guitar case in the other. I looked at my brother in shock saying, 'What are we going to do now?' If they tried to do something to Jimi, it wouldn't be fighting. These guys had guns. If there *was* trouble, we would have had to kill those guys, because if we hadn't, they would have come back and killed us. Hendrix was screaming, 'How dare you do this? You don't have the right to do this!' This guy was looking at him like he was crazy. Then he looked at us, because he knew we understood who he was, and said, 'You two better straighten this motherfucker out.' Hendrix wouldn't let up, though; he was a man of principle. He kept pointing to the advertisement saying, 'What right do you have to do this?' We were waiting for the guns to come out, but Jimi never backed down, he stood his ground. Finally, the guy told Hendrix that he was going to do the show with him or without him. As his crew escorted him away, Hendrix kept after him, yelling, 'My lawyer will be talking to you guys! You don't have a right to use my name on this!' They never hassled him again, but he was lucky he wasn't killed."

Hendrix's next aggravation took its form as a benefit concert staged at Downing Stadium on Randalls Island in New York. Portions of the proceeds, artists had been informed, were to be split among RYP-OFF, a coalition of militant left-wing politicos, and the Young Lords, Spanish Harlem's equivalent of the Black Panthers. Getting Hendrix's involvement had been a complicated process. First, festival promoters Don Friedman and Robert Gardiner had asked Alan Douglas if Hendrix might be persuaded to perform. Douglas had then forwarded the request to Hendrix, who agreed; though Michael Jeffery was reluctant, he was unable to dissuade his star and unwilling at this time to batter their bruised relations further, so he ultimately consented.

Arguably Jimi's worst performance of the 1970 U.S. tour, the Randalls Island festival was a disaster, plagued by violence, gate crashings and drug abuse. Nearly 8,000 of the estimated 25,000 in attendance had not paid to see the show. "That was something I got him into, sorry to say," says Alan Douglas. "It should have been great but it wasn't. Hendrix got up on stage in front of a pretty raunchy crowd."

"It was a complete mess," recalls Gerry Stickells. "We weren't going to go on, but the Young Lords held us at knife point and wouldn't allow us to leave. When we finally did get out of there, we all jammed in a van and the boat taking us over to Manhattan got stuck in the mud. A total disaster."

In Seattle on July 26, 1970, Hendrix's last visit home, Concerts West staged their biggest homecoming yet, booking the Experience into Sicks Stadium. "Seattle had always been a big money market for us and Hendrix was up for the challenge," remembers Tom Hulett. "On the plane from San Diego, I spoke to Jimi about the weather forecast for Seattle. A steady rain was threatening our walk-up sales and I was afraid we were going to lose our ass – remember, it was both Hendrix's own money and ours at stake that night. I was thinking about canceling, but Hendrix said no. He instructed Stickells to cover the stage floor with rubber, a process, he explained, to ensure that the band wouldn't be electrocuted."

After Seattle, Hendrix and his entire crew flew to Hawaii to join Michael Jeffery, immersed in the myriad of production requirements of *Rainbow Bridge*. "Jeffery had fallen in love with the stoned California-Hawaii lifestyle," recalls Stickells. "Just sit back, moan and smoke dope. This Maui thing was the end of that era. He had a real fear of growing old and clung to the dying throes of the hippie movement, all while trying to be hip himself. Chuck Wein's people were involved with surfers who would smuggle dope to the island in surfboards; it was outrageous. We were staying at a girls' school in Maui, which, of course, served only vegetarian food. The film crew from Warner Bros. were staying there as well, and they were freaking out, having just come from shooting a Burt Lancaster movie in Spain to do this. The crew would be sleeping in the middle of the night when someone would rush in saying, 'The vibrations are right in the church! Come right now!' They thought you could just rush right in and film it. It was a complete shambles. Hendrix wanted nothing to do with the entire thing but, again, it was a case of Jeffery convincing him to do it. Hendrix was into hanging out and smoking dope, but this was ridiculous."

Chuck Wein heartily refutes these charges, and remains convinced that a large measure of blame should lie with Michael Jeffery for not communicating the film's central premise to either Warner Bros. or his own staff. Had that happened, Wein argues, the crew would have come prepared to shoot a cinema verite-style documentary rather than a feature film. "*Rainbow Bridge* was prophetic in many ways," explains Wein. "We were talking about environmental issues way before it came into vogue. The people in the film weren't all stoned-out space cadets and surfers: what we were documenting was an alternative lifestyle that Hendrix's predominantly New York-based associates couldn't relate to."

Hendrix's lack of commitment to the project rippled throughout the ranks of his associates, fast creating an atmosphere of sheer lunacy that soon cloaked the entire production both on and off screen.

"We were staying at this huge, rented mansion, complete with servants and a cook," recalls Bob Levine. "One evening, we staged a big, formal dinner for some executives of Warner Films who had flown in to check up on the movie's progress. Unbeknownst to any of us, Mitch Mitchell had gone into the kitchen and dumped a potent mix of marijuana and hashish into the batter of the dessert. After dinner and dessert, as we sat drinking coffee, we all started tripping. I got up – so I'm told – and yelled, 'Does anybody want to do the chicken dance!' These Warner Films representatives, stiff and very proper in their three-piece suits, started screaming, 'Yes!' Hendrix was under the table laughing, but he decided to do me one better, he started clucking like a chicken behind me! One of the servants, an older, dignified Hawaiian woman, had eaten one of the tarts, heard all of the commotion and started to get down and boogie with us. Later, we all sat down to watch television. *A Hard Day's Night* was on and we all saw it in color. We couldn't believe the Beatles would have a red chicken in so many scenes. I distinctly remember discussing that with the people from Warner Films – hoping that they could give me the industry insider's reason for the chicken. The next day, we were talking about the movie with some of the servants, who were dumbfounded. Not only was *A Hard Day's Night* made in black and white, so was the TV set we watched it on!"

Although Levine and company escaped their spiking unscathed, one member of the Hendrix entourage, tour accountant Arthur Johnson, wasn't so lucky. "Johnson was a straight guy who had never been to a rock concert before he worked for Hendrix," explains Ron Terry. "In Hawaii, a nurse slipped some acid into his drink at a bar and he just flipped out." "He was in way over his head," echoes Bob Levine. "We were very worried because he had been wandering around the beach all night. When we found him, he was swimming in his clothes. He came walking out of the water fully clothed in his three-piece suit. I asked him if he was all right and he asked me what was for dinner. I *knew* this guy was in trouble." "We took him to the hospital," remembers Terry, "because no one could explain to him what was happening. It was scary."

With Jeffery growing increasingly aware that *Rainbow Bridge* was nothing more than a cash sinkhole, it was decided that the film should feature a performance by the Experience. "In the end," remembers John Jansen, "when all of the money had been spent and they realized that this movie wasn't a movie, Jeffery had to talk Hendrix into performing. Up until that point, he hadn't bought any of the nonsense and had refused to write a note of music for the film." To save the feature, the Experience reluctantly agreed to perform in front of the cameras. "Of course, now that a concert was necessary, it *had* to be shot atop one of the highest points in Maui," complains Jansen. "With nothing but blue sky behind him, they could have filmed him playing in Staten Island and no one would have known the difference."

"The classic for me," recalls Gerry Stickells, "was hauling all the shit to the top of the mountain in four-wheel-drive jeeps." Says Gene McFadden: "We were in this meadow atop the mountain; the wind was howling, with gusts close to fifty miles an hour. We didn't have any wind screens, so I cut foam out of the instrument cases and wrapped them around the microphones."

"As you can imagine, there was no hard-wired power available," explains Mike Neal. "We had to share the film crew's generator. It was totally unorganized. I couldn't see why we couldn't rent the proper equipment to record the show correctly. I had rented an eight-track machine from a studio in Hawaii and stuck it in the back of a rented U-Haul – which doubled as our sound truck."

"It was a four-camera, 35mm shoot," remembers Stickells. "Chuck Wein would say, 'Roll all cameras!' but each shooter only had one 1,000 foot magazine [roughly eleven minutes] of film. Then Wein got on stage to address the 'audience' and we started having trouble with the multitrack tape machine. I said, 'Whoa, stop! It's not recording properly!' Barry DePrendergast, standing next to me, was livid. 'You can't stop it now!' he told me. 'Chuck is creating the vibrations to make everything good.' I looked out the back of the truck and there, as thousands of dollars were rolling away, was Wein chanting *om* on the edge of the stage."

Aside from a brilliant medley of "Hey Baby" and "In

From the Storm," little usable material was actually captured on tape, as technical gremlins prevented Mitchell's drums from being properly recorded. "I wasn't in Hawaii," explains Eddie Kramer, "but the tapes were all shipped back to me at Electric Lady. We had to rerecord all of the drums because, save for an overhead microphone, they hadn't been recorded. To salvage the material, Mitch later overdubbed all of the drums in the studio, listening through headphones as I watched the visuals in the control room on this makeshift movieola."

"Mitch actually did a brilliant job," John Jansen believes. "It was as good as it was ever going to be. Later, when they were assembling the final print, the film editors disregarded everything and didn't cut the picture to the music. They just cut the picture to what they thought looked good, and, as a result, the entire performance sequence was totally out of sync."

"The whole thing was an unmitigated disaster and certainly not much of a show," says Mike Neal. "No one – neither the band nor crew – were happy with what had gone down. The next night [August 1,1970], we were playing our normal show in Honolulu at the International Center. *That* was a great show, but no one was there to film or record anything."

The events of the previous few days had rattled Hendrix's composure, and he desperately needed a respite. "I walked into his dressing room before the Honolulu show and Hendrix grabbed me," recalls Tom Hulett. "He said, 'Tom, you have to get me out of here. I'm staying over in Maui and I'm not happy. I have to do this film, I haven't eaten any meat and these people are making me eat this crazy shit.' I had never seen him like this, so I told him to jump in my Hertz station wagon after the show and I would take him to a hotel. He didn't want anyone to know where he was. I went to Stickells, confided in him and he gave me some of Hendrix's clothes to pack in a small bag. After the show, Hendrix, Pat Hartley (star of *Rainbow Bridge*) my wife

Charlene and I hopped into the station wagon and took off. Backstage, everyone was panicking. They thought that Hendrix had gotten lost; meanwhile, we had checked him into a hotel. Hendrix went upstairs, showered, changed and wanted to go out. He was as straight as a whistle and in great spirits, as if we had sprung him from jail. He asked if I knew Don Ho; I said sure, I had booked him all over the West Coast when 'Tiny Bubbles' first hit big. So I called the maitre d' at the Duka, where Don and his band were playing, and they reserved us a table. When we arrived, Don came over and welcomed us and we watched his show. After he finished, Don came over to our booth with his girlfriend and talked with us until four in the morning. He and Hendrix talked music for hours over mai tais and zombies."

Upon returning to New York, disgusted with the recent events in Hawaii, Hendrix initiated yet another attempt to distance himself from Michael Jeffery. "My brother and I had formed a publishing company, West Kenya Music, and a production company, Rainbow Brothers Productions," explains Arthur Allen. When they got started, Hendrix called a meeting at his place on 12th Street. "He wanted us to get a lawyer, so we called Kenny Haygood in Harlem. My father had suffered an injury when he worked for the railroad and Haygood had represented him, so that was how we knew him. Haygood and Ed Howard [Haygood's law partner] came down to Hendrix's place, where he told them he wanted to become part of our two companies. They told Jimi that they didn't want to make any moves until they spoke with Michael Jeffery. Hendrix was getting pissed off because they kept telling him that they had no choice but to consult Jeffery. He finally exploded. 'What are these niggers talking about!' he screamed while he looked directly at us. 'I'm saying what *I* want and he [Haygood] wants to speak with Michael!' That was just what he didn't want to hear. 'Fuck this,' he hissed, 'and fuck them [pointing to Haygood and Howard]. When I get back [from a brief September European tour], I'll get a lawyer and set this whole damn thing straight!'"

Returning to Electric Lady, Hendrix took stock of his progress in the studio, creating yet another list of songs he wanted to include on his next album. "Songs for the LP *Straight Ahead*," he titled the memo before proceeding to list the following: "'Ezy Ryder,' 'Room Full of Mirrors,' 'Earth Blues Today,' 'Valley of Neptune,' 'Cherokee Mist' that's going to be an instrumental, 'Freedom,' 'Stepping Stone,' 'Izabella,' 'Astro Man,' 'Drifter's Escape,' 'Angel,' 'Bleeding Heart,' 'Burning Desire,' 'Nightbird Flying,' 'Electric Lady' – slow, 'Getting My Heart Back Together Again,' 'Lover Man,' 'Midnight Lightning,' 'Heaven Has No Tomorrow' – slow, 'Sending My Love' – slow to medium, 'This Little Boy,' 'Locomotion,' 'Dolly Dagger' and 'The New Rising Sun' ['Hey Baby']."

With a framework now in mind for the shape of the album, Hendrix's August 1970 sessions were primarily reserved for mixing. "We spent a great deal of time overdubbing and mixing, and trying to finish tracks," recalls Kramer. "Some of the material, such as 'Room Full of Mirrors,' required a great deal of work. I was never happy with the drum sound on the original master, as it sounded squashed; therefore, that track required a considerable amount of time. In a continuing series of overdubs and remixes, we added guitars and created some intricate panning effects before finishing."

"Ezy Ryder" was another Band of Gypsys-era track extensively retooled. "The basic tracks had been done at the Record Plant almost nine months before," remembers Kim King. "We overdubbed eight tracks of guitar, everything in pairs – four tracks of lead and four tracks of rhythm – all at Electric Lady. Eddie had also asked Stevie Winwood and Chris Wood to contribute some backup vocals as well. This work took weeks and involved a number of intricate punchins. During the song's final mixing session, we were using two tape machines and Eddie and Jimi were doing a four-handed mix on the console while I was doing the flanging – actually holding my thumb on the tape reel and varying the flange. This manuever controlled the tape machine's pitch, and by varying that by microcycles, the notes were beating against each other. I had terrible blisters on my thumb, but the sound was fantastic, in fact the entire mix was magical. Eddie, Jimi and I were rocking and leaning back in our chairs throughout. Right near the end of the song, we leaned back too far and all fell over. We were scrambling around the floor before Eddic got to the board, grabbed the master fader and brought it up full to make sure we had hit the end of the tune correctly. Actually we hadn't, there was some garbage there at the end, but the mix worked and Jimi thought the whole thing was hilarious, so we left it in!"

Hendrix's final sessions at Electric Lady were dedicated to many of the songs that would ultimately form *Cry of Love*. Beginning on August 20 and continuing through the 24th, his last documented session, Hendrix and Kramer mixed "Straight Ahead," "Room Full of Mirrors," "Nightbird Flying," "Astro Man," "Belly Button Window" and "Dolly Dagger." Some tracks – "Dolly Dagger," "Freedom," "Nightbird Flying," "Ezy Ryder," "Room Full of Mirrors, "Stepping Stone" and "Izabella" among them – were to all intents and purposes finished. Others, such as "Straight Ahead," "Earth Blues Today" and "Bleeding Heart," were close, lacking only final vocals or overdubs.

In spite of his obvious progress, touring beckoned once more, this time in Europe, effectively stalling his completion of the album, a fact not lost upon Hendrix. With Hendrix's mood soured by the impending tour, Electric Lady president Jim Marron grew concerned that Jimi might boycott the studio's lavish opening party scheduled for August 26, 1970. "We had a hard time getting him to come," says Marron. "I appealed to him directly, telling him that I had been breaking my balls trying to open this place for him. I said, 'You can't have an opening party for Jimi Hendrix's studio without Jimi Hendrix.' He complained about having to go on tour and I cut him off, asking what exactly – between him and me – it would take to get him to the party.

He said, 'Well, I have to leave for England after the party and I've never had a police escort to the airport. If you get me a police escort to the airport, I'll come to the party.' For me, that was simple. I knew a lieutenant in the Village police precinct who had been cooperating with me and I called him, asking for a favor. I didn't care what it cost, I just needed an escort to Kennedy. My connection said, 'No problem, I'll arrange for two motorcycles.' With that, I got Hendrix to come."

The party was a smash success, and though Hendrix did appear, he kept a low profile, eschewing the mingling so common at such affairs, choosing instead to remain with his own small band of friends. "Just before Hendrix was to leave," recalls John Veneble, "I saw him in Jeffery's office upstairs. I remember thinking to myself, 'Boy, this guy doesn't want any part of this tour.' I couldn't say anything, as Hendrix barely knew I worked there, but I'll never forget that feeling. That was the last time most of us saw him."

# 15 A TRAGIC LOSS

*"I've turned full circle. I'm back where I started. I've given this music everything, but I still sound the same. When the last American tour finished, I just wanted to go away and forget everything. Then I started thinking about the future, thinking that this era of music, sparked off by the Beatles, had come to an end. Something new has to come and Jimi Hendrix will be there."*

— Jimi Hendrix

Awaiting him in England was yet another in a long line of impersonal performances at festivals both over-crowded and poorly managed. The Isle of Wight would be no different. Using borrowed equipment (a similar WEM system to the one that had plagued their last U.K. performance at the Royal Albert Hall), the Experience, and Hendrix particularly, offered a half-hearted, lackluster performance, which, regrettably, would be filmed, recorded and ultimately released after his death. As with all Hendrix concerts, the Isle of Wight show did have its highlights, most notably "Red House" and "All Along the Watchtower," as a sense of desperation seemed to power his vocals.

Over time, Hendrix's performance at the Isle of Wight has

taken on cult status, often inaccurately referred to as his final concert. It was neither his last nor his best, as the *Isle of Wight* album (issued in 1971) and a recently released film of the show painfully prove.

Things would soon worsen. After an equally dismal performance in Stockholm the next evening, the entourage traveled to Gothenburg, where Billy Cox's unusual behavior began to attract attention. "It had come on slowly," remembers Gerry Stickells, "and at first, everybody thought he was joking, but he wasn't. It didn't seem drug related because Billy wasn't really into drugs. In America, he had been fine, always friendly and very reliable."

Explains Mike Neal: "On the Cry of Love Tour, there were times when Cox seemed very shy. But in Europe, he just came unglued. This was a straight guy, liked by everyone. I don't feel he was dosed because, at that time, *I* had done a lot of acid and knew what people who were tripping acted like. He sure didn't come across to me as someone who had ingested LSD. His paranoia was incredible."

The September 2, 1970, show in Arhus, Denmark, took place in a sunken gymnasium, the audience in the pit with the band. By this time, Billy Cox had grown worse and Hendrix's mood was terrible. "The first time most of us felt that Billy Cox had a serious problem was there," explains Mike Neal. "Cox was afraid of almost everyone, including the people he had been working with for six months."

Unnerved by Cox's condition, and in no state – mentally or physically – to do the show, Hendrix stumbled clumsily through "Freedom," "Message to Love" and an aborted "Hey Baby," which, after he had unstrapped his guitar and left the stage for good, developed into a lengthy drum solo by Mitchell, Cox having also ventured off, trying unsuccessfully to make Hendrix return. Gerry Stickells, fearful of a riot, instructed Gene McFadden to take the stage and reclaim Jimi's instruments before any were stolen. "Stickells told me to put the guitars away without being conspicuous," says McFadden. "They were all still in the full view of audience. I went out there, pretended to tune each one and then set them back in their cases. We got everything out of there, but it was very scary for a while."

The next night, in Copenhagen, Hendrix rebounded with a strong performance; "Hendrix played for nearly two hours," recalls Gene McFadden. "He even came out and did 'Hey Joe' and 'Fire' for an encore."

Following a stop in West Berlin on September 4, the Experience remained in West Germany, booked for a show at the Isle of Fehmarn. Originally, they had been scheduled to perform on the 5th, but, as had been the case with Woodstock, inclement weather pushed their start time back a full day. "The Isle of Fehmarn festival was a total nightmare," recalls Gerry Stickells. "All of the musicians and crew had been booked into one hotel; when the performances on the 5th were canceled, the bar was a madhouse, people fighting and smashing chairs. Later that night, when the bar ran out of liquor, the owners packed up and left, leaving people to fend for themselves."

Billy Cox's mood worsened. The action in the bar downstairs seemed to unnerve him. "Cox lost it completely at this point," says Stickells. "He swore that people were trying to kill him and wouldn't stay in his room on his own. He was so paranoid that he ended up sleeping on the floor by the side of my bed. To convince him to play the gig, I had to promise to stand behind him on stage."

On a cold, damp German night, amid brawls between rival factions of machine-gun-toting Hell's Angels, the Jimi Hendrix Experience played what would be their last concert. "We were the last to perform," recalls Stickells. "As soon as our gear was off the stage, the Hell's Angels burned it down. We escaped to Hamburg and then flew back to London."

While in London, with Cox's immediate future uncertain, the tour's remaining dates were canceled. "At this point, to communicate with Cox," says Mike Neal, "you would have to say, 'Billy, you remember me. We're friends. We did this

and that together ...'" Seeing Cox in such a state greatly
affected Hendrix, who had a doctor visit and prescribe his
bass guitarist some tranquilizers, but Cox was convinced
they were poison. "Billy would promise to take them and try
to sleep," explains Neal, "but we would find them hidden in
the bathroom or hear him flush them down the toilet."
"Finally," explains Gerry Stickells, "I had to convince him to
get on an airplane – alone – and fly back home." Once back
in the States, Billy quickly returned to form.

With Cox away indefinitely, Mitchell and Hendrix considered replacements. As insurance, Noel Redding was
contacted, although most doubted Hendrix would hold the
slot open for him. Rich Grech, formerly of Blind Faith, was
one of the potential candidates, says Gene McFadden.

In the interim, Hendrix hooked up with Devon and Alan
and Stella Douglas, who were staying with their friend
Daniel Secunda at his London flat. Douglas Records was
enjoying its first hit album, *The Last Poets* having cracked
the *Billboard* top 30, peaking in late August at number 29.
With Hendrix as dissatisfied as ever with Jeffery, Douglas
again made his services available. "We started talking a lot
about his business," Douglas remembers. "He didn't want
to go out on the road that much anymore. I had a
multimedia company and he loved that. We dealt with
books, films and records and he wanted to express himself
in the multimedia fashion." Douglas's plan to curtail
Hendrix's oppressive touring schedule was similar in style
to an idea Michael Jeffery had long wished to implement.
"My plan was to do four concerts a year," says Douglas,
"film them in 35mm and distribute the prints around to
theaters, many of which were just getting into stereo. I
knew about this system because of my background at
United Artists."

Having sparred with Jeffery in the past, Douglas advised
Hendrix to take the path of least resistance. "I told him to
forget about Jeffery, and that I would help him find another
manager. I wanted Hendrix to tell Jeffery that he didn't have

to work anymore, he could just stand aside and collect his percentage." Let him collect his money, Douglas implored Hendrix. Don't be crazy and try to break his contract.

Jeffery himself had made a brief stop in London en route to Spain to check up on his nightclubs. "I had seen Jeffery myself the day before [September 13, 1970] in Danny Halpern's office at Track Records on Old Compton Street. He burst in saying, 'Alan, you have to get me in touch with Jimi.' I pretended not to know anything because I didn't want to get in the middle of it all. Jeffery was desperate, saying he had urgent business and had to see him. I said, 'Look, I'll try to get in touch with him.' I told Hendrix the next day and he blew me off."

Jeffery's pressing concern was a meeting with Ed Chalpin and solicitors for both Yameta and PPX. Chalpin's action in the High Court of Justice was still pending. Unlike Warner Bros., which – in exchange for Hendrix's signature on an exclusive recording contract – had settled the U.S.-Canadian action, Track Records could boast neither the deep pockets nor expansive artist roster to back PPX down and force a settlement. With the Experience being Track's largest-selling act, Chris Stamp had a vested interest in fighting Chalpin to the bitter end. "People kept telling me to settle with him and end it, but I said no, I knew we could beat that contract he had if we could just hang in there long enough." Though Hendrix had pledged to his London solicitor John Hillman that he would attend the meeting, he backed out, leaving Chalpin in the lurch.

Having devoted the evening of September 14 and the early morning hours of the 15th to discussion with Hendrix about his career and ideas for prospective projects, Douglas was due to return to New York. "Hendrix climbed into the cab taking me to the airport and came along to see me off," he recalls. "I was going back to tell Henry Steingarten that this was Jimi's position, and that from now on, Jeffery would no longer be involved. A separate attorney and accountant would draft a new arrangement. That's what we agreed when he dropped me off at the airport. I thought it was that simple."

Though Douglas left convinced of Jimi's intentions, Hendrix himself had reservations. Financially crippled by Electric Lady's cost overruns and Jeffery's subsequent advances and loans against forthcoming royalties, and emotionally distraught over Billy Cox's inexplicable collapse, Hendrix sought out the one person whose belief in him had never wavered: Chas Chandler. Like the son who left the nest with grand ambitions only to return empty-handed, Hendrix had to check his pride and seek advice from the man who had first recognized his great ability.

Though Hendrix's management contract with Jeffery was set to expire on December 1, he would nonetheless – lacking the necessary cash reserve to buy out his many interests – have to remain associated with Jeffery, not only as co-owner of Electric Lady Studios, but as party to the many agreements he had yet to fulfill, including his current Warner Bros. recording contract, which extended through 1972, and an obligation to provide a soundtrack for *Rainbow Bridge*. A Chandler warning had fallen on deaf ears nearly two years before, though: Electric Lady Studios had indeed become Jeffery's emotional pawn, a way to rescind any potential change in management. Firing Jeffery could have dangerous repercussions and Hendrix had watched those – such as Douglas and Buddy Miles – who had pit their will against Jeffery only to lose. Alan Douglas, as well as Stella, Colette and Devon, may have thrown their full support behind Jimi, but what exactly did that represent in the face of his massive debt and responsibility to those, such as Mitch Mitchell or Gerry Stickells, who had worked so tirelessly for him?

Though Douglas was a friend, his brief tenure as Hendrix's advisor during the fall of 1969 had been a failure, marred not only by scrapes with Jeffery and Steve Weiss but by Hendrix's own indifference. What Douglas might accomplish without interference from the incumbent, powerful management team was anybody's guess, but the future of

Hendrix's career hung precariously in the balance and Jimi, as indicated by his actions on the 16th, could not commit himself to Douglas.

"Douglas was trying to take Hendrix away again," explains Bob Levine. "But Hendrix felt a certain thing for Jeffery. He couldn't bring himself to step on him. He didn't feel he was right for his growth musically, but he did have mixed emotions. It had gotten to the point where Hendrix wanted change, but his options were limited."

Perhaps clouding these options was the notion that a move to Douglas – or any other potential suitor – would represent not a lateral change, but rather a step down. Compounding Hendrix's frustration was the fact that Jeffery's tactics *had* given his talent the exposure he needed. For all of Jeffery's flaws, this *was* the top. Few rock artists and, with the possible exception of James Brown, no black entertainer could boast of his many accomplishments. In comparison to Douglas's scrappy one-man operation, Jeffery ran a machine. Though Douglas had a rapport with many jazz greats intrigued by Hendrix's talent, his role as go-between really wasn't necessary. "Douglas didn't have to set up any meetings for Hendrix," says Buddy Miles. "They were happening naturally. [Jazz] musicians like Miles Davis loved his music."

Perhaps the most damaging blow to Douglas's offer to restructure Hendrix's management was Jimi's own unwillingness to entrust a professional relationship with him. "Quite frankly, I don't think Hendrix wanted to take the financial risk that a management change represented," explains Jim Marron. "He would have much preferred to [tinker] with his current situation rather than go broke. Douglas's taste in music leaned heavily toward American jazz, and quite honestly, Hendrix could have been a great jazz player, but he had been a starving artist before and wasn't interested in going that route again. There was no money in jazz at that time. There still isn't."

So, desperate for direction, Hendrix visited Chas

Chandler. "I was still living in the same apartment we had shared in London," Chandler says. "Out of the blue, he just rang the bell, never phoned to say he was coming. The reason he had come – his excuse if you like – was that he hadn't seen my baby son Stephen. When Jimi and I had split, Lotta had just found out she was pregnant. He sat talking with Stephen on his knee and, for old times' sake, asked to play a game of Risk. Over the course of that evening he asked me to produce him again, saying that he had lost his objectivity and couldn't really see what he had in the can. He wanted to put the old team back together: him, myself and Eddie Kramer. I offered to book time in Olympic and listen to what he had done. I just wouldn't believe that he could have spent so much time in the studio and not have good stuff. At that point, he called Eddie Kramer in New York about coming over with the tapes."

Back at Electric Lady, Kramer had been awaiting Hendrix's return. "I was in the studio, observing," recalls John Jansen, "because I was going to be Kramer's assistant on Hendrix's next string of sessions. Eddie was doing some rough mixes, bouncing guitars and generally getting the tapes ready for Hendrix's return."

"I distinctly remember the call from London," says Kramer. "I was working on some Hendrix stuff in the control room of Studio A when the red [private] phone rang. It was Jimi and he was asking if I could bring all the tapes over to England. I sensed something was up, but I said, 'Jimi, don't be crazy. We've built this beautiful studio for you. You'll be here on Monday.' There was a long, drawn-out pause on the line until he said, with a touch of resignation, 'Yeah, you're right. I'll be back on Monday and we'll get it together.' He sounded disappointed that I couldn't or wouldn't bring the tapes over to England. It seemed as if he wanted me to drop everything and come over."

"My brother and I had been in the studio watching Kramer work," explains Albert Allen. "Eddie handed us the phone and said, 'Hey, it's Jimi. Do you want to say hello?' So

I got the phone and Hendrix small-talked, saying that he thought someone had drugged Billy Cox with LSD, and, as a result, he had had to stay over there a little longer than expected. Kramer got back on the phone with him for a little while and then that was it. I do remember Eddie telling us, looking a little confused, that Hendrix had asked him to come over to England. Next thing we knew, Jimi was dead."

"I've thought about that phone call many times over the years," says Kramer. "He never mentioned Chas or Olympic – probably because he didn't know who might be around me in the control room – but I wish he had. It did seem as if he couldn't talk, but I had no idea as to his intentions. Initially, I just figured he couldn't wait to get started again."

"He ended the night by saying that he was going to go back to New York and bring all the tapes back to London," says Chandler. "I told him that I had already made arrangements to bring the baby up to Newcastle and see my parents over the weekend. I told him I would see him Monday or Tuesday."

To facilitate Chandler's return as producer, Hendrix knew he would have to put distance between Jeffery and Chandler – as well as Jeffery and himself – if the move was to be successful. If needed, Hendrix told Chandler, his friend Alan Douglas had pledged his support. "The first time I ever heard the name Alan Douglas was that Wednesday night," explains Chas. "Hendrix told me that he had spent the previous night with him at Douglas's friend's flat in Knightsbridge, and that this guy would be available to help if we decided to ease out Jeffery. Then he said to me – and I remember the sentence – 'He can help, but I don't want that guy to have anything to do with my music.'"

Following his consultation with Chandler, Hendrix traveled to Ronnie Scott's Club, hoping to sit in with Eric Burdon and War. Hendrix had been to the club once before that week, joining Alan and Stella Douglas, Devon Wilson and a group of friends. At that time, however, Terry McVay, formerly road manager for the Animals and now with War, refused to let him take the stage. "When he came in here the first time," says McVay, "I wouldn't let him jam. He looked disoriented [several members of War would later say Hendrix looked slightly "smacked out," a possibility considering Wilson's presence and the unrelenting grip heroin had over her]. When he came back [September 16], he was alone, looking clean and sharp. With a smile, Jimi asked, 'Can I play now? I've even brought my own cord!' I told him I would consider it a pleasure. He plugged into Howard Scott's [War's guitarist] Yamaha GE 12 and those two went at it all night. Hendrix played well, and that was one of Scott's best nights ever."

On that night Hendrix phoned Gerry Stickells. "He was very enthusiastic," says Stickells, "saying he wanted to get back to New York and finish the album. He was very positive about returning to the music and the studio."

"Gerry Stickells told me that I would be flying back to New York with Hendrix," recalls Gene McFadden. "Since we weren't going to be touring for a while, management wanted me home. As it turned out, I flew back to New York beside an empty seat."

Hendrix spent most of September 17 with Monika Dannemann, a girlfriend from West Germany living on Lansdowne Crescent in London. Shuttling between his suite at the Cumberland Hotel and Dannemann's garden flat, Hendrix spent a skittish day running errands and making business calls, the most important of which, remembers Dannemann, was to his attorney, Henry Steingarten. Hendrix, she explains, had decided to reinstate Chas Chandler as his manager, and wanted Eddie Kramer to bring all of the tapes they had been working on to London. Jimi, she says, informed Henry Steingarten of this and instructed him to begin whatever procedures were necessary to entirely eliminate Michael Jeffery from his affairs. "Steingarten asked Jimi if he had given the consequences of such an action enough consideration," remembers Dannemann. "As he answered I had never seen him so determined. He told the lawyer that he was completely sure and wanted him to start proceedings right away. After he hung up he told me that if he [Steingarten] didn't do it, he'd just find another lawyer to do as he asked."

Dannemann's details of the evening of September 17, as testified to Westminster City Coroner Gavin Thurston, are sketchy, but remain the only firsthand account of Hendrix's last hours:

"He got up and had something to eat, then I took some photos of him for my work. We met some people at his hotel, where he telephoned New York. He went to the flat of a person we had met and stayed for about one hour. We arrived home at about 8:30 in the evening. [There] I cooked a meal, and around 11 P.M. we drank a bottle of wine. I washed my hair and we listened to music. He told me that at 1:45 A.M. he had to go see someone at their flat, they were people he didn't like. I dropped him off in my car and picked him up an hour later. During the time we were apart, we spoke three times on the telephone. Just after 3:00 A.M. we went back to my flat. We talked and I made him two fish sandwiches. At 7:00 A.M., I took a sleeping tablet. I woke at 10:20 A.M. and could not sleep anymore. Hendrix was sleeping normally so I went to get some cigarettes. I came back and looked to see if he was awake and I saw that he was sick, [with] vomit around his mouth and nose. I listened to his breathing and took his pulse, it was no different than mine. I tried to awaken him but he would not and then I saw that he had taken some of my Vesparax sleeping tablets. I thought he had taken ten, but later I found one on the floor. He was still breathing and his heart was beating. I telephoned a friend and she advised me to send for an ambulance. I suppose this came about twenty minutes later."

Unable to awaken Jimi, Dannemann became nervous. Wanting to consult with close friend Alvenia Bridges before she took any action, she dialed the flat of Dick Fontaine and Pat Hartley – then still on location in Hawaii filming

*Rainbow Bridge* – where Bridges, Judy Wong, Andrew Coburn, Amanda Leer, Johnny Moke and Graham Bell were staying. Awakened by the ring, Judy Wong answered immediately. "Monika was looking for Alvenia," remembers Wong. "I told her that she had spent the night with Eric Burdon. She wouldn't tell me what was wrong but she did say, 'If I can't reach Alvenia, I'm going to need your help.' When Monika called back sometime later, she and Alvenia were at the hospital crying hysterically."

Dannemann did reach Alevnia, but she had no idea who Hendrix's London doctor was. "I knew Jimi's doctor's last name was Robertson, because Jimi had taken Billy Cox to see him," she remembers. "I looked in his phone book, but there were too many Robertsons listed. I called Alvenia because she knew Jimi and had lived in London for some time. She didn't know Jimi's doctor's name either. Eric Burdon then got on the phone and asked what was happening. I told him Jimi was sick and wouldn't wake up, and that I wanted to call an ambulance. He told me to wait, and that maybe he would wake up on his own. I insisted and he said, 'Then call your fucking ambulance.'"

Eric Burdon's account differs from Dannemann's. In his autobiography, he claims to have phoned Dannemann back, imploring her to call an ambulance without further delay. Dannemann, says Burdon, told him, "I can't have people around here now, there's all kinds of stuff in the house." Burdon insisted, saying, "I don't care, get the illegal stuff and just throw it down the toilet, do anything you can, but get an ambulance now, we're on our way over."

Resting on his side, his head at the edge of the bed, Hendrix lay prostrate in his own vomit for *nine* minutes – the time it took for the ambulance to arrive. During this time, Dannemann again tried, without success, to awaken him. "I knew he hadn't tried to commit suicide because he had only taken nine out of the forty [sleeping pills] that were still in the cupboard."

Notting Hill police sergeant John Shaw confirmed the

grim details. Hendrix "had been found by Monika Danne-mann at 11:00 A.M. to have been sick in his sleep, lying in a pool of vomit. The ambulance was called at 11:18 A.M. and arrived at 11:27 A.M. I went to St. Mary Abbot Hospital where I saw the lifeless body of Jimi Hendrix at 11:45 A.M."

If the testimony of Shaw is accurate, Hendrix went without medical attention for at least twenty-seven minutes (the time span beginning with Dannemann's return to the flat, estimated by Shaw to be between 10:45 and 11:00), too much time for his overburdened heart. Hendrix clung to life until the ambulance reached the hospital: there, his heart swelled and spinal column congested, his system too slowed by the combination of alcohol and barbiturates to recover. At twenty-seven, Jimi Hendrix was dead.

As Hendrix lay dead in St. Mary Abbot Hospital, Gerry Stickells was roused by a frantic phone call, instructing him to go there at once. Though he raced to the hospital from his Elgin Crescent flat, all he could do was identify the body for local officials.

Dazed and saddened by Hendrix's unexpected death, Stickells slowly set about collating the morning's fateful events and informing his co-workers of the tragedy amid the fog of shock and disbelief that shrouded the hospital's emergency-reception area. Michael Jeffery was in Spain and had not left a phone number. Instead, Stickells reached Bob Levine, still asleep (because of the U.K.-U.S. time difference, Stickells's call was placed between 6 and 7 A.M. New York time) at his home in Manhattan. "I was stunned," recalls Levine. "I was wondering if I was dreaming. I wasn't."

Though no member of Hendrix's management team was able to reach Jeffery, he still managed to learn of his artist's untimely end. "I was in Spain with Jeffery and we were supposed to have dinner that night in Majorca," remembers Jim Marron. "He called me from his club in Palma saying that he would have to cancel. I said, 'Mike, we've already made reservations.' He said, 'Well ... there is good reason. I've just got word from London. Jimi's dead.' I said, 'What!'

He said, 'I always knew that son of a bitch would pull a quickie.' I was stunned. 'A quickie?' 'Yeah, look at that! He's up and done it!' Basically, he had lost a major property. You had the feeling that he had just lost a couple of million dollars – and was the first to realize it. My first reaction was, 'Oh my God, my friend is dead.'

"The next day," continues Marron, "I met with Jeffery to assess what exactly had happened. Being away from London, and having traveled in such shady circles himself, Jeffery didn't know if Hendrix's death had been a hit or just his own misadventure. He told me that he was going to conduct his own investigation and that I should trust no one."

From Spain, Jeffery secretly flew to London in an effort to clarify the circumstances that had led to the death of his star client. First and foremost on his agenda was a confrontation with Devon Wilson and her cadre of Colette Mimram and Alan and Stella Douglas. On September 20, Jeffery phoned Alan Douglas and requested that he come to his hotel. "When I arrived, he was bent over, in misery from a recent back injury," remembers Douglas. "We started talking and he let it all out. It was like a confession. The one thing he said that I'll never forget was, 'Every time I had a woman I cared for, at some point I would realize that she was with me only to get to him.' In my opinion, Jeffery hated Hendrix because Jimi had slept with [Jeffery's girlfriend] Lynn Bailey. Being so open, Hendrix couldn't have understood why Jeffery might be upset."

Back in New York, the question of Jeffery's whereabouts remained unanswered. "We tried calling all of Jeffery's contacts – from [his club] Sgt. Pepper's to the Hotel Victoria in Majorca – trying to reach him," remembers Bob Levine. "We were getting frustrated because Hendrix's body was going to be held up in London for two weeks and we wanted Jeffery's input on the funeral service. A full week after Hendrix's death, he finally called. Hearing his voice, I immediately asked what his plans were and would he be going to Seattle. 'What plans?' he asked. I said 'The funeral.' 'What funeral?' he replied. I was exasperated: 'Jimi's!' The phone went quiet for a while and then he hung up. The whole office was staring at me, unable to believe that with all of the coverage on radio, print and television, Jeffery didn't know that Jimi had died. He called back in five minutes and we talked quietly. He said, 'Bob, I didn't know,' and was asking about what had happened. While I didn't confront him, I knew he was lying because I had spoken to people who saw him at a party Track Records had staged in London the night before Hendrix died. I knew everybody who had attended, from Douglas's pair – Stella and Colette – to Devon, as well as friends from Harold Davison's office. It was impossible for him to have slipped incognito into Spain without hearing about Jimi's death."

Fleet Street press had a field day with Hendrix's death, blazing headlines informing readers of the "Wild Man of Pop"'s lurid personal life. So cleverly manipulated by Jeffery and Chandler during Hendrix's lifetime, the newspapers, true to form, now seemed bent on destroying his memory. Tales of Hendrix's "last hours" and "lost days" were standard fare. One such article invented its own dramatic scenario:

"I need help bad, man." These words, gasped into a telephone-answering machine in an empty office, are the epitaph of Jimi Hendrix, idol of millions and prophet-in-chief of the drug generation.

They were spoken at 1:30 A.M. on Friday morning and discovered on the tape when the office opened at 10:00 A.M.

Charles Chandler of the Robert Stigwood show business empire and Hendrix's former manager, made a frantic phone call to the Notting Hill number the pop idol had given.

But Hendrix, a cocaine addict, was already near death. "Call me a bit later, man," he groaned.

Within hours he was dead. At 24. A victim of the pop-and-drugs culture he helped perpetuate.

Further damaging Hendrix's reputation was Eric Burdon's bizarre "revelation" that Jimi may have committed suicide. In an interview broadcast on September 21 with Kenneth Allsop for the BBC television program *24 Hours*, Burdon described Hendrix's death as "deliberate," adding that Jimi had "made his exit when he wanted to." Citing a poem Hendrix had allegedly crafted the evening before his death, Burdon surmised that Hendrix "had used the drug to phase himself out of this life and go someplace else."

Burdon's comments caused a firestorm in Britain and abroad, increasing the already intense scrutiny and speculation over the final sketchy hours of Hendrix's life. In addition, Burdon's allegation temporarily jeopardized the Lloyd's of London insurance payout to Warner Bros. "We had a big insurance policy on Hendrix that covered the money we lent him for the studio," explains Reprise vice president Joe Smith. "We were preparing to approach Lloyd's of London when Eric Burdon went on television saying that Hendrix had killed himself. I remember calling him and saying, 'You fucker, don't open your mouth again! That's our insurance policy!'"

Burdon's evidence, a sensitive, albeit rambling work of original Hendrix poetry given to him by Dannemann, suited his purpose more successfully in part than in whole, as the poem-song's last verse seemed open to interpretation. Many fans and writers, searching to solve the riddle of Hendrix's undignified death, accepted it as Jimi's own acknowledgment of his impending demise.

> The story of
> life is quicker
> than the wink of an eye
> The story of love
> is hello and goodbye
> Until we meet again.

While Burdon would later repudiate his suicide claim, citing, in his own autobiography, the Allsop interview as a regretful, shameful exercise, his initial claim ignited a destructive thought process that has dramatically shaped the posthumous Hendrix legend. "The Story of Life," his fabled "last" work, curiously, like "Black Gold," has emerged as a cipher of sorts, one of the clues or signposts that Hendrix enthusiasts are not to ignore should they wish to fully understand the true Hendrix. In the years following Hendrix's death – especially during Alan Douglas's reign as steward of the Hendrix tape closet – great emphasis has been placed on such ciphers while seemingly discounting Hendrix's achievements with the Experience, creating a bizarre dichotomy best described by critic Dave Marsh in 1980:

> [Hendrix] was a prophet who had known some honor,
> almost all of it exactly the wrong kind, a prolific and
> profligate creator who left almost everyone who heard or
> saw him with the distinct impression that the heartcenter of
> his work remained tantalizingly out of reach. So even today,
> as scraps of his music never intended for public
> consumption are steadily dredged up, each one is greeted
> with nervous anticipation, as if the right six hundred feet of
> tape might open up and clarify the dimensions and secrets of
> his ambition, recasting his music in comprehensible fashion,
> reducing it to something intellectually explicable.

Douglas's initial foray into the Hendrix legacy was principally based on two such ciphers – his attempt to remodel Hendrix as a frustrated jazzman mired amid the trappings of psychedelia, and the promise of "Black Gold," described by Douglas as "a kind of musical autobiography."

Burdon's suicide claim further cheapened Hendrix's already fragile legacy. Though touted initially by Burdon's supporters as the missing link, "The Story of Life" is remarkably similar to a number of other Hendrix compositions – released and unreleased – in which themes of God, love and death are frequently prevalent. In fact, his boasts within "Voodoo Chile" and "I Don't Live Today," namely,

"I'll see you in the next world and don't be late" and "I don't live today, maybe tomorrow I just can't say," could both be interpreted as foreboding and perhaps even more menacing than any verse within "The Story of Life."

Casting aside Burdon's claims, Michael Jeffery concluded his private investigation unable to find any evidence of foul play. Gnawing at him was the notion that Hendrix's death had resulted from a reckless oversight that could have been prevented. Says Jim Marron: "Jeffery found Jimi's death hard to accept. As his personal manager, the image of his million-dollar rock star drowning in his own vomit was ugly and hard to dismiss. Though he knew Hendrix had neither committed suicide nor been murdered, he never went public with his feelings because they would have hurt his record sales. Jeffery didn't want to tell the truth – as ugly and simple as it was – because he was afraid that it would pop the bubble. He believed in mystique; it was the basis of his entire management-marketing technique. When people didn't know the answers, they created mystique, and Jeffery felt that to keep them interested, you always had to keep them guessing."

In New York, a New York City Surrogate Court approved Al Hendrix's request that Henry Steingarten be named the administrator of his son's estate, conservatively estimated to be worth some $500,000. Because Jimi had died without a will outlining the disposal of his assets, Al Hendrix was named sole beneficiary. While in Manhattan, Al Hendrix also tried to take account of his son's possessions, visiting Michael Jeffery at Electric Lady Studios and Jimi's modest 59 West 12th Street apartment. "Jimi's dad was a proud, gentle man," remembers Jim Marron. "Jeffery and Stickells were being as polite as they could, a 'Yes, Mr. Hendrix, no, Mr. Hendrix' type of thing. They took him to Jimi's apartment and Al Hendrix was horrified. He said, 'Where is everything?' Instead of this monumental Hollywood or Las Vegas style of wealth he had envisaged, all he found were tapestries on the wall and Indian pillows on the floor.

Inside the vault at Electric Lady, where we had stored Jimi's guitars and tapes, Al saw them and asked if he could take them back to Seattle. Jeffery offered to package them up and ship them to him." (Shortly thereafter, Marron alleges, when the cases arrived in Seattle many were empty – the guitars had vanished and were never found.)

In keeping with New York state law, Henry Steingarten began converting all of Jimi's known assets to cash. This process, set in place immediately, included a blind auction of many of Hendrix's personal possessions. His Corvette and a number of Stratocasters were among the items unceremoniously sold to the highest bidder. In all, Al Hendrix was presented with some $21,000 in cash, a pittance considering the Experience's recent U.S. and European tour revenues. Jeffery had taken Hendrix's share of the European funds and funneled it back into Electric Lady Studios, which, although nearly completed, was in dire need of operating capital. Though Al Hendrix now controlled his son's many valuable publishing and recording contracts, as well as a 50 percent share in Electric Lady Studios Inc., Jimi's personal finances were in shambles.

The destiny of Electric Lady Studios was now a pressing concern to both Al Hendrix and Michael Jeffery. Whereas Warner Bros. had succeeded in garnering Hendrix's signature on a multimillion-dollar insurance policy, Jeffery had had no such luck. "When we were in Hawaii filming *Rainbow Bridge,* Jeffery was trying to get Jimi to sign a million-dollar insurance policy," recalls Bob Levine. "I had bad feelings about it and warned him not to sign. I then later confronted him in Oahu, asking if he had signed any agreements, and he said, 'Just some performance contracts that I was behind on.' I was relieved, but I still warned him to look out for it. I knew Jeffery not only had power of attorney over Jimi, but, in trying to finish the movie, had borrowed himself to the limit. I was afraid Jeffery would try to get money against *Jimi's life,* using the policy as collateral."

The policy Jeffery so desperately wanted Hendrix to sign, says Jim Marron, is commonly known in the business trade as key-man insurance. Explains Marron: "He wanted a key-man insurance policy that – should one partner die – made one million dollars available to either partner to buy out the full interest in the company."

Overwhelmed by the week's events, a bereaved Al Hendrix returned home to Seattle. There, with the help of his family, and logistical support from Concerts West's Tom Hulett, funeral services, to be held at the Dunlap Baptist Church, were planned for October 1, 1970.

On that dreary, overcast afternoon in Seattle, all of Jimi's immediate family, joined by his bandmates and associates from New York, attended the memorial services, crowding the small church to pay their final respects. Freddie Mae Gautier, a friend of the Hendrix family whose care and love for Jimi dated back to his early childhood, read both "Angel" and Jimi's liner notes for the Buddy Miles Express album *Expressway to Your Skull* with heartfelt sincerity, a quality the Reverend Harold Blackburn's sermon lacked. "The reverend didn't know anything about Jimi," says Bob Levine. "When he started with, 'We have to remember the great guitar player in the sky ...' we all broke up laughing. It helped ease the tension."

The open casket ceremony unnerved many, including Mitch and Noel. Michael Jeffery, remembers Bob Levine, never approached Jimi's casket, choosing instead to remain in the limousine. As Jimi was laid to rest, Devon Wilson, in a fit of hysteria, tried to throw herself into the open grave.

Later that day, an informal jam session in Jimi's memory was staged at the Seattle Arena, and Noel and Mitch joined Buddy Miles, Johnny Winter and others in a half-hearted exercise. Though George Harrison and Paul McCartney were rumored to appear, neither they nor any other such stars materialized and Jimi's wake ground to a sad halt. For many of Hendrix's closest associates – who had been in New

York when he died – the funeral had driven home the reality of his death. Jimi was no longer among them, gone forever, his death a terrible waste and his spirit irreplaceable.

# 16 HIDDEN TREASURES

*"When Jimi died, apart from having a big piece of our lives torn away, a big chunk of musical history suddenly disappeared."*

—Eddie Kramer

Overwhelmed and clearly overrun by his son's manager and legal team, Al Hendrix sought assistance in clarifying Jimi's complex web of contracts and commitments. Acting on the advice of Herbert Price, an acquaintance of Jimi, Leo Branton was hired and instructed to sort out his son's business affairs. Branton, later to represent noted black activist Angela Davis, had some experience in entertainment law, most notably through his association with the Nat King Cole estate.

During Branton's first trip east on Al Hendrix's behalf, he sought out Ken Haygood and Ed Howard, the same attorneys Jimi had disagreed with during the secret August 1970 meeting held at his apartment. "Leo Branton came to New York," remembers Arthur Allen, "wanting to know if any lawyers [apart from Steve Weiss and Henry Steingarten] had ever had any affiliation with Hendrix. My brother and I, like fools, even though Jimi hadn't wanted their services, volunteered Kenny Haygood and Ed Howard. Next thing you know, Haygood was in charge of the estate."

Not exactly, but Haygood's alliance with Branton did

have a pronounced effect on the course of Hendrix's post-humous legacy. Their first order of business dealt with the future of Electric Lady Studios. Al Hendrix had little interest in the facility and, as a result, negotiations to sell Jimi's share in the studio to Michael Jeffery were set in motion. Though Hendrix – through his own cash contributions and portion of the Warner Bros. loan – had invested nearly a half million dollars in the project, Jeffery was able to secure full owner-ship of the facility for $240,000 in cash and the promise to fulfill the outstanding balance of the Warner Bros. mortgage. "As a good businessman, Jeffery knew the estate wouldn't want to continue their relationship with the studio now that Jimi had passed away," explains Jim Marron. "He placed his own investment to date at $500,000, not including the interest on the Warner Bros. loan and the good will created by the Hendrix name. Jeffery felt he could buy out Jimi's share for less than fifty cents on the dollar and, as a result, his first offer was $200,000. While he ended up paying $240,000, he got them to accept the payments in installments – just to twist the knife a bit. Basically, he was hoping that the studio could pay off the debt without having to take out another personal mortgage."

Hamstrung by Jimi's existing contracts, the estate was forced to continue its relationship with Michael Jeffery. Only the slightest measure of good faith existed between the parties, each shackled by suspicion over each other's motives. Ken Haygood investigated each facet of Hendrix's management team, looking to purge those who may have looted his famous client. As dire as Hendrix's financial condition had been at the time of his death, its future prospects were even worse. Jeffery's 30 percent commission of all Hendrix revenues bound the estate significantly, creating a situation that, coupled with the still bitterly ensnarled Yameta-PPX British action and Hendrix's indebt-edness to Warner Bros., effectively limited their ability to generate the amount of revenue needed to revive Jimi's moribund financial standing.

One of Michael Jeffery's biggest, and perhaps most important, remaining responsibilities concerned the many reels of recording tape tucked away in the confines of Electric Lady Studios. Though Jimi had made progress toward finishing his fourth studio album during the previous summer, all of the material had been left in various stages of completion. After Jimi's death, Jeffery had clamped down on his remaining assets, guarding them in house under his watchful eye. "Jeffery had a definite philosophy about the tapes," explains Jim Marron. "He wanted to secure everything we had – and could get our hands on – in Electric Lady's vault on the third floor, and ordered very tight security."

In addition to sequestrating Hendrix's unreleased material, Jeffery also devised a plan for their eventual release. "He wanted to elicit the best of whatever music remained and burn the rest," recalls Marron. "He said, 'Let's not put out shit, because now that Jimi's dead, people will buy anything.' He was hoping to see three albums out of all that stuff." While this rationale might suggest a sudden care for the memory of his artist, Jeffery's primary concerns – as they had been during Hendrix's lifetime – were centered squarely on the business aspects of Jimi's posthumous career. With Jeffery's reign of power effectively set to expire along with Hendrix's Warner Bros. pact in 1972, he wanted to dictate the terms in which Jimi's final works would be issued before his ties with the estate were permanently severed.

The parameters of Jeffery's posthumous release schedule were framed by two obvious unfinished works: the *Rainbow Bridge* soundtrack album and what ultimately would become *The Cry of Love*. There would be no double album issued, as Jeffery wished to carefully dole out the very best of what music remained. While he would place no creative restraints on Eddie Kramer – entrusted, with the able assistance of Mitch Mitchell, to craft these albums – Jeffery envisioned a number of separate releases, each maximizing the potential of such expensive and heretofore unrealized efforts as *Jimi Plays Berkeley* and *Rainbow Bridge.*

For Eddie Kramer, the mere thought of poring through hours of unfinished Hendrix masterworks was a terribly sad and difficult exercise. That Jimi had come so close to seeing finished the fruits of nearly two years' labor, before passing away, made the task even more arduous. Hendrix had made tremendous strides during the summer, when, while flying in the face of his own turbulent personal and professional life, the creativity he felt had abandoned him returned. While the cumulative effects of outside pressures could not be discounted, Hendrix's music – at least the material the Band of Gypsys or Gypsys Suns & Rainbows were unable to realize – was no longer entrenched within meandering jams. Where Hendrix had seemingly been unable to complete a single track to his satisfaction during the fall of 1969, at Electric Lady he had brought many songs to fruition, including "Dolly Dagger," "Freedom" and "Night Bird Flying." Moreover, Hendrix seemed to have matured as a producer, first in reestablishing Kramer in the position he had been most effective in, and then admitting to Chas Chandler during their meeting in September that, indeed, he *had* lost his objectivity and needed help.

Despite these considerable creative strides, none of Hendrix's close associates feel he had fully escaped the demons that had dogged not only his progress as an artist but his quality of life. Gerry Stickells echoes the sentiments of many: "You can't say his crisis was over just because he would have been able to finish *The Cry of Love.* He was happy with what he had in the can and knew what he had to do to finish it. Yes, he would have been pleased with *that* record, but who knows about the next one. Jimi might have written a couple more good rock n' roll albums, but the thrill wouldn't have been there for him, and the whole cycle would have started all over again."

That cycle, says Linda Keith, drew its roots in Hendrix's aversion to personal commitments. "Jimi's elaborate double life backfired on him because there was no depth to any of his relationships – certainly with women as far as I know. You can't survive in that world without knowing that when the chips are down, there is *someone* committed to helping you. He would never forge these relationships because he feared putting himself in a position where he could be hurt."

Had Hendrix lived to fully complete and issue what all involved considered to be a masterwork at the very least equal to his previous achievements, his legacy would bear few similarities to the one that shrouds his image today. *The Cry of Love* (incorporating the bulk of *Rainbow Bridge* and select portions of *War Heroes*) signaled a musical evolution for Hendrix, and had he lived to see its release the album would have served his memory well, its contents not cheapened by speculation as to what might have been. While splitting the unreleased material into separate albums may have been the prudent financial option, each new issue featured lower-quality material and lessened public expectation and anticipation for additional releases.

Having assigned Kramer to evaluate the studio tapes and shape them into an album, Jeffery moved to organize either a tribute film or television special. Aside from the Maui (July 30, 1970) performance, which he owned outright, material from festivals such as Woodstock, the recent Isle of Wight concert and various promotional films, the most promising footage available was controlled by Peter Pila-fian, who – with Jeffery's permission – had filmed Hendrix's two concerts in Berkeley (May 30, 1970).

Though besieged by debt and his commitment to *Rainbow Bridge*, Jeffery had promised Pilafian and his crew that they would be compensated for their efforts. However, after both performances were filmed, considerable expenses incurred, and without viewing as much as a single frame of film, Jeffery reneged on his promise, refusing to forward any payment. With his limited resources, Pilafian was unable even to develop his film, carefully storing the negatives and working through legal channels to recoup expenses totaling some $22,000. "Shortly after Hendrix's death I received a call from Jeffery about the footage," remembers Pilafian. "He was anxious to resurrect the project and release it, but he still refused to pay until I finally negotiated a deal where I gave up my percentage in return for immediate reimbursement of my expenses to date. Of course, he paid me with a bad check that didn't clear for a month."

Though Pilafian's team edited in various scenes of recent riots across America, including footage of Berkeley's own bloody People's Park insurrection, *Jimi Plays Berkeley* was still too short to be considered a feature film. "I had never edited a film in my life," explains John Jansen, "but Jeffery asked me to change the film from a documentary to a full-length movie. Primarily, I was adding more footage to the film and, because they had originally cut it so weird, reediting different shots to the songs already included. Eddie Kramer remixed the audio and we finally synched it up properly."

While Jeffery busied himself with securing available concert footage, work on *The Cry of Love* progressed quickly. After an initial period of confusion, Kramer and Mitch Mitchell had isolated the best of what remained in Electric Lady's vast tape closet. With many songs incomplete, Mitchell had to overdub drums and additional percussion onto various tracks, one being "Angel." John Jansen, assistant engineer on the session, recalls the tension that hovered over the control room, as Mitchell readied himself for the emotional task. "Mitch was around the control room listening to playbacks and I was wondering if he was up to it. Then he got behind his kit and doubled his original drum line in one take. It was amazing."

Explains Eddie Kramer: "Mitch had always intended to overdub tom-tom [drums] with mallets, because that was a sound we were particularly good at getting. This was an idea that had been discussed originally, something we all – Jimi included – felt would embellish the track. Therefore, I had no problem with Mitch adding the overdub at all."

As Eddie Kramer explains, not all of Electric Lady's staff shared Mitch Mitchell's resolve. "I was working on 'Drifting' late one night in Studio A when I realized that I only had a DI [direct-injection] guitar track for this very important lead-rhythm part. Originally, wanting a very clean guitar sound, Jimi had put this part on tape to act as a guide. There was no amplifier track, so in order to create the amplifier sound, I ran the DI out of the console, through the cue system into the studio, fed it through a transformer into Jimi's Marshall stack and miked it up. All of the lights were out in the studio, save for the glow of the Marshall headstack, and it sounded just as if Jimi was playing through the amplifier. The back door to the studio had been open and in the midst of transforming the sound to tape, an assistant engineer was startled to hear Jimi's screaming guitar in Studio A. He came running into the control room, flustered, his face white as a sheet, sure that he had heard Jimi playing again, before he realized what I had been doing."

"Drifting," another Hendrix ballad too strong to exclude from the collection, posed a more intricate challenge for Kramer and Mitchell. Where Mitchell's drum overdub for "Angel" solidified an existing rhythm pattern, "Drifting" required considerable construction, for while its original basic track included the combined efforts of Hendrix, Mitchell and Cox, the song's delicate melody was framed by just two guitar lines and buttressed by generous insertions of Jimi's backwards guitar. Having studied rough stereo mixes incorporating all of the available elements, Kramer and Mitchell also recruited Buzzy Linhart to contribute a charming, tastefully muted vibes overdub. Explains Linhart: "Eddie Kramer and Mitch Mitchell called me up and told me they had one track where Jimi hadn't been sure if he wanted vibes playing the song's chords or an additional rhythm guitar, and would I play on this song for them? It was just so touching to be in the studio he built, playing back this tape and hearing Jimi's beautiful voice."

While the version of "Drifting" that graces *The Cry of Love* may or may not have conformed to the vision of its composer, Kramer and Mitchell's modest assist in no way defiled Hendrix's intent, as the producers correctly placed Linhart's contribution in a supporting role behind Jimi's melodic guitar and endearing lead vocal.

Of all the tracks considered for *The Cry of Love*, only one, "My Friend" – a leftover from a one-off March 1968 session featuring Hendrix-Scene Club compatriots Paul Caruso, Stephen Stills and the Fugs' Ken Weaver – had neither been mixed nor recorded by Hendrix during his spring and summer 1970 sessions at Electric Lady. Many, like "Freedom," "Night Bird Flying," "In From the Storm" and "Dolly Dagger," had been built front to back at the studio. Others, such as "Ezy Ryder," "Room Full of Mirrors" and "Stepping Stone," were the subject of extensive mixing and overdubbing sessions, typical of Hendrix's penchant for perfection.

Save for "Dolly Dagger" (originally considered as a single release) and "Room Full of Mirrors" – reassigned to the *Rainbow Bridge* sound track album and substituted at the last minute with "Straight Ahead" and "My Friend" – *The Cry of Love*'s final ten songs were compiled on December 3, 1970, and readied for release.

Perhaps the most obvious victim of Jeffery's scattershot attention was *Rainbow Bridge*, the film for which he had harbored such grand visions, but which dissipated into a disastrous, embarrassing failure. "He couldn't believe that he was broke and still without a finished project," remembers Jim Marron. "That project sucked up all of his cash and left him with a cinema verité documentary of nothing."

Recalls John Jansen, assigned to pore through the Hendrix tape library to find music beds for the film's soundtrack, Jeffery and Wein's original vision of an orgasmic collage of sex, drugs and rock n' roll Jimi Hendrix-style never translated to the finished product. "I went to the screening of the first rough cut and it was four hours long. There was a lot of leader [blank film] edited in where the special effects were going to happen. When they would appear on the screen, someone would say, 'This is when the smell of hashish will fill the theater.' I'm sitting there with my mouth hanging open thinking, 'What the fuck have I committed myself to?'"

The film's sole asset remained its short passage of the Experience's concert atop the volcano. Desperate to recoup the fortune he had invested in the project, Jeffery ordered Wein to extract maximum mileage out of whatever performance footage the crew had shot. "We had a meeting," recalls Marron, "and Wein said that we should reassess the whole Hendrix part in the movie. Jeffery exploded, 'You're damn right we're going to!' He owned the footage and told Wein to stretch or expand the performance section – even if it meant shifting the focus away from this quasi-spiritual travelogue through Maui to a film based on Jimi Hendrix."

Educated at Harvard and Oxford, as well as a "graduate" of the Warhol avant-garde film clique, Chuck Wein bitterly refutes charges that he simply set out to squander Jeffery's considerable investment. "The version that was released was totally disjointed," he explains. The problem, says Wein, originated in the editing room. The correct version, he explains, was 123 minutes long and, aside from the initial screening held at the Aquarius Theater in Los Angeles, the general public has never been afforded the chance to see the finished film in its proper context. According to Wein, what unsuspecting audiences endured – having been alerted to the film via a shameless advertising campaign that trumpeted Hendrix's minor "contribution" – was a version (usually seventy to ninety minutes in length) edited to satisfy theater owners and drive-in operators who coupled the film with other celluloid rock n' roll attractions.

Wein freely admits to using nearly every piece of Hendrix footage he had at hand. "No matter what people say, what you see in the finished film is all that existed. I had to go to some length just to get that." As if to add insult to injury, Jimi's sole speaking scene, an embarrassing and obviously stoned rap sequence, was inserted into the final print. "I had to bait him into doing that small scene with Pat Hartley," admits Wein. "It was about 2 A.M. and both of them were ripped, but what came out of Jimi was his true imagination."

Perhaps, but regardless of its length (or even the Hendrix content), *Rainbow Bridge* was a dismal critical failure. Doubly cruel was the injury to Hendrix's reputation, which, lent to the production without his consent (at least Hendrix had originated the music released on posthumous albums), further stained his image. Of the many mistakes Michael Jeffery committed during his final phase of stewardship, the close association of Hendrix with Jeffery's first, futile foray into the jungle of cinema would perhaps be the most critical. Wein's "documentary" apart, Jeffery's attempt to rescue his own personal finances via Hendrix's memory was disgraceful. While Jeffery may have made what seemed to him to have been the most prudent financial option available, his brazen decision to highlight – not merely incorporate – an obviously substandard Hendrix performance rejected by both Mitch Mitchell and Eddie Kramer, left Jimi's shrinking fan base utterly dumbfounded.

With the exception of "Dolly Dagger" and "Room Full of Mirrors," plucked from *The Cry of Love* to bolster the content, work on the film's soundtrack album, a second posthumous record release, was notably more difficult. Where *The Cry of Love* had been predominantly drawn from the best of the Electric Lady sessions, material to merit a second release simply did not exist. To augment their base of "Dolly Dagger," "Room Full of Mirrors," "Izabella," "Hey Baby (Land of the New Rising Sun)" and "Stepping Stone," producers Kramer and Mitchell pressed Jeffery to reclaim master tapes Warner Bros. had been reluctant to turn over. The great majority of these tapes had been recorded at the Record Plant throughout 1969. Since he had intermittently participated during that time, Mitchell could only surmise that the lion's share came from the Band of Gypsys' many sessions. Work on the *Rainbow Bridge* album slowed until, in early February 1971, Reprise vice president Mo Ostin relented, and ordered all master recordings within his label's vaults shipped to Electric Lady.

Warner Bros.' cache of 186 reels of multitrack tape offered Kramer and Mitchell surprisingly little in terms of finished studio masters. The most promising tapes had been recorded at TTG Studios during October 1968, when the original Experience staged their final rally to record a fourth album as a cohesive unit. From these, only "Look Over Yonder," with the three-man Experience lineup intact, was an early consensus choice. Just one other *Rainbow Bridge* track would be unearthed from these tapes, Jimi's studio interpretation of "Star Spangled Banner," taken from a March 18, 1969, Record Plant session.

To fill the balance of the album, the producers turned to "Earth Blues," a flawed but inspired original Hendrix had not lived to finish. Though work on the song dated back to sessions throughout November and December 1969, the track that graces this collection was cut at the Record Plant with the Band of Gypsys on January 20, 1970. While Hendrix had shipped the master over to Electric Lady, "Earth Blues" had been overlooked amid the spate of new compositions recorded that spring and summer. The version from January 20 was remixed and Buddy Miles's original drum parts replaced with a new Mitchell overdub.

"Hey Baby (Land of the New Rising Sun)," another noteworthy Hendrix original, suffered from the same structural problems as "Earth Blues," and Jimi's "Is the microphone on?" – purposely left in the song's final mix – conveys that point. A staple of the Experience's 1970 U.S. and European concerts, "Hey Baby (Land of the New Rising Sun)" had been an early contender for inclusion on *The Cry of Love* before being passed over.

John Jansen revived "Pali Gap" and put forward the instrumental for a slot on the album. It has since been reported that "Pali Gap" was the result of a deliberate attempt by Hendrix to record an instrumental dedicated, as its title might suggest, to the Hawaiian goddess of the volcanoes. Not so. "Pali Gap" was christened by Michael Jeffery, who thought the title might help wed the song to the film's Hawaiian locale. As for the recording, neither the Experience nor Eddie Kramer seriously considered the song's prospects during Hendrix's lifetime. It was only during Jansen's exhaustive searches through Electric Lady's tape vaults that the track resurfaced.

As had been the case with *The Cry of Love*, two tracks were withdrawn from *Rainbow Bridge* during the production's final stages. Where "Dolly Dagger" and "Room Full of Mirrors" had been pulled from *The Cry of Love* to bolster the film's soundtrack, "Izabella" and "Stepping Stone" were held back in favor of a live version of "Hear My Train A Comin'" from the Experience's May 30, 1970, Berkeley performance. Though their inclusion would have been more appropriate, this Jeffery decision was not as coldly commercial as the first had been. Because the final print of *Rainbow Bridge* featured a live version of "Hear My Train A Comin'," the accompanying soundtrack album had to have one too. The rendition depicted in the film had been recorded under miserable technical conditions, and, with no acceptable studio version having ever been completed, Kramer substituted the vastly superior Berkeley performance in its place.

Having committed a major effort to screening and remixing *Jimi Plays Berkeley*, there was not, in Eddie Kramer's opinion, enough worthy tracks from the two concerts to merit a soundtrack release in its own right. An album of live Hendrix recordings had been designated by Michael Jeffery as the next posthumous release, and if a *Jimi Plays Berkeley* soundtrack couldn't be fashioned, Kramer was instructed to craft an album incorporating the best from Berkeley blended with other pristine Experience live performances.

In the opinion of the producers, this meant gleaning songs from three sources: San Diego, Berkeley and London's Royal Albert Hall. (Additional tracks from the group's brilliant performance at the Monterey Pop Festival were not made available to Kramer.) The May 24, 1969, San Diego recording offered one true gem, a magnificent rendition of "Red House." Berkeley's prospects were open-ended, as a number of tracks were strong contenders, the electrifying rendition of "Johnny B. Goode" being an obvious choice. The most promising recordings of all, however, seemed to be from the February 24, 1969, Royal Albert Hall performance. While Jeffery *possessed* master tapes of the concert, it wasn't particularly clear who *owned* the recordings in question. The debate stemmed from Jeffery's failed television production venture with Steve Gold and Jerry Goldstein. Post-production on the original presentation had foundered when Jeffery failed to secure adequate distribution for the finished product. The film's budget had soared over original estimates, and Jeffery had flinched at investing additional revenue into the project. But with Hendrix dead and Gold and Goldstein sitting on thousands of feet of pristine 16mm Experience footage, Jeffery was forced to come to the table and settle with his former partners, now adversaries.

Recalls Jim Marron, "By this time, Jeffery hated Gold and Goldstein with a passion. During one meeting at Electric Lady, they so enraged him that he hit one of them with a two-inch tape box. Their main argument was over visual rights to the Royal Albert Hall concert. Gold and Goldstein claimed this to be theirs. Jeffery exploded. 'You have no fucking rights to either my artist or any footage of him!' he ranted. They insisted otherwise, so he threw the tape box at them. Right after that, he had Steve Weiss threaten them with an injunction."

Though rebuffed by Gold and Goldstein, Jeffery refused to back down, deciding instead to release portions of the Royal Albert Hall soundtrack *apart* from the film. "Initially, as we were putting together the live album, we knew that Gold and Goldstein had refused Jeffery permission to use anything recorded at the Royal Albert Hall," explains Eddie Kramer. "I remember Jeffery walking into the control room with brown, unmarked tape boxes saying, 'Use these.' While he offered no explanation, John Jansen and I both knew where they had been recorded. We confronted him about it, but he specifically said, 'Go ahead and use them, it's okay.'"

Jansen concurs: "Jeffery told us not to worry and that he would take care of it, but when the album came out, the two tracks we'd used were listed as having been from San Diego and not the Royal Albert Hall. Soon after, I went home one day to find a letter naming me, Eddie Kramer and Michael Jeffery in a multimillion-dollar lawsuit filed by Gold and Goldstein. I just laughed and threw it out, thinking, 'You sure took care of it, Michael.'"

As it turned out, *Hendrix: In the West* proved to be a misnomer of sorts, as three of the album's seven tracks (the third, "The Queen [British National Anthem]," was from the August 30, 1970, Isle of Wight festival) had been recorded in Britain. While the title was a holdover from the all-Berkeley concept, Jeffery, much to the contempt and disbelief of his onetime partners Gold and Goldstein, did indeed mislabel the album's credits. Nonetheless, the LP was a strong and steady seller, reaching number 12 on *Billboard*'s chart while attaining RIAA gold album status.

As for the multimillion-dollar lawsuit, Jansen and Kramer were dropped from the action, which was partially resolved in 1979 via a modest out-of-court settlement between Gold and Goldstein and Warner Bros., only to see the inclusion of additional Royal Albert Hall material on the 1982 album *Jimi Hendrix Concerts* resurrect the dispute anew. Gold and Goldstein's footage – and an accompanying soundtrack album featuring such Experience standbys as "Fire" and "Foxey Lady" – remains unreleased at the time of this writing.

Still needing more product to satisfy Hendrix's 1968 agreement with Warner Bros., Jeffery pressed Kramer to produce another release, preferably a live album, this time featuring material selected from the Experience's August 30, 1970, Isle of Wight performance. To this end, Kramer did

indeed review and remix the entire Isle of Wight performance; however, he was adamant that its contents were
decidedly inferior to Hendrix's standard, let alone those the
producers had tried to set via *Hendrix: In the West.* Jeffery
was unimpressed with this opinion, fully aware of the
legendary status – especially in Britain – that the festival
performance had curiously cultivated.

The sales possibilities that could be realized by marketing
"Hendrix's last recorded performance" were considerable,
and Jeffery refused to be dissuaded, deciding instead to
license the Isle of Wight album to Polydor and Barclay –
Hendrix's foreign record companies – and rush-release the
album in time for Christmas 1971. Jeffery took the tapes to
Carlos Ohlms, a British-based engineer for Polydor, who
fashioned the release. In doing so, Jeffery's clumsy, greed-
driven maneuver landed in the marketplace simultaneous
to Warner Bros.' *Rainbow Bridge,* not only competing for
sales but infuriating WB officials, who – having screened
the disastrous finished film – desperately needed a strong
sales performance from the album to recoup the conspicuous debt Jeffery's folly had incurred.

*Isle of Wight* proved to be a miserable failure, dropping
quickly – after brisk initial sales – out of the British album
charts. Ohlms had inexplicably selected – especially for the
album's first side – clearly inferior Hendrix material. The
"Midnight Lightning–Foxey Lady" medley meanders
pathetically out of musical time, tune and direction. Why
anyone would saddle the bleating feedback that hampers
"Foxey Lady" atop the memory of an artist known for his
inventive manipulation of the same is beyond comprehen-
sion. While the album's second side is stronger – specifically
"All Along the Watchtower" and "Freedom" – *Isle of Wight*
remains second-rate Hendrix by any measure. "I thought the
album was awful," recalls Kramer, "and while I couldn't
stop its release, I told Jeffery that under no circumstances
was my name to be credited or associated with it in any
way."

While neither Mitchell, Kramer nor Jansen would deny that the three posthumous albums featured material Hendrix might not have approved for release, the issue of *Isle of Wight* set a dangerous precedent: greed – not artistic quality – was now the standard bearer. Explains Kramer: "Many of those tracks on the posthumous albums were incomplete, even if they don't sound like it. The point is that we never finished working. Hendrix was such a perfectionist that I'm sure he wouldn't have permitted some of that material to be issued. Putting those albums together was so painful because Jimi had only just started to find those new sounds and ideas that had been eluding him. We are talking about the greatest guitarist that ever lived, a man I would have to beg not to erase guitar parts I thought were fantastic but which he considered poor."

The *Isle of Wight* debacle behind them, work on *War Heroes* – described at the time as Hendrix's last posthumous release – began in earnest. At first, there had been a tentative plan to make *War Heroes* a combination of live and studio material, but this idea soon ran out of steam. Having plucked the best of the unissued studio cuts for the first two posthumous LPs, assembling a third studio album was a formidable assignment.

With only two surefire tracks – "Izabella" and "Stepping Stone" – to act as centerpieces, the multitrack tapes acquired from Warner Bros., as well as those still stored at London's Olympic Sound, were meticulously combed to wring out enough hidden gems to fill out the release. Another two "Hendrix-approved" tracks were slated for inclusion, "Highway Chile" and "The Stars That Play With Laughing Sam's Dice," both former UK B sides produced by Chas Chandler. ("The Stars That Play With Laughing Sam's Dice" was dropped at the last moment, later resurfacing as part of Polydor's 1973 *Loose Ends.*) After that, there was little in the form of finished masters acceptable for release. "Midnight," arguably *War Heroes'* most pleasant surprise, had been recorded at TTG Studios during October 1968. "Bleeding

Heart" and Mitch Mitchell's "Beginnings" were holdovers from *Rainbow Bridge* mixing sessions, and both "Tax Free" and "Three Little Bears" were outtakes from the 1968 *Electric Ladyland* sessions.

"Catastrophe–Peter Gunn Theme" was a snippet from summer 1970 sessions at Electric Lady, included by Eddie Kramer to provide a glimpse of Hendrix's spontaneity and playful sense of humor. While Kramer's intentions may have been good, however, this fourth posthumous release arrived without liner notes (which perhaps, among other things, could have explained why "Catastrophe–Peter Gunn Theme" or "Three Little Bears" had been included) or even the slightest detail as to when or where any of the material had been recorded. Interest in this release was limited compared to the first three posthumous albums and it enjoyed only modest sales, some 180,000 units – less than half of the figure for *Hendrix: In the West* – and peaking at just number 48 on the *Billboard* chart.

Given the lukewarm critical and financial reception afforded *War Heroes,* it finally did seem as if the "bottom of the barrel," as Eddie Kramer described it, "had been scraped clean." With Mitch Mitchell already out of the picture, having left the studio to renew his career, Kramer put away the Hendrix tapes for good. A meeting to determine the future course of Hendrix's posthumous career was called by attorneys for Jimi's estate. There, Kramer was asked if more albums could be issued from the hundreds of tapes remaining in the vault. "I told them how difficult it had been to complete *War Heroes* and that Jimi wouldn't have approved any of it because it simply was not up to his standards. Nonetheless, they were persistent, so I had to say that unless better-quality material could be found, I was no longer interested in issuing new albums. I tried to stress the quality issue very clearly – and while they politely thanked me for my opinion, the meeting ended without a clear resolution."

Unbeknownst to Kramer, who now quietly excused himself from Jimi's last affairs, there were two more very different Hendrix projects already under way. One had been originated by Leo Branton, who, besieged by calls from frustrated parties holding film footage and multitrack tapes, took his case to Warner Bros. Meeting with Warner Bros.' executive. Ted Ashley, Branton described what had become a ritual since his appointment as executor of the Hendrix estate: regularly fielding calls from persons in possession of Hendrix materials but estranged from Michael Jeffery. What Branton described to Ashley rang a bell, for Joe Boyd, in charge of film scores for Warner Films, was himself in just such a position. Explains Boyd: "Leo Branton was referred to me, and over lunch in the Warner commissary, I informed him that I owned one-third of John Marshall's *Experience* film. What he revealed to me – and what I knew vaguely – was that John Marshall's situation was similar to many others who had filmed Hendrix. Jeffery would allow *anybody* to film Jimi, but when producers would ask for a [talent] release, he would demur. When the production was complete, he wouldn't grant them a release unless control *and* ownership was handed over to him. For this, he would offer producers royalties off the back end – a deal no one would ever accept. As a result, a number of people owned film negatives and had no contract."

Branton's meeting resulted in Warner Films granting Boyd some $20,000 in development funds to study the possibility of producing a feature film. Fearful of the many Hendrix factions having an axe to grind, Branton asked Boyd to produce the project as an independent. The next step for Branton and Boyd was to procure a full budget to begin production. Though Warner Films had fostered the idea, their enthusiasm was decidedly lukewarm, principally because, while *Woodstock* had made a fortune, subsequent similar attempts had failed to generate similar dollars. Warner Films, Boyd was instructed, made a practice of risking $3 million to make $13 million, not $500,000 to help sell Jimi Hendrix albums. To combat this mindset, Boyd approached Mo Ostin, hoping that his considerable influence within the company would sway the project's many doubters. Indeed he did, and with the promise of an accompanying soundtrack album to be issued by Reprise, Boyd was given $575,000 to make his *Film About Jimi Hendrix*.

Incensed that he be left out of such an important project, Jeffery had little recourse. By now, his contract with Warner had expired, Polydor remaining his only outlet for the release of Hendrix product. "Eddie Kramer had lost interest," remembers John Jansen, "but Jeffery kept pressing for 'just one more.' Previously, I had been giving Kramer and Jeffery tapes simultaneously whenever I came across something that seemed promising. At that time, I had listened to every tape Jimi had played and each one was filed and renumbered. Now, with just Jeffery to answer to, anything that remotely sounded like music was worth going to Polydor and getting money for an album."

That album – Polydor's aptly titled *Loose Ends* – was a callous and shameful exercise. So embarrassed was he that Jeffery would actually issue this mediocre collection of jams and demos, Jansen refused to allow his name to appear as part of the album's credits, adopting instead the pseudonym "Alex Trevor." Apart from "The Stars That Play With Laughing Sam's Dice," the sole authorized track, the remainder offered nothing to enhance or define Hendrix's unparalleled artistic genius. Even the cover, a shoddy, stop-frame depiction of Hendrix seemingly nodding off to sleep, or worse, vandalized his memory. Warner Bros. refused to issue this release in the U.S. and Canada. On the heels of the admittedly uneven *War Heroes* (which, because of "Stepping Stone," "Izabella," "Highway Chile" and "Tax Free," was worthy of release in some form), *Loose Ends*, coupled with Michael Jeffery's sudden death on March 5, 1973, signaled the need for someone else to step forward and assume control of the Hendrix tape vaults.

Jeffery's death came as a tremendous shock, one of forty-seven victims of a violent midair collision between an

Iberian Airways DC-9 bound for Majorca and a smaller aircraft, a Spandex Coronado. The crash was partly attributed to pilot error and poor coordination by military air traffic controllers substituting for their striking French civilian counterparts. Jeffery's death fulfilled his private phobia that he would perish in an aircrash. Jeffery was notorious for making as many as seven different flight reservations – on as many airlines as possible – all in an effort to deceive fate. "Flying was Michael Jeffery's greatest fear," remembers Bob Levine. "On the plane, he'd grip the arm rests so tightly his knuckles would turn white. During take-off, he'd grab your hand so hard you'd think it was broken. Eric Burdon used to hum Glenn Miller's 'In the Mood' just to wind him up even more."

Having requested a brief recess during the final stages of the British PPX-Yameta legal action, Jeffery was in the process of purchasing a castle in Spain, and needed a few days to secure the property. Before he left, he stopped in to see his attorney John Hillman. Explains Hillman: "He came into my office and told me that he was packing it all in. He wanted to buy this castle he'd been considering, retire and try to have a baby with his girlfriend Melissa. He wanted to route whatever business that remained through my office, but I told him I couldn't possibly handle all of his affairs. He tried to reassure me, saying, 'Don't worry, I'll deal with the artists, but I want to do it from a distance. I'm moving to the castle. When I'm there, I'll call you and we'll work things out.'"

Jeffery's proposed retirement, says Jim Marron, was actually a ruse to give him time to develop a film script he had recently acquired. "Jeffery wanted to make an espionage film based on Michael Collins, the IRA agent British Intelligence had unsuccessfully tracked for nearly two decades. He loved the script, and the plot line was right up his alley. The plan was for the four of us [Marron, his wife Paulette, Melissa and Jeffery] to live in Spain and film the movie on location in Ireland. In London for the PPX-Yameta trial,

Jeffery was told that there had been some lighting problems at his club in Majorca. A friend of Melissa's volunteered to fly back with him and handle the repairs if Jeffery would cover his rent and expenses. They never made it. Paulette and I came back to New York, but Melissa was so devastated that she went to live in an ashram somewhere in India and was never heard from again."

# 17 RE-ENTER ALAN DOUGLAS

> *"The whole point was to restore the Hendrix legend, put the whole thing back into perspective and restore the financial condition of the estate. The public has accepted and purchased the records. That's the only gauge we have to go on. There has been a lot of criticism by many of the major critics about the way we did it, by overdubbing new people and so on, but that is what the record business is all about."*
>
> —Alan Douglas

Alan Douglas first approached Michael Jeffery almost immediately after Hendrix's death, but was rebuffed. He was not the only outsider who broached Jeffery at this time, expressing interest in overseeing the release of posthumous albums. The actual number, Mitch Mitchell quipped only half jokingly, was somewhere in the teens. Now, partly out of guilt for including Douglas's brief and unflattering interview in the finished cut of *Film About Jimi Hendrix* (reduced to a quick sound bite, Douglas's sole comment regards Hendrix's drug use), Joe Boyd sought to make amends by bringing Douglas before Mo Ostin and Leo Branton. Douglas had a small number of Hendrix tapes in his possession, mainly Record Plant sessions billed and

393

shipped to his company, Douglas Communications. Explains Boyd: "When we interviewed him for the movie, Douglas had taken us to Media Sound and played those tapes of Jimi jamming with people like Buzzy Feiten. I kept that in mind and later set up a meeting with Branton and Ostin."

This second Douglas foray was also fruitless, however, as Jeffery remained steadfast against him having any involvement. But though he had failed again, Douglas had at least established his name as a front runner among those disgruntled with Jeffery's totalitarian control of Hendrix's musical affairs. After Jeffery's death in March 1973, full control of Hendrix's creative affairs was thrust solely into the hands of Leo Branton. Of all those displeased with Jeffery's decisions, Warner Bros. stood at the head of the list. Already dismayed by *War Heroes'* lackluster chart performance, the label rejected *Loose Ends* out of hand. There were clear indications that public interest in Hendrix music was on the wane, his record sales slowing at an alarming rate. Even *Film About Jimi Hendrix*, trumpeted by Boyd to hesitant Warner Film executives as both a sales incentive for the Hendrix record catalogue and a surefire box office winner, failed on both counts and was greeted largely with disinterest.

Reluctant to cut the company's losses and place the Hendrix legacy quietly to rest, Warner Bros. executive Don Schmitzerle actively began to seek out those parties that might still be harboring quality Hendrix music. One such person, he remembered, was Alan Douglas. By early 1974, Douglas's career had been placed in a self-imposed limbo, with Douglas Communications, the umbrella corporation under which he had operated since breaking from United Artists, dissolved. Recalls Douglas: "At the end of 1972, my audience seemed to have disappeared. Douglas Records had the counterculture audience and the support of underground newspapers – that was our medium. We had been selling underground product as if it had been pop product.

When the counterculture got absorbed and no longer existed, I closed up the company and let everybody go. In early 1974, Don Schmitzerle called to ask if I knew of any more Hendrix material. I didn't, but I did remember that Jimi had recorded a lot of tracks at the Record Plant."

Those Record Plant tapes – the very same cache Warner had shipped to Electric Lady in February 1971 – had since been placed in a New Jersey storage warehouse. On February 8, 1974, production rights to these tapes were sold by the Hendrix estate to Presentacione Musicales, S.A. (PMSA), a Panamanian corporation, guaranteeing them all revenues in any future use. Jimi's estate, then strapped for cash, thought them useless, proven by the mediocre quality and poor sales of *Loose Ends*. Privately, Douglas had another idea, and with Warner's blessing, formed Depaja Productions with the estate and the Panamanian corporation.

Having now finally ascended to the position he had longed to occupy, Douglas had all of the tapes forwarded to Shaggy Dog Studios in Stockbridge, Massachusetts, to evaluate exactly what he had to work with. There, with the assistance of staff engineer Les Kahn, Douglas duplicated the efforts that Eddie Kramer and John Jansen had completed just three years prior, combing the tapes for scraps suitable for release. While Douglas had supervised, or at least attended, a handful of Record Plant sessions where versions of such songs as "Room Full of Mirrors," "Dolly Dagger" and "Izabella" had been cut, Hendrix had scrapped each during his lifetime, choosing instead to add further overdubs or rerecord a new master take. Those new versions had since been issued as part of the Jeffery-supervised posthumous releases. All that remained in the library now were stark demos and sketches of various songs. An album might possibly be fashioned from these fragments, but it would require all new instrumentation.* Douglas felt the task of recording the new instrumentation he thought was necessary could be accomplished by only one person, engineer Tony Bongiovi.

"Alan Douglas approached me because I had done a repair job on *Devotions*, an album he had produced for John McLaughlin in 1969," explains Bongiovi. "There, the session tapes had actually been destroyed, so I had to manufacture pieces to create the final master. Having successfully completed that process, Douglas had been somewhat impressed. He called me again in 1974 and told me about this Jimi Hendrix project."

To prepare for his meeting, Douglas and Les Kahn selected the best material remaining in the tape library, and came armed with a stack of recordings for Bongiovi to audition. What Douglas carried to Media Sound in New York was a series of two-track tapes that contained Hendrix's guitar and lead vocal, and whatever accompaniment by Mitch Mitchell, Noel Redding, Buddy Miles or Billy Cox existed. Under no circumstances were these unfinished tapes suitable for release in their present form. "Douglas asked if there was anything I could do with them," recalls Bongiovi. "I thought there were some great songs there and told him that I could come up with something similar to what we had done with the John McLaughlin project." What Bongiovi was prescribing seemed unthinkable: in order to salvage these song fragments, he would have to erase all of the original

*CRASH LANDING: *Unreleased Version*
According to longtime Douglas associate and Track Records executive Daniel Secunda, there *was* an album – complete with Hendrix's original accompaniment – of unreleased material prepared before Douglas opted to add new instrumentation. Their original *Crash Landing* was as follows:
*Side One:*
Crash Landing [H-256 Record Plant 4-24-69]/Somewhere [H-124 3-68]/Anything Is Possible (With the Power) [H-36 Record Plant 1-21-70] New Rising Sun [H-264 TTG 10-22-68]
*Side Two:*
Message to Love [H-34 Record Plant 1-20-70]/Scat Vocal-Lead 1-Scat Vocal 2 Lead Vocal 2 [H-273 Hit Factory 8-28-69]/Stone Free [H-255 Record Plant 4-7-69]/Peace in Mississippi [H-282 TTG 10-24-68]/Here Comes Your Lover Man [H-248 TTG 10-29-68]

backing tracks – save for Hendrix's guitar and voice – to make way for new instrumentation.

Before such a process could even be attempted, Bongiovi needed every note of music committed to paper so that session musicians would be able to follow each song. "I hired Brad Baker, an arranger, to transcribe everything on Douglas's tapes – note for note. I didn't want the [session] musicians to be creative, I just wanted them to take what was on the tape and finish it. When you have 75 percent of a bass track, you pretty much know how it was going to go from there. In order to assimilate that, you have to write each individual part out very carefully so that the musicians can follow."

Further hindering Bongiovi and Douglas's efforts was the fact that nearly every Hendrix master required a great deal of work just to carry it to the point where new overdubs could be effected. Explains Bongiovi: "In some instances, there would be eight or nine versions of one song spread over five reels of tape. Each one might have a guitar solo, but the band might not be playing all the way through every take. What I had to do was find and piece together the best semblance of a rhythm track. When I got that done, I went back to the other versions and lifted Jimi's guitar solo and mechanically put it in place."

Clearly, Douglas's discovery had not been tracks from a lost Hendrix album left unfinished and hidden in some secret vault. He and Bongiovi were forced to create composite masters from song fragments and demos rejected by Kramer, Mitchell and Jansen as unfinished.

"It was taking us an average of sixty hours to pull each original track together," recalls Bongiovi. "Recording new bass guitar overdubs normally took three to four hours, recutting drum sections usually averaged seven. For songs where we didn't have a complete drum track, what we did was have [session musician] Alan Schwartzberg play along with Mitch Mitchell. In a lot of instances, the *Crash Landing* album features Mitchell with a lot of Schwartzberg punched in. I was able to match the new recording with the sound of the original take, so whenever Mitchell's [musical] time wavered, I could just punch in Schwartzberg and let him take it to the end. Since we had everything written out for him, all he had to do was listen to the playback and count the bars to know where he was anywhere in the song."

But the most dangerous part of the entire production centered not on the producers' handling of Jimi's sidemen, but Hendrix's original contribution. "For guitar," continues Bongiovi, "we often had to finish up some of the rhythm track because Jimi hadn't recorded it all the way through. What we did was write out everything Hendrix had done and have [session musician] Jeff Mironov practice it over and over. Not only did I have to match the original Hendrix guitar sound, but I had to join the rhythm sections while preserving Jimi's sound and style." If asked if he felt that such overdubs defiled Hendrix's original musical intentions, Bongiovi defends his actions. "We were not trying to infringe upon Jimi's creativity, just extend it. All of the important Hendrix solos and personality remained intact. Remember, the style was already there, we weren't being creative, saying, 'Well, this is how Jimi would have played it.'"

Douglas described his criteria for these new Hendrix songs as such: 'What we were basically interested in was a good vocal track and a good guitar track from Jimi. When Hendrix recorded his first rhythm guitar track, that pretty much indicated the arrangement of the tune. On occasion, we found double or single lead guitar lines, and if those worked we used them and went from there. If we found tracks that featured other musicians [e.g., the Experience or Band of Gypsys] but didn't work, we overdubbed new musicians in their place."

If new instrumentation was to be added posthumously – an extremely delicate issue under any circumstances – why then weren't Hendrix's original sidemen, especially Mitch Mitchell, who had performed admirably under difficult yet similar circumstances, given first crack at the job? Co-producer Bongiovi explains his motive: "Douglas had the idea to do these records and the foresight [to overdub the tracks], but once the project was turned over to me, I had to behave and call the shots like the director on a film. To be perfectly honest, that scenario was considered. Whether Douglas could have worked out all the business aspects in time, I'm not sure. My criterion was that the musicians had to read music and be trained in the art of precise overdubbing. Certainly Jimi's old sidemen could have *tried* it, but I don't think they would have had the time, patience or endurance to punch in a single note at measure 15 and letter 2."

As if his decision to bypass Jimi's former sidemen wasn't insensitive enough, as part of the tidal wave of publicity for *Crash Landing*, Douglas often cited the failures of Hendrix's past bandmates as one of the primary factors in his decision to replace their original parts. "In the first place, Jimi was having problems with his rhythm section constantly. It was obvious at the time," Douglas told Michael Cuscuna in 1975. Further: "Hendrix's basic problem was that he used to pull the rhythm section all the time," he explained on the BBC *Profile* radio program. "Of course, in the studio you can't tell because of cutting and editing, but if you watched him live, he constantly had to go back into the rhythm patterns himself to keep it moving at the intensity he wanted."

Regardless of whether Douglas's explanations carried any merit, his sharp words rankled and humiliated those, like Redding and Mitchell, inspired by Hendrix's great talent to contribute to his music, while exacerbating the growing rift between Douglas's camp and those who had once been Hendrix's associates. "I had no idea I was stepping on someone's pride," confesses Douglas today. "I was just trying to make a record. I had a problem and I went and fixed that problem. That was my motivation, to get tracks of Jimi's vocal and his lead and rhythm guitar that worked."

Months of difficult production work had reduced Douglas's twenty-odd original candidates down to a mere

eight. "Some of those new master tapes had so many edits –
as many as fifteen to twenty on a single two-inch tape – that
it made overdubbing new material very tricky," recalls Ron
Saint Germain, assistant engineer on the *Crash Landing*
project. One example was the album's title track. While the
best overall take had been cut on April 29, 1969, it remained
uncompleted. To salvage the track, Bongiovi deftly
incorporated portions of a previous version, recorded on
April 24, to create a final take onto which the overdubbing
of new instrumentation could be effected. "I couldn't get the
rhythm track to fit the solo quite right," explains Bongiovi.
"Therefore I had to keep editing both sections so that they
would end and start at the same time. I ended up with a solo
that had a 9/8 bar and a 5/7 bar and, since I wasn't a
guitarist, I just cut the tape where I felt it would work. The
kind of editing I did inside the solo did not destroy its
artistic integrity; in fact, the song was later written up in a
music magazine touting the genius of Jimi Hendrix. Make
no mistake, Jimi was truly a master, and this solo had been
purely the result of an accident, yet the magazine raved
about its transcription!"

The overdubbing of new instrumentation was an
extremely arduous task that took months to complete and
frayed the nerves of all parties involved. "Those sessions
were sheer torture," remembers Douglas. The album's
budget ultimately topped $100,000 and costs for the new
overdubs alone ran between $60,000 and $70,000 – the same
amount spent to create *Electric Ladyland.*

"*Crash Landing* was probably the most difficult project of
my career," recalls Bongiovi. "There was so much cutting
and pasting because we didn't have the tools we have today.
We couldn't change pitch, but I still had to bring sections in
tune. I had to vari-speed tape machines and then create little
pieces to extend Jimi's notes and make them fit. I would
have to copy parts, one at a time, in increments of a quarter
inch, to extend a note. This mechanical altering took forever."

The eight tracks on *Crash Landing* comprised material originally recorded over a two-year span (October 1968–July 1970), with a variety of sidemen and at a host of different studios. "Message to Love" (which, save for Jimmy Maeulen's incidental percussion, is the album's sole unadulterated track) and "With the Power" are obvious Band of Gypsys era tryouts; "Somewhere Over the Rainbow" and "Peace in Mississippi," the latter an offshoot of *War Heroes'* "Midnight," were Experience era rejects, as was the insipid "Stone Free Again." The inclusion of a refitted "Come Down Hard on Me" was particularly curious, considering Douglas's stated disgust with Hendrix's previous posthumous issues – especially *Loose Ends*, where this song had first debuted. However technically competent *Crash Landing*'s new overdubs might have been, though, they could do little for a group of second-rate Hendrix material never intended for public consumption.

Aided immensely by an aggressive PR campaign spearheaded by Ken Schaffer, the voracity of which rivaled past efforts by Jeffery and Chandler, the so-called lost tapes that created *Crash Landing* became the project's central premise. (Oddly enough, though, the Hendrix jam with jazz guitarist John McLaughlin, the discovery of which Douglas most often boasted, was never released, though nearly every writer willing to interview Douglas or Schaffer was afforded a listen.) The spokesman for this new music became Alan Douglas, self-described as Hendrix's producer. His own self-promotional zeal aside, Douglas exaggerated his original role when forced to justify his new position as creative director of the Hendrix archives. While he had certainly enjoyed a friendship with Hendrix, their professional relationship had been largely undefined, a fact few would surmise from his public posturing. "Of course, I was there with most of these [*Crash Landing*] things," Douglas informed syndicated radio host Michael Cuscuna in 1975. Worse still was Douglas's insistence that *Crash Landing* as well as other forthcoming Hendrix recordings, was actually linked to a new, all-revealing musical progression. It was no such thing, a fallacy perhaps best exemplified by the album's strongest track, "Captain Coconut."

Where tracks like "Crash Landing" and "Somewhere Over the Rainbow" had required Douglas and Bongiovi to fuse various components together in order to create a master take, "Captain Coconut" had needed no such attention. During their exhaustive review of the Hendrix tape library, Douglas and engineer Les Kahn came across a two-track mixdown of an instrumental cryptically titled "MLK." A composite track combining pieces from three different sessions, Kahn was unable to locate, save for the middle section, the song's original master. But not wanting to exclude it from *Crash Landing,* Tony Bongiovi simply transferred the original two-track to a new sixteen-track master, where Alan Schwartzberg overdubbed percussion.

The reason neither Kahn nor Douglas could locate the multitrack masters to "Captain Coconut" was because they didn't exist. "Captain Coconut" had actually been the creation of John Jansen, acting under the pseudonym "Alex Korda." When the task of screening each tape in the Hendrix library had been his, Jansen had dual motives: one was to locate finished tracks, the second was to find instrumental passages that could possibly be linked together to score various scenes for *Rainbow Bridge.* Explains Jansen: "By that point, I had begun to feel like a vampire. I would go into the library and pull out bits that were good, including this great passage titled 'MLK' [contrary to recent reports, this jam was neither a paean to slain civil rights leader Martin Luther King nor even the writing of Hendrix himself, as the three letters were just the stray, unexplained markings of the tape operator] that had been recorded on really thin tape from a 1969 Hit Factory session."

This Jansen find did indeed appear in the *Rainbow Bridge* film (it can be heard as Chuck Wein makes his invocation speech), albeit longer and in its original key. "Then I came across this great jam piece with Buddy Miles from the

Record Plant," continues Jansen, "as well as another separate passage from Electric Lady that could serve as a beginning. I fused the three sections together and had to vari-speed each until the tempo and key were perfect."

Before Jansen could proceed to the final mixing process, Kramer took notice of his handiwork and confronted him. Recalls Jansen: "Eddie came into the control room and said, 'John, what the fuck are you doing? This is not right.' I agreed, and thought I must have lost my mind. I had actually put three pieces of music together that had nothing to do with each other. That was the end of all that."

So Jansen thought, but when *Crash Landing* reached record shops in March 1975, it arrived with a surprise in store. Jansen's "MLK" had now transformed into "Captain Coconut," reputedly one of the album's more salient examples of Hendrix's now clarified musical direction. By either moniker, "Captain Coconut" wasn't even a true Hendrix composition, rather a composite master initially created by Jansen and then *enhanced* by Douglas and Bongiovi's tinkering. "I was pissed off because I knew those tracks cold," says Jansen. "They had found the two-track I had mixed down and then overdubbed on top of that."

Jansen's objections aside, *Crash Landing* – the total running time of which was a paltry 29:46 – proved to be a phenomenal sales success, ultimately reaching the number 5 spot on the *Billboard* album chart. While most critics were hostile and highly aggrieved by the album's controversial production techniques (which, incredibly, were neither explained nor mentioned on either the album's sleeve or jacket), Hendrix fans initially snapped up more than 450,000 copies, which, while well short of *The Cry of Love*'s early tally of some 700,000 units, more than doubled the sales of *War Heroes* and surpassed *Rainbow Bridge* by some 10,000.

Central to the amazing success of *Crash Landing* was Ken Schaffer's all-out publicity onslaught, which, quite cleverly, began *before* the album was released. Hendrix fans, via *Time, Rolling Stone* and even WABC-TV's Geraldo Rivera, were inundated with reports of Douglas's "discovery." So impressed with the quality of these "warehouse tapes" (which was strange because the great majority had actually been those transferred by Warner Bros. to Michael Jeffery in February 1971), Mo Ostin, now president of Warner Bros. Records, issued the following statement: "In recognition of our excitement over *Crash Landing* and the other albums coming from the newly found tapes, and out of deference to the quality of the new records we'll be issuing, Warner Bros. Records is recalling all previously issued posthumous Hendrix albums from distributors and retail stores. The best cuts from these albums will be reconsolidated and released in the future. This way, we believe all available Hendrix, both the original and the ones from this new series, will be of consistent quality, and that the Hendrix legacy will, at last, be intact."

In one swift stroke, and to the delight of the Hendrix estate, Ostin deleted *Rainbow Bridge, Hendrix: In the West* and *War Heroes* from the catalogue, purging – save for *The Cry of Love* – Michael Jeffery's postmortem efforts (as well as reducing the number of albums paying him his hefty royalty cut) to make way for *Crash Landing* and its follow-up, *Midnight Lightning,* already in production.

Originally to have been titled *Multicolored Blues, Midnight Lightning* was to provide Hendrix fans with a showcase for Jimi's blues playing as *Crash Landing* had attempted with pop-styled compositions. In theory, the album's premise was cause for optimism, but in actuality most studio recordings of Hendrix playing blues consisted of jams, not structured songs. For example, his jam with Johnny Winter, another celebrated warehouse find, produced only an ineffectual remake of Guitar Slim's "Things I Used to Do," which was eventually left off the album.

Not only were the producers short on blues material, there was a paucity of quality tracks capable of sustaining new overdubs. Explains Tony Bongiovi, "*Crash Landing* had been made up of the best material Douglas had found at

Shaggy Dog Studios, but that album was so successful that Warner Bros. called for a second release. I wasn't as enthused, because *Midnight Lightning* was going to be made from the stuff rejected for *Crash Landing*, but commercially speaking, and the way record companies go, I had no choice but to do it."

Even Douglas, aided by hindsight, acknowledged the shortcomings of *Midnight Lightning*. "I was forced to make more records — from a business perspective — than I wanted to make," he says. "The material itself was a little bit light, and I think I forced the issue in a couple of instances. It's just not thoroughly enjoyable, and it's not the best of Hendrix," he later admitted to *Guitar Player* magazine.

With so little to work with in terms of Hendrix material, overdubbing sessions for this second release were much more difficult, and fraught with tension. Recalls drummer Alan Schwartzberg: "I got so frustrated trying to stay with all of the [musical] time and tempo problems that I just threw my drumsticks across the studio."

Schwartzberg endured, but guitarist Jeff Mironov, whose task of matching and bolstering Hendrix's rhythm guitar lines was arguably the most difficult of all, left before the project was completed and was replaced by Lance Quinn. "Working on those records was hard, exacting work," recalls Mironov. "As time went on, that second album was the dregs, and the material was just not that strong. We were working on music that was, by and large, spontaneous jams. The original tracks were raw and the playing had a lot of freedom. Jimi, without any restrictions, was obviously stretching for something. Our roles were totally opposite, we had to come in and methodically take the original idea and do it better, especially the bass and drums. That was very difficult to do."

The shortcomings of the eight *Midnight Lightning* tracks were painfully obvious. "Blue Suede Shoes" had been one of *Loose Ends'* more prominent embarrassments, and no amount of studio redressing could possibly have justified its inclusion. The album's title track was just as shameless, which, with its risque nursery rhyme lyric, was obviously a tongue-in-cheek jam never intended for release. Maeretha Stewart, Hilda Harris and Vivian Cherry's vocal overdubs, specifically their doubling of Jimi's "stoop down ..." were particularly gratuitous.

The inclusion of a refitted "Beginnings" seemed curiously insensitive, as Mitch Mitchell, the song's composer (Mitchell had sold his copyright, along with all of his claims to the Hendrix fortune, for some $300,000), was still alive. Certainly, this track, not discounting the entire content of *Midnight Lightning,* was ample proof that the material necessary to neatly clarify the blues aspects of Hendrix's genius simply did not exist.

This second Douglas-sponsored LP was, again, critically lambasted following its release in November 1975. Without the benefit of the *Crash Landing* "lost tapes" marketing strategy, *Midnight Lightning* had only its contents by which to sell itself and, by that yardstick, fared poorly. Despite the success of its predecessor, *Midnight Lightning* limped only to number 48 on the *Billboard* album chart and proved a poor replacement for the three Jeffery-authorized albums then deleted; *Hendrix: In the West* sold more units in its two-year shelf life than *Midnight Lightning* has been able to muster in more than fifteen.

Stung by the repeated critical jabs, Douglas shifted gears, reaching back to a more proven tactic, and one that had helped launch his own company. Echoing *The Essential Lenny Bruce,* Warner Bros. issued two greatest hits compilations, *The Essential Jimi Hendrix Volume One* in July 1978 (followed the next year by *The Essential Jimi Hendrix Volume Two*), though, surprisingly, both generated only modest sales.

Needing one final album to fulfil the deal for three new albums the estate had struck with Warner Bros. in 1974, Douglas next initiated  work on *Nine to the Universe,* his long-promised compilation of Hendrix's various explorations with such jazz stalwarts as John McLaughlin and Larry Young. Once more, despite the 1975 promise of enlightenment and ultimate deliverance from Hendrix's psychedelic trappings, Douglas's latest effort to recast Hendrix, this time as a frustrated jazz man, sputtered when he failed to deliver his much touted goods. While there were literally hours of Hendrix jamming with his *Band of Gypsys*, no such recordings with the likes of either Miles Davis or Roland Kirk – both acknowledged Hendrix influences – were forthcoming.

Hindering Douglas's claims still further was that, of the select few tapes that *did* exist, each found Hendrix simply shredding the efforts and good intentions of his fellow musicians, such as McLaughlin, who did their utmost just trying to keep pace. The mere thought of Hendrix collaborating with Miles Davis, Gil Evans or Quincy Jones was tantalizing, but the release of *Nine to the Universe* offered preciously little, in terms of hard evidence, of any such "embryonic fusion of jazz and rock."

Lacking enough tracks needed to continue issuing records even in the tradition of *Crash Landing* and *Midnight Lightning*, Douglas now shifted gears for *Nine to the Universe*, featuring unfinished, instrumental Hendrix recordings designed to intimate music that he may have had on his mind, the scope of which lay beyond the pop song format. Under this criterion, buttressed by a liner note that specified that, indeed, the album's contents were never meant to be issued, this third Douglas-sponsored LP was, by far, the least tampered with Hendrix compilation of his tenure to date. Where *Crash Landing* and *Midnight Lightning* had both been cloaked within the premise of supposedly clarifying Jimi's heretofore undefined musical legacy, *Nine to the Universe* made no effort to interpret its five jam sessions as anything more than what they were: uncharted Hendrix forays fusing blues, jazz and rock in his own inimitable style.

Though *Nine to the Universe* may indeed have been

intended to show "Hendrix having fun, the master at play," the producers betrayed their concept by editing all five jams, thus creating composite song structures rather than exposing Hendrix at his "free-est, freshest." "We did tons of test edits," explains Ron Saint Germain. "It ended up being a judgment call by Douglas, because that stuff jumped around so much there was no way to make it work. The material just didn't lend itself to being cut as well as the stuff on *Crash Landing*." The difficulty in editing spontaneous recordings so that they do not lose this very spontaneity was best exemplified by Buddy Miles's drum solo in the "Earth Blues – Message to Love" hybrid title track. Explains Saint Germain: "I had been working for a solid week on that track, trimming, pasting and retrimming Miles's drums and Jimi's guitar, trying to find a way to make it work. Buddy Miles happened by Media Sound one day while we were working on it and upon hearing his drum 'solo' smiled broadly and said, 'Ain't I a motherfucker!' I didn't have the heart to tell him how long it had taken me to tidy up and cut the original down to that."

Despite the inherent concept problems, each track, for better or worse, did illustrate particular Hendrix methods in composition and recording, "Nine to the Universe" itself being indicative of Jimi's circa 1969, Band of Gypsys songwriting approach. Oddly, though, despite that band's notorious appetite for jamming, this title track marks Buddy Miles's sole contribution to the LP (though it certainly sounds like him, and not the credited Mitch Mitchell, supporting Hendrix and organist Larry Young on "Young–Hendrix"). "Easy Blues" was a pleasant surprise, a glimmer at the potential Hendrix's big band, Gypsys Suns & Rainbows, held in store. But while "Drone Blues" was yet another tribute to Hendrix's virtuosity, this was only mildly revealing. "Jimi/ Jimmy Jam" was simply unnecessary.

"Young/Hendrix," another much ballyhooed warehouse "discovery," stands as the strongest track on *Nine to the Universe*, remaining, to date, the most concise example of

Hendrix's grasp of fusion and the wedding of his unique talents to jazz.

Absent, amazingly, from the album, yet again, was its most eagerly awaited cut, the fabled Hendrix–McLaughlin jam! Explains Saint Germain: "There was so much talk about that, but there just wasn't that much material there, just the one jam." Irrespective of McLaughlin's concerns (during the jam he had struggled with a seemingly intermittent pickup manually attached to his acoustic guitar), even a condensed portion of the recording would have strengthened *Nine to the Universe* immeasurably, as the raucous enthusiasm of the jamming was clearly evident and Jimi's performance superb. For his part, McLaughlin – as is his prerogative – dismisses the jam out of hand, content merely with his memory. He has not, and likely will never, sanction its release.

With most critics still suspicious of Alan Douglas's motives, and the album's extended selections being unsuitable for FM radio airplay, *Nine to the Universe* failed to crack the *Billboard* top 100, peaking at number 127 before quickly exiting the 200. While an album of fusion-styled jam sessions was hardly expected to be a winner, initial sales were soft and they never rallied. *Nine to the Universe* struggled to pass the 100,000 unit mark, ultimately selling fewer copies in its first five years than *War Heroes* did in two. At this point, fully ten years after Hendrix's death, the well, by all measures, had finally run dry.

During the next decade, Douglas assumed the role of estate caretaker, opting to stick, with varying degrees of success, to the issue of compilations of studio material or live Experience performances. His efforts to finally collate Hendrix's magnificent Monterey performance into both disc and videotape was commendable, as was the careful transfer of the Experience's great works to compact disc during the latter stages of the 1980s. (Ironically neither Douglas nor Warner Bros. possess the original multitrack tapes to *Are You Experienced?*, *Axis: Bold as Love* and portions of *Electric Ladyland.* These tapes, as well as master tapes from nearly all of Hendrix's early recording sessions in London, are still controlled by Yameta and Chas Chandler. To facilitate the CD release of these Hendrix hallmarks, two-track protection masters were utilized.)

Following *Kiss the Sky,* a fine 1984 compilation counterpart to *Smash Hits,* Douglas switched labels, leaving Reprise, Hendrix's U.S. label of eighteen years, for Capitol. His two subsequent Capitol releases, *Johnny B. Goode* and *Band of Gypsys 2,* represented the absolute nadir of Hendrix's posthumous career. Both of these live compilations were drawn from poor Hendrix performances, the only criterion for their release being that they represented some of the last professionally recorded concerts remaining in the tape vaults. But even those guidelines were stretched, "Foxey Lady" and "Stop" from *Band of Gypsys 2* being lifted from the mono soundtrack of an amateur videographer there to document a Fillmore East concert. (All the multitrack tapes from the four Band of Gypsys shows at the Fillmore are missing, last seen when Hendrix and Eddie Kramer mixed the album in February 1970.) Worse still was the concept betrayal rampant in *Band of Gypsys 2.* Side two *does not feature* the original Hendrix–Cox–Miles Band of Gypsys lineup at all! The substitution of Buddy Miles for Mitch Mitchell was something that *did* matter, not a trifling factor meriting simple dismissal in the album's one-paragraph liner note. It was this very personnel change that had paved the way for the group's formation in 1969.

In the aftermath of these two appallingly shoddy issues, Douglas switched labels once more, landing with Rykodisc, a small Massachusetts-based independent, and scoring with two consecutive releases, *Live at Winterland* and *Radio One,* a collection of the Experience's spirited 1967 BBC radio performances. Though musically suspect (*Live at Winterland,* for example, would have been better served as a single album compilation), both were sales winners that reawakened critics and reactivated interest in Hendrix music.

*

This very interest in Hendrix music continues unabated to this day, with new generations keen to discover Jimi's amazing talents. Unlike his late 1960s dead contemporaries – Jim Morrison, Brian Jones, Janis Joplin *et al.* – Hendrix's achievements and, perhaps most importantly, his influence, has neither diminished nor grown outdated. So who are the present-day practitioners of Jimi Hendrix's pioneering innovations? The list may surprise you. As a guitarist, Jimi provided the showman persona that Prince has so successfully extended. He has repeatedly acknowledged Hendrix's considerable influence on his music. (While *Graffiti Bridge*'s "Tick Tick Bang" is perhaps the most obvious nod of all – with its inventive sampling of Jimi's own "Little Miss Lover" – somewhere, reportedly, within Warner Bros. tape vaults lies Prince's own rendition of "Purple Haze," cut during sessions for the guitarist's magnificent *1999* album.)

While Prince may stand as an obvious Hendrix successor, succeeding – as did Jimi – as a guitarist, composer, showman and producer, not to be discounted is the undeniable imprint Hendrix has left upon black music in general. The Time, Cameo, Parliament/Funkadelic, Nile Rodgers, the Eric Gales Band, Chris Thomas, the Gap Band, Living Colour, Ernie Isley, Digital Underground and Jon Butcher represent just a few of the black acts to have collected various fractured images of Hendrix and incorporated his unique talents into their own compositions. Whereas Jon Butcher pays tribute via his fine ballad work, the Time – whose versions of "Skillet" and "Blondie" from their magnificent *Pandemonium* album seem merely an extension of the Band of Gypsys' molten mix of rock and R&B – re-create the energy, humor and sheer audacity so prevalent in many of Hendrix's finest performances.

In what is now called heavy metal, Hendrix created the vocabulary of the guitar – from the shaping of feedback to whammy bar action, neck tapping and sustained harmonics – that informs the style of so many of today's leading guitarists, from Eddie Van Halen, Joe Satriani and Steve Vai to such modern blues interpreters as Robert Cray, Donald Kinsey, Joe Louis Walker and the late Stevie Ray Vaughan.

To so many, Jimi Hendrix was simply the ultimate star – the guitar hero of all time, frozen forever at his peak. That he also played the pivotal role of musician-composer, shaping the future of electric blues and beyond, is too often blurred or forgotten. And if people consider virtuosity as an electric guitarist was his sole contribution to rock n' roll, his memory is suffering an undeserved slight, for the manner in which he wed his talent and personality to also inspire his supporting cast, musically and professionally, and broke down barriers in the recording studio, on the concert stage, and also in the rich but hitherto uncharted world of rock n' roll business, was just as profound.

Jimi Hendrix was, without doubt, the most innovative guitarist of his, or any other, era. While many have attempted to emulate his feats, none have been able to enlarge upon, or even match, his incredible achievements. His collected works, specifically his first five groundbreaking albums, stand among those by Robert Johnson, Charlie Parker, Miles Davis, Muddy Waters and Howlin' Wolf as consummate contributions to American music culture.

*"It's funny the way most people love the dead. Once you have died, you are made for life. You have to die before they think you are worth anything. And I tell you, when I die, I'm going to have a jam session. [I'll] have them playing everything I did musically, everything I enjoyed doing most. The music will be played loud and it will be our music. I won't have any Beatles songs, but I'll have a few of Eddie Cochran's things and a whole lot of blues. Roland Kirk will be there and I'll try to get Miles Davis along if he feels like making it. For that, it's almost worth dying, just for the funeral." – Jimi Hendrix*

# Appendix A

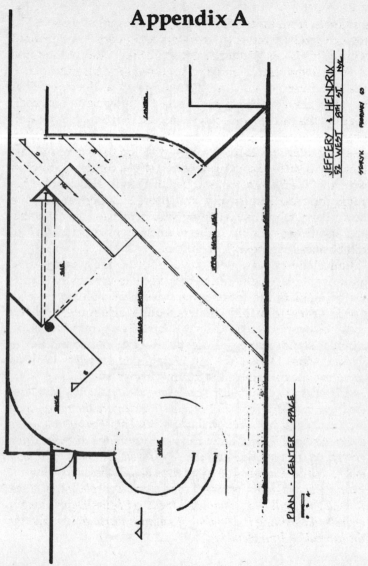

The evolution of Electric Lady Studios: Architect John Storyk's first submission to Michael Jeffery and Jimi Hendrix, outlining the layout of their proposed nightclub/recording studio. (*John Storyk*)

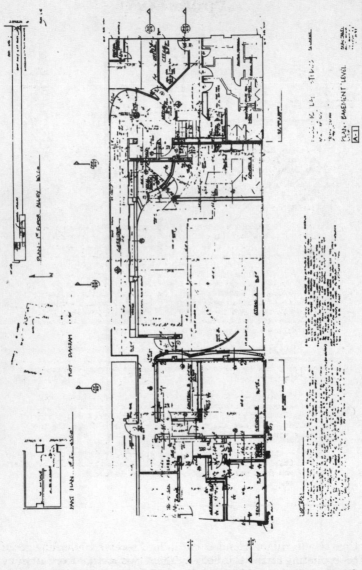

By May 20, 1969, the nightclub concept had been dismissed. (*John Storyk*)

# Appendix B

STEINGARTEN, WEDEEN & WEISS
ATTORNEYS AT LAW
444 MADISON AVENUE
NEW YORK, N. Y. 10022

HENRY W. STEINGARTEN
ALBERT A. WEDEEN
STEVENS H. WEISS
PHILIP BARASH
BARRY JAY REISS
THOMAS E. CONSTANCE
HENRY HORR KALOW

CABLE ADDRESS-STWEEDS
—
PLAZA 2-1330

November 11, 1969

Mr. Jimi Hendrix
59 West 12th Street
New York, N.Y.

### Re: Miscellaneous Matters

Dear Jimi:

I was disappointed that you did not show up yesterday for our meeting. I tried to get you at the Hotel
but you were out. There are several things that we have
to straighten out, and soon. These are as follows:

1. The Toronto case is scheduled for trial on December
1st. We are all to meet at the Royal York Hotel in Toronto
the evening of November 29th. We will spend the following
day with O'Driscoll preparing the case. Sharon Lawrence,
Leslie Perrin, Bob Levine, Mike Jeffery and possibly Chaz
Chandler will all be there. I want to talk to you about
this before we go up to Toronto.

It may be of interest to you that Mark Stein's case
for possession of narcotics was tried on October 24th, in
Montreal, and he was acquitted. His was a more difficult
case than yours.

2. In your absence yesterday, I signed an agreement
with Warner Bros. whereby if you fail for a period of three
months to deliver an album to them, as required under your
contract, they may mix one from your reels. There are two
albums now due, one for Capitol and the other for Warner.

The editor is subject to your approval, as is the
album itself, and you have the right to substitute for material
which you find unsuitable, but all this is under a tight
schedule.

Contrary to rumor, Hendrix did indeed receive counseling about
his escalating financial problems. These two memos from attorney
Henry Steingarten dramatically outline the mounting pressure
created by Jimi's mounting debt and unfulfilled commitments.

Mr. Jimi Hendrix          -2-          November 11, 1969

Warner will pay immediately $100,000 plus approxi-
mately $100,000 to Sea Lark, and upon the release of any
album will pay an additional $20,000 against recording costs.
The advances are, of course, recoupable out of royalties.

3. I was in London last week to meet with four of the
lawyers who represent you in the action brought by PPX against
you, Polydor, Track, Chandler and Yameta. The legal expenses
are rapidly becoming enormous. I made a deal whereby Lord
Goodman, your lawyer, would represent Yameta, Jeffery
and Chandler at no extra cost to you. I also put a stop to
other expenditures they were contemplating.

In my opinion, the case should be settled, but unfortunately, Chalpin is a very difficult person with whom to
negotiate.

In any event, I must meet with you to have you sign
the necessary papers to transfer the representation of the
case against the other defendants to Goodman's firm.

4. Your failure to keep the Boston date, as well as the
dates agreed to by you on which Concerts West began work, is
costing you approximately $25,000 in reimbursement of expenses.
This was a very unwise move on your part, and one for which
you alone are responsible.

5. The damage to the Woodstock house you rented came to
$5,000., which also has to be paid.

During your stay in Woodstock, you ran up a limousine
bill of more than $5,000 which has to be paid.

6. We do not have the money at this time to meet your
obligations, and a good part of what you will be receiving
from Warner and from Sea Lark will go to meet these expenses.
I have repeatedly tried to get you to understand the serious
situation in which you find yourself, and to urge you to cut
down on your spending. I must repeat this is vitally necessary,
and I should like to take some of the money and invest it for
you so that it is not available for immediate spending.

7. I received proposed material concerning you which is intended to be included in a book entitled "Groupies and other Girls". You are quoted at several places in the book, and because of the nature of the language attributed to you, the publisher wants your written authorization to include them in the book. Personally, I do not think they do you any credit, and if publicized as they inevitably will be, will detract from your image as an artist. Whatever opinions one may have of another person is one thing - but for that person to give them his own quotations on the subject does him no credit. We must talk about this.

8. Mike requires your written authorization to complete his contract negotiations with Polydor for the countries outside the United States and Canada. I would like to discuss this with you.

9. At the time you retained me, it was agreed that if by the end of the year the work done by me justified an additional fee, we would agree upon the amount, or you would have the election of terminating the arrangement. I believe I am entitled to receive an additional $5,000 for 1969. Hardly a day passes when I do not spend at least an hour discussing or trying to straighten out some problem. We can talk about this when we meet.

Please let me hear from you as soon as possible. There are important things to decide.

Sincerely,

HWS:mf

STEINGARTEN, WEDEEN & WEISS
ATTORNEYS AT LAW
444 MADISON AVENUE
NEW YORK, N. Y. 10022

HENRY W. STEINGARTEN
ALBERT A. WEDEEN
STEVENS M. WEISS
PHILIP BARASH
BARRY JAY REISS
THOMAS E. CONSTANCE
HENRY NORR KALOW

CABLE ADDRESS-STWEEDS

PLAZA 2-1330

December 24, 1969

Mr. Jimi Hendrix
59 West 12th Street
New York, New York

Dear Jimi:

Following our conversation over the telephone
yesterday, you instructed me to do whatever was necessary to
re-establish your position as a one-half owner in Electric
Lady Recording Studio on an equal basis with Mike Jeffery,
and Jeffery & Chandler, Inc.

During our conversation, I outlined to you the
reasons why Mike Hecht and I approve of this commitment by you.
I nevertheless believe it desirable for me to repeat them in
written form for your further consideration and review.

1. It is clear beyond question that you are dissi-
pating the substantial sums of money you are earning, and will
continue to earn in the future, and that it is desirable to
involve you in a business venture which will be financially
rewarding in the future.

Although the cost of construction of the studio is
more than in my opinion it should be, the studio represents,
on the basis of figures submitted, a desirable investment,
returns from which should be substantial and long-lasting.

2. However, it is estimated that it will cost $344,000
to build the studio, and require approximately $275,000 to finish
and put it into operation. Presently, you have $109,000 in-
vested and Jeffery $260,000. In order to equalize the investment
by each of you and to complete construction, Jeffery has to come
up with approximately $62,000 and you with $213,000.

3. It is proposed to raise the necessary capital in
one of two ways; (a) by obtaining an advance of royalties from
Warner in consideration of the extension of your recording.

Mr. Jimi Hendrix          -2-          December 24, 1969

agreement until 1975 at a royalty rate of 8% instead of 5% until 1972, and thereafter, at 11% until 1975, and the granting of sound track rights at 13% royalty, or (b) preferably, by obtaining a loan from Warner, secured by the assets of the recording studio, and additionally secured by the royalties to be earned in the future.

The amount of money you are committing yourself to invest is very sizable, particularly if you have to pay taxes on it, and it is important for you to realize that you must continue to produce albums and to make personal appearances because it will be some time before the monies advanced by Warner under either approach will be repaid and you will resume receiving royalties.

If you do not take this commitment seriously, your entire career can be seriously hurt, if not destroyed. The answer lies entirely in your hands. You must stop wasteful spending and sacrifice unnecessary things for the long-term benefit which the studio represents.

We have already begun discussions with Warner, and these will continue as rapidly as the situation permits. I will keep you informed of developments.

Sincerely,

Henry

HWS:mf

# DISCOGRAPHY

*"Don't be overwhelmed by the minutiae."*

## —Michael Goldstein

Jimi Hendrix's majestic reputation rests on a handful of carefully prepared, "authorized" recordings. Unfortunately, these few works are dwarfed by a catalogue top-heavy with inferior posthumous releases which have fundamentally altered public perception and understanding of his great talents. What follows is a selected discography detailing Hendrix's finest work, his most notable recordings as a sideman, stints as a guest guitarist or producer during his Experience career and a listing of Hendrix recordings issued posthumously.

## The Albums:

**ARE YOU EXPERIENCED?:** Track 612 001 Release Date: May 1967
Producer: Chas Chandler; Engineer: Eddie Kramer; Additional Engineering: George Chkiantz, Mike Ross, Dave Siddle; Studios: Pye, CBS, De Lane Lea, Regent and Olympic [London].

Foxey Lady/Manic Depression/Red House/Can You See Me/Love or Confusion/I Don't Live Today/May This Be Love/Fire/Third Stone from the Sun/Remember/Are You Experienced?

An invaluable introduction into the Hendrix legacy, and undoubtedly one of the best debut albums in rock history, this European release omits Hey Joe/Stone Free, Purple Haze/51st Anniversary and The Wind Cries Mary/Highway Chile, the band's first three singles.

**AXIS: BOLD AS LOVE:** Reprise RS 6281 Release Date: January 1968
Producer: Chas Chandler; Engineer: Eddie Kramer; 2nd Engineer(s): George Chkiantz, Andy Johns, Terry Brown; Studio: Olympic [London].

Exp/Up From the Skies/Spanish Castle Magic/Wait Until Tomorrow/Ain't No Telling/Little Wing/If Six Was Nine/You Got Me Floatin'/Castles Made of Sand/She's So Fine/One Rainy Wish/Little Miss Lover/Bold as Love

**ELECTRIC LADYLAND:** Reprise 2RS 6307 Release Date: October 1968
Produced & Directed by: Jimi Hendrix; Additional Production: Chas Chandler; Engineer(s): Eddie Kramer, Gary Kellgren; Additional Engineering: Tony Bongiovi; Studios: Olympic [London], Record Plant, Mayfair and Bell Sound [New York].

And the Gods Made Love/Have You Ever Been (to Electric Ladyland)/Crosstown Traffic/Voodoo Chile/Little Miss Strange/Long Hot Summer Night/Come On (Part 1)/Gypsy Eyes/Burning of the Midnight Lamp/Rainy Day Dream Away/1983 (A Merman I Shall Turn to Be)/Moon, Turn the Tides ... Gently Gently Away/Still Raining Still Dreaming/House Burning Down/All Along the Watchtower/Voodoo Child (Slight Return)

**SMASH HITS:** Reprise MS 2025 Release Date: July 1969
Producer(s): Chas Chandler, Jimi Hendrix; Engineer: Eddie Kramer.

Purple Haze/Fire/The Wind Cries Mary/Can You See Me/Hey Joe/All Along the Watchtower/Stone Free/Crosstown Traffic/Manic Depression/Remember/Red House/Foxey Lady

Hendrix's most popular release, *Smash Hits* was further improved in 1989 when, to add extra incentive for fans who had switched to the compact disc format, "Highway Chile" and "51st Anniversary" were added as bonus tracks.

**BAND OF GYPSYS:** Capitol STAO-472 Release Date: April 1970
Producer: Heaven Research Unlimited [Jimi Hendrix]; Engineering & Remixing Supervision: Eddie Kramer; Live Recording: Wally Heider, Jimmy Robinson; Edited & Mixed: Juggy Sound [New York]; Recorded Live: Fillmore East 1/1/70.

Who Knows/Machine Gun/Changes/Power of Soul/Message to Love/We Gotta Live Together

**WOODSTOCK:** Cotillion SD 3500 Release Date: June 1970
Producer: Eric Blackstead; Engineer(s): Eddie Kramer, Lee Osbourne; Recorded Live: Woodstock Festival 8/19/69.

Star Spangled Banner/Purple Haze/Instrumental Solo

**WOODSTOCK II:** Cotillion SD 2400 Release Date: March 1971
Producer: Eric Blackstead; Engineer(s): Eddie Kramer, Lee Osbourne; Recorded Live: Woodstock Festival 8/19/69.

Jam Back at the House/Izabella/Getting My Heart Back Together Again

**THE CRY OF LOVE:** Reprise MS 2034 Release Date: March 1971
Producer(s): Jimi Hendrix, Eddie Kramer, Mitch Mitchell; Engineer: Eddie Kramer; 2nd Engineers: Dave Palmer, Kim King, John Jansen; Additional Engineering: Jack Adams; Studios: Electric Lady, Record Plant [Basic tracks: "Ezy Ryder"], Mirasound or Sound Center [Basic tracks: "My Friend"].

Freedom/Drifting/Ezy Ryder/Night Bird Flying/My Friend/Straight Ahead/Astro Man/Angel/In From the Storm/Belly Button Window

**EXPERIENCE:** Ember 5057 [Not Released in U.S.] Release Date: August 1971
Producer(s): Jerry Goldstein, Chas Chandler; Recorded Live: Royal Albert Hall, London 2/24/69.

Sunshine of Your Love/Room Full of Mirrors/C# Blues [Bleeding Heart]/Smashing Amps

A particularly curious release, followed some seven months later with a sequel, *More Experience* [Ember 5061]. Never issued in the U.S., both albums featured bootleg quality recordings purportedly from the soundtrack of the forthcoming film of the same name. Most of this material – save for "Room Full of Mirrors" and a spirited rendition of "Fire" from *More Experience* – have resurfaced, properly mixed, on later compilations.

**MORE EXPERIENCE:** Ember 5061 [Not Released in U.S.] Release Date: March 1972
Producer(s): Jerry Goldstein, Chas Chandler; Recorded Live: Royal Albert Hall, London 2/24/69.

Little Ivey [Little Wing]/Voodoo Chile [Voodoo Child (Slight Return)]/Room Full of Mirrors/Fire/Purple Haze/Wild Thing/Bleeding Heart

**THE FIRST GREAT ROCK FESTIVALS OF THE SEVENTIES: ISLE OF WIGHT\ATLANTA POP FESTIVAL:** Columbia G3X 30805 Release Date: September 1971
Producer: Ted Macero; Engineer(s): Don Puluse, Stan Tonkel, Russ Payne; Recorded Live: Isle Of Wight 8/30/70.

Power to Love [actually Message to Love]/Midnight Lightning/Foxey Lady

Though this three-disc compilation featured inspired performances by such prominent CBS Records artists as Miles Davis, Johnny Winter and Sly & the Family Stone, these three Hendrix tracks – poorly mixed and edited Isle of Wight performances – were the first real chink in his armor. "Power to Love" was a vastly inferior alternative to the "Message to Love" that had graced *Band of Gypsys*, while "Midnight Lightning/Foxey Lady" was simply miserable.

**ISLE OF WIGHT:** Polydor 2302 016 [Not Released in U.S.] Release Date: November 1971

Producer: Michael Jeffery; Mixed: Eddie Kramer – Electric Lady Studios July 29 1971-August 21971; Remixed & Compiled: Carlos Ohlms – Polydor Studios [London] September 1971; Recorded Live: Isle of Wight 8/30/70.

Midnight Lightning/Foxey Lady/Lover Man/Freedom/All Along the Watchtower/In From the Storm

While it can be argued that these renditions of "Freedom," "In From the Storm" and certainly "All Along the Watchtower" are worthy of release in some form, "Midnight Lightning/Foxey Lady" is not. Had this release been filled out with "Red House" and "Machine Gun," later to grace *Soundtrack Recordings From the Film: Jimi Hendrix, Isle of Wight* would have been upgraded considerably. Without them, it remains a mediocre document of a less than stirring Hendrix performance.

**RAINBOW BRIDGE:** Reprise MS 2040 Release Date: October 1971 Producer(s): Jimi Hendrix, Eddie Kramer, Mitch Mitchell, John Jansen; Engineer: Eddie Kramer; Additional Engineering: John Jansen, Abe Jacob, Dave Palmer, Kim King, Tony Bongiovi; Studios: Electric Lady, Record Plant [Basic tracks: "Star Spangled Banner," "Room Full of Mirrors," "Earth Blues"], TTG [Basic tracks: "Look Over Yonder"]; Live Recording: "Hear My Train A Comin'" Berkeley, California 5/30/70 first Show.

Dolly Dagger/Earth Blues/Pali Gap/Room Full of Mirrors/Star Spangled Banner/Look Over Yonder/Hear My Train A Comin'/ Hey Baby (The Land of the New Rising Sun)

Out of print for more than fifteen years, *Rainbow Bridge* and, to a lesser degree, *War Heroes*, document Hendrix's unfinished work, fascinating sketches and ideas he never lived to complete. To properly collate Hendrix's remaining studio recordings, *Rainbow Bridge* should be coupled with *War Heroes* onto a single compact disc (the live "Hear My Train A Comin'" could be added to *Hendrix: In the West* – another long out of print gem – where it would fit perfectly).

**HENDRIX: IN THE WEST:** Reprise MS 2049 Release Date: February 1972

Producer(s): Eddie Kramer, John Jansen; Engineer(s) Eddie Kramer, John Jansen; Recorded Live: Berkeley, San Diego, London, Isle of Wight.

Johnny B. Goode [Berkeley 5/30/70 first Show]/Lover Man [Berkeley 5/30/70 second Show]/Blue Suede Shoes [Berkeley S/30/70 Afternoon rehearsals]/Voodoo Child (Slight Return) [Royal Albert Hall, London 2/24/69]/God Save the Queen/Sgt. Pepper' s Lonely Hearts Club Band [Isle of Wight 8/30/70]/ Little Wing [Royal Albert Hall, London 2/24/69]/Red House [San Diego 5/24/69]

**WAR HEROES:** Reprise MS 2103 Release Date: December 1972
Producer(s): Jimi Hendrix, Eddie Kramer, John Jansen; Engineer(s): Eddie Kramer, John Jansen, Dave Palmer, Kim King; Additional Engineering: Gary Kellgren, Tony Bongiovi; Studios: Electric Lady, Record Plant [Basic tracks: "Izabella," "Stepping Stone," "Three Little Bears," "Bleeding Heart, "Tax Free"], Juggy Sound ["Izabella," "Stepping Stone"], TTG ["Midnight"], Olympic ["Highway Chile," "Tax Free"].

Bleeding Heart/Highway Chile/Tax Free/Peter Gunn/Catastrophe/Stepping Stone/Midnight/Three Little Bears/Beginning/Izabella

Coupled, as suggested earlier, with *Rainbow Bridge* and filled out with such odd tracks as "51st Anniversary" and "The Stars That Play With Laughing Sam's Dice," *War Heroes*'s more prominent triumphs – namely "Izabella," "Stepping Stone" and "Highway Chile" – would vastly improve *Rainbow Bridge* and help correct Hendrix's posthumous legacy.

**SOUNDTRACK RECORDINGS FROM THE FILM: JIMI HENDRIX** Reprise 2RS 6481 Release Date: June 1973
Recorded Live: Berkeley, Monterey, Isle of Wight, Fillmore East, London, Woodstock [as well as interviews with Hendrix and other associates].

Rock Me Baby [Monterey 6/18/67]/Wild Thing [Monterey 6/18/67], Machine Gun I [Isle of Wight 8/30/70]/Interviews I/Johnny B. Goode [Berkeley 5/30/70 1st Show]/Hey Joe [Monterey

6/18/67]/Purple Haze [Berkeley 5/30/70 1st Show]/Like a Rolling
Stone [Monterey 6/18/67]/Interviews II/Star Spangled Banner
[Woodstock 8/19/69]/Machine Gun II [Fillmore East 1/1/70 First
Show]/Hear My Train A Comin' [London 12/19/67]/Interviews
III/Red House [Isle of Wight 8/30/70]/In from the Storm [Isle of
Wight 8/30/70]/Interviews IV

**LOOSE ENDS:** Polydor 2310 301 [Not issued in U.S.] Release Date:
February 1974
Producer: Michael Jeffery; Engineer: Alev Trevor [John Jansen];
Additional Production: Jimi Hendrix, Chas Chandler; Additional
Engineering: Eddie Kramer, John Jansen, Dave Palmer, Kim King,
Gary Kellgren, Jack Adams, Tom Flye, Jim Robinson; Studios:
Electric Lady, Record Plant [Basic tracks: "Blue Suede Shoes," "Jam
292," "Burning Desire," "I'm Your Hoochie Coochie Man"], May-
fair ["The Stars That Play With Laughing Sam's Dice"], Olympic
["Electric Ladyland"].

Coming Down Hard on Me/ Blue Suede Shoes/Jam 292/The Stars
That Play With Laughing Sam's Dice/Drifter's Escape/Burning
Desire/I'm Your Hoochie Coochie Man/Electric Ladyland

The last – and worst – release of Michael Jeffery's tenure, *Loose
Ends* is an aptly titled, patchwork collection of decidedly inferior
Hendrix material.

**CRASH LANDING:** Reprise MS 2204 Release Date: March 1975
Producer(s): Alan Douglas, Tony Bongiovi; Arranger: Brad Baker;
Engineer(s): Les Kahn, Tony Bongiovi, Ron Saint Germain; Studios
(1974): Shaggy Dog [Stockbridge, Ma.], Track [Washington, DC],
Media Sound [New York]. Message to Love [Record Plant
12/19/69]/Somewhere Over the Rainbow [Mirasound or Sound
Center 3/68]/Crash Landing [Record Plant 4/24/69, 4/29/69]/
Come Down Hard on Me [Electric Lady 7/14/70]/Peace in Mis-
sissippi [TTG 10/24/68]/With the Power [Record Plant 5/15/69]
/Stone Free Again [Record Plant 4/9/69]/Captain Coconut [Three
composite pieces from Electric Lady, Record Plant and the Hit
Factory]

The first release of Alan Douglas's tenure, *Crash Landing* was, and remains, a highly controversial project. Casting the issue of eliminating the contributions of Hendrix's original sidemen aside, *Crash Landing*'s eight tracks seem tepid, conspicuously devoid of the energy so prominent in Hendrix's finest recordings – including such posthumously issued material as "Dolly Dagger," "Izabella" and "Stepping Stone." Without having the appropriate material to work with, Douglas (and Tony Bongiovi) are left to interpret what were merely formative musical explorations.

## CRASH LANDING: UNRELEASED VERSION
Crash Landing [H-256 Record Plant 4/24/69]/Somewhere [H-124 3/68]/Anything Is Possible (With the Power) [H-36 Record Plant 1/21/70]/New Rising Sun [H-264 TTG 10/22/68]/Message to Love [H-34 Record Plant 1/20/70] Scat Vocal-Lead 1-Scat Vocal 2-Lead Vocal 2 [H-273 Hit Factory 8/28/69]/Stone Free [H-255 Record Plant 4/7/69]/Peace in Mississippi [H-282 TTG 10/24/68]/Here Comes Your Lover Man [H-248 TTG 10/29/68]

## MIDNIGHT LIGHTNING: Reprise MS 2229 Release Date: November 1975
Producer(s): Alan Douglas, Tony Bongiovi; Arranger: Brad Baker; Engineer(s): Les Kahn, Tony Bongiovi, Ron Saint Germain; Studios (1974-75): Shaggy Dog [Stockbridge, Ma.], Track [Washington, D.C.], Media Sound [New York].

Trash Man [Ohlmstead 4/3/69]/Midnight Lightning [Juggy Sound 3/23/70]/Hear My Train [Record Plant 4/9/69]/Gypsy Boy [Record Plant 3/18/69]/Blue Suede Shoes [Record Plant 1/23/70]/Machine Gun [Hit Factory 8/29/69, Record Plant 9/23/69]/Once I Had a Woman [Record Plant 1/23/70]/Beginning [Electric Lady 7/1/70]

## MULTICOLORED BLUES: UNRELEASED VERSION
Seven Dollars in My Pocket /Hootchie Cootchie Man [Record Plant 12/18/69]/Midnight Lightning/Lee Blues [H-396 Hit Factory 8/28/69]/Izabella Blues [H-276 Hit Factory 8/29/69]/Blue Suede Shoes [H-38 Record Plant 1/23/70]/Farther on Down the Road [Electric Lady]/Winter Blues [H-309 Record Plant 5/7/69]/Slow Time Blues [H-39 Record Plant 1/23/70]/Blues for Me and You [H-242 Hit Factory 9/6/69]/Last Thursday Morning [H-83 Electric Lady 7/20/70]/Comin' Down Hard [Electric Lady]

## ESSENTIAL JIMI HENDRIX VOLUMES ONE AND TWO:
Reprise 26035-2 Release Date: Album: Vol. One July 1978, Vol. Two July 1979; CD: Vol. One & Two November 1989

Are You Experienced?/Third Stone from the Sun/Purple Haze/ Hey Joe/Fire/Foxey Lady/The Wind Cries Mary/I Don't Live Today/Little Wing/If 6 Was 9/Bold As Love/Little Miss Lover/ Castles Made of Sand/Gypsy Eyes/Burning of the Midnight Lamp/Voodoo Child (Slight Return)/Crosstown Traffic/Still Raining Still Dreaming/Have You Ever Been (To Electric Ladyland)/ All Along the Watchtower/House Burning Down/Room Full of Mirrors/Izabella/Freedom/Dolly Dagger/Stepping Stone/Drifting/Ezy Ryder/Wild Thing [Recorded Live: Monterey 6/18/67]/ Machine Gun [Recorded Live: Fillmore East 1/1/70 First Show]/ Star Spangled Banner [Recorded Live: Woodstock 8/19/69] /Gloria [Unreleased studio track: TTG 10/68]

While the pairing of Volumes 1 and 2 for issue on compact disc eliminated the lionshare of complaints initially lobbed at this compilation, some "essential" tracks ("Red House," "Angel," "Nightbird Flying") were conspicuously absent. Worse still was the glaring absence of Hendrix's blues masterworks. Aside from the aforementioned "Red House," superb live renditions of "Hear My Train A Comin'" and "Bleeding Heart" were bypassed.

## NINE TO THE UNIVERSE: Reprise HS 2299 Release Date: March 1980
Producer: Alan Douglas; Assistant Producer: Les Kahn; Engineer: Ron Saint Germain.

Nine to the Universe/Jimi-Jimmy Jam/Young–Hendrix/Easy Blues/Drone Blues

## JIMI HENDRIX CONCERTS: Reprise 22306-1 Release Date: August 1982
Producer: Alan Douglas; Associate Producers: Daniel Secunda, Albert Koski; Engineers: Bob Potter, John Porter, Les Kahn, Buddy Epstein, Rino Roucco; Recorded Live: Winterland, San Diego, New York, London, Berkeley.

Fire [Winterland 10/12/68 First Show]/I Don't Live Today [San

Diego 5/24/69]/Red House [Randall's Island, NY 7/17/70]/Stone Free [Royal Albert Hall, London 2/24/69]/Are You Experienced? [Winterland 10/10/68 First Show]/Little Wing [Winterland 10/11/68 Second Show]/Voodoo Child (Slight Return) [Winterland 10/10/68 First Show]/Bleeding Heart [Royal Albert Hall, London 2/24/69]/Hey Joe [Berkeley 5/30/70]/Wild Thing [Winterland 10/12/68 First Show]/Hear My Train A Comin' [Winterland 10/10/68 First Show]/Foxey Lady [San Diego 5/24/69]

*Jimi Hendrix Concerts* would have been a magnificent single album, had "Little Wing," "Voodoo Child (Slight Return)," "Hey Joe" and "Wild Thing" been deleted (and "I Don't Live Today" from the Experience's 4/26/69 L.A. Forum performance substituted for the 5/24/69 San Diego version enclosed in this collection). When evaluating Hendrix recordings, Douglas seemingly continues to devalue, or worse, overlook the contributions – good or bad – of Mitchell, Cox and Redding. Throughout "Voodoo Child (Slight Return)," Mitch Mitchell's drumming lacks the power and precision of past performances, and his playing on "Little Wing" is nowhere as dramatic as the version recorded at London's Royal Albert Hall and included as part of *Hendrix: In the West.*

**KISS THE SKY:** Reprise 25119 Release Date: October 1984 Compilation
Producers: Kevin Laffey, Chip Branton, Alan Douglas.

Are You Experienced?/I Don't Live Today [Recorded Live: San Diego 5/24/69]/Voodoo Child (Slight Return)/Stepping Stone/Killing Floor [Recorded Live: Monterey 6/18/67]/Purple Haze/Red House/Crosstown Traffic/Third Stone From the Sun/All Along the Watchtower

**JIMI PLAYS MONTEREY:** Reprise 25358-1 Release Date: February 1986
Producer: Alan Douglas; Associate Producer: Chip Branton; Additional Production: Lou Adler, John Phillips, Wally Heider, Eric Weinbang; Engineer: Mark Linett.

Killing Floor/Foxey Lady/Like A Rolling Stone/Rock Me Baby/Hey Joe/Can You See Me/The Wind Cries Mary/Purple Haze/Wild Thing

Certainly the best release of Douglas's tenure to date. Audio production throughout is first rate and the Experience's performance superb. An invaluable document.

**JOHNNY B. GOODE:** Capitol MLP 15022 Release Date: June 1986 Producers: Alan Douglas, Chip Branton; Remix Engineer: Mark Linett.

Voodoo Child (Slight Return) [Atlanta Pop Festival 7/4/70] /Johnny B. Goode [Berkeley 5/30/70 First Show]/Along the Watchtower [Atlanta Pop Festival 7/4/70]/Star Spangled Banner [Atlanta Pop Festival 7/4/70]/Machine Gun [Berkeley 5/30/70 Second Show]

**BAND OF GYPSYS 2:** Capitol SJ-12416 Release Date: October 1986 Producers: Alan Douglas, Chip Branton.

Hear My Train A Comin' [Fillmore East 12/31/69 First Show]/ Foxey Lady [Fillmore East 1/1/70 First Show]/Stop [Fillmore East First Show]/Voodoo Child (Slight Return) [Atlanta Pop Festival 7/4/70]/Stone Free [Berkeley 5/30/70] Ezy Ryder [Berkeley 5/30/70]

Both *Johnny B. Goode* (technically a "mini-album") and *Band of Gypsys 2* are mediocre compilations. Hendrix fans would be best served if "Hear My Train A Comin'" – *Band of Gypsys 2*'s only worthwhile track – was added to *Band of Gypsys* when that album is ultimately issued on compact disc. "Foxey Lady" and "Stop" are both poorly performed and recorded, while "Ezy Ryder" is hardly the definitive Band of Gypsys version. To fill out *Johnny B. Goode*, Douglas opted for "Voodoo Child (Slight Return)" and a ragged "All Along the Watchtower," two of Hendrix's weaker Atlanta Pop Festival performances, curiously bypassing "Room Full of Mirrors," "Freedom" and a magnificent "Stone Free."

**LIVE AT WINTERLAND:** Rykodisc RCD 20038 Release Date: May 1987 Producer: Alan Douglas, Chip Branton; Mixing Engineer: Mark Linett.

Prologue/Fire [10/11/68 First Show]/Manic Depression [10/12/68

Second Show]/Sunshine of Your Love [10/10/68 Second Show]/ Spanish Castle Magic [10/12/68 Second Show]/Red House [10/11/68 First Show]/Killing Floor [10/10/68 Second Show]/Tax Free [10/11/68 Second Show]/Foxey Lady [10/11/68 Second Show]/Hey Joe [10/12/68 First Show]/Wild Thing [10/12/68 First Show]/ Epilogue

Not the best of the Experience in concert, but hardly the worst, this compilation of the group's six Winterland performances was an overwhelming critical and commercial success. As with *Jimi Hendrix Concerts, Live at Winterland* would have made a superb single album. Audio quality, as well as the album's packaging, is laudable.

**RADIO ONE:** Rykodisc RCD 20078 Release Date: November 1988 Production Supervisor: Alan Douglas; Remix Engineer: Mark Linett. Mono BBC Radio Recordings.

Stone Free [2/13/67]/Radio One [12/15/67]/Day Tripper [12/15/67] Killing Floor [3/28/67]/Love or Confusion [2/13/67]/Catfish Blues [10/6/67]/Drivin' South [10/6/67]/Wait Until Tomorrow [12/15/67] /Hear My Train A Comin' [12/15/67]/Hound Dog [10/6/67]/Fire [3/28/67] /I'm Your Hoochie Coochie Man [10/17/67] /Purple Haze [3/28/67]/Spanish Castle Magic [12/15/67] /Hey Joe [2/13/67] /Foxey Lady [2/13/67]/Burning of the Midnight Lamp [10/6/67]

Long a favorite of collectors and bootleggers alike, these BBC recordings were fun, spirited performances, full of the vitality and spirit that made *Are You Experienced?* and *Axis: Bold as Love* so endearing.

**RED HOUSE: VARIATIONS ON A THEME:** Hal Leonard HL00660040 Release Date: November 1989 Producer: Alan Douglas.

Red House [Berkeley 5/30/70 First Show](Electric Church) Red House [TTG Studios 10/29/68]/Red House [L.A. Forum 4/26/69]/Red House [Randall's Island, NY 7/17/70]/Red House [Royal Albert Hall, London 2/24/69]/Red House [Winterland, 10/10/68 First Show]

Though inaccurately annotated, this compact disc release highlights seven different renditions of "Red House" including one by blues giant John Lee Hooker, a longtime Hendrix admirer. Oddly enough, Hendrix's own studio rendition – the track on which these live performances was based – was omitted.

**LIFELINES:** Reprise 9 26435-2 Release Date: 1990
Producer (Radio): Bruce Gary; Producer (Compact Disc): Alan Douglas.

This strange release is actually a radio program transferred verbatim to disc and coupled – perhaps to justify its hefty retail price tag – with an uneven Experience concert (LA Forum 4/26/69). At least the commercials have been edited out.

**STAGES:** Reprise 9 26732-2 Release Date: November 1991
Producer: Alan Douglas; Mixing Engineer: Mark Linett; [Stockholm 9/5/67-Paris 1/29/68-San Diego 5/24/69-Atlanta 7/4/70]

While the concept behind this release – essentially documenting the evolution of Hendrix's stage performances over four years – is intriguing, *Stages* is hardly, as its liner notes suggests, the "performance pillars upon which a master's legacy rests." Such lofty praise would better describe such Experience triumphs as Monterey or the Royal Albert Hall. There are a number of gems marbled within these four discs – enough certainly to fill two discs (and command a much smaller retail price tag) – however, too many of the tracks find Hendrix and company dreadfully out of tune (no amount of 1991 studio trickery can rectify the tuning problems that dog Paris's "Fire" or San Diego's "Hey Joe") and compromised by primitive and often woefully inadequate sound and monitoring systems. If servicing the demands of hardcore Hendrix fans – who might instead turn to bootleggers in order to hear these performances – is a motivation for releasing sets like *Stages*, then, less discriminating fans would be better suited by sticking with such acknowledged masterworks as *Band Of Gypsys* and *Jimi Plays Monterey* or even an import copy of *Hendrix: In the West*.

## HENDRIX AS A GUEST AND/OR PRODUCER: SELECTED HIGHLIGHTS

While Hendrix is deservedly hailed as a giant of electric guitar, his guitar reputation did not often show in his work as a session guitarist. A listen to his guest appearances – from Curtis Knight to Love – will show that the spark so prevalent within his own recordings was often muted elsewhere. Listed below are selected examples of his appearances as a session guitarist and/or producer. To spare Hendrix fans, this list omits a great many variations – all contain the same material – that usually sport an attractive cover and dubious, if any, liner notes.

## LONNIE YOUNGBLOOD

While fans should not expect to hear any traces of Hendrix's guitar genius, these 1963 recordings with R&B journeyman Lonnie Youngblood represent Hendrix's first-known recording sessions.

Like his later sessions with Curtis Knight & the Squires, hundreds of albums have been fashioned from the fifteen-odd tracks Hendrix actually recorded with Youngblood. Perhaps the most notorious example was 1971's *Two Great Experiences Together*. Blessed by an attractive cover photograph featuring an Experience-era Jimi Hendrix jamming with Lonnie Youngblood, Youngblood's original 1963 mono recordings were enhanced with new, 1971 stereo overdubs of a pathetic Hendrix-soundalike. Arriving in record shops almost simultaneously with Hendrix's "official" album, *Cry of Love, Two Great Experiences Together* actually broke into the *Billboard* top 200, peaking at number 127 – a remarkable feat for tiny Maple Records, the album's label – before quickly exiting.

To get as honest an appraisal of Hendrix's first known recording sessions as possible, these two 45 singles should suffice:

Lonnie Youngblood: "Go Go Shoes"/"Go Go Place"
Fairmont Records F-1002

"Soul Food (That's What I Like)"/"Goodbye Bessie Mae"
Fairmont Records F-1022

## ISLEY BROTHERS
Hendrix participated in three different recording sessions with the Isley Brothers (two in 1964, the other in 1965), lending rhythm and lead guitar to six songs. Released on three singles, they are:

Isley Brothers: "Testify (Part I)"/"Testify (Part II)"

"The Last Girl"/"Looking For A Love"
Atlantic 2263

"Move Over And Let Me Dance"/"Have You Ever Been Disappointed?"
Atlantic 2303

Neither of these three singles cracked *Billboard's* Top 40 chart. Contrary to rumor, Hendrix did not appear on the Isley Brothers 1962 chart hit "Twist and Shout."

In 1971, the Isley Brothers issued *In the Beginning,* a compilation on their own T-Neck label featuring Hendrix's recordings with the group. "We remixed [Hendrix's tracks] so that Jimi is more upfront," an unabashed Ronnie Isley explained in 1971. In addition to remixed versions of "Move Over and Let Me Dance" and "Have You Ever Been Disappointed?," a new take of 1964's "Testify (Part 1)" was also introduced.

## ROSA LEE BROOKS
According to Rosa Lee Brooks, Hendrix co-wrote "My Diary" at the Wilcox Hotel on New Year's Day 1964. The song was later recorded in a converted garage for tiny Revis Records. Arthur Lee – later to form the seminal Los Angeles psychedelic band Love – arranged the session and contributed background vocals. Also contributing to this session were musicians from Major Lance's band, recruited by Hendrix from Ciro's, the famed L.A. nightspot. "Utee" was a spontaneous effort inspired by a dance then popular in Detroit.

Rosa Lee Brooks: "My Diary/Utee" Revis Records 1013

## LITTLE RICHARD
What exactly Jimi Hendrix may have actually contributed to any

Little Richard single or album is a matter of considerable debate. By 1965, Little Richard's popularity had noticeably waned. Having hired Hendrix to join The Upsetters, his support group, Richard concentrated on touring, recording infrequently.

While in Los Angeles, Hendrix, using the pseudonym Maurice James, did contribute guitar parts to one Little Richard single, "I Don't Know What You've Got But It's Got Me (Parts 1 & 2)." Indicative of Richard's withering following, the single barely dented *Billboard*'s Hot 100, peaking for a single week at number 92 before exiting as quickly as it arrived.

Little Richard: "I Don't Know What You've Got But It's Got Me (Part 1)"/"I Don't Know What You've Got But It's Got Me (Part 2)" Vee Jay 698

## KING CURTIS

In addition to touring briefly with the famed saxophonist and his band, the Kingpins, Hendrix also contributed lead guitar to King Curtis's 1966 single "Help Me," recorded at Atlantic Studios.

King Curtis: "Help Me (Part 1)"/"Help Me (Part 2)" Atco 6402

## CURTIS KNIGHT & THE SQUIRES

While Hendrix's intermittent tenure as lead guitarist for Curtis Knight & the Squires was relatively brief, more than 100 albums have been crafted from some forty studio recordings and a handful of live appearances. None of these albums justify the extravagant claims their titles boast, and most feature low-fidelity variations, remixes, edited versions and instrumentals of the same material – often with their song titles changed. All of Hendrix's studio sessions as a member of Curtis Knight & the Squires were produced by Ed Chalpin at Studio 76 in New York.

The following two singles were licensed in 1966 by Chalpin to RSVP Records, a New York-based independent label owned and operated by Jerry Simon. Neither cracked *Billboard*'s elusive Hot 100 chart.

Curtis Knight & the Squires: "How Would You Feel"/"Welcome Home" RSVP 1120

"Hornet's Nest"/"Knock Yourself Out" RSVP 1124

[Hendrix, listed as "Jimmy Hendrix," received his first label credit as co-composer of both these instrumentals.]

When Chalpin approached Capitol Records in the fall of 1967, he offered the label thirty-three master tapes featuring Hendrix as a member of Curtis Knight & the Squires. These masters had been recorded during sessions in October and December 1965, as well as two later, highly controversial, sessions, July 17, 1967, and August 8, 1967. As outlined in PPX's November 21, 1967 contract with Capitol, these songs were:

Gloomy Monday [vocal]/No Business [vocal]/Get That Feeling [vocal]/Day Tripper [vocal]/Hush Now [vocal]/Hush Now [instrumental]/Hush Now [second vocal master]/Future Trip [vocal]/Flashing [instrumental]/Flashing [second instrumental master]/Happy Birthday [vocal]/Level [instrumental]/Love [instrumental]/You Don't Want Me [vocal]/You Don't Want Me [second vocal master]/How Would You Feel [vocal]/Ballad of Jimmy [vocal]/Fool for You Baby [vocal]/Hornet's Nest [instrumental]/Got to Have a New Dress [vocal]/Knock Yourself Out [instrumental] /Simon Says [instrumental]/Simon Says [vocal]/Love Love [vocal]/Strange Things [vocal]/Odd Ball/UFO/My Heart Is Higher/Welcome Home/Welcome Home [second master] /Don't Accuse Me/Don't Accuse Me [second master]/How Would You Feel [second master]

**Get That Feeling:** "Jimi Hendrix Plays and Curtis Knight Sings" Capitol ST 2856 Release Date: December 1967
Producer: Ed Chalpin; Engineer: Mickey Lane; Studio: Studio 76 [New York].

How Would You Feel/Simon Says/Get That Feeling/Hush Now/Welcome Home/Gotta Have A New Dress/No Business/Strange Things

*Get That Feeling* compiles the "best" of Hendrix's studio efforts with Curtis Knight & the Squires. "How Would You Feel" is the album's strongest selection, a spirited knockoff of Dylan's "Like a Rolling Stone," a mainstream hit from the previous summer.

**Flashing:** "Jimi Hendrix Plays and Curtis Knight Sings" Capitol

ST 2984 Release Date: October 1968
Producer: Ed Chalpin; Engineer: Mickey Lane; Studio: Studio 76
[New York].

Gloomy Monday/Hornet's Nest/Fool for You Baby/Happy Birthday/Flashing/Day Tripper/Odd Ball/Love Love/Don't Accuse Me

While somewhat better identified and annotated, *Flashing* remains, at best, a tepid collection of tracks seemingly cut from the jam that created *Get That Feeling*'s interminable title track and older R&B workouts. Of the latter, "Hornet's Nest" and "Don't Accuse Me" – both "pre-Experience" recordings – offer fans an interesting glimpse inside Hendrix's evolving technique.

**What'd I Say:** MFP 5278 Release Date: 1973
Recorded Live: 12/26/65 George's Club 20, Hackensack, NJ, various venues in New York & New Jersey.

Drivin' South/California Night/On the Killin' Floor/What'd I Say/I'll Be Doggone/Bright Lights Big City

**Birth Of Success:** MFP 50053 Release Date: 1973

Recorded Live: 12/26/65 George's Club 20, Hackensack, NJ, various venues in New York & New Jersey.

I'm a Man/Sugar Pie Honey Bunch (I Can't Help Myself)/Get Out of My Life Woman/Ain't That Peculiar/Last Night/Satisfaction/Land of 1000 Dances/UFO

**In The Beginning:** Ember NR 5068 Release Date: 1973

Recorded Live: 12/26/65 George's Club 20, Hackensack, NJ, various venues in New York & New Jersey.

You Got Me Running/Money/Let's Go, Let's Go, Let's Go/You Got What It Takes/Sweet Little Angel/Walkin' the Dog/There Is Something on Your Mind/ Hard Night

Of all the live material licensed by Chalpin for release, these raw, mono recordings capture Hendrix's difficult, yet undeniable transformation from sideman to band leader. There's no "Gloomy Monday" or "Love Love" here, as Hendrix's renditions of "Killing Floor," "I'm a Man" and "Drivin' South" are refreshingly robust. To measure Hendrix's amazing growth from this humble stage in his career, one needs only to compare this "Killing Floor" with Hendrix's volcanic interpretation of the song at Monterey some eighteen months later.

While the fidelity of these live Curtis Knight & the Squires recordings are sub-standard (additional overdubs without Hendrix – recorded in stereo – were added to some albums in an unsuccessful effort to upgrade quality), they remain intriguing documents, marking Hendrix's increasing confidence and ability.

**McGOUGH & McGEAR:** Parlophone PCS 7047 Release Date: October 1968
Producer: Paul McCartney; Studio: De Lane Lea.

Hendrix, along with Mitch Mitchell, Noel Redding and a host of other British rock luminaries, contributed to this UK only release. Jimi overdubbed lead guitar on two tracks: "So Much" and "Ex Art Student."

**EIRE APPARENT:** *Sunrise* Buddah Records 2011-117 Release Date: May 1969
Producer: Jimi Hendrix; Engineers: Eddie Kramer, Gary Kellgren, Tony Bongiovi [Record Plant], Jack Hunt [TTG], Carlos Olms [Polydor]; Studios: Record Plant [New York], TTG [Los Angeles], Polydor [London].

Production for *Sunrise* began at the Record Plant in August 1968 and moved to TTG Studios, as Eire Apparent accompanied the Experience and Vanilla Fudge as their opening act. The group's debut single, "Rock n' Roll Band," was the last track to be finished, as Hendrix, in early January 1969, nipped into Polydor Studios to overdub and mix his lead guitar overdub.

**CAT MOTHER & THE ALL NIGHT NEWSBOYS:** *The Street*

*Giveth ... And The Street Taketh Away* Polydor 24-4001 Release Date: June 1969
Producers: Jimi Hendrix & Cat Mother; Studio: Record Plant; Engineers: Gary Kellgren, Tony Bongiovi.

Another group in the Michael Jeffery stable, Cat Mother & the All Night Newsboys enjoyed modest chart success on both *Billboard's* single and album charts, as "Good Old Rock 'n' Roll", the group's debut single, peaked at number 21 in July 1969.

**BUDDY MILES EXPRESS:** *Electric Church* Mercury SR-61222
Producer: Jimi Hendrix ["Miss Lady," "69 Freedom Special," "Destructive Love," "My Chant"]; Studios: Record Plant [New York], Mercury Studios [New York].

During February and March 1969, Hendrix produced these tracks for the Express's second Mercury release (Jimi also wrote the liner notes for *Expressway to Your Skull*, the group's debut album, issued in January 1969).

**TIMOTHY LEARY:** *You Can Be Anyone This Time Around* Douglas Records 1 Release Date: April 1970
Producer: Alan Douglas; Engineer: Stefan Bright; Studio: Record Plant.

Recorded first as a jam session (with Hendrix on bass), then later edited and mixed to underscore the more salient comments from Leary's post-jail press conference held at Douglas's 55th Street office, Hendrix, like fellow contributors Stephen Stills, Duane Hitchings, John Sebastian and Buddy Miles, had no further involvement following their initial "Woodstock" jam.

**LIGHTNIN' ROD:** *Doriella Du Fontaine* Celluloid/Douglas Records CEL166 Release Date: July 1984
Producer: Alan Douglas; Engineer: Stefan Bright; Mixdown: Material & Dave Jerden; Studio: Record Plant [basic tracks], RPM [1984 mixing].

This 12-inch single (the B side is an instrumental take) marks the first marriage of Hendrix's music to rap, a music form in which

Alan Douglas – through his work with the Last Poets – enjoyed commercial and critical success.

**STEPHEN STILLS:** *Stephen Stills* Atlantic SD 7202 Release Date: November 1970
Producers: Stephen Stills & Bill Halverson; Engineer: Andy Johns; Studio: Island [London].

While Hendrix lent his lead guitar to a series of different songs, only one, "Old Times Good Times," made the finished album. In recent years, Stills has stated a desire to release "White Nigger," another track from these March 1970 sessions, on an upcoming solo project.

**LOVE:** *False Start* Blue Thumb BTS 22 Release Date: December 1970
Producer: Arthur Lee; Session Date: March 1970; Studio: Olympic [London].

Hendrix added lead guitar to "The Everlasting First," a composition, says Love's Arthur Lee, that was written about Jimi. Though long rumored, Hendrix does not play on either "Ride That Vibration" or "Slick Dick." The session, explains Lee, was dedicated to "The Everlasting First" and versions of Hendrix's own "Ezy Ryder."

**GHETTO FIGHTERS:** *Ghetto Fighters* Unreleased
Producers: Jimi Hendrix & the Ghetto Fighters [Albert & Arthur Allen]; Engineer: Eddie Kramer; Studio: Electric Lady.

Arthur and Albert Allen, two longtime friends of Hendrix, performed professionally as the Ghetto Fighters, an R&B combo. With Hendrix and Kramer's assistance, a number of tracks were recorded (some with Hendrix on lead guitar) at Electric Lady Studios during the summer of 1970. Following Hendrix's death, work on their debut album continued through 1972, before the project was ultimately shelved.

# Jimi Hendrix on Video:

**FILM ABOUT JIMI HENDRIX** Warner Home Video
Originally released in 1973, this 103 minute documentary tried to join the many strands of Hendrix's much misunderstood life and legacy. Producer/directors Joe Boyd, John Head and Gary Weis managed to interview most of the right people, but struggled to balance the many diverse, yet crucially important issues – namely Jimi's musical direction, his turbulent relationship with Michael Jeffery, the planning, construction, or even future of Electric Lady Studios – that raged within Hendrix.

While some, including Noel Redding, Chas Chandler and Michael Jeffery, refused to participate, all of the initial interviews conducted by Boyd, Head and Weis in London were shipped back to Warner Films in Burbank, California and inadvertently thrown away. While the producers later supervised a frantic search of a local landfill, complete with heavy equipment trucks turning over thousands of pounds of earth, lengthy conversations with the likes of Mitch Mitchell and Pete Townshend were lost (Townshend and Mitchell did agree to be interviewed again, but neither afforded Boyd, Head and Weis the time or candor each had displayed during their first encounter). "It was embarrassing to have to go back to these guys and explain that we somehow had lost all of the film footage from our interviews with them", remembers Joe Boyd. "Townshend gave us one day," continues Boyd, "and the interview – if it was going to happen – would have to be conducted after he had finished shooting a promotional film clip with The Who. At the end of a long, frustrating day having not exposed a single frame of film, Townshend emerged from his dressing room and told us that the interview would last until the magazine currently loaded in the camera ran out." True to his word, Townshend gave Boyd and crew nearly ten minutes of quality material before drawing the conversation to a close.

Mitch Mitchell's second interview was not as successful. In fairness to Mitch, Boyd, Head and Weis seemed poorly prepared to decipher Mitchell's cryptic, yet prophetic insights. To his credit, Mitchell gave his inquisitors a number of chances to stray from standard questions about, for example, the Monkees tour, to more obtuse reflections about Hendrix's character. In fact, Mitch's sole onscreen appearance – questioning Hendrix's supposed naivete – was one such example.

By chance, Boyd shared a London cab with Devon Wilson during the early stages of production. Though she consented to an interview, Devon's death came before one could be properly arranged.

Musically, by dint of Hendrix's magnificent Monterey, Berkeley and Fillmore East performances, *Film About Jimi Hendrix* is enjoyable. Jimi's impromptu 12 string, accoustic rendition of "Hear My Train A Comin'" is charming, as is his 1969 appearance on the *Dick Cavett Show*. Even the Isle of Wight footage – especially that of "Red House" – capture a sense of frustration and desperation in Hendrix that the film's interviews are unable to convey.

**JIMI PLAYS BERKELEY** Warner Home Video
This much flawed, 55 minute documentary features haphazardly edited selections from two inspired Hendrix performances intercut with dated (if not downright silly) political observations from various Berkeley residents.

**JIMI PLAYS MONTEREY** HBO Home Video
The Experience's magnificent Monterey performance, as well as two songs, "Sgt. Pepper's Lonely Hearts Club Band" and "Wild Thing" (where Jimi's vocals seem strangely out of sync), from the group's December 22, 1967, Christmas on Earth performance in London. An indispensable document.

**JOHNNY B. GOODE** Sony Home Video
Save for "Johnny B. Goode" from Berkeley, reproduced here for the third time (*Jimi Plays Berkeley* and *Film About Jimi Hendrix*), the remainder of this 26 minute collection is filled out with mediocre renditions of "All Along the Watchtower" and "Star Spangled Banner" from Hendrix's July 4, 1970 Atlanta Pop Festival appearance. Unsuspecting fans beware.

**RAINBOW BRIDGE** Rhino Home Video
Of interest only to the morbidly curious. Even the performance "section," with the possible exception of "Hey Baby – In From the Storm," is decidedly substandard Hendrix.

**WOODSTOCK** Warner Home Video

Hendrix's renditions of "Star Spangled Banner," "Purple Haze" and "Instrumental Solo" dramatically close this three-hour documentary.

**JIMI HENDRIX AT THE ISLE OF WIGHT** BMG Home Video
While most of the highlights included here were originally featured in 1973's *Film About Jimi Hendrix*, the medley of "God Save The Queen" and "Sgt. Pepper" (including a wonderful backstage scene where Gerry Stickells, to remind Hendrix of its melody, hums the opening bars of "God Save The Queen") and a powerful rendition of "All Along the Watchtower" outweigh a strong, but poorly edited "Freedom" and subpar versions of "Voodoo Child (Slight Return)" and "Dolly Dagger".

**JIMI HENDRIX AT WOODSTOCK** BMG Home Video
This condensed sampler of Hendrix's celebrated Woodstock performance includes superb versions of "Voodoo Child (Slight Return)," "Star Spangled Banner" and "Purple Haze".

**JIMI HENDRIX EXPERIENCE** Warner Home Video
Narrated by Alexia Korner, this short (33 minutes) film was originally produced for BBC television in 1968. Highlights include interviews with Jimi, spirited live performances of "Purple Haze" and "Wild Thing" and a stellar, accoustic 12-string version of "Hear My Train A Comin'."

# Index